CMS Security Handbook

The Comprehensive Guide for WordPress®, Joomla!®, Drupal™, and Plone®

Tom Canavan

WILEY

Wiley Publishing, Inc.

CMS Security Handbook: The Comprehensive Guide for WordPress®, Joomla!®, Drupal™, and Plone®

Published by
Wiley Publishing, Inc.
10475 Crosspoint Boulevard
Indianapolis, IN 46256
www.wiley.com

Copyright © 2011 by Wiley Publishing, Inc., Indianapolis, Indiana
Published simultaneously in Canada

ISBN: 978-0-470-91621-6
ISBN: 978-1-118-09174-6 (ebk)
ISBN: 978-1-118-09175-3 (ebk)
ISBN: 978-1-118-09176-0 (ebk)

Manufactured in the United States of America

10 9 8 7 6 5 4 3 2 1

For general information on our other products and services please contact our Customer Care Department within the United States at (877) 762-2974, outside the United States at (317) 572-3993 or fax (317) 572-4002.

Wiley also publishes its books in a variety of electronic formats. Some content that appears in print may not be available in electronic books.

Library of Congress Control Number: 2011922796

This book is dedicated to my wife, Carol Ann. Thank you for your support and love. You are more appreciated than I can likely ever tell you.

And I dedicate this book to you, dear reader, that in it you may find support in these trying cyber-security times.

Credits

Executive Editor
Carol Long

Project Editor
Kevin Shafer

Technical Editor
David A. Chapa

Production Editor
Kathleen Wisor

Copy Editor
Paula Lowell

Editorial Director
Robyn B. Siesky

Editorial Manager
Mary Beth Wakefield

Freelancer Editorial Manager
Rosemarie Graham

Marketing Manager
Ashley Zurcher

Production Manager
Tim Tate

Vice President and Executive Group Publisher
Richard Swadley

Vice President and Executive Publisher
Barry Pruett

Associate Publisher
Jim Minatel

Project Coordinator, Cover
Katie Crocker

Proofreader
Jen Larsen, Word One New York

Indexer
Robert Swanson

Cover Designer
Ryan Sneed

Cover Image
© Fuse / GettyImages

About the Author

Tom Canavan has enjoyed an extremely successful career in the technology sector for more than 24 years, working for companies such as Dell Computer and Texas Instruments. He has served in the roles of Director of IT, CIO, and many other valued and highly sought-after positions throughout his career. Having worked at all levels from field technician to senior management, he brings distilled knowledge and wisdom from the *enterprise level* down to the small and medium business world. Canavan has a degree in Robotics and Computer Numerical Control. His background includes many years in the computer hardware industry, and extensive experience in data center operations and the information security sector. Canavan has authored several books, and is a frequent public speaker on the topic of IT/information security. He is co-founder of `SalvusAlerting.com`.

About the Technical Editor

David A. Chapa is a Senior Analyst with the Enterprise Strategy Group, a research and strategic consulting firm. He has invested more than 25 years in the computer industry, focusing specifically on data protection, data disaster recovery, and business resumption practices. He has held several senior-level technical positions with companies such as Cheyenne Software, OpenVision, ADIC, Quantum, and NetApp. He has been a featured speaker at a variety of industry events covering various topics related to disaster recovery, compliance, and the use of disk, tape, and cloud for recovery and backup strategies. He is recognized worldwide as an authority on the subject of backup and recovery. Chapa is also a member of SNIA's Data Protection and Capacity Optimization (DPCO) Committee, whose mission is to foster the growth and success of the storage market in the areas of data protection and capacity optimization technologies.

Acknowledgments

For those who have never written a book, you never see the cast of many behind the author. While the writing belongs to the author, the quality of the writing is often enhanced by the team of people behind the author that make him or her look good. In my case, I believe I'm a decent writer, but with the editorial staff of Wiley, I look like a great writer. That "greatness" comes through the hard work and skill of the editors I had the honor to work with.

I wish to thank my Project Editor, Kevin Shafer, and his team for helping me to produce what I hope to be a truly great work. I wish to thank Carol Long, my Executive Editor, for putting up with multiple delays, and for the opportunity to put my experience on paper and bring it to you. I especially would like to thank the Technical Editor, David Chapa, for his most excellent and challenging technical peer review of this work.

Thanks to Jeff Star of `perishablepress.com` for his help with the art of `.htaccess`, and Doug Vann of `dougvann.com` for his valuable assistance with Drupal questions.

Special thanks go to my good friend Mark Turner of Walt-Disney Corporation, who inspired the original idea for this work some time ago.

I thank my beautiful wife, Carol Ann, who has endured me writing yet another book and putting up with an unfinished remodel of our home during this time.

In my 20-plus years in the technology industry, I have met and learned from so many people that I cannot begin to recall them all. Please know you are not forgotten. I appreciate your wisdom and guidance.

And I wish to acknowledge and thank my Lord and Savior, Jesus Christ, who gave me the wisdom in this book and the ability to write it. Without Him I would not have ever embarked on this effort.

Lastly, I wish to thank you, dear reader, for purchasing this book and reading it. I truly hope that you will find answers to questions about your security that will keep you safe and operational.

Contents at a Glance

Contents

Introduction

As a business owner, you are probably faced with hundreds of decisions that must be made weekly. Diving headlong into a technical effort might be scary. Diving into a *security and operations* effort is something you likely don't know how to do.

That's where this book comes in. This book helps you fill in the blanks for often-overlooked operational and security aspects of your business that lead to security breaches, downtime, excessive financial costs, and more bad things that go bump in the night.

This book is written in a very straightforward manner, and is oriented toward the owners of small and medium-sized businesses. You won't need a degree in computer science to follow along. Rather, this book has been written for the average person who utilizes technology in his or her business.

Business owners are often misled when it comes to technical and security matters because of a lack of knowledge. This is a handbook of distilled knowledge. It's not meant to make you a technical expert. Rather this book has been geared toward business owners to help alleviate that lack of knowledge.

Within these pages, you will find a number of valuable lessons:

- Choosing proper hosting for your business
- Choosing the *right* CMS to use for your business
- Recovering when a hacker attacks your site
- Reading your log files to spot and prevent trouble
- Writing a simple (but effective) plan for disasters
- Learning how, why, and when to patch your websites
- Hardening the web server against attack

- Writing an effective information security policy
- Discovering how to *prevent* problems before they start

This handbook is designed to help owners of small and medium-sized businesses run a more efficient IT group. It focuses on the more popular Content Management Systems (CMSs) in use today. These CMSs are all *open source*, meaning they are *free* to download, modify, and use. The dark side to open source applications is that clients often choose them for their low cost of implementation, but often fail to realize that "free" means freedom to change, modify, and use the code. "Free" does not mean free from vulnerabilities, hackers, or financial costs of support.

For the tactical aspects of your server and your CMS, you'll find this book to be packed with wisdom often reserved by specially trained technical staffers.

This book can help to keep your web-enabled business running smoothly and safely — free from cyber thugs or random disasters that could take out your website.

Overview of the Book and Technology

Today, cyber-crime has evolved from the typically introverted teenager stereotype into a billion-dollar crime business. Wherever there's that much money, organized crime gets involved.

Today's average website is under constant assault, with many of those attacks resulting in great successes for the hackers. Likewise, the number of vulnerabilities continues to grow, but website owners practicing good patch management are not keeping pace.

This book focuses on the open source CMSs that offer many free add-ons from developers. Often, the add-ons, the core CMSs, and even the web servers will become vulnerable or be misconfigured. This can lead to small or medium businesses being hacked, suffering the loss of customers through reputation damage and much more. This book addresses all the needs of the non-technical business owner to help you understand *why* you must shore up your CMS or web server defenses, and how to establish your information security policy.

The following technologies are covered in this book:

- Joomla!, Drupal, WordPress, and Plone CMSs
- Linux security
- Wireless security
- Security tools such as Nessus, Nmap, and WireShark

Following are operational topics covered in this book:

- Choosing the *right* hosting company for your needs
- Starting with the right CMS for your business needs
- Building a baseline for your site
- Establishing a password policy
- Learning to read and use your web server logs
- Establishing a disaster-recovery plan
- Applying patches to keep your system up to date
- Securing your wireless networks
- Establishing an information security policy
- Building information security awareness

In essence, this book provides you with the tools to help you operate in a similar manner as a large enterprise IT shop.

How This Book Is Organized

This book is written in a manner that weaves process with technical concepts. Each chapter builds a specific set of knowledge that bridges you into the next topic of discussion.

Following is a brief synopsis of how this book is organized:

- *Chapter 1, "Introduction to CMS Security and Operations"* — Planning and executing a good operational plan for your website and business will keep things moving smoothly. This chapter begins by introducing a number of the concepts that most business people don't know and can ill-afford to misunderstand.

- *Chapter 2, "Choosing the Right Hosting Company"* — Because of the many options available to you for hosting companies, choosing the *right* hosting company is important. This chapter teaches you how to identify the various types of hosting, the estimated costs, and the key issues with each type of hosting. Additionally, you'll learn how to discuss proper security with the host to determine whether that host is right for your needs. You'll also learn about accepting payments via your website, and the technologies involved.

- *Chapter 3, "Preventing Problems Before They Start"* — Many business owners jump into building a website without proper consideration of how their CMS or design choices will affect security. This chapter takes you through several decisions that must be made, starting with helping you choose the right CMS for your particular needs. You'll review four key tenets related to choosing the right CMS. The rest of the chapter guides you through the cost and support decisions, as well as post-install tasks.

- *Chapter 4, "Baselining Your Existing Website"* — If you have an existing website, determining where you stand is vital to your security. In this chapter, you'll learn how to develop a baseline report that will provide not only a snapshot of your site's security, but also a road map to guide you when updating and patching your site. If you are just now building your site, then capturing that baseline will help with proper documentation of the new site, as well as implementing strong cyber-safety measures.

- *Chapter 5, "Hardening the Server Against Attack"* — This key chapter is a detailed look at how to protect your server against attack. There are many areas that can be easily strengthened on any server. These include protecting your FTP server, ports on the machine, operating system settings, and more. You'll learn how to eliminate common problems and how to add a strong defensive layer to your web server.

- *Chapter 6, "Establishing a Workable Disaster Recovery Plan"* — Things can (and will) eventually go wrong with your website or your server operation. Something will fail, and that's when you need a recovery plan. In this chapter, you learn about building your team, installing the proper backup software, developing your written disaster plan, and, of course, conducting proper testing. By the end of this chapter, you'll have a framework on which to build and document your own plan.

- *Chapter 7, "Patching Process"* — By its nature, software is forever being changed. New features are offered and new vulnerabilities are discovered on a regular basis. No matter the size of your operation, you'll need to develop a *patching plan*. This teaches you how to implement the patching processes and how to craft proper documentation related to patching. You'll additionally gain an understanding of why and when to patch your software.

- *Chapter 8, "Log Review"* — Log files provide an historical record of activity on your site. The traffic, the activity, and the statuses of your site are all recorded dutifully in various log files. Learning how to read those log files will help keep you safe. This chapter familiarizes you with the Apache and FTP log files, and teaches you how to interpret them, as well as how to react to problems. This is one of the more important chapters in the book, because log files are often ignored, never captured, or are deleted — all without a single look at them. During or after an attack, the log files may be your very best source of information. Take the time to absorb all this chapter has to offer.

- *Chapter 9, "Hack Recovery"* — Websites are hacked every day. What's worse is the loss of time, money, and reputation among your customers that you can suffer from such an event. In this chapter, you'll learn a very hands-on approach to recovering from an attack. You'll be introduced to the proper tools and procedures needed to restore your site's operation after a devastating hack attack on your site.

- *Chapter 10, "Wireless Networks"* — As more and more devices become enabled wirelessly, more and more attacks will find their way into your systems via wireless networks. Thus, vulnerabilities in wireless networks are being used as a means to attack CMS websites. This chapter provides a high-level examination of the concepts for managing security with wireless access in your building or office. You'll learn about some tools to help track down rogue systems, and some information on securing wireless networks in your environment. This chapter also touches briefly on Bluetooth devices and security.

- *Chapter 11, "Information Security Policy and Awareness"* — In this chapter, you learn about crafting a good information security policy for your business. This is a vital to protecting you and your clients, as well as your employees. In addition to the policy discussion, the subject of security awareness is also covered. Many social engineering attacks would fail if the person being manipulated were simply more aware.

- *Appendix A, "Security Tools, Port Vulnerabilities, and Apache Tips"* — Available for free or for very low cost are literally hundreds of security tools. This appendix describes a few key tools with which everyone who runs a website or network should be familiar.

- *Appendix B, "Acronyms and Terminology"* — The computer and technical industry runs on acronyms. Acronyms provide a means for techies to reference specific technologies or to communicate in a brief manner with each other. The average person who does not work every day in the technical sector might not be able to understand the normal "geek-speak." This appendix provides a reference for a number of popular acronyms and common terminology.

Who Should Read This Book

The intended audience for this book is for owners of a small to medium-sized business. The reader may have some technical experience, or none at all. This book is not intended for someone with a deep technical background.

If you are the manager of a company, but not necessarily the technical person, you may benefit from reading the process chapters and working with your technical staff to ensure that they review and read the entire book.

Overall, if you are a small business owner, you, too, will likely want to read the book in its entirety.

Tools You Will Need

Following are a number of tools that you may find useful while reading this book:

- *Putty* — This is an SSH client used to connect to servers.
- *FileZilla* — This is an FTP client used to connect to websites and servers.
- *WireShark* — This is a packet sniffer used for troubleshooting.
- *Nmap* — This is a network mapping tool used for troubleshooting and for reconnaissance (among other things).
- *Nessus* — This is a vulnerability scanner.
- *Notepad ++* — This is a Windows-based text editor that has superior features to the default text editor.

These tools are readily downloadable from the Internet for free. Some of them (such as Nessus) offer a professional support package.

Summary

As you read through this book, keep in mind that, in terms of learning, technology is no different from your chosen profession. Non-technical people sometimes act as if becoming familiar with technology involves *magic*. It doesn't, and in your line of work, you would likely be as impressive with your knowledge base.

Don't let technology be a frightening thing for you. Rather, realize that it is simply a tool like a hammer or a screwdriver. If you get lost while reading this book, take a few minutes to do an Internet search and read up on the topic that confuses you.

After reading this book, you should have a base knowledge about CMS security, and be familiar with the tools that you need to make your site and your operations run smoothly and without interruption.

# CHAPTER 1

Introduction to CMS Security and Operations

As a business owner, you may face the struggle of spending money for things that your information technology (IT) personnel may request. After all, you've grown this business from an idea to where it is today. What could the request for more money possibly do for increasing sales? Why would you need a written policy, or to spend money and time writing and practicing for a disaster?

If you are the IT person in that situation, you may not understand the pressures faced by senior management, or possibly you may not have spelled out your case. You may be faced with a limited budget, and unlimited projects from marketing.

You may actually be wearing both hats, balancing the objectives of running the business, making sales, and reconciling the books. Thinking about site security will likely be low on your list.

In all cases, you must clearly understand the objectives of your business. Specifically, if you are running one of the open source Content Management Systems (CMSs) such as Joomla!, Drupal, WordPress, or Plone, you may feel that the low cost of these systems means that you can get by without the added time and expense required to grant the IT person's request.

This book can assist you with preparing your business and your technical operations. For the manager, ensuring that your security is tight and safe from hackers is important. You do this via processes such as patching, using a backup site, and performing tasks such as log reviews. The technical person will gain knowledge built upon information presented throughout this book to enable a process framework that can be bolted on to most any business model.

This chapter lays the groundwork for discussions throughout this book by helping you assess where your security needs may arise within your organization. You will learn about various types of security threats, how the bad guys try to penetrate your computer systems, how to prepare your workers for good security practices, and how to begin formalizing a disaster recovery plan. Later in this chapter, you will discover some of the key terms and concepts essential for understanding the information presented throughout this book.

Target Acquired

Today's website is not just an ordinary stop on the Internet. It is a target for hackers. The use of your server and site could serve as a jumping-off point to attack other sites. Compromised sites may be used to host *phishing* scams that house near-mirror copies of bank websites. They may be used to house *drive-by malware*, or to house Internet Relay Chat (IRC) communications channels, which is a form of instant messaging.

As this chapter is being written, a current media report cites the capture of a portion of the *ZeuS* gang. This notorious criminal element has successfully gathered into its fold several hundred thousand machines. These "zombies" (as they are called) are fully under the control of the ZeuS criminals. Among other things, their aim is the theft of money. And they have been very successful at their goal.

Another big name making recent news headlines is the worm known as *Stuxnet*. This highly sophisticated worm has been responsible for working its way into electrical generation systems in many countries. According to some reports, it has been found in Iran, China, and the United States. Stuxnet is a very advanced worm (or virus) and has proven to be very formidable.

The challenge is that many systems on the Internet have weaknesses and vulnerabilities. These weaknesses often are the result of a default password or weak passwords guarding the door providing entry to websites.

In addition to banks and utility companies, the small or medium business owner is also at great risk. As one of these owners, you probably have your hands full with growing and managing your business. You might have even had someone build your site for you. After all, why not? You may not be in the technology business, and keeping up with security may be over your head.

Guarding your website and your data is not simply important. You have a moral imperative to do everything you can prevent the loss of your data. Loss of data can occur through poor operations such as not being prepared for a hard drive crash, or it could occur through a cyber-attack.

This book may not prepare you for all contingencies, but it can help you develop a framework to deal with catastrophes ranging from the occasional outage of your CMS all the way through a full-blown disaster.

Operational Considerations

The operation of your site will vary greatly as determined by its usage model and the type of CMS you have. If you are running a small WordPress site that has little traffic and its crashing wouldn't matter much, then, operationally, you have nothing to be concerned about. However, if you were running a large Joomla! or Drupal site that supports an active and profitable customer base, you are likely tweaking and caring for it regularly.

The operations for your site will consist of many items, including the following:

- *Disaster recovery and business continuity plan* — This represents the procedure and plan for how you will react to various types of problems that could hit your website or operations. This disaster and business continuity plan should contain all the elements needed for successful restoration and recovery of your web business and online systems.

- *Backup and offsite storage of data* — Making a backup is clearly important. After you make a backup, the next step is to actually copy it to a local drive or media such as CD-ROM, DVD, or a USB drive. Other types of operations may require backup tapes. In all cases, making an offline copy of data from the server to a local machine or storage system is paramount.

- *Patching* — This is the term used in the technology space to apply updates to software. The application of patches in a small organization is usually done periodically, and depends on your setup. A medium-sized business will have to manage the patching process more frequently because there will simply be more to keep up with.

- *Setting up a test and development platform* — You will almost always need a test and development platform for your site. The "test and dev" environment is used to test patches, try new code, and design a new site that could be used as a mirror copy in an emergency.

- *Log reviews* — Normally, all the traffic and activity on your site and server is recorded in a special file called a *log file*. Your normal administrative activities should include the review of the various log files. This task is not fun and is often ignored because of the mundane nature of it. Yet, a consistent and detailed review will yield any warning signs associated with oncoming attacks. Site issues such as bandwidth consumption, low disk space, and any other events that need your attention can be quickly dealt with.

- *Taking action on log data* — Finding questionable entries in your log files is reason enough to take further action in review of your operations. This doesn't mean that some kiddie-scripter in a cafe somewhere in the world attempting to break in warrants alarms. It does mean that a simple block of the IP address is necessary if it becomes a nuisance. Another example is if you see (via your logs) unauthorized access to your FTP site, indicating you have a compromise on your hands. The actions in the logs will dictate and warrant the proper actions needed.

Educating Your Employees and End Users

If your business is a very small one-person operation, security awareness training won't be as difficult as it will be for a larger business. Just practice good cyber security, and you should be fine. If yours is a "larger" small business all the way to a medium-sized business, then you need to implement a program to train and make your employees aware of cyber security.

For maximum impact, ensure that your security awareness has the following elements:

- *Information security policy* — A good start is a well-developed IT security policy that reflects your businesses needs measured against the known risks to your business. For example, suppose your business uses an *instant messaging* (IM) program to communicate with clients. If this IM application can accept or send files, the risk is that something could be allowed in, or something such as confidential documents could be allowed out. Weighing that IM application's benefit against the need to accept or send files would dictate your IM policy.

- *Make IT security everyone's concern* — Ensure that your staff understands that personal IT security is their responsibility. Ensuring that the employees understand (and not just sign-off on) the policies and procedures should be the role of management. Often, things such as ethical training or IT security are met with passive disdain and eye-rolling by employees. However, IT security awareness is something that an employer must take seriously, and ensure that the staff does as well. Enforcing disciplinary action for non-compliance is one method of ensuring compliance.

- *Monitor* — Establish a process for monitoring and reviewing the information security policies. No one should be exempt from security awareness training. This means that it should become part of the company culture, starting at the top. Management in any organization sets the tone. Thus, managers from the top boss down should demonstrate proper IT security behavior.

Raising Security Awareness

According to www.dictionary.com, being *aware* is having knowledge, being conscious, or being cognizant. It can also mean being informed, alert, and knowledgeable. Awareness of potential security risks is vital to the success of any web-oriented business. This implies that programs should be designed to bring awareness to the threats and dangers of cyber-attacks to your employees and business partners.

Educational efforts are more specific in nature than mere campaigns promoting employee awareness. Where awareness deals with potential threats, education should include elements that give the employees a means to support your security. The following sections take a look at a few proven ways to educate your employees about the security of your operation.

Training on Information Security Policies

Training your staff on information security policies provides them with the actual nuts and bolts of what they can and cannot do. For example, if you prohibit browsing adult-related content sites, then state it in the policies.

This training is your opportunity to have a frank discussion about online safety and how it relates to your policies. Discuss the penalties associated with violating the policies.

Providing a Standard Protocol for Threat Reporting

In this day and age, terrorism can appear in many forms. Cyber-terrorism is likely in its infancy, but will not remain so for much longer. Because of the "nation stateless" nature of the Internet, an attack or threat may not originate from the place you think it has.

Your staff should be aware of when to report events such as viruses being found on their desktops. They must know what the documented process is. There should be a documented process for lost or stolen computers that includes password changes, identifying the data that was stolen, and potential exposure of the company. For example, many larger companies have procedures for dealing with disasters related to weather, fire, floods, and even for reporting bomb-threats.

Consider establishing a similar reporting process for cyber-threats.

Ensuring E-mail Security

By far, e-mail is one of the most prominent places to introduce threats to your infrastructure. In fact, more than 80 percent of the e-mail that flows across the Internet today is *spam*. Much of that spam has the potential for harm.

As of this writing, spam was circulating that informed recipients that the government had *rejected* their electronic tax payment. The spam looks very official and important. It directs recipients to a link that then collects all their information to complete the payment process. Of course, it is a scam used by hackers to steal personal information.

Amazingly, many people still fall for this advanced form of scam. Educate your employees on how to identify a link in an e-mail (for example, right-click it, copy the URL location, and paste it in a text editor such as Notepad). Most of the time, malware e-mail says one thing and directs the browser to another site altogether.

Applying Patches and Updates

If your employees are responsible for doing any form of updates, ensure that they follow only instructions that you offer. Or, ensure that they are able to identify where the updates are coming from. Provide employees with a trusted, intranet, or verification program that will enable them to apply *trusted* patches.

In essence, your education program should reinforce the lessons everyone learned as children: "Don't talk to or get in a car with a stranger," "Do not accept candy from a stranger," and so forth.

Being Aware and Staying Safe

As your program matures, be sure you institute an update program to educate and counter modern threats. Threats change on a frequent basis, and what exists today may not tomorrow. Threats tend to follow in complexity and level of power with the current level of technology.

Employees should go through training on security very regularly (meaning more than one time in their career).

NOTE For a good blueprint on setting up training, see "Building an Information Technology Security Awareness and Training Program" written by Mark Wilson and Joan Hash, and produced by the National Institute of Standards and Technology. You may find it at `http://csrc.nist.gov/publications/nistpubs/800-50/NIST-SP800-50.pdf`.

Looking at Your Site Through the Eyes of a Hacker

In the book, *The Art of War* (New York: Oxford University Press, 1971), Sun Tzu writes about planning a military strike:

"The General who wins a battle makes many calculations in his temple before the battle is fought. The General who loses a battle makes few calculations beforehand. Thus do many calculations lead to victory, and a few calculations allow defeat. It is by attention to this one point that I can foresee who is likely to win or lose."

In essence, what he is saying is that the more a military planner *knows* about the potential situation, and has planned for it ahead of battle, the greater chance he'll have in winning.

Hacking a website or gaining illegal access to a computer system requires the same planning effort. The stronger the target, the more planning it takes; the weaker it is, the less effort it takes.

If you have a horribly unsecured website, then kiddie-scripters will gain and retain access of your site until you get rid of them. However, a well-secured site is a great deterrent to the average hacker.

If they want in, good hackers will take great pains to learn about you and what weaknesses exist. Following *The Art of War,* the more a hacker knows before he or she attempts to break in, the better his or her chances are of success. Inversely, the more you know about *your own security* and site, the better chances you'll have of defending against the bad guys.

Very good hackers are the kind you never know were there. They are the digital equivalent of mist. They can enter, get what they need, and never leave tracks.

Breaking into a secure site means that you must first gather intelligence on its operations. Knowing the defenses that are in place, the weaknesses that exist, where tracking systems are, and who can be compromised are all part of the planning.

The start of intelligence gathering is often a passive activity — one not easily detected and that is done before any active probing of your network. The passive steps can divulge a lot of information needed to get in.

Mapping out the elements of your network, your firewall, your CMS, and your applications are part of the pre-attack phase. Hackers finding a weakness in the previous stage can then penetrate your defenses, and secure their access by adding backdoors and wiping out their tracks.

In the underground world of the Internet, bad guys are known as *blackhats.* Their tools are powerful and dangerous, and their skills are nearly without compare.

An interestingly well-written and dangerous program is the *C99 Shell.* Written in PHP, this "blackhat" tool gives hackers a great deal of control over your server environment. After it is planted on a server, the bad guy can control files, change permissions, open up ports, eavesdrop, send e-mail, upload data, add an IRC application, or simply shut down and wipe your site. Figure 1-1 shows a partial image of the C99.php control program. This very powerful application can easily be used to conduct any number of malicious attacks on a site.

The best means of defense is to look at your site through the eyes of your enemies. What you see, they will see, and you seeing it first is best.

WARNING As you read through this discussion, remember that you must stay fully within the bounds of the law. *Do not take any illegal actions.* Moreover, do not use any of these techniques on computer systems or websites you do not have permission to touch. In other words, this is for your education, and not meant to arm you as a bad guy. If you do use any of the material presented here for illegal means, you do so at your own risk.

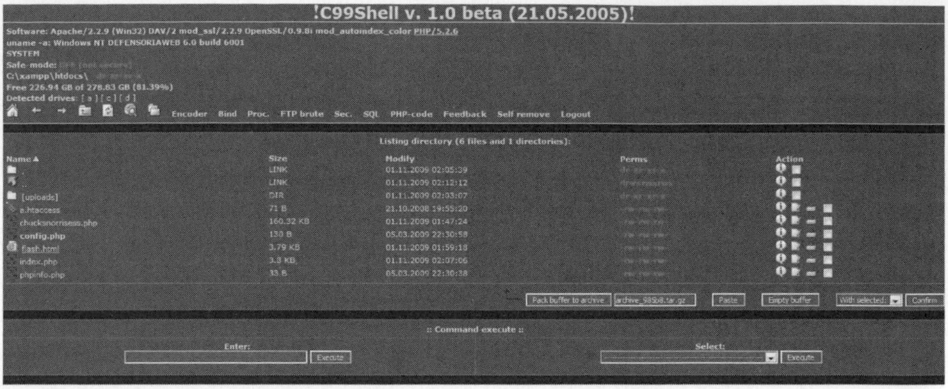

Figure 1-1: Partial view of C99 Shell

Steps to Gaining Access to Your Site

Now take a look at the basic steps a hacker might follow to gain the needed knowledge to attack your site.

WARNING As a caveat, understand that the information presented here is meant to show you how to *defend* yourself. You should not use any of what is outlined here for illegal access to any computer systems.

Researching

Attackers first want to know about your site — what server it's on, the operating system, what applications are running, the specific versions, and so on. Knowledge about defense systems and intrusion detection will also help the bad guys evade getting caught. After they have all that, they can begin the work of researching for vulnerabilities.

For example, if you are running a vulnerable piece of software, they will target it to get in.

Attacks known as SQL injections could use a well-crafted SQL statement that could divulge the *administrator user name* and *password*, thus giving the attacker administrative access to your site.

As an example of research, assume you have a website with a good web hosting company, and that you're running some type of CMS site on a Linux server.

If you were the attacker, you would first determine what software this site was running. You can do this passively or actively in a number of ways, including the following:

- View the page source using the browser of the website. This would help you to learn what its running. Is it Joomla!, WordPress, Drupal, or Plone (or any number of other web systems)?

- Run the scanning tool Blind Elephant on the site to determine the type and version. (You'll learn a bit more about Blind Elephant shortly.)

- Attempt to gain access to the administrator portion of the CMS.

- Write a note from a web e-mail account and praise the developer. Ask what the site was written in because you want to have such a nice site, too! This is an example of social engineering.

- Use a Google search such as "Allinurl: Powered by Joomla!" and see what shows up.

- Many CMSs will show a Favicon with their logo. This makes identification very simple.

You can see that a number of methods are available to learn about the CMS running your site.

Next, the attacker would want to learn about your company, what it does, and where your business is located to essentially build a profile about you. For this task, the attacker may consider the following tools:

- *Google* — This tool can tell an attacker quite a bit about your company because a Google search may turn up press releases, news items, and other information.

- *Domain Name System* (*DNS*) — The attacker could review DNS records to see who your technical contact is, telephone numbers (in some cases), physical address, and your net block. The attacker could also use a tool such as NSLOOKUP (which you will learn more about shortly) to learn about the DNS information of your website.

- *Physical location* — If you have a physical building, an attacker might dig in the garbage can for tossed-out knowledge. This could include customer lists, internal memos, "media" (such as CDs), and more. If the attacker wants to gain access to your operations, he or she may pose as an insider via phone.

Having access to all this and other tidbits of information such as employee names, products you make or sell, and more could allow the attacker to fool someone.

Googling Away

Google is a great tool for everyday use to find information you need. It's equally good for building a profile on a potential target. Let's take a run at it and see what can be discovered.

Suppose a hacker has decided to break into your site. First, the attacker needs to gather some information about the target. What could Google tell the bad guy?

- *Your building address* — This is a great way to do some low-level reconnaissance of the employees, the perimeter, guards, and more. A dedicated attacker could use this opportunity to do some *war driving*, which means the hacker sniffs the external building for wireless access points.

- *Officers or managers of a company* — These employees are a favorite target of social engineers. Through these employees, the attacker can learn all about the upper management. In turn, hackers can use this information to fool other unsuspecting employees into assisting them.

- *Positions you may be hiring for* — Through job postings, a would-be attacker can learn a lot about the infrastructure in place, languages, hardware, systems, and servers in use. The best course of action is to give as little information out as possible for employment ads beyond what will attract the right talent. Ensure that phone interviews are carefully handled so as to not reveal the inner workings of your office and IT operations.

- *Potentially posting passwords on support forums* — Although this point may seem obvious, it's surprising how often passwords get revealed in this manner. What's more shocking is that if you know how to use Google, you can occasionally find lists of passwords in use. Of course, the best stopgap is not to publish or give out passwords and user IDs. The next-best defense is to institute a policy that requires changes to passwords on a regular and frequent basis. This ensures that if a password escapes into the wild, it will be changed soon.

Employment ads for your company are a particularly vulnerable area. For example, suppose the hacker wanted to learn more about a fictitious company called *The Center for All Knowledge*. A search on a job board might yield something like the following:

```
The Center for All Knowledge, a nonprofit publisher, is seeking a Drupal
Developer to work at its headquarters in Chicago, Ill.

The Web Developer will help lead development and redevelopment of
websites on the Drupal platform. Maintenance of existing websites
on other platforms, such as Oracle, will also be required. This
position reports to the CIO of the company.

Required Qualifications:
* Minimum 2 years experience developing in Drupal.
* Strong PHP knowledge.
* XML, CSS and Web Standards experience and knowledge
* Demonstrated ability to produce code
```

The attacker could submit a fake resume to this firm and discuss the job opportunity by phone with the employer. The attacker might even interview for the job personally. Or, the attacker may just add it to the data pile, knowing from this job posting that the company runs Drupal and has something with Oracle running.

This information would enable the attacker to start down an easy path of locating weaknesses that may exist in Drupal sites. So far, nothing that has been done is illegal. It's simply the act of gathering intelligence.

Using Google Hacking Tools (Dorks)

Several years ago, security researcher Johnny Long set up an online database of cut-and-paste Google searches to reveal previously unknown information. According to his website, "Hackers for Charity" (www.hackersforcharity.org/ghdb/), these searches are called "googledorks," or "dorks" for short — meaning "inept or foolish people as revealed by Google."

Many of these searches can reveal things like passwords. One such dork, people.lst, will sadly find many different "lists" of people. Although the intent was probably not to let such lists roam the open Internet, the troubling fact of the matter is that they are there. The dorks on Long's site are very out of date, but, surprisingly, many still yield results. Other sites and dorks have now sprung up.

WARNING Be cautious about these types of searches. You may find unpleasant or offensive content.

Take the time to run various dorks to see whether your website shows up to ensure that you are not revealing sensitive information.

Footprinting

After the hacker has gathered a wealth of details and developed a profile of your site, he or she will move to the *footprinting* phase. This is the phase where the attacker attempts to develop a map of your site, server, and network.

As mentioned previously, the fictitious company, *The Center for All Knowledge*, is running a Drupal site or sites. Mapping out the company's Drupal modules and versions is the first step in footprinting.

Identifying your CMS is fairly easy, and today a few tools are available to help an attacker determine your site's CMS.

Blind Elephant (mentioned earlier) from Qualsys makes this type of work very easy. This Python-based tool is known as a *web application fingerprinter*. Blind Elephant attempts to discover the version of (known) web applications such as CMSs. Through comparisons of static files that exist at known locations, it can check to see what application you are running.

This tool discovers the versions of the following:

- Drupal
- Joomla!
- Liferay

- Mediawiki
- Moodle
- MovableType
- osCommerce
- phpBB
- phpMyAdmin
- phpNuke
- SPIP
- WordPress

In addition, it reveals more than a dozen plug-ins for Drupal and two dozen for WordPress. The obvious implication for this is easy identification of your CMS.

Next, the hacker needs the web server version. Given Apache is by and large the most popular web server out there, a likely chance exists that the site is being run under Apache. But the attacker must verify that is the case, and identify the version.

One quick method to do this is to send the web server a request for a bogus page. The attacker could type in a non-existent web page at a site to see what error results. For example, suppose that, at the browser, the attacker entered the following for a political website:

```
http://www.domain.com/candidates.html.
```

The hacker would then receive back from the server the error message shown in Figure 1-2.

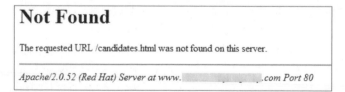

Not Found

The requested URL /candidates.html was not found on this server.

Apache/2.0.52 (Red Hat) Server at www._____.com Port 80

Figure 1-2: Error showing web server version

From the web server's point of view, the request made is not a huge deal, and it's certainly a valid request. The browser asked for the Candidates.html page, and because it didn't exist, the server could not produce the page. It gave the default error of Not Found and the other information.

Notice that the hacker was not directed to a "404 page" offering other information — for example, another page that may contain helpful information such as links on the site. The web server did not even send the attacker to a page explaining that the information requested does not exist.

The reason it is a troublesome message is that it shows the website's Apache version. In this case, this site is running Apache/2.0.52 (Red Hat).

Searching the Apache 2.0 branch (currently up to 2.0.63) *changelog,* the attacker can now see that 19 security patches are between this version the site is running and the current version. That's 19 methods the hacker may use to attempt an attack, which includes the following:

- Four Cross Site Scripting (XSS) vulnerabilities
- Two buffer-related issues (potential buffer overflow)
- Two Secure Socket Layer (SSL) vulnerabilities
- Three specific memory-related errors
- Various other security fixes

As you can see, a quick search of the changelog was all that was needed to discover this information.

Attackers also have at their disposal the diagnostic tools of the operating systems. Several exist, and the following are a few that tend to be universal:

- *AngryIP* — This is a simple IP scanning tool. You can learn more at `www.angryip.org`.
- *DIG (Linux)* — This tool helps you query DNS records. You can learn more at `www.linux.com/archive/feature/113992`.
- *hPING* — hPING is a command-line-oriented TCP/IP packet assembler/analyzer. You can learn more at `www.hping.org`.
- *NMAP* — This is a network mapping tool. You can learn more at `www.insecure.org`.
- *NSLOOKUP (Windows, Linux)* — This is another DNS-related tool. You can learn more at `www.kloth.net/services/nslookup.php`.
- *TraceRoute (or Tracert)* — This tool enables you to track the number of hops to a destination. Using this tool can enable mapping of a network. This tool is built into today's operating systems. Windows users can reach it using the Start ➢ Run ➢ CMD option.

Several vulnerability scanning tools are also available, such as Nessus from Tennable (`www.nessus.org/nessus/`).

NOTE None of these tools were written or are supported for the purposes of ill-gain or criminal activity. They are all used every day in very legitimate operations. That does not prevent a criminal from using them to learn about you. Knowing these tools yourself can give you a view that will help you defend your business.

Using NMAP for Nefarious Means

Take a look at the use of the NMAP tool. Suppose a scan of an example website produced the results shown in Figure 1-3.

1	tcp	open	tcpwrapped	
21	tcp	open	ftp	PureFTPd
22	tcp	open	ssh	OpenSSH 4.3 (protocol 2.0)
25	tcp	filtered	smtp	
53	tcp	open	domain	
80	tcp	open	http	Apache httpd
110	tcp	open	pop3	Courier pop3d
111	tcp	open	tcpwrapped	
143	tcp	open	imap	Courier Imapd (released 2008)
443	tcp	open	http	Apache httpd
465	tcp	open	smtp	Exim smtpd 4.69
993	tcp	open	imap	Courier Imapd (released 2008)
995	tcp	open	pop3	Courier pop3d
3306	tcp	open	mysql	MySQL 5.0.91-community-log
8009	tcp	open	ajp13	Apache Jserv (Protocol v1.3)
8080	tcp	open	http	Apache Tomcat/Coyote JSP engine 1.1

Figure 1-3: Ports found on web server using NMAP

This information is valuable to an attacker. Of course, the value will vary on what the hacker finds and what the planned attack might be. At a minimum, the attacker knows the following from this scan of the server:

- Apache web server
- MySQL (version 5.0.91)
- Apache TomCat and Jserv
- FTP and SSH
- Various mail servers
- Open port 53, which may be a problem if this DNS were to allow *zone transfers* (which you will learn about later in this chapter).

As shown in Figure 1-4, NMAP has identified this server as having a 95 percent chance of being Linux 2.6.24, Gentoo distribution. As shown in Figure 1-5, the tool discovered several "probable" named devices.

⊟ Operating System	
Name:	Linux 2.6.24 (Gentoo)
Accuracy:	95%

Figure 1-4: O/S identification using NMAP

OS Class Type	Vendor	OS Family	OS Generation	Accuracy
general purpose	Linux	Linux	2.6.X	95%
firewall	IPCop	Linux	2.4.X	95%
WAP	Linux	Linux	2.4.X	93%
WAP	Linksys	Linux	2.4.X	91%
WAP	Linux	Linux	2.6.X	90%
broadband router	Linux	Linux	2.6.X	90%
telecom-misc	Avaya	Linux	2.6.X	88%
firewall	Check Point	Linux	2.4.X	88%
WAP	AVM	embedded		86%
general purpose	Linksys	Linux	2.4.X	88%
specialized	Linux	Linux	2.4.X	88%
proxy server	Riverbed	embedded		88%
storage-misc	D-Link	embedded		87%
WAP	Linksys	embedded		87%
remote management	Dell	embedded		87%
switch	HP	embedded		87%

Figure 1-5: Devices found by NMAP on an IP address

As you can see, an attacker can tell a lot about this environment, including the probability of the Voice Over IP (VoIP) phone system being an Avaya (88 percent chance), the probability of a Linksys wireless access point (more than 90 percent chance), and the incorporation of Dell and Hewlett-Packard switches. All in all, this would not be a bad haul of information.

Using Traceroute

One common tool used in the footprint phase is called *traceroute* (on Windows machines, it's called *tracert*). Traceroute can determine the path from the source (you, for example) to the destination system. With traceroute, an attacker could gain enough information to put a decent network diagram together. (However, this result would take several runs of the traceroute tool and some other tools.)

In addition to traceroute (Linux) or tracert (Windows), several tools exist to gather this type of information:

- DnsStuff (www.dnsstuff.com)
- 3D Traceroute (www.d3tr.de)
- GEOSpider (www.oreware.com)

The route an attacker is likely to take is to scan the network using one of these tools, many of which are freely available. The purpose of this active scanning is to gather information about the system to see how it responds to the probes, and to gather what information the scan produces. Using tools such as AngryIP, NMAP, and others (all created for purposes of right and good), an attacker can effectively map out your network.

Keep in mind, however, that a single scan by a tool such as NMAP could trigger various alarms at the server and its defense network. Bear this mind if you intend to test your servers.

Finding Subdomains

Another way a bad guy might attempt to gain access to your site is to hunt for subdomains such as `http://subdomain.example.com`. The gathering of subdomain data can help an attacker form a better picture of your network. Often, attackers can gather this information using tools to search the DNS of the site. For example, sites such as `www.magic-net.info/dns-and-ip-tools.dnslookup` can provide a detailed map of your subdomains.

If you find that your subdomains are showing up at these sites, and you do not want to be exposed, then you can use methods such as `.htaccess` to prevent access. Other means exist as well, but exploring those is beyond the scope of this book.

Enumeration

The next step, *enumeration*, essentially entails putting all the gathered data into a map of some kind. The process of enumeration (or naming of the resources that have been found) is conducted just before an attack.

Mapping through enumeration could show as much (or as little) of the network as the attacker can find, including items such as the firewall IP, intrusion-detection system (IDS), operating system, other IP addresses, and anything else the attacker may have found.

Attacking and Owning the Site

If the attackers have found a weakness to exploit, and they are successful, then they will carry out their agenda. They may possibly leave a *back door* in place. This means that they can use the back door to get back in when they want very easily. This application is usually a small program that is buried on the system (such as the C99 Shell described earlier in this chapter). They may even replace critical applications on the server to evade detection.

The purpose of the site attack may not always be to gain information. Attackers may use the attack to *deny service* (DOS attack), delete data, or deface the system.

Wiping Out Their Tracks

After attackers have gained a way into a site, the last typical activity is to wipe the activity logs. By doing so, they eradicate any paths that show they were there.

> **NOTE** Chapter 8 examines log files much deeper, but for now, it's worth noting that a regular review of log files is a great way to catch the bad guys. Seeing an irregular gap of time missing from your logs is a bad sign.

Examples of Threats

When you think of Internet threats, viruses and possibly scams come to mind. And certainly those are part of it, but there are many more. Threats are becoming more and more sophisticated. These threats include variations on age-old scams, such as snake-oil salesmen or spies.

Let's examine a few of the more common ones.

Social Engineering

Social engineering techniques are used to gain unauthorized information or access from someone through social contact. This common ploy can be quite effective; after all, employees are supposed to be helpful to clients and customers. Although you certainly do not need to change your customer service policies to be less helpful, you should look to see where you could be exposed.

Social engineering is one of the most common and effective means a hacker can use to gain entry to your site. It often plays out as a request for help, and through that request, the attacker can get the necessary information, get a virus into the system, or open a door. The possibilities are quite unlimited.

Calling into Your Office

One easy-to-imagine scenario is for an attacker to call into the office of the CEO. The attacker would already have a lot of information about the CEO, including the officer's background and other important data. When an executive assistant takes the call, the attacker would simply feign being transferred to the wrong extension, and ask the assistant to kindly transfer the call to technical support (or wherever the attacker may get the information needed).

Internally, a very good possibility exists that the extension would show the call as being transferred from the CEO's office. Or the attacker could say that he or she was sent from the CEO's assistant — after all, who is going to call upstairs and ask?

The rest is easy to imagine. The attacker requests information such as logins, passwords, and other secret information. This method doesn't always work, but it has a great probability of working.

Train your personnel on the latest in social engineering tactics, and ensure that they are empowered to request positive identification of the caller.

Sending in a Trusted Friend

Sending a friend into your office posing as an unsolicited sales person can be a risky move if it goes wrong. It could cause a trust issue with your employees, or could have legal ramifications.

However, if the ploy is orchestrated properly by a real attacker, it can give him or her a good deal of information about how your employees follow procedures.

In a legitimate test, this type of penetration testing is done during "black-box" security testing to see whether the "tester" can gain access.

The best way to conduct this type of operation is to engage a professional penetration testing company.

Using USB Keys

During 2010, the news was filled with stories centering around all kinds of mischief and stupidity related to the misuse of USB keys. These small devices are relatively cheap and are capable of storing many gigabytes of information. A 4GB USB key, for example, could easily store a full operating system to boot a server and place a Trojan horse on a unit in short order.

For example, imagine a scenario where an employee arrives for work, and finds a USB key that someone has apparently dropped in the parking lot. What a lucky day! A new USB key someone lost! Imagine further that if that same key had *your logo* on it, it would be all the more enticing. However, for this scenario, suppose that the "lost" key contained a powerful Trojan horse program meant to work its way in from behind the firewall, where it would not be far from getting into your systems.

Although this scenario may sound like a fantasy event, it did happen, where someone scattered a lot of USB keys in a parking lot of a building. And, yes, they were infected.

Another scenario might be when an employee has brought a key from home — for convenience and to do some work. His or her home desktop unit is not well-protected, and a virus is transferred over to the key. Again, a virus or Trojan sneaks past your defenses.

The idea is not to discourage use of this wonderful technology. Rather, these scenarios should make you aware of the dangers. Here are a few suggestions to keep your infrastructure safe:

- *Educate* — Bring your employees' awareness up to par with the threat. Make sure they know the basic rules of using keys in the office environment.

If an employee finds a key lying in a parking lot, it could be okay — or it might be filled with evil.

■ *Virus control* — Ensure that your desktop and servers (if you manage them) scan USB keys automatically, and not give the user operator the chance to decline a scan.

■ *Lock the USB ports* — Disabling the USB ports will lower the chances of infections reaching your network, or data escaping. However, this is becoming less and less possible because of the use of USB keyboards and mice requiring the port.

Indiscriminate Browsing or Instant Messaging

Indiscriminate browsing and instant messaging are two vulnerabilities that can result in dangerous exposure of your internal systems. Although your IT policy *should* dictate what employees can or cannot do on the business network, employees do not always do as they are told.

In the case of indiscriminate browsing, an employee may browse plenty of sites either intentionally or by accident. These websites could contain harmful malware or content that could put your site and network at risk.

Instant messaging has been responsible for passing harmful code through to an unsuspecting employee in at least one well-known cyber-attack case that occurred in 2010.

NOTE For more information on this attack, see `http://www`
`.information-age.com/channels/security-and-continuity/`
`news/1278213/worst-ever-pentagon-cyber-attack-came-from-usb-`
`drive.thtml`.

The awareness you must bring to the table is echoed by the Department of Homeland Security's latest campaign for cyber security — *Stop, Think, Click*. People are generally lured into a false sense of security and will click links that are designed to play on that. Get your employees to a level or sense of awareness about dangers to the network, your website, and company information.

External Media

External media can include USB keys, CD-ROMS, DVDs, or even a mobile smartphone. All of these can represent threats to your system.

Using something as simple as the Knoppix Linux kernel, a computer system could be booted on a USB key, potentially bypassing the security. Given that this kernel is small, fast, and easily obtained, combined with the very dense USB keys available, you have the perfect *spy* tool.

Other media may be innocent enough, but could be virus-laden.

Your policy should be that no external media is allowed in without a solid defense in the form of virus scanning of it.

Vendors or External Clients/Customers as the Threat

When a hapless salesperson comes into a company office, he or she may need to connect to the Internet. Keeping in mind that a vendor or salesperson would not necessarily knowingly transmit a virus, you don't know what level of protection is installed on that "outsider" machine.

Ensure that you provide either a special connection to the Internet that is firewalled away from your network, or do not allow these types of Internet connections. The awareness is for employees to follow your policies regarding plugging in computers to your network.

Reviewing Your Perimeter

If you have a single website or a full brick-and-mortar operation, reviewing and securing your digital and physical perimeters will keep you safe. Knowing where you're vulnerable (and to what it is vulnerable) is the first step in shoring up your defenses.

You can use a few common defenses, such as strong passwords, frequent change of passwords, virus protection, firewalls, and other devices. Brick-and-mortar businesses may face an even greater challenge in the wireless space. As part of your perimeter review, checking and disabling rogue wireless access points reduces the chances of unauthorized activity on those devices.

The following sections provide a good primer to get you started down the path of perimeter review.

Using Virus Protection

What is your current virus scanner? Is it set for automatic scanning and updates? Have you renewed the licenses? Can it be disabled without a password? These are just a few of the common issues surrounding virus scanners.

Depending on the configuration of the machine, scanning can take some time. This may lead to employees simply disabling it *for now* because they are *busy*. Locking down your virus scanners to run at specific times and removing the capability to easily disable it will keep your digital fence up.

Periodically review the machines to ensure that nothing is in the quarantine. Should you have a rash of infections, then the possibility exists that something sneaked in through a USB key or other media.

Banning Passwords on Desks

Believe it or not, a known practice in some office environments is to have passwords taped to monitors, under keyboards, and tucked away in desk drawers. Consider implementing random checks to ensure that your security is not compromised by a simple thing such as a sticky note with a password.

People tend to write down passwords, because they are difficult to remember. Of course, having a paper copy defeats the purpose of having a difficult password. You should set a policy that prohibits writing down of passwords. If you're in an office environment, periodically do a random look around to see whether passwords are taped to yellow sticky notes.

Enforcing a Password Complexity and Change Policy

Passwords should be difficult, using a mix of numbers, letters, and symbols. The passwords should be comprised of a mix of non-repeating letters in both uppercase and lowercase letters. By all means, never use a word that's in a dictionary.

Passwords that are words appearing in a dictionary are subject to a particular attack known as a *dictionary attack*. The dictionary attack simply tries a password over and over using words from a dictionary. Many free and powerful tools are available on the Internet that enable an attacker to take this route.

Passwords should be cycled in all systems at least every 30 days, and should never be reused in less than a year (if ever). If you are hacked, you should cycle all passwords immediately. If you have other systems connected to your network (such as a VoIP phone), then consider the passwords for the VoIP server as well.

> **NOTE** At the end of the day, an attacker could enter your system or obtain passwords through rogue or misconfigured wireless routers. This style of attack was responsible for a large department store being penetrated between May and December 2006. The result of the attack was hundreds of thousands of consumer's identities stolen and millions of dollars lost because of the attackers gaining access to sensitive data.

Policing Open Wireless

In an office environment, employees sometimes feel that they know better than IT. Sometimes employees feel that they need an "easy to access" wireless access point. Often, it is set up when policies and procedures are in place to route requests through the IT department. Small companies that grow large may implement policies that centralize the control of technology aspects, and those companies tend to run into these situations.

A quick trip to the local electronics store to purchase one inexpensive wireless router and cable equips the rogue employee. Returning to the office and plugging it into your local area network (LAN) provides this employee with the desired "easy access" wireless access point. Believe it or not, this situation is not infrequent, and should be handled quickly and firmly.

As part of your effort, defining your wireless policy upfront will help prevent this situation. Draft an IT policy that clearly outlines what an employee can and cannot do. Chapter 11 further discusses IT policies.

As with the case of passwords that are written down, take the time to look for any wireless access points that should not be there.

Tools for Wireless Detection

A low-cost laptop computer with a wireless card can be an easy wireless detection tool to check for rogue wireless systems. Installing a tool such as NetStumbler can enable you to record and identify the rogue systems and shut them down.

If you have an iPhone or iPad, a very interesting tool is available from a company called `dynamicallyloaded.com` for those devices called WiFiFoFum. This powerful tool is a Wi-Fi scanner and locator tool that scans for 802.11 wireless (WiFi) networks and displays information about each network it detects. The scans results include the following:

- Service Set Identifier (SSID)
- Media Access Control (MAC) address
- Received Signal Strength Identifier (RSSI)
- The security mode of the access point
- The available transmission rates

Figure 1-6 shows how WiFiFoFum displays all the available networks, the channel ID, the SSID, and the RSSI of a local coffee shop and surrounding area. As you can see, it found 12 networks available.

Figure 1-7 shows a WiFiFoFum radar view that provides a graphical representation of nearby WiFi access points. This screen shows the positions of the access points with the highest signal strength near the center. The identified access points that have lower signal strength are positioned on the periphery, providing an easy-to-use method to approximate the location of an access point.

Figure 1-6: WiFiFoFum showing networks

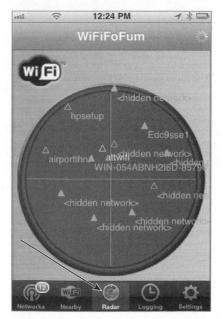

Figure 1-7: WiFiFoFum radar screen

As shown in Figure 1-8, WiFiFoFum can create logs of access point locations as they are discovered. You can then view these logs directly on an iPhone's map application, or e-mail them so that you can view them on your desktop or laptop. To view e-mailed logs, you can simply paste the link in the e-mail into the Google Maps site.

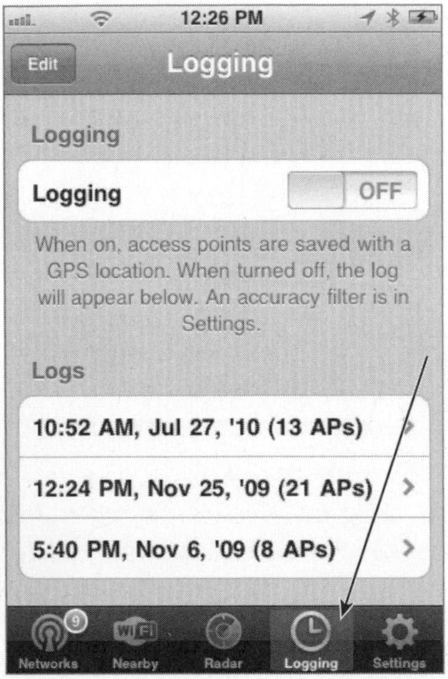

Figure 1-8: WiFiFoFum logging mode

WARNING   This tool may not be legal for all applications. It may also have specific restrictions on its use, based on where you are located. Consult with an attorney regarding the legality of using this tool if you have any concerns.

Another means to check your premises is to see whether your site has been listed on www.wigle.net. This site provides a map of reported wireless access points found by people who reported them to the site. You can drill down to the street level on this map, as well as browse and search by various data points, as shown in Figure 1-9.

Using the wigle.net website, you can verify whether your access point is listed. If you do find your wireless systems listed, you can request removal of them from the site's database.

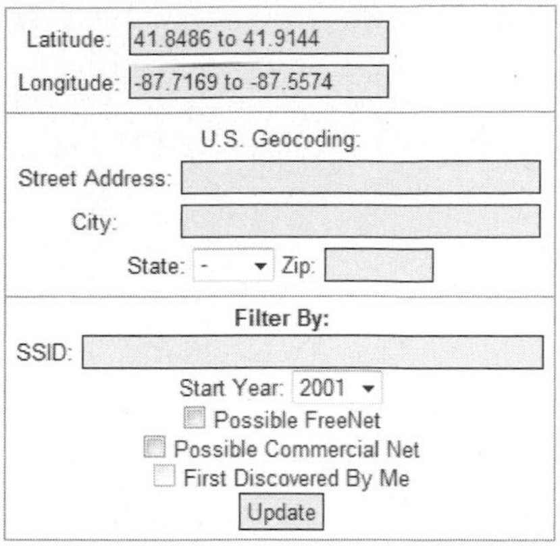

Figure 1-9: Locating physical addresses on Wigle.net

How Will You Respond to an Incident?

According to an August 2010 survey in *InformationWeek* magazine, 17 percent of those surveyed did not have a disaster-recovery plan. Businesses often cite that they do not have a plan for various reasons, such as *lack of resources,* or they find it *too difficult*. Other reasons given by these businesses include the fact that they were "not sure where to start," "we're too small," or "we have backups." You should have a disaster-recovery plan no matter what size your business is. If you're a very small company, then, clearly, formulating a disaster-recovery plan should be easy.

Of course, the types of potential disasters vary with different businesses. For example, you may feel that you are immune from natural disasters because your data center is safely tucked away far from you. You may want to rethink that view. For example, you may think that earthquakes only occur on the West Coast, but you may be surprised to discover that, according to the U.S. Small Business Administration, earthquakes have also occurred in Mississippi, Missouri, Arkansas, Illinois, Tennessee, and South Carolina. Consider the impact to you if your data center were hit by an earthquake.

Chapter 6 works through how to put together an entire disaster-recovery plan. However, in the context of this discussion on assessing your security risks, let's take a look at some important preliminary questions you should answer.

Does Your Plan Exist?

"Does your plan exist?" is a simple "yes" or "no" question. Your plan can be something as simple as a set of steps on a yellow pad of paper. It can be as complex as a full-blown effort designed for a small to medium-sized business.

If your plan does not exist, or rather if you have no plan at all, then developing one will take some time to complete. The plan should be comprehensive, yet easy enough to follow.

The reason for the ease of use is twofold:

■ During a disaster, stress and other factors lower a human's capacity for rational thought. Messaging is best done at lower reading levels that are easy to mentally understand.

■ In the event an untrained person must take the reins and follow the plan through, it should be clear.

Is the Plan Up to Date?

Suppose you have some plan or even a full-blown plan. Check the dates to see when it was last updated. A good recovery plan should be updated every six months, and no more than year should pass between updates. The reason is that new threats arise all the time. Changes in your business, your systems, and your personnel are always in flux. Capturing those changes quarterly or semi-annually keeps a surprise away when you need the plan.

Items you want to look for (also known as *deltas*) are things that can sneak up on you because they changed or were added without your knowledge. These include the following:

■ *New versions of an application suite* — Do you need or have the license keys for restoration?

■ *Updated operating systems on your desktops and server(s)* — Perhaps you haven't changed the operating system in a while, and when you do, it changes the procedures. Capture these changes in your disaster-recovery documentation.

■ *Changes in support policies of an important piece of software* — Maybe the person or company who did the development has gone out of business. The great part about open source code is that you can bring a developer in to change and update your application stack. But again, when those changes are made, then update the documentation.

Be careful of the downstream effect. An example is Joomla! 1.5 versus Joomla! 1.6. These two versions share a lot of similar functionality, but keep in mind that the screens are different. The procedures for doing things are very different.

These differences could cause major changes downstream. Items such as PHP must be at a specific level. The introduction of the Joomla! access control list (ACL) manager and other changes will be cause to review your documentation. Drupal, WordPress, and Plone are ever-changing and improving as well.

The downstream effect would also involve systems that interact with other systems. Do you have custom code? Does your solution interact with other systems? Will a change to one impact a completely separate system, such as a change to a database schema?

Take care that you treat your disaster plan and your site as a *whole*, not just a point solution for just your CMS. Consider the items the CMS runs on, who it touches, and what the outcome will be if it's gone.

Where Are Your Backup Tapes, Disks, and USBs?

Your operation might be small enough to warrant just backup disk, tape, or USB key. Immediate considerations for these media are as follows:

- *If you had to use the media, do you know where it is*? — The answer to this question should be, "Yes, it can be found at *x* location." You surely will be on vacation sometime. If you have an administrative assistant, he or she will be on vacation at some point as well. If you or the assistant are the only ones with the knowledge of where the backup is, then you're sunk if the backup is needed.

- *When was the backup media was last made*? — If you have had zero changes since the last backup (highly unlikely, and believing that you wouldn't is naïve), then you needn't worry. Meanwhile, here in the real world, websites, servers, and applications are constantly evolving, changing, and being patched. Thus, your backup media should reflect that.

- *Was it tested*? *In other words, did you run a test restore*? — An untested backup is about as effective as having no backup whatsoever. Running a test (using your procedures) and ensuring that the backup will restore is wise. This procedure confirms that the backup is intact and will, in fact, restore. It also highlights any changes or updates you need to make to your written documentation.

- *Is your backup encrypted*? — Although this measure is prevalent in mainly tape-type backups, nothing says you cannot encrypt your backups on other media. Issuance and use of the passwords should be documented and guarded.

If you create a plan, even a simple one, you and your staff will indeed know what to do and be ready to respond under the worst of circumstances.

Summary

Planning for and executing a good operational plan for your website and business will keep your business going. In this chapter, you learned about the various components that comprise small and medium business site operations. The importance of viewing yourself through the eyes of hackers can give you a sense of where you are weak.

The various tools discussed (such as NMAP and traceroute) represent some of the many fine tools available to defend yourself.

Disasters or outages do happen, even though your site may be at a very reputable host. Planning in advance for these events will keep you prepared for the day you need it.

Chapter 2 guides you through how to choose a good hosting provider.

Choosing the Right Hosting Company

Choosing the proper hosting for your website or business is akin to selecting a place to live. You may seek a certain part of town that has lots of entertainment, or specific services. You may wish for a quiet home on a nice parcel of land in the country. If you have school-aged children, you will likely want access to the best schools in the area.

Each of these choices is as individual as you are, yet they share a key attribute that crosses all these boundaries. You want a place to live that is safe and secure. Safety in our residence is what we all want.

This chapter provides an abundance of information that will enable you to make the right choice for your particular hosting needs. Making the right hosting choice for your website is vital. Your website or web application may be the only interaction a customer has with you. Making that good first impression is key to having a second interaction, a third one, and so on. Settling for a poor hosting company may result in downtime, hacked servers, or spotty service, which will result in loss of customer satisfaction.

The goal of this chapter is to educate you with an insider's view of hosting — the good and the not so good. Making you a smarter customer will ensure that you make the right choice for hosting.

Types of Hosting Available

To continue with the analogy of living arrangements, you have many different choices for where you want to live. You could rent an apartment, flat, or townhouse, or you could buy a condominium or a house.

Let's compare different types of home choices to website hosting. Table 2-1 provides you with a metaphorical comparison for residences and website hosting. For example, shared hosting is like renting an apartment — you are not responsible for much, other than your own dwelling. Yet, a dedicated server is like owning a home — you must take care of it all.

Table 2-1: Simple Comparison of Residences and Hosting Equivalents

RESIDENCE	WEBSITE HOSTING EQUIVALENT
Apartments (multifamily)	Shared hosting
Condominium/Town homes	Virtual Private Server (VPS)
Owning your own home	Dedicated server
Spectacular time share	Cloud hosting (for example, Amazon)

This section begins with an overview of basic concepts, and then digs into some areas that sales web pages do not tell you about hosting companies.

Various types of hosting are available to choose from, including the following:

- Shared hosting
- Virtual Private Server (VPS)
- Dedicated server
- Cloud hosting

Shared Hosting

Today's average server hardware has much more power than most users consume. *Shared hosting* spreads both the cost and the user load out over many clients in order to make it affordable. The hosting company can put more people on a single box, lowering its cost.

With shared hosting, your website is being served off a single server, along with many other web clients. Although many websites share the hardware, they live in their own *partitions* — much like an apartment unit.

With a properly configured web server, one client cannot see any other clients on the system. The host will maintain the machine, the core operating system, and web server components. The site owner need only worry about running his or her business, and maintaining his or her site.

What that essentially means to you is that you do not need to worry about patching, updating, or configuring the machine. This is the most common hosting platform available. It is also one of the least secure types of hosting you can buy. The average cost for shared hosting per month runs from free ($0) all the way to about $40 a month.

Following are some considerations to keep in mind for shared hosting:

- Hosts that are improperly maintained or misconfigured may allow neighboring websites to be hacked — thus allowing you to be hacked.

- Shared hosting tends to have several sites on each machine. This can be a performance issue. The systems are limited in memory, CPU, and disk space; thus, they provide limited performance. The limitation is based in load versus capacity.

- A shared IP address could get you marked as a spammer, if a site on the server using the same IP address is spamming.

- Configurations may vary by host. This can result in many security-related and performance issues.

- Secure Sockets Layer (SSL) is typically a challenge to install and use on shared hosting. (However, exceptions do apply.)

- Failure of the physical machine will bring down your site.

- If you have too much traffic, your host will ask you to upgrade.

- Backups are usually 100 percent your responsibility.

Virtual Private Server (VPS)

Virtual Private Server (VPS) hosting is shared hosting of a sorts. It runs a special operating system that allows many "guest operating systems" to be loaded. Each guest operating system is treated as if it were the only one on the server(s). A VPS could be a single machine or a group of machines acting as one. This particular hosting is becoming very popular because of plummeting hardware prices.

Running a VPS is more secure than traditional shared hosting because your neighbors on the machine are in a different partition, each with its own guest operating system. Hackers may target and successfully penetrate a neighbor's site, but won't necessarily be able to break into yours. Your site is, for all intents and purposes, a separate server. Depending on the hosting company, the VPS operating system you use will be either maintained by the host, maintained by you, or a mix of both.

One key attribute of a VPS similar to shared hosting is that you are sharing a physical machine with others. The sharing of the machine is accomplished using *virtualization software* such as XenCenter available from `citrix.com`. The disk, memory, CPU, and network resources are divvied up among all the virtual servers using the virtual software.

The capacity of the machine will be used to measure out what you are allowed to consume. In other words, if you exceed a specific load limit on the machine, the host will ask you to purchase either more resources, or to move to a different plan.

When you move to a VPS, you can expect a much higher per-month cost than shared hosting. You will need to have more technical skill to operate and maintain it than you would with shared hosting. The monthly costs typically start at $12.00 per month and up.

Following are some considerations to keep in mind for a VPS:

- Monthly or annual costs will be higher.
- The administrator will need more technical skill than is needed for shared hosting.
- A crash or loss of the physical machine will likely will bring down your site. (However, some exceptions do apply.)
- A VPS is generally more secure than common shared hosting.
- You have the capability to configure the "virtual" machine in any manner you want.
- A wide range of control panel choices is available.
- The physical machine will be shared across many clients. Thus, resources will be allocated over a large pool of sites. However, it typically contains many fewer clients per machine than with shared hosting.
- You have more memory, CPU, and disk space available.
- Backup of your server and sites data will be your responsibility.

Dedicated Server

The *dedicated server* in its most basic form is one you rent or buy, and place into a co-location facility. You can rent a dedicated machine from a hosting company as well. The dedicated server has the highest cost and highest maintenance requirement. However, this option is also the most flexible.

The dedicated server means that *you* are the only one on the machine. You do not share the resources, nor do you have to worry about another site on the server being hacked and exposing you to attack. The **dedicated** box is one you should choose if you have a very busy site, or if you **are** concerned about security and uptime.

Security for a VPS and dedicated server is typically comparable. In some situations, you might have slightly more control over the security of a dedicated server versus a VPS.

You can expect to pay anywhere from $70.00 a month all the way to $500 to $600 a month, depending on the provider and the configuration.

Following are some considerations to keep in mind for a dedicated server:

- You will most likely be required to perform administrative tasks.
- Use of a dedicated server requires a comprehensive disaster plan.
- Typically, this is by far the most expensive of options.
- A dedicated server can provide you with a great deal of computing power.
- If you have purchased your machine, keep in mind that hardware ages, and must be replaced over time.

Cloud Hosting

Cloud hosting is a popular technology model. It has been gaining a lot of press attention and seems very sexy. The basic concept is very much like a United States electrical grid, where many power companies provide electricity to the grid. As the consumer, you can consume as little or as much power as you need. You pay only for what you consume.

This model has a lot of promise for sites that may experience uneven or spiky traffic. Retail sites at Christmas time see a lot of traffic spikes. With cloud hosting (such as that sold by Amazon or Rackspace Cloud), increasing the capacity on demand is simple — thus providing more resources to the web visitors.

As with all technology, cloud hosting has a dark side. The biggest concern with cloud computing is security, with privacy of the data following very closely behind.

> **NOTE** If cloud computing is an area you are interested in using, review the Cloud Security Alliance guidance document at `www.cloudsecurityalliance .org/`. This security guide will help you get on the right track before you start.

If you are choosing cloud hosting because it's "hot" or it's what the technical guy told you to buy, keep in mind the following considerations for cloud computing before buying:

- Although not necessarily a new concept, cloud computing is new enough in this application that administrators are facing "old" problems as if they were new.
- You should understand the billing model and rates before buying. Not understanding the individual costs might cause you to end up with a surprisingly large bill.
- If you are handling or storing credit card data, be sure your cloud provider is able to prove compliance with Payment Card Industry (PCI) requirements.
- Failures are no longer as big of a deal. A failed server in a cloud will not take down the whole grid.
- Plan for data security — it is by far the biggest risk your business will face.

Security of Data in a Cloud

Data must be secured when not in use. It has the potential to be moved (or stay in motion) in a cloud. You should determine how your cloud vendor does this. Here are some considerations:

- If data is moved, it must be moved securely, and not intermixed with other client's data.

- Hackers can run with wild abandon through sites on a cloud if the cloud is not properly secured.

- Ask your host how you can access and audit your logs.

- Just because you are on a cloud doesn't mean you are backed up. Data loss is still data loss. Be sure you have a documented means to restore data.

- You should review and understand the contractual obligations from your cloud host provider. Carefully review areas such as uptime and the afore-mentioned privacy concerns in order to understand the obligations of each party.

NOTE For a detailed review of cloud computing, check out the book *Cloud Computing*: *Implementation, Management, and Security* (Boca Raton, FL: CRC Press, 2010) by John Rittinghouse and James Ransome. Rittinghouse and Ransome are highly regarded experts in the field of security, and, in particular, the area of cloud computing security. Additionally, you may refer to, *Cloud Security*: *A Comprehensive Guide to Secure Cloud Computing*, by Ronald L. Krutz and Russell Dean Vines (Indianapolis: Wiley, 2010).

Selecting the Right Hosting Option

Choosing a hosting provider and a plan can be a bewildering experience. You don't want to buy too little or pay too much. Add in the fact that technological capabilities are always changing, often increasing potential while dropping costs, thus making your entry point a tough decision. You may be wondering what direction you should go, or even whether you are on the right path. The only constant with technology is that it's always changing.

Let's take a look at how you can choose the right hosting for your situation.

Budget Considerations

To be in business today most likely means that you need a website. Very few exceptions to that rule exist. Spending a few dollars or hundreds of millions of dollars a year on a website is a business and budget decision. As a business owner, you can have your site online for as little as $75 a year, including the domain name and website. Establishing a budget is really driven by your business needs.

The first part of your budget you may want to establish is *domain names*. Several top-level domains are available — `.com`, `.org`, `.net`, and even the new `.co`. Many more exist for various countries and specific applications such as `.mobi`.

Determine how many top-level domains you need beyond your normal choice — such as `example.org` or `example.mobi`. Each of these carries with it an annual commitment cost of registration. Depending on your registrar, you may pay from $9.00 a year or more. Remember, this does not include any extras, such as private registration and other domain-related services.

Of course, you'll be hosting some or all of these, and the costs per month or year must be calculated in. You can get barebones hosting starting at $4.00 to $5.00 per month, or go for premium, affordably priced hosting at a company such as `Rochen.com` or `LunarPages.com` all the way up to a dedicated server, which can run you hundreds of dollars a month. Determining this cost is solely based on your requirements, and then you find a host that meets the requirements within your budget.

Many software packages have annual license maintenance costs, which should be disclosed to you before you purchase any package. Although nothing is wrong with an annual software license, be sure that you understand what the license fee is for.

Going hand in hand with license costs is support costs. Some hosts charge an extra fee for assistance on a dedicated box, outside of the hardware and base operating system install. This value-added service is never cheap.

Choosing to physically own the hardware incurs not only the costs to acquire the machine, but the costs of repair as well. Factor in the warranty costs and the out-of-warranty costs of buying a machine. Include in that extra cabling, minor items (such as mounting it in a rack), and other miscellaneous items you'll need.

If you are conducting any type of e-commerce transactions, you'll need to purchase an *SSL certificate*. This cost starts at just under $30 and increases from there. Renewing the certification has an annual cost.

Developing a budget around an open source CMS such as Joomla! or Drupal can fool you into thinking that development *for* the CMS should be at or near zero. Do not mistake the fact that the framework is free with the costs to develop graphics, code, or setup of these platforms. The lure of open source is the capability to get in inexpensively. Don't fall into the trap of wanting an `ebay.com` clone and setting a budget of $200. Believe it or not, that sort of nonsense is a rampant on freelance development sites.

The costs of development include the expertise and the time it takes. After those costs are settled, and your project is complete with your site running, you'll have a cost of maintaining the content. This maintenance can be done by an administrator-type person who makes the changes, or it can be a team. It all depends on your site.

The best way to keep these costs under control is to do lot of paper exercises in both function and form, as well as proposed content. The costs tend to rise if you suddenly find a project switching in mid-design. You can determine additional financial considerations by asking whether the changes in the future will be programming-based, or can be done some by other means. By identifying your goal, you'll be more likely to stay within your financial boundaries.

One other hidden charge you do not want to encounter is the maintenance of the code. Suppose that after testing, it seems fine, but after it's in production, it has a few bugs that make it difficult to use. Set out in advance how those things are handled. Do not expect the developer to continue developing and fixing bugs forever.

When putting together your technology budget, include items such as CD-ROMs and a CD burner to store your backup data. Or if you want to use Flash drives, then add that cost in. Factor in the cost for a fireproof safe, or a safety deposit box to store your data backups in.

Surprise charges such as restoration of files may have a large price tag. Check with your hosting company to find out the cost for restoring a backup. You may be shocked at the cost and turnaround time for the hosting company to do a restoration.

Other costs to consider are any fees that may creep in the mix, including various business services a host may offer, such as search engine optimizing (SEO) of your site, validation of your domain, and other value-added services.

Determining the Appropriate Server Size

Most (if not all) hosting plans described here will suffice for many small to medium applications. However, as applications grow in power, and, hopefully, as your site grows in popularity, you must keep in mind a few sizing rules. The sizing of the application is complex, and will not necessarily be tied to the number of users, but rather the load that is required per user.

Let's begin this analysis by defining a few basic items common to any website/hosting platform.

All computers use *random-access memory* (RAM), and servers tend to require more RAM because of the higher load they take on. Currently, RAM is measured in gigabytes (GB). Typically, the more RAM a system has, the better it performs.

The analog to RAM is *hard drives*, which perform the long-term storage of data. The measuring stick for hard drives is *disk space*, and it will be listed as gigabytes, and soon you'll see it listed in *terabytes* (TB). Note that 1,000GB equals 1TB.

The *CPU* is the heart of any computer. It is the computer chip that is measured traditionally by speed. Today you see advertisements for dual, quad, or hex core CPUs. The designations indicate how many CPUs are present. Note the speed and other technical specifications present. Taking these specs into account is important. For example, you may see "CPU: Intel Core 2 Quad — 2.50 GHz," which means that it has four CPUs working. This particular system would be a great workhorse.

Although it's not listed in most traditional hosting plans, *redundancy* is a consideration for performance and uptime. Many servers have a "dual-drive" mirrored system, which means that it utilizes two disk drives. If one fails, then the other has a copy of the data. Although this setup is perfect for safety, keep in mind that you are only reading and writing data (there's *lots* of reading and writing that happens) to a *single* drive. Thus, if your site is a medium or heavy transaction site (such as a heavily trafficked forum site, or an e-commerce site that has many people writing data), you'll incur a performance penalty while waiting on the drive to complete the writes to the disk. Stated quite simply, more hard drives working tend to cause the entire system to perform better.

Bandwidth is a measure of the amount of data transfer to and from your server. For example, every time someone visits your home page, you consume a certain amount of bandwidth. That measure is calculated in a peak period using a measurement called the *95th Percentile*. This means that you can consume bandwidth as needed as long as you remain below an average "peak" level over the month.

Now that the basics have been covered, take a look at some example scenarios and how to estimate them.

NOTE Cloud computing is not covered in these models.

Case 1: Light Website Traffic (Shared Hosting)

Case 1 entails a small website acting as a placeholder for a business, consisting of approximately ten total pages. Traffic is light, around 200 to 250 visitors a month. In this example, the obvious choice would be the smallest shared hosting plan your web host offers. There is no need for more. This server can easily be offline for maintenance and not impact the business.

This website would require an external backup. For the cost of this type of site, the host will not be handling the backup. However, the host will maintain the operating system and associated parts.

As an administrator of a shared hosting website, you need a very basic understanding of hosting applications such cPanel or WHM and other control panel systems. You must have a light level of knowledge for setting up your database. Three of the four CMSs this book focuses on requires a database.

Communications with the server are typically done through a protocol known as *file transfer protocol* (*FTP*). Using an FTP client such as *Filezilla* will be a normal and possibly daily task.

Backing up your site will rest squarely on your shoulders, with few exceptions. Learning to use the available backup tools from your host will save you on the day you need it.

Finally, you must learn the skill of patching your site and keeping it safe from hackers targeting any of the site's weaknesses.

Case 2: Medium Website Traffic (VPS)

For this example, this medium-trafficked site hosts a popular forum discussing hot political topics of the day. It hosts a fair amount of graphics and text. The site administrator will need to monitor the bandwidth to avoid overage charges. Traffic is 50,000 to 70,000 visitors a month. Security is a concern here because of the fact that the site was hacked on a shared hosting account when the business first started. The business also needs more control over the server environment. This site's primary source of revenue is advertising displayed on the site. For this client, a VPS would be in order.

With virtual systems, the bigger concern is the amount of RAM that is on the system, because most modern servers have more CPU power than they normally use. In a VPS or any virtual system, the more RAM you install on the physical server, the better it can perform. As a result, costs will be much higher than traditional shared hosting. This system will be equipped with 12GB to 16GB of RAM.

The administrative skills needed on a VPS could be higher, depending on the hosting company of choice. For example, `Rochen.com` offers a great deal of support for its virtual server offering. Other hosting providers may offer the same, more, or less. Take this into consideration as you shop. Choosing a fully managed provider will take care of a lot of issues surrounding server management.

If you are tasked with caring for your VPS, then the skill set should include the same as needed for shared hosting, as well as few additional skills. These skills could include light management of your firewall, scripting for your `mod_security` or `ConfigServer and firewall` applications. You'll need some command-line Linux skills (or the equivalent Windows skills), as well as knowledge of using the *Secure Shell* (*SSH*) protocol. This is a safer means to connect to your server than FTP. Tools such as Putty or WinSCP are two popular choices for SSH.

Lastly, you'll want to gain some knowledge of using `phpMyAdmin` to manage your databases. The time may come where you have to edit or change items in the database. This is the best method to do so, unless you are a database administrator and can use advanced command-line skills.

The good news is that, with most VPS offerings, the technical support group is there to assist you.

Case 3: Heavy Website Traffic

The example website for a heavy website traffic scenario is a revenue-generating site that distributes training videos on demand. This popular site serves around 250,000 unique visitors a month. They consume more than 1TB to 1.5TB of bandwidth a month. Given that the site runs run 24 hours a day, 7 days a week, the business has little room for downtime, and it needs maximum performance.

The optimal solution for this client would be a pair of machines, with one acting as the primary server. The other machine would be available for development, and would contain a copy of the first system. In the event of an outage, the second system would be put into action. One budgetary consideration here is that the host is doing minimal maintenance of this system.

This solution requires a dedicated server and a trained administrator. Most hosting companies will assist with the software, but for a fee. This is based on the fact that, as a dedicated client, you are expected to know how to administer a server. The tasks at a high level are configuration and updating of the server, which sounds simple in a point-and-click world, but in a Linux world means that being able to perform several difficult tasks is required, including the installation and configuration of PHP, Ruby, Python, Perl, and various other compiler and software tools.

Installation and configuration of your Apache web server, log file rotations, and various other features are not trivial tasks, nor is the setup of your MySQL database server. In most cases, these are handled at a command-line prompt using SSH.

Security is an area the administrator of this machine would spend a great deal of time on. Setting up the various layers of protection requires a strong knowledge of the tools and, in some cases, scripting. Because your dedicated server may likely be running a *Secure Sockets Layer* (*SSL*) *certificate*, the administrator will need to configure and install the certificate.

Having a dedicated machine usually implies a dedicated person with the proper skill set and trustworthiness to be operating at the innermost levels of your business operations.

Using Backups

These generic work models have provided you with a view of each of the needed skills. One common task across all the models is the need to back up the data to an offsite location. That can be as simple as using a tape or CD-ROM. Or it could be a commercial solution such as `www.AkeebaBackup.com` that does the backup to an offsite cloud.

In all cases, depending on the host, performance of the website during backups may be impacted. Find out how the host conducts backups and ask about the effect on the performance of your site. Remember, in all cases, it's your data, and it's your responsibility to ensure that it is backed up — no matter what.

What to Look for in Web Host Security

Choosing a hosting company does not typically require a multi-year agreement. Generally speaking, the fees for web hosting are charged on a monthly basis. Co-location might be an annual commitment, but, typically, terms are included that allow you to break the agreement. Even so, choosing the wrong company for your hosting needs could be costly.

This section examines a topic of growing importance — security. When selecting a host, you want to have a clear understanding of the finer points that are not typically considered. This discussion is broken down into the following topics:

- Physical security
- Cyber security
- Environmental support

Each of these shares common ground and can clearly have an impact on each other.

Physical Security

The phrase *physical security* likely conjures up mental images of contract security guards on patrol, or the guard in the lobby of a business admitting visitors. The truth is that these are examples of the physical security of a hosting company, but there is much more to security in your hosting company.

Glass Windows

Let's start with the simple example of the building in which the host is located. Many areas could be a huge concern. If you tour a web host or co-location facility, make note of your surroundings. Does it have glass windows in the building allowing light, heat, and prying eyes into the data center?

Of concern with glass in a data center would be things like the temperature of the building. Glass tends to let heat in via solar radiation. If your data center resides in the Southwest region of the United States, then it will be subjected to high temperatures during the long summer months. This can impact the cooling capacity of the building. The high temperatures would make the cooling systems work harder, costing more, and creating potentially more maintenance for the air-conditioning systems. Higher temperatures in the data center caused by the addition of an unwanted heat source is not a good alternative.

Additional concerns abound regarding secrecy of data. In one real-world case, a private data center had windows. Located on the front of the rack was the username and password for a specific system, which was visible from the outside.

Civil unrest in a populated city is also a concern. The unrest could result in a brick, fire bomb, or other incendiary device being tossed through the glass windows into the data center.

The forces of nature can also raise concerns. One threat that people in the Southwest and Midwest tend to live with is tornadoes. The building might be rated for a F5 tornado, but flying debris will break through the glass windows, potentially causing unnecessary damage to systems in the data center.

One final minor consideration is the cost to upkeep the hosting company's building. Windows leak air, get dirty, and get broken. All these things require maintenance, which is a cost. That cost is not absorbed by the hosting company, but rather trickles its way down to you.

Flooding

Water in the forms of rivers or steams tends to be part of the reality of many landscapes. When water levels rise, the water occasionally gets into buildings — especially those built in a flood zone. Some areas are thought to flood only every 500 years, others every 100 years, and some when it rains for only a few days.

Asking the hosting company about its building's proximity to flooding areas is wise. If the company is located in a flood zone, ask when the last time the water approached, and ask how high it got. Check out the U.S. Government's database on flood data at `http://msc.fema.gov`.

Signs

People are often inundated with marketing messages, and building signs are no different. Although marketing may be vital to your success, advertising a data center with big splashy signs may not be the best idea. To be fair, a dedicated attacker will take the time to locate a facility, even if it's a non-descript, concrete building. Making a security breach easier for the attacker by providing lots of signage pointing the way is not a great idea.

People

Like any business, hosting facilities will admit a lot of visitors and guests for various reasons. Your due diligence should include an understanding of the types of controls put in place for monitoring visitors and guests.

Entries are the only legitimate ingress and egress from a building. Controlling those is of primary importance to perimeter security. Find out what processes are in place for check-in and check-out of visitors to the building. Are they escorted? Do they require a government-issued photo ID? Will the photo ID be retained during their visits? Although low-tech, these types of controls are highly effective to deterring bad guys.

One common means of entrance to a facility is what's known as a *man trap*. A man trap is a dual-door room that typically requires a key to enter, and another key or permission to enter the main room. Literally, it traps you in this room. The idea is that, if you get into one door, the second one is locked. Most data centers operate some form of a man trap to help control the flow of traffic in and out of sensitive areas. Other technologies may include some form of biometric scanning.

Patrolling guards are also a strong deterrent to crime. If you are headed toward a co-location facility, ask about how the company handles the monitoring of the data center floor, the perimeter, cameras, and so on. Some smaller facilities may be lightly staffed, with only a few guards having to watch the door, attend to unlocking cabinets, or attending to client needs. This is where adding in the strong authentication and deterrent systems comes in handy.

Many cyber breaches occur from insiders who use their knowledge to attack the data in the servers. Insider attacks typically rank at or near the top of many breaches. As a client, you have the right (and duty to your company) to ask about criminal background checks. While a mistake in the past should not prohibit a person from obtaining work, it should be a factor in the employment. In other words, if an employee has a history of risky behavior, then no guarantee exists that the employee will not still be a risk. Find out what background checks are performed. If you have any doubt about the legal right to ask this question, check with your legal counsel.

Dumpster Diving and Social Engineering

Employees (and people, in general) tend to leak information. One big area of concern is the disposal of private information on hard drives, paper, and CD-ROMs. These are great sources of information. If you are touring hosting facilities, make note of whether you see locking recycle or destruction bins for paper and CDs. The careless disposal of customer lists and account numbers has resulted in security breaches, theft, and more.

If you are hosting with a company, feel free to ask how that company decommissions disk drives. If the drive cannot be repaired and completely wiped, then it should be sent to an authorized destruction facility where it will be ground up.

One of the more simple ways to break into a company is through the front door during working hours. This does not mean "tailgating" in behind someone, which is an issue for sure. However, in this case, it means asking for information. As noted in Chapter 1, social engineering is one of the more powerful ways to gain knowledge about a company. Find out from your host about its training procedures for the prevention of social engineering intrusions.

Breach Response

Hopefully, you won't be the victim of a break-in at your data center or host. But it can happen, so ask your host what the procedures are for dealing with it. Discover in your discussions what the processes are for cleanup and ensuring that no criminal activity happened to your equipment or website.

Terrorists

The world we live in today must grapple with terrorism. The challenge with terrorism is that if it's not dealt with swiftly, it tends to grow and change. Tactics shift, and terrorists tend to become bolder and more aggressive. Businesses of all types are probably working on (or amending existing) plans to account for this new threat.

Hosting companies are a unique target, because they may experience *hacktivism*, or hacking for a political cause as a form of terrorist attack. The host may also be subjected to a physical assault such as a bomb threat. Asking about the host's contingency plans is fair, but do not expect full disclosure. You mainly want to gain a sense of the host's level of planning.

Access to Equipment

In most (if not all) cases, physical access to machines should be limited. Inquire as to who has access to your equipment or the server your machine is on, when and why they have access, and how this access is granted. In a shared hosting situation, you have zero say as to how this is handled. In a co-location situation you should have 100 percent control over the access to the machine.

Water Detection

Data centers typically have a raised floor with removable tiles composing the flooring. This gives access to underfloor cabling, power, and other supporting infrastructure needs. Occasionally, cooling is routed underfloor to the cabinets. In researching your host or co-location facility, ask about water-detection sensors under the raised floor. One broken water pipe could ruin your day. Rest assured that this safeguard is pretty typical for most modern installations.

Fire Suppression

If a fire does occur, then putting it out as quickly as possible is clearly the only correct action. In your research, you may hear a few terms such as *pre-action*, *dry pipe*, and *wet pipe*, and, in some cases, you may hear *Halon*. All of these are different types of fire extinguishing systems, and are governed by the local laws and jurisdictions of the townships in which the buildings are located.

> **NOTE** Note that Halon is likely not in use in any modern hosting facilities.

Emergency Procedures

In an emergency, people, not your business, matter most. The websites, servers, data, and the building are secondary to human safety. In this regard, you want to have a high-level understanding of the procedures used to protect the people.

After the threat has passed, then all the websites and servers should be the primary focus. Assuming that the emergency brought your sites down, then you'll want an idea of the time that it will take (either in hours or days) for service to be restored. Knowing this, you can measure your tolerance for downtime in your business against the projected time.

Reasons for an emergency evacuation could be fire, flood, tornado, earthquake, bomb threat, hurricane, or other unforeseen activities.

Disaster Recovery and Business Continuity

As mentioned previously, in a shared hosting model, you are most likely 100 percent responsible for your backups. This means that even if the server fails and the hosting company replaces it, to restore your data, you must have a backup. Do not expect the hosting company to spend time discussing its disaster plans with you if you're paying $3.99 per month. Build your own disaster-recovery plan.

If you are co-locating or buying a dedicated server, then learning more about your host's disaster planning and business continuity plans are paramount. Chapter 6 covers this topic in detail. However, here are a few questions to get you started in your business conversations:

- Where is your backup facility?
- How often do you test your disaster plan?
- Are the procedures updated after the tests?
- How will you communicate with the host in a disaster situation?
- Who should you call during a declared disaster? Will this be an internal person, or an external disaster recovery provider?
- Will the external company levy a disaster declaration fee?
- When was the last disaster declared?
- If an evacuation is necessary, where does your staff operate from?
- What is the Service Level Agreement (SLA) of the hosting company? Many hosting companies do not offer a lot in the way of guaranteed uptime.

As you can see, try to ask questions that cover the typical who, what, when, where, why, and how aspects of disaster planning.

Cyber Security

As you read this, some untold number of servers and websites have been hacked by malicious people. Cyber security should be at the top of your list of important things when it comes to protecting your sites. This includes putting up a good fence between you and the criminal element on the Internet.

In terms of that defense, the best method is a *layered approach* to security. Literally, layering involves using different protection methods for the network, server, and websites. This requires many pieces of technology to secure your operations. The following discussion provides an introduction to each of the items.

Firewalls and Intrusion Detection

On the surface, both firewalls and intrusion-detection systems could appear to be the same thing. They differ in that a firewall works to keep two networks separate, allowing only traffic that is authorized. Because the Internet is a giant network of networks, firewalls are a must. They look "forward" — in other words, outside the firewall — for danger. Intrusion-detection systems work to look at the traffic patterns and signatures, and work to detect malicious behavior so that the administrators can be notified about it.

Software firewalls (such as `SecureLive.net`) work at the application level, which represents almost the last line of defense against attackers. Other types of security software include `ModSecurity`, `ConfigServer`, `Firewall`, and `ipsec`.

When looking for a new host, ask how the host prevents and detects attacks.

Log File Auditing

The *log file* is typically a catch-all phrase for several different files that are used to store information. They may contain access logs, hardware information logging, application or operating system logs, and error logs. These records are valuable for tracking down any number of problems. Because most site owners are not aware of them, or don't know how to read them, many times they are not even stored.

Ask your host what logging access you have and how to obtain the logs. In that discussion, you'll probably hear about several different logging types. Following are a few of the more important ones you should keep up with:

- *Error logs* — These logs record all sorts of vital information about your website. In a PHP environment, these files will capture quite a bit about the health of an application. These logs can lead you to hacked or damaged files, and should be reviewed at least weekly.

- *Access logs* — These files can often be unwieldy because of their size, especially on an Apache web server. The process used to keep them at a manageable size is called *log rotation*. The access logs record all activity on your website, and can be used to reconstruct activity from a specific IP address. You'll learn more about the Apache logs in Chapter 8.

- *Firewall logs* — These can encompass many forms, depending on the hardware or the application. For example, for the CSF firewall software, these logs maintain a list of recent attacks. Keeping an eye on these logs will make you aware of the failed attempts to get in. Remember, a successful attempt may appear as normal traffic.

- *Hardware logs* — If you own a dedicated machine, you may have access to the hardware logging of the server box, which will provide many valuable data points — things such as temperature of the machine, information about the CPUs, or the speed of the fans. These logs can even tell you whether a hard drive is getting close to failing. Today's hardware logging is very powerful. For what it's worth, do not expect to get this type of logging in a hosting model.

Spam, Virus Scanning, and Prevention

Another security front you want your host to be on top of is spam filtering, virus scanning, and prevention. These tasks can be done in a number of ways, depending on the operating system, the hosting company, and more. In fact, some companies will filter and clean your inbound and outbound mail for you in flight. That means that as mail reaches your infrastructure, it has been cleaned of viruses and spam. This method may be well worth looking at. Have your host explain how it prevents infections from outside sources such as e-mail.

Many hosting companies take a hard line against hacked websites. They really have no choice in the matter. One hacked website can infect many others, both in the network and out in the wild. Find out what your host's plan is if you were to be attacked.

Patching for Weaknesses

Weakness and vulnerabilities appear daily in all types of software and hardware systems. Using services such as SalvusAlerting.com, you can stay apprised of new vulnerabilities in a timely fashion. After these vulnerabilities are out in the open, then the attacks start up. Your host should have a process and a plan to apply patches according to priority. Hackers keep an eye on released vulnerabilities as well, and they will try to break into your site through a variety of means. Do not give them an opening by not patching.

VoIP

The Voice Over IP (VoIP) protocol allows telephone calls to be made on the Internet. It is also a very big threat to any infrastructure if not configured properly. VoIP traffic can travel over the same networks that the data runs on. Tools exist today to launch malicious attacks on VoIP. Ask the host whether it uses VoIP, and how it segments this protocol off from the rest of the network traffic.

Web Servers

Enough cannot be said about maintaining your web applications. Today, a significant number of attacks occur at the web application layer — literally, at the website. In terms of your host, ensure that the *easy-to-install* items it offers (such as Joomla! or WordPress) are up to date. Many hosts do not keep versions of these ready-to-install applications up to date.

Ask the web host how it protects shared servers from your neighbors. If you recall, the shared server actually is many websites on a single physical machine. If a hacker breaks into a neighboring site, he or she could affect yours.

Environmental Support

Humidity in the great outdoors can sometimes be aggravating in the summer. In data centers, keeping humidity levels around 45 percent to 55 percent to maintain a low static-electricity environment is important.

Network Redundancy

In the hosting world, the terms *pipe*, *power*, and *ping* refer to bandwidth, electricity, and connectivity to the Internet, respectively. Unless you are dealing with a company that only leases a few boxes, or has a "single-cabinet" in an office that it calls "hosting," these items should be set up in a redundant fashion.

The network includes the pipe and ping portion of the data center. A sales representative should be able to easily articulate to you what systems are in place to offer network redundancy. You should hear a few common answers here, such as redundant telecom providers for the main Internet trunks. Other redundancy systems may be known as *load balancers*, which can serve to route a failed connection in the event of an issue. To add another layer, routers should be able to fail over or be taken out of service for updates and maintenance without impacting the overall service level of the network. Find out from your prospective hosting company what the standard operating procedures are to ensure network uptime.

An example of a host that may not be able to provide you a very good uptime is one who offers a single connection (or backbone) to the Internet. If a backhoe cuts the fiber to the host's location, or if the route fails, you are down until that connection can be restored.

Electrical Service

Electrical service is something you are no doubt familiar with. You simply expect it to be there. In a huge consumer like a host, several data points must be considered that underlie the host's capability to maintain electrical service. These include the following:

- Multiple electrical providers to the building
- An onsite generator that supports a full load for long periods of time
- The capability to support single or multiple electrical feeds per cabinet
- On-premise emergency battery power

Larger data centers often are serviced by more than one electrical provider. The area of the country you are in will dictate the number of providers. This is important because of outages. You may recall the August 2003 Northeastern U.S. blackout and the rolling blackouts in California. Data centers without redundant electrical providers may not be your best choice.

If you are considering working with a small hosting provider or data center, find out what the limits per rack for power (amperage) are per the local city codes. The purpose of discovering this information is to see whether enough electricity (power measured in amps) will be available for your needs. Limiting racks to a lower power availability keeps them from being fully utilized, thus causing *server sprawl*. Generally, this is something to avoid.

Another consideration to ask about is emergency power. This can come in two forms: battery generated and diesel generators. Battery power can take the form of a small, in-rack, *uninterruptible power supply* (*UPS*), or a large battery cluster housed in the building. The generator is typically paired with the large battery cluster to provide power for the few minutes of time the generator takes to come on and power the building.

When shopping for your host, ask how the host powers the building during a power outage. Be sure to check the *service-level agreement* (*SLA*) for specific terms that the host agrees to follow. Check the terms closely for how you are compensated, and how you might file a claim should the host not meet its uptime obligations. For example, does the guarantee spell out what power will be available for your server? Or will power only be available to critical systems, and you are expected to provide your own UPS to your server?

It's worth noting that this likely will not be something you would be concerned with on a low-cost, shared hosting provider. Other scenarios may mean that the hosting provider will power your equipment down during (or as part of) the outage. Again, in more modern facilities, this is not typically a problem.

Ask how long (measured in hours) the generator can power the facility in the event that electrical service is interrupted. In essence, if the generator has fuel, it should be able to run as long as it needs. In reality, this means it should be able to run until the local fuel storage is depleted. Many data centers and hosts have about 48 to 72 hours of fuel on site. This, of course, varies, and should not be used as a measure. Ask the hosting provider about the refueling process. Ask about guaranteed fuel delivery (sometimes known as *fuel contracts*, which means that the provider can get refueled, guaranteed in "X" hours).

Find out about a generator test plan. Again, on average, the generator should be tested approximately every 30 days.

Most modern data center facilities have some form of battery power. Hosting facilities, or co-location companies, most likely have a battery room, which is a room with huge batteries in it to power the building for a few minutes. If you tour a facility, ask to see it.

Technical Support

In a time of crisis, good technical support is worth its weight in gold. Sadly, many technical companies skimp in this area. Companies such as `wiredtree.com` that excel in providing superior technical support are the kind to look for. Having said that, how do you know?

When you ask a potential hosting provider, "Do you have good support?" the answer will always be "Yes." Putting the provider to the test by purchasing isn't always the best approach. Fortunately, some methods are available that will help you reach the right answer.

One popular method to find out about pricing, uptime, service, or whatever is to ask around by networking with other business people. This is preferred over relying on reviews in a printed magazine or website. The business people you network with likely do not have any vested interest in the hosting company. Thus, you will get a honest answer in the form of their opinions based on experience.

Of course, online reviews have value in the form of reader comments. Review comments on Twitter, Facebook, web host reviews, and other forms of non-printed media. This method can provide a dynamic, living model from which you may form your own opinion.

One mistake to avoid is assuming that a company provides great support because it is huge. It seems that the bigger the company gets, the worse its support may get. Although that may be a bit of a blanket statement, take it as a metric. The bigger a company gets, the more the urge exists internally to cut costs. Services (which are sometimes viewed by the bean counters as not turning a profit) are often reduced, or even outsourced to countries that offer significant cost savings or other incentives. The company often ends up with a poor customer experience and a disenchanted client base. However, not all big companies get it wrong, just as not all small companies get it right. Just consider this as a metric to measure in your plan.

Take time to read the online support documentation a company offers. Well-written documentation can easily keep a company's internal "people" costs down, while maintaining a high customer satisfaction rating. Reviewing the documentation gives you an idea of the company's technical skill. Here are a few points to consider when reading online documentation:

- How relevant to your day-to-day tasks is the support being offered?
- Is the documentation timely?
- When was the documentation last updated?
- Are there plenty of articles?
- Can you follow along and understand the documentation?

Many times, online documentation is used as an *RTM* (or "read the manual") situation. If the technical support is going to default to that, then the documentation had better be good.

You can put technical support to the test by submitting a trouble ticket and judging the response. This may not be possible in all cases, but where it is, you should use it. By using this technique, you can find out whether the technical support is thorough, timely, helpful, and, most of all, friendly. If the company doesn't treat you right before you're a client, then you can't expect to be treated right after you become a client.

One final method is to call the competition of your primary choice. When you call, tell them you are thinking of going to with hosting choice "A" and you would like to know about theirs. They will go out of their way to tell you how much better they are, how much more qualified their technical support staff is, and all the sales pitch material. In the processes, they may have a lot of negative or positive things to say about their competitor. Listen to those things. Vendors know things about each other that you may or may not know. Dig in and find out why one company seems better than another. It may just be noise, or something may be there that you wouldn't find out otherwise. Who knows? You may find that hosting choice "B" has a better deal for you in the end.

Technical support represents your remote hands at the machine and with the software. During a crisis, you want the technical support staff to be as effective as they can be for you.

Emergency Planning for the Host

Emergency planning is as important as security of your site. Making several backups has a purpose beyond simply being paranoid. The prime reason for maintaining several backups is peace of mind that if something happens, you have a copy of your data.

Being able to restore can make the difference in keeping your website in business or going out of business. If a machine is confiscated by law enforcement because of illegal activity by a neighboring shared hosting website, or something as simple as a hard drive crash occurs, it doesn't matter — you're off the air.

This introduces the "$64,000 question" for your host: Who is responsible for backing up and restoring the server? If you are responsible (per the host), then work that into your disaster-recovery planning. If the host is responsible, then plan for the host to fail at it. In essence, at the end of the day, it's your data, and, thus, your responsibility, to ensure that you have a plan to restore. That plan can be in conjunction with the host, but plan it nonetheless.

If the host is managing your backups, then find out how often the backups are run. In the case of Rochen.com, each plan includes a twice-daily backup with the capability to restore to most any point in time. This type of backup-and-recovery process is what any business should demand.

If your host doesn't offer any backup-type services, don't worry. In your disaster-recovery plan, you can build out the necessary processes.

The frequency of your backups should reflect the rate of change in your data. If your data only changes once a week, then weekly backups should suffice. If your data changes more frequently, then a daily backup is in order. The bottom line is that if your host suddenly were not there, you would need the most recent copies of your data. Explore emergency plans in depth.

The abuse factor from employees and external persons should be part of the host's emergency processes. If an employee goes crazy and deletes whole servers, what is the plan? If you are hit with a Denial of Service (DoS) attack, then what is the host's plan for action?

NOTE A Denial of Service (DoS) attack is the prevention of authorized access to resources or the delaying of time-critical operations. ("Time-critical" may be milliseconds or hours, depending upon the service provided.)

The ultimate emergency planning item is if the host must evacuate the building, where will the people go? Does the host have staff in another location that can monitor the servers remotely? If not, what is the plan to regain control of the network? The "where will people work" question is one that is very often overlooked.

Learn as much as you can about the host's emergency planning processes. You will need to fill in the gaps where the host leaves off in order to protect your business.

Location of the Host's Data Center

You may wonder why the location of the host's data center matters. After all, the Internet is everywhere! You should care because this location can have some wide-ranging implications.

Technical talent is abundant in most cities in the United States, as well as abroad. The quality of the talent may vary. Take into account where your host is, and ask a lot of questions about the local talent. Asking about local talent is important, because the technician on the night shift may be a terrific Windows guy, but you are running Linux.

Major interstate highways and rail lines in the United States are often the same path major portions of the Internet run along. Consider the cost if you needed a point-to-point connection with another data center, or if you need a very high-speed connection. Although it is likely present, it may cost more because of factors such as distance or the local telephony provider.

Weather and geographic conditions can be an issue. Is your provider in an earthquake-prone area? What about tornadoes or hurricanes? These can all impact the daily operation of your host.

Lastly, the political climate could impact you financially. For example, think about cities that are way overboard in their green thinking. They may view a data center as a threat to the Earth and enforce taxes for the emissions of carbon dioxide. This will not be paid by the host. It will be paid by you in the form of higher taxes and fees on your hosting.

Processes

Certain processes are important to the healthy operation of your site(s) and server(s). Although some of these have been discussed in various contexts, you must ensure that you understand these processes for shared, VPS, dedicated, and cloud hosting.

Backups

As mentioned previously, looking at the processes that involve backing up is important. Depending on the technology being used to conduct the backup, these processes can slow down your web server. The time of day is important. For example, if, for some strange reason, the host wants to back up during the day, and your site has a lot of traffic during the day, then this practice introduces a conflict.

NOTE It's worth noting that a *backup* differs from a *snapshot*. Snapshots are simply pointers to the original data. Snapshots allow you a quick means to restore a lost file or files. One critical point is that if you do not make an off-disk copy, then a snapshot is irrelevant if the hard disk crashes. Having said that, snapshot technology is highly valuable, and should be part of your recovery plan.

Many software packages are available (both commercially and in the open source world) to conduct backups. If you are on a Windows machine, you might easily be using a commercial package. If you are on Linux machine, an equally good chance exists that you use an open source package. You should care if you need to move media from one operating system to another. You must know whether the encryption and backup software will be able to read the other format.

One extremely popular method for backing up data is called a storage area network (SAN). This does not mean the data leaves the data center. It means that it's stored (with exceptions) onsite. If the host is using a SAN or a network attached storage (NAS) device, find out how it protects that storage — encryption, tape software, and so on.

Offsite Procedures

Offsite procedures should include the safe transport and retrieval of the data. Plenty of instances exist where important data was lost and used nefariously. If backups are removed from a server and taken anywhere, they should be encrypted to prevent the data from being read by unauthorized persons. Find out whether the data is taken offsite, and how it is encrypted. Who has the key to unlock the encryption?

As a real-world example, consider a mortgage company that sent backup tapes off site. The courier from the tape company lost the tape. The tape contained all the personal information of mortgage holders (including Social Security numbers, home addresses, dates of birth, and so on).

The concern was that this tape was unencrypted. Mortgage holders received a year of free credit monitoring and a form letter from some vice president who expressed his "deep regret." The company eventually recovered the tape and all was well. The moral of the story, of course, was that if data leaves a hosting facility in any form (tape, disk, USB key, and so on), then it should be encrypted.

Accepting Credit Cards on Your Website

Most businesses accept some form of payment on their websites. Doing so requires that a number technical parts be put into place, such as SSL certificates, some form of a shopping cart, and, of course, a means to accept money through a special bank account that allows you to accept money via credit cards, known as a *merchant account*.

The simplest form of payment acceptance is PayPal. It offers the merchant a very low risk and is simple to use. This type of payment system does not require you to be *payment card industry* (*PCI*) compliant.

Some hosts offer PCI compliance assistance. `Rochen.com` is one host that will assist you in the process. When shopping for your host, ask what experiences the host has had with PCI. Find out how much assistance the host can provide you when your site fails to pass the technical and security tests. Note that this advice is for *when*, not *if*. This is because new vulnerabilities discovered regularly can and will impact your security. If you're impacted, then you will not pass PCI compliance testing. It's important to stay on top of vulnerabilities and correct them as soon as possible.

> **NOTE** `SalvusAlerting.com` **is a good source to use to keep up with ever-changing vulnerabilities.**

If the host does not offer much in the way of assistance, and you need to be PCI compliant, then find a new host.

It's important that you understand the basics of what PCI is, and how to obtain it.

Understanding PCI

Payment card industry or *PCI*, actually refers to the industry group that formed the cyber security standards for payment acceptance. It also represents the *standard*. In this discussion, the term *PCI* will be used interchangeably to represent this standard. The intent of this security standard is to protect financial institutions and card holders against fraud. The PCI security standards are designed to give a common set of security safeguards against all types of threats.

> **NOTE** **The discussion here is not meant to be a comprehensive guide to PCI, but rather as a means to give you a sense of the standard. For the most complete and up-to-date information about PCI, see** `www.pcisecuritystandards.org`**.**

If you read the PCI documentation, it can be confusing. It is a complex set of rules and procedures to cover a variety of merchant payment-acceptance situations. It covers everything from the card swipe on a gas pump all the way to the bank that accepts the card and makes payment to the merchant. In other words, if payment by card is accepted, then the device, website, gas pump, or whatever, is required to be PCI compliant.

Today, if you want to accept credit card transactions (with the exception of certain services such as PayPal), then you must be compliant with PCI.

PCI Terminology

As with any technology-based industry, knowing the terminology associated with PCI will help you understand the solution. Let's take a look at a few terms that you will hear when pursuing or discussing PCI.

Depending on your merchant level, you may need to hire a *Qualified Security Assessor* (*QSA*). The QSA is a person (or persons) working for a company who is responsible for validating your compliance and creating a report of compliance.

NOTE Not all merchants will interact with a QSA. For an up-to-date list of QSA persons and companies, see www.pcisecuritystandards.org/pdfs/ pci_qsa_list.pdf.

All websites accepting payment by credit card are required to use an *approved scanning vendor* (*ASV*). This is a third-party company that has been certified to perform external vulnerability scans for merchants and service providers. The ASV will scan your website and your hosting server to determine what potential weaknesses exist. The ASV is typically contracted on an annual basis with fees based on services provided. Because the ASV is working from a standard, shop around and find the best deal. These vendors all must provide the same service.

NOTE You can find an up-to-date list of ASVs at pcisecuritystandards .org/pdfs/asv_report.html.

The term *acquirers* refers to the bank or other financial entity with whom you, as a merchant, have a contractual relationship. Additionally, they may be a referred to as a *bank*, a *merchant bank*, a *process*, or an *independent sales organization* (*ISO*). They hold the ultimate responsibility for a merchant's compliance. At the end of the day, you both bear the liability for non-compliance.

You are considered a *merchant*. Merchants accepting payment over a scan terminal with a PIN pad may range from the dry cleaners all the way to an online e-commerce store.

Becoming PCI Certified

Gaining PCI certification is not a simple matter. It involves several steps and is time-consuming. PCI compliance is required, and thus, it is very important. The importance comes in via financial penalties if you are breached and found to have been non-compliant at the time. Theft of cardholder data carries a large price — so be sure you stay compliant.

WARNING If you don't have a reason to store credit card data, then don't do it. Some merchant providers will store card data for you as part of their service. This shifts the risk from you to them.

To help ease you into the PCI experience, let's examine the moving parts that you must have in place (technically speaking) as a basic merchant.

Installing an SSL Certificate

The most basic element of conducting an online credit card transaction is to purchase and install an SSL certificate. The SSL certificate ensures that a session between the visitor and the server is encrypted. It does not mean that the information on the server is encrypted — only information from point A to point B. This prevents an eavesdropper from capturing the credit card or other information in flight. This is a huge source of confusion for consumers and business owners alike. Part of the confusion comes in the different price levels, levels of encryption, and other features of various certificate vendors. The SSL certificate is an annually renewable process, and must be installed by your host.

Testing by ASV

The ASV will scan your website and server. To pass the certification requirements, your server and website must be up to date and "risk free." "Risk free" means that the website is free from a certain category of risks.

To achieve PCI compliance, you contract with an ASV to test your server. The ASV will provide you with either a passing certificate or a failure report. The failure report will detail the elements (such as open ports, out-of-date software, or other items) that are considered to be a threat. Provide your host with this report for mitigation.

After the host feels the threats have been mitigated, run the test again. This process is repeated until the website passes. This can be a frustrating process. If you find a host that is accustomed to dealing with PCI to start with, then this process will be much easier. Additionally, you must attest that the machines you use are in a secure facility — that is, proper controls have been put in place to physically guard the machine. This eliminates hosting an e-commerce site on your nephew's home-built server in a basement.

Choosing a Shopping Cart

Selling goods and services requires a shopping cart or other similar system. PCI requires that you to use an approved shopping cart. These are referred to as *validated payment applications* by the PCI council. As of this writing, the PCI website listed 377 approved vendors and 732 approved payment applications (last updated on July 8, 2010). This can present a challenge to a new business owner. Who do you pick?

Sadly, how to make this choice is often a "buyer beware" problem. The merchant providers expect that you understand all the fees and terminology. They may point you to "their" carts. This can lead to you paying more for a service than you should.

Shop around until you find a merchant processor who will take the time to clearly explain the details. You should also find shopping carts that do what you need them to do. Because this is a book about CMSs such as Joomla!, Drupal, and Plone, you may want to look for carts that are both PCI compliant and work within those frameworks.

Let's examine a few things to look for in a cart:

- *Is it on the PCI-approved list for accepting payments?* — This question may not be a show-stopper, but you should still consult with your bank and find out.

- *Does the cart have good reporting?* — As a merchant, having good reporting makes for knowing where you are in your business. Though not strictly a PCI function, having detailed reporting is a good idea.

- *Does the cart have any added security features that might augment your PCI efforts?* — This can be any number of things, including an encrypted database, Captcha, and other spam deterrents.

- *Does it offer download functions?* — Offering digital downloads means that your clients will be interacting with the cart to download. Ensuring that the download functions are vulnerability free will keep you on the right track with PCI.

- *Is the cart easy to integrate with your site?* — You should find out how easy the shopping cart is to bolt on to your website. If it is difficult, then you may find an unexpected vulnerability lurking in your site.

- *How often does the vendor update/upgrade the cart?* — This can involve an update of features, or more importantly, for vulnerabilities found. If the last update was years ago, look for another cart. Remember, the vendor should be there for you if you run into PCI trouble. A recent real-world example was a shopping site that, out of the blue, failed PCI compliance on the website. Tech support determined that it was a false positive. The ASV was able to ignore the failure because it did not pose a real threat. Without any support, this problem would have been impossible to discern quickly.

Storing Data Securely

Storage of your data should be secure and safe. The idea is that if you store credit card data, specific steps surround it in terms of what you can store, how it should be stored, and more. If you are using a backup service, then *that service* must be PCI-compliant as well.

PCI Vulnerability Management Plan

PCI requires that you have a vulnerability management program, which means that you must stay on top of vulnerabilities, and not wait until they are discovered in a scan. However, a vulnerability may occasionally be flagged by the ASV that is false (as shown in the earlier example) or has been fixed. This can be handled by what is called *compensating controls*, which are technologies or processes put in place to compensate for weaknesses. For example, good reasons may exist as to why you fail a scan. Sometimes certain operating systems will patch a vulnerability, but not update the version number. The scan detects it as a vulnerable version. Your host should be able to provide documentation that shows you are "backported," which means that the changes have been made to a software package, but the version is not updated. However, if the software has not been backported, you must patch it.

Avoiding Common ASV Testing Pitfalls

You may encounter a number of problems when ASV testing, and mitigating them before you start the process will make things go much smoother. Here is a brief list of a few common issues:

- Ports that are open and should be closed are a common problem in websites. This can be for any number of reasons, such as poor setup or being intentionally left open. In any case, the general rule is to close ports *not in use*. Although it's a very generic rule, it stands up to the test.

- Having the OpenSSL be out-of-date or vulnerable on the server can also be a problem. In the Linux operating system, it is part of the SSL security. Updating it does not take long, but is often overlooked.

- Because the SSL certificate must be renewed annually at a minimum, an expired SSL certificate will be flagged as non-compliant. Likewise a *self-signed* certificate is one you create and establish yourself. Although technically viable, it's not acceptable for compliance.

- Many means are available to block a vulnerability scan on your site. This is not a bad practice, because it prevents bad guys from looking for weaknesses. However, if your scanning company is being blocked, your site and server likely will fail to meet certification requirements.

- Control panels (host side) that are out-of-date or not configured correctly can be a source of problems.

- Web mail or control panel systems that are accessible from the Internet may require an additional SSL certificate.

After Certification

Staying certified in PCI is not a one-time event. In fact, you must certify every quarter. This task is easily handled by a QSV who provides not only quarterly scanning, but on-demand scanning as well. You should scan every 30 days (or more often), and in the event you discover you are vulnerable, you can address it immediately. Staying on top of the scanning effort and catching problems as they are detected is important.

You will likely have a training requirement for you and your staff to complete. This typically involves handling of the credit card data, refunds, disputes, and other items. What training you receive really depends on your merchant account provider. Check with the provider for specific training requirements for you and your staff.

As a business, you want to grow and make a healthy profit while serving the needs of your customers. Staying on top of the PCI certification is a duty and an obligation. What this is really all about is preventing a breach of your security, and thus, the loss of credit card data.

DEALING WITH BREACHES

Dealing with breaches is an unpleasant and costly event, one you do not want to experience. As a word of caution, each state in the U.S. has a different set of laws and penalties that govern the loss of consumer data. This book *does not* set out any legal advice. Check with your attorney to understand the regulations and laws you must comply with in the event your server is breached, and credit card or other consumer privacy data is stolen.

Senators Tom Carper and Bob Bennet introduced the 2010 Data Security Act. This bill, if enacted, would affect any entity that maintains personal data of individuals, including financial institutions, retailers, and federal agencies. Along with this bill, two other bills were introduced. As a merchant, you would be very wise to keep apprised of these bills. Their status should be well-known by the time this book reaches your hands.

NOTE PCI compliance is generally good thing for all industries. It gives the merchant some protection, and it clearly provides the consumer some peace of mind. Many people, while afraid to swipe their card on a website, will have no problem at a gas pump or a brick-and-mortar merchant. Yet, without PCI, they are vulnerable in either area. Although this book *is not* a guide to PCI, the information has been presented to give you a bit of a taste and some guidance. Refer to the official PCI website at www.pcisecuritystandards.org for full guidance.

Domain Name System Servers

The domain name system (DNS) is essentially the Internet's telephone book. DNS is the map that browsers follow to reach websites and other computers on the Internet. Normally, you don't have much worry about with DNS after it's set up and running. The biggest concern you should have about DNS is maintaining the software on the machine and protecting it from attack.

DNS is probably one of the most critical pieces of technology on the Internet. Without it, there simply would not be an Internet, only a collection of machines with little capability to communicate.

This section dives into the shallow end of the DNS pool to help you learn about how it works, and how to protect it.

Understanding DNS

Today's Internet is vastly different, more complex, and more populated than the original implementation known as ARPANET (Advanced Research Projects Agency Network).

Back in the day, computers would be connected point to point — in other words, they were connected directly to one another. ARPANET enabled the computers (early servers) to use a *network* to reach any of the other computers on the network. The scientists working on the system maintained a list called the *host* list. To connect, the systems would look at that list, and then discover the route. As the early Internet (formerly the ARPANET) grew, that list quickly became too large to manage. Out of that was born DNS.

DNS is a distributed database of hosting information. In simple terms, it's a giant version of the old host list. It maintains the path to all top-level domain (TLD) websites. The actual DNS servers themselves (known as the *root servers*) are maintained in Virginia. If any local DNS server has trouble locating a website for you, it can ask the root servers for the location.

Your hosting account has a machine that serves as the local DNS. Its job is to keep track of your site (and others) at the host. If an attacker could fool the DNS server into thinking the attacker's site was the destination for your domain, the hacker could take over your website.

Threats to DNS

The DNS server is what makes our highly connected world work. It resolves the IP address of a server to the domain name, allowing visitors to type `example.com` rather than 10.100.10.8, which would be impossible to remember, and no fun at all. Because the DNS server (or *name server*) in a host represents websites to the "WWW" world, it stands to reason that maintaining and protecting it is as important as protecting your business or home from crime.

Although there are likely several more threats to the DNS servers in your host, here are a few that could impact you:

- DNS (name server) failure
- Poorly maintained and unpatched DNS servers
- DNS poisoning
- Zone transfers

DNS (Name Server) Failure

Most of the time, hosts ensure against failure of your DNS (or *name server*) by using multiple physical boxes. However, if you have DNS deployed on a single machine, think about how you will respond and react to a server failure.

Using tools such as those found at www.dnsstuff.com, you can quickly determine whether the host has a redundant DNS server setup. Using a single server as the DNS exposes you to loss of that server. The effect would be your site disappearing.

Find out from your hosting company what its plan is in case of DNS server failure. There have been cases where a single machine was configured for DNS. You can also look at online tools (such as the previously mentioned dnsstuff.com) for verification. You should see NS1.domainname.com and NS2.domainname.com as an example of multiple name servers. However, verify that they are not on the same physical machine. This is a very low-level concern, unless you are affiliated with an extremely small host.

Zone Transfers

DNS servers exist to maintain both an internal and external mapping of networks, known as *zones*. The zone information about the IP addresses, machine names, and so on is extremely valuable to dedicated attackers. They can literally build a map of machines on the network. This gives them an effective edge in an attack. Today, although it's not common, many badly configured servers do exist.

Zone transfers are a means of gathering information about your infrastructure. The type of information that can be obtained is quite detailed *if* hackers can get in. The zone transfer is normally used to copy DNS data such as IP address, CNAME, name servers, and more across one or more DNS servers or backup files. When a zone transfer occurs, it provides all the information about the internal workings of your network in a text file — which is easily read by anyone.

Preventing zone transfers is a matter of proper configuration of your firewall, DNS server, and ports, among other things.

Figure 2-1 shows a list of ports on a test server. A high number of ports are in a state of "open" that should not be. However, in the case of a zone transfer, these open ports would give the attacker a place to start. Port 53 is "open" on this server. The attacker could potentially copy the zone files out from that port.

The host should ensure that steps are taken to protect the DNS from unauthorized zone transfers. Following are a couple of items that you want to be aware of:

- Close (depending on your DNS setup) port 53
- If your host has "external" DNS servers and "internal" DNS servers, then port 53 should be closed. Internal DNS servers should forward their requests to the external servers. They, in turn, should be configured to talk to the root servers.

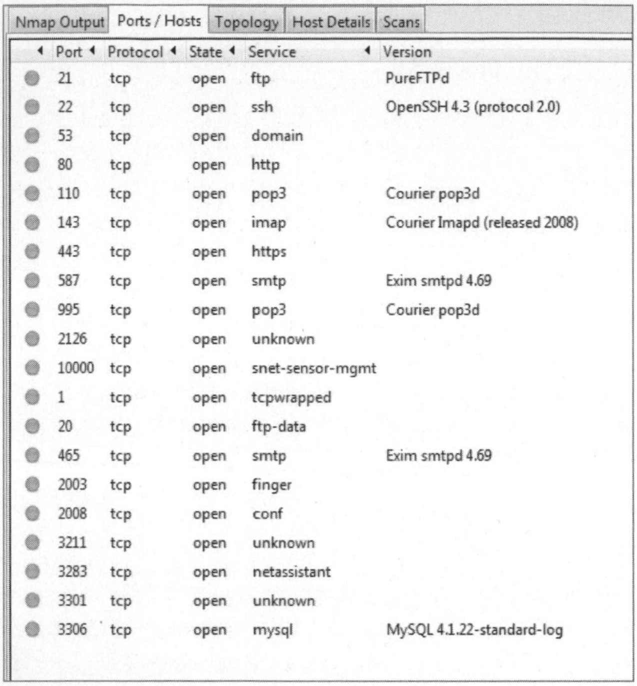

Nmap Output | Ports / Hosts | Topology | Host Details | Scans

Port	Protocol	State	Service	Version
21	tcp	open	ftp	PureFTPd
22	tcp	open	ssh	OpenSSH 4.3 (protocol 2.0)
53	tcp	open	domain	
80	tcp	open	http	
110	tcp	open	pop3	Courier pop3d
143	tcp	open	imap	Courier Imapd (released 2008)
443	tcp	open	https	
587	tcp	open	smtp	Exim smtpd 4.69
995	tcp	open	pop3	Courier pop3d
2126	tcp	open	unknown	
10000	tcp	open	snet-sensor-mgmt	
1	tcp	open	tcpwrapped	
20	tcp	open	ftp-data	
465	tcp	open	smtp	Exim smtpd 4.69
2003	tcp	open	finger	
2008	tcp	open	conf	
3211	tcp	open	unknown	
3283	tcp	open	netassistant	
3301	tcp	open	unknown	
3306	tcp	open	mysql	MySQL 4.1.22-standard-log

Figure 2-1: Ports open on a server

Lack of Patching DNS Servers

One of the most (if not *the* most) popular DNS server software platforms is *Berkeley Internet Name Domain* (*BIND*). Like all other software systems, BIND will become vulnerable at some point in the future. Applying updates or patches (as you do with the rest of your software) is the best way to stay safe.

As of this writing, a recent update to BIND v9 fixed a dangerous threat called *DNS poisoning* (discussed next). This is an example of why the host and you should keep up with patching.

DNS Poisoning

One of the more nefarious means of attacking a website is to poison the information in the DNS server. Literally, this means the attacker forces the DNS server to accept incorrect information, and thus, the server gives out malicious or wrong website addresses instead of yours.

On December 18, 2009, the microblogging service, `Twitter.com`, suffered a DNS server compromise by political activists. The hackers redirected all requests for Twitter to a web page on a server they controlled. They did not have to get to Twitter's server to conduct this attack, only to the DNS servers.

If you are being stalked by a really knowledgeable and determined attacker, the DNS server will be one of the prime targets. The DNS server is a terrific place to gather information about a network's internal infrastructure, passwords, usernames, internal IP addresses, and much more. All of this information can be gained from an improperly configured DNS server. Think about it in the manner of a criminal who might case an office before breaking in. The criminal wants to know where the alarms are, the exits, the cameras, and so forth. The dedicated attacker would view DNS in the same way.

NOTE To learn more about DNS, pick up the book *DNS and BIND, Fifth Edition* (Sebastopol, CA: O'Reilly, 2006) by Cricket Liu and Paul Albitz. It is one of the best references for DNS available.

Hosting Your Own Website Server

Occasionally, you will hear about a person who is hosting a web server at home. As a small business, you may very well be based in a home office. Hosting a server at home may seem like a good idea, but it is not. You should drop that idea and find proper hosting.

However, if you are a business with a technical staff, then hosting internally is a viable option. This brief section touches on the highlights of handling your own web server.

Getting Ready

You first must determine what size of physical server you'll need. If your website is a high-transaction store, then you'll want to look at a fast-processing, low-latency drive system. If you are in a low-volume, but high-bandwidth consumption business (for example, a training video server), then having the proper network bandwidth is where you will focus your budget dollars.

Determining your application stack, such as e-mail, web server, languages, and website software (for example, Joomla!, Drupal, Plone, or WordPress), will drive your hardware decision. Next up is the choice of operating systems. Although several are available, this book focuses on Linux primarily.

Each of these decisions will change your cost model in some fashion. For example, Linux will cost less, because it is an open source choice versus going with a major company like Microsoft that has higher-priced commercially licensed choices. Price should not be the deciding factor. Rather, choosing the right tool for the right job is the correct decision.

In the category of safety falls security and backups. The security of the network will be handled by physical hardware such as a Cisco firewall or software firewalls, as previously mentioned.

With the general framework laid out, let's get started learning about hosting your own web server.

Making Your Shopping List

Most low-end server hardware on the market today can accomplish what you need. To achieve the minimum web server setup, you'll want to look for the following in a machine:

- A single or dual-core CPU server
- Dual network interface cards (NICs)
- RAID 1 capability with three drives (one serving as a hot spare)
- Dual power supplies
- Backup software
- CD-ROM drive
- 4 hour × 7 days a week × 365 days onsite service
- Uninterruptible power supply (UPS)

REDUNDANT ARRAY OF INEXPENSIVE DISKS (RAID)

RAID was invented many years ago, and has become standard in servers worldwide. Different levels of RAID exist, starting from 0 and going to 5. RAID 5 is very common in the enterprise world and is considered one of the safest. With RAID 5, you can actually lose a single hard drive and not lose any data. RAID 1 is also known as *mirroring*. With that configuration, you can lose a single drive and it will continue to run. However, be sure to get that drive replaced as soon as possible.

This list represents a fairly plain vanilla setup, and should not be too much burden for your budget. However, perish the thought of running internal mission-critical applications (such as accounting) on this system. That is simply a bad idea. Keep the web server as a web server.

The next hardware components are the internal network and the Internet service brought to you from the telephone or cable provider. This will be connected to a router they provide to your internal network.

You'll need to pick up a small managed or unmanaged 10/100/1000 switch with proper connections to fit the router being brought in. This switch connects all the machines in your office to the server, and potentially, to the outside world.

Note that this is a general description of your internal network, and does not necessarily represent a configuration that you should deploy. You must consider factors beyond the scope of this book for proper network configuration.

When speaking to the Internet service provider (ISP), find out a few things such as its SLA, which spells out the penalties, responsibilities, and legal terms. Additionally, find out who is responsible for connection of the ISP's equipment to your network. Most of the time, it will be you. If you do not have the in-house network expertise, then ask the ISP about the costs to connect it.

Choosing an Operating System

Choosing the operating system to run on the web server can have a great impact on your operations and your budget. Your choice includes either Linux or Windows in this example.

Each choice requires different skill sets of personnel to handle it. Each has license choices such as open source versus commercially licensed apps. Table 2-2 outlines a few points to help you make a decision about your operating system.

Table 2-2: Considerations When Selecting an Operating System

COMPONENT	LINUX	WINDOWS
O/S	Free	Fee-based
Web Server	Apache is free	IIS ships with server software
Support	Fee-based and free	Fee-based and free
E-mail	Postfix, Squirrel, Horde	Exchange
Backup	Open source, commercial	Commercially available
Extras/add-ons	Open source, free	Commercially available
Security	Strong when configured	Strong when configured

As you can see, both operating systems sport equal functionality in the areas you are likely to need it.

After you have made the decision about the operating system, setting up and configuring the machine, establishing the web server, and connecting to the outside world are your next steps.

NOTE Choosing your CMS is independent of the hardware choices, and should not have a bearing on your decisions. The usage model of the CMS will be a bigger factor. An example is a high database transactions website that requires a machine that can support higher disk I/O to service the database requests.

Ensuring Security

Some of your security will be inherent in the network in the form of your firewall and other security-oriented hardware. Protecting your servers requires that you add on software to protect the following vulnerable areas:

- Mail servers
- Web servers
- Web applications
- Operating system
- Virus prevention
- Spam prevention
- Physical protection of the machine and network

Although more areas exist, these are some to pay particular attention to when hosting your own machine.

Patching

Maintaining your own systems and network means that you must stay on top of patching on your site, server, switches, routers, and applications.

Developing a schedule to check for and update your network will make it easier and keep you from falling behind. On Windows, many patches require restarting your machine. On Linux, while occurring less often, sometimes your server may require a restart after patching. The reason this is important to remember is that you will want to schedule that restart in off hours. Servers can take a few minutes to reboot and come back to a running state. During that time, your site will be offline.

NOTE Chapter 7 covers patching in more detail.

Consider strongly whether or not it's worth it to you to bring hosting in house. Although the upside is that you have nearly unlimited freedom to do things the way you want, you also have the nearly unlimited chance to miss something very important because it probably isn't your core business.

Summary

In this chapter, you learned several important points about choosing the host that is right for you. The central idea is clearly to maintain a suitable level of security, stay within budget, and keep things easy to use and maintain. The chapter introduced the basic concepts of PCI to help you get started down the e-commerce path. You also learned about hosting your own web server.

Based on all this data, you are now armed with the knowledge you need to make a decision on where to host, what to look for, and what plan you should select.

Chapter 3 examines how to prevent problems before they start through the proper installation of a CMS and the handling of post-installation security issues.

Preventing Problems Before They Start

You have a lot to discover and learn before you start building a site. Although this is not a design book, the initial design you choose can have a positive or negative effect on your security. One big way website owners get into trouble is not planning their sites ahead of time. Rather, they plan as they build, and that is not the best situation.

In fact, the general attitude for inexperienced website owners is summed up in the book, *Joomla! Start to Finish: How to Plan, Execute and Maintain Your Web Site by Jen Kramer* (Indianapolis: Wiley, 2010) in the title of Chapter 1: "I Want a Web Site and I Want it Blue — How Much Will That Cost?" Although this sounds like a parody, it's a situation that web developers face all the time.

One decision you'll make early on is what content management system (CMS) framework to choose. Each has its own unique approach to securing the CMS. Following are a few questions that you may want to research as they relate to your security profile:

- Will you use SSL? (If you are supporting any kind of e-commerce, you will.)
- Will you need a Virtual Private Server (VPS), or will shared hosting work?
- What method of backup do you need, and will your CMS support it?
- Have you verified that the third-party add-ons you have chosen are secure?

- In the CMS of choice, do you understand the Access Control Lists (ACL) options? (This is important to control access to the site's resources.)
- Does the CMS provide adequate core tools, or are proper third-party add-ons available that you can use to solve your business problem?
- Will the third-party add-ons cause any problems with each other?

This chapter can help guide you through learning about each CMS and how to properly install it with proper security in mind. Let's begin by looking at how to choose the appropriate CMS for your business application.

Choosing an Appropriate CMS for Your Needs

You may not necessarily share that same passion for a particular software (or hardware) platform that seems to be the status quo of open source projects and their fans. Although acknowledging the passion that the developers and the community bring to each of these is good, the passion for your business should supersede that.

You should view CMSs just as what they are — tools. Take a look at each CMS addressed in this book and choose the one that best helps you achieve your business goals. Making a list of the features and functions you need, as well as the skills you have to manage the solution, can help you with that choice. Each of the CMSs covered in this book can help you solve the goal of getting your business on the web. For that matter, a high school student could do the same thing by building an HTML page. But is that what you really want?

The real key is what you want the platform to do for you. What business goal will it solve? Start there, and make the right business decisions for the project software you choose.

Making the Right Business Decisions

The first business decision you must make is defining what your site is being built to do. Is it a corporate *brochure site*? Is it an *e-commerce site*? Will your solution need live customer service chat capabilities? Identifying the purpose of your site will lead you to a number of other questions. Asking these questions first will guide your design choices.

Secondly, you must consider the intangibles involved with this effort, both before and after it's built. For example, if you have a technical staff, do they have the technical programming skills to support the site? Do you have a trusted technical developer who can work with the code, should it need it? What about the server operating system and associated moving parts?

Three of the CMSs covered in this book (Joomla!, Drupal, and WordPress) are all written in PHP. Plone is written in a different language called Python.

In most cases, choosing one or the other CMS will necessitate a developer with skills equal to the chosen CMS.

You should also consider the ecosystem in which the CMS lives. Joomla!, Drupal, and WordPress enjoy a very large third-party development community. All three are easy enough to use.

Plone has a much smaller market share and, hence, a smaller ecosystem of developers. What Plone lacks in market share, it makes up with a hearty, solid CMS and a spirited community. Plone has a much heavier technical requirement than the other three, and, as such, having a strong community backing is a good thing.

Let's take a look at a bit of background about each of the CMSs covered in this book.

Joomla!

In the world of Open Source, when a group of developers wishes to redistribute code with their changes and likely a new name, it's called a *fork*. Joomla! is one of the more successful forks of the open source project that was known as *Mambo*. Over the last several years, it has grown dramatically, and has become one of the most popular CMS platforms around. Joomla! has a very active ecosystem of third-party developers, many of which offer commercial products and support.

By and large, you can use Joomla! for everything from simple websites all the way to collaboration websites.

You can find practically any type of *extension* (as add-ons are known in Joomla!) for almost any need. The development community for templates (that is, skins that change the look) is very deep and wide, offering literally thousands of templates. The Joomla! extensions site (`http://extensions.joomla.org`) lists hundreds and hundreds of extensions covering a vast variety of categories. For example, in the e-commerce category, more than 20 third-party developers offer shopping carts alone.

The Joomla! commercial development community is a very innovative group. One developer (`www.corephp.com`) even offers an extension that enables you to run almost any Drupal module on a Joomla! website.

Joomla! is well-documented, and many published authors have written about the platform. It is considered medium-difficulty software for the beginner.

Drupal

Drupal's install base is nearly as large as Joomla!'s, but with a number of key differences. Drupal is considered to be more technically challenging than Joomla!. Unlike Joomla!, most *Drupal modules* (the term for Drupal add-ons) are *free*, rather than for sale. This represents a cultural difference between the Drupal and Joomla! communities.

Drupal is very robust and is being used in some very high-profile websites (such as www.whitehouse.gov). It enjoys an excellent third-party development community, and offers a host of module add-ons.

In terms of complexity and technical challenge, Drupal just might rank above Joomla!. Drupal 7 seems to have eased a number of the challenges of previous versions by building in a number of modules in the core installation. Drupal 7 marks a great forward step toward easing some of the technical challenges for the average user.

WordPress

WordPress is the most popular of all the CMSs in this book. It has the largest install base of all CMS platforms. WordPress began its life as blog software, but has moved into the CMS space.

WordPress is the right choice if you need a company blog. It's easy to use, with an intuitive interface conducive to writing blogs. The community offers several themes (the name for the skin of WordPress) for free, and many more are commercially available.

Plug-ins (the WordPress term for add-ons) are abundant, and, for the most part, free. Although e-commerce is possible with specific plug-ins on WordPress, you may find the other CMS platforms more suited to the task using other third-party add-ons.

WordPress is very easy to install, and a fairly secure system. Many websites you visit are probably running on WordPress.

Plone

Of the four CMSs discussed in this book, Plone is clearly the most technical to set up and manage, but it is as easy (or perhaps easier, in some ways) to add and manage content to it as WordPress or Drupal, both of which have a fairly robust and user-friendly means for adding content. This CMS appears in this book in an effort by the author to expand the horizons of the business community.

Plone does not have as big of a community as the other three CMSs discussed in this book, but plone.org offers an abundance of *add-ons* (the Plone term for add-ons). You may also visit www.contentmanagementsoftware.info/plone/ for additional add-ons.

Plone is built on top of the Zope framework, and works on many operating system platforms.

Which CMS Offers the Best Security?

You're reading this book, therefore, you've no doubt pondered the question, "What's the best CMS from a security perspective?" The somewhat tongue-in-cheek answer is that all CMSs are safe until you install them and put them online. The reality of this is that *all* the CMSs covered in this book can and *do* suffer from vulnerabilities from time to time.

Since March 2009, `SalvusAlerting.com` has tracked a number of different applications and projects. What was discovered in looking back over nearly two years of data was that the CMS with the *fewest* vulnerabilities was Plone. The rest are all within a hundred or so vulnerabilities of each other. That does not mean that Plone is the most secure, and that Drupal or Joomla! or WordPress are vying for the distinction of "the CMS voted most likely to fail." It simply means that Plone has the fewest number of published vulnerabilities.

The development teams of all these CMSs take security very seriously. The area in which you should focus your research includes the third-party extensions developers. This is where you are more likely to run into security issues.

Four Factors to Consider from a Business Point of View

Overall, you should use four key tenets to form your decision on which CMS to use. Consider these guiding principles as you move into the selection phase.

- *Supportability* — Can you or your staff *support* it? Can you answer user questions? Do you know how to add content? From time to time, all of these CMSs will require updates, add-ons, and more.

- *Viability* — Although these four CMSs are not really at risk of going away because of their following and installed base, the question still should be asked: Will the CMS of choice maintain bug fixes and patches? If *any* commercially available or open source software platform stops the support, are you prepared to migrate to a new platform, or continue to care for and feed the technical needs of the old system?

- *Functionality* — In the core platform or with third-party add-ons, does the CMS you choose offer the functions you need? When you draw up your selection criteria on paper, create a spreadsheet and list the *function* or *process* you need it to support. Also list the core software or third-party add-ons to support the CMS.

- *Security* — Although the four CMSs examined in this book do offer strong default levels of security, many other tools also offer enhanced levels of security. So, the security question to ask is *what* does the CMS and its third-party offerings have to protect your site from attacks?

Considering Development Costs

Development costs can quickly get out of control, and then the security becomes relegated to a *nice-to-have* status.

When you prepare to develop your site, or have a third-party developer handle this for you, approaching the entire effort holistically will yield better benefits. The site will be highly survivable in an attack if you plan upfront for security.

Calculate the cost for backing up the system — including any utilities and time it will take you or your staff to use the necessary tools. If you want to include specific security functions or tools, define them upfront, or get the web developer to provide you with an accurate cost.

Another cost you may consider budgeting for is a code audit in the event that you have software written by a third-party developer. What this amounts to is hiring another software developer (in addition to the primary developer) who will review the code. The items you may want the auditor to look at could be any number of things, but following are some key areas:

- SQL injection vulnerabilities
- Cross Site Scripting (XSS) vulnerabilities
- Remote file inclusion vulnerabilities
- Backdoors
- Trojan code
- Debug code

For the most part, these areas should not be a real issue. But if a project is fully custom-written, then having a second pair of eyes on the code won't hurt.

Considering Support

Support is often overlooked or "underplanned." Sadly, this often results in the *"I need support and I need it now!"* situation. When you choose a firm to hire for software development, take the time to understand its support policies for post sales. Here are some guiding questions:

- Does it offer post-sale support?
- If not, does it have a company it recommends?
- If the firm makes modifications to the core CMS code, how is it documented? How will upgrades take place?
- What are the costs associated with the firm's support?
- What warranties (if any) does it offer on its work?

Assuming the software development firm does provide post-sale support, how are problems and questions handled? This often is done through a ticketing system, but not always. Finding out upfront is best.

Following are a few options to consider:

- Few commercial firms offer *only* support, such as `OpenSourceSupportDesk.com`, which offers support of WordPress and Joomla!.

- You may choose to run your WordPress site directly with `www.WordPress.com`, and it will manage the core software for you, thus relieving you of that burden.

- If your site is built on Drupal, you may opt for `www.drupalgardens.com`, which offers support for updates and more.

- Plone has a healthy community with more than 300 companies that offer some form of Plone support. Visit `www.plone.net/providers` for more information.

Support is a multi-faceted issue, and keeping up with it can be costly. When you are in the CMS selection process, following are some support questions to consider:

- How will you discover whether the CMS or an add-on has vulnerability?

- How quickly does the CMS respond to security issues?

- Does the add-on developer offer support? If so, what is the cost, and how quickly will the developer respond to problems?

- Does the third party charge for updates?

- What is the difficulty level of updating?

- What security features are built in the *core* CMS?

- What third-party security applications are available?

Building It Before You Build It

It has been my experience that people tend to get wrapped up in the details of the look and feel of a site, instead of how it works. Although the look and feel is very important, you should spend time designing the workflow of the site and system first.

For starters, here are some considerations about the functionality of your site:

- Will the end users need to, or be required to, register?

- Will the site automatically allow them to log in?

- What information will the end users need to provide?

- What will they do after they log in?

- What is the lost password policy?
- What features should the login have?
- What permissions or access will the users get?
- Will you have more than one administrator of the site?
- What will these administrator roles be?

As you can see, these are the detailed questions that do not involve the actual colors, pictures, or text on the site. They are designed to help you get the site workflow in place.

A low-tech (but effective) method to approach site planning is to lay out the functions on index cards and then list the potential third-party extensions (add-ons) that can fulfill those functions. If you settle on an add-on, record the URL, support information, or telephone number on the index card for future reference.

Additionally, take a look at the track record of the developer via the change logs to see a record of security fixes. If the developer has a lot of fixes, it could mean the company is proactive, and you may feel good about using that company. It could also mean that the company is not that good at coding. No good metric exists to depend on for this determination; it's more of a matter of intuition.

Use the paper method to run through a workflow. Verify the ACL for each resource, and run through any potential holes you might be creating.

Lastly, you want to decide on paper what environment you will develop on — a server or your desktop. Let's take a detailed look at both options.

Developing on a Server

When you develop on a server, you will be accessing it either over your internal network or over the Internet. Protecting the development site from prying eyes is important. The easiest method to do this is to use the Apache `.htaccess` file. You can very easily set up a method to allow only authorized persons into the site.

NOTE   Appendix A provides more detail on using the `.htaccess` file.

The summary of the process is as follows:

1. Create a password for your `.htpasswd` file.

2. Save the `.htpasswd` file upload to a non-public portion of your server. In most cases, that is the directory above `public_html`.

3. Write out a short bit of `.htaccess` code and place it in the root directory of your site that calls the password file and checks the given password against the stored version. The following is an example of the `.htaccess` code:

```
AuthName "Restricted Area"
AuthType Basic
AuthUserFile /home/mysite/public_html/.htpasswd
```

```
AuthGroupFile /dev/null
require valid-user
```

Anyone browsing to the site will see the screen shown in Figure 3-1.

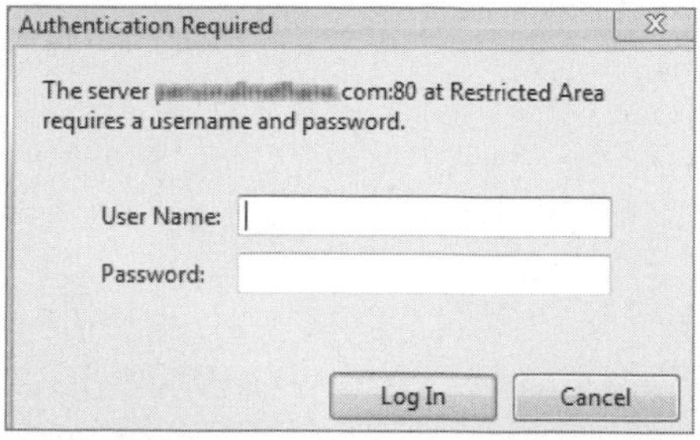

Figure 3-1: .htaccess password dialog box

NOTE A good site is available that can assist you with everything you need to do to set up the password system via `.htaccess`. Visit the site `http://tools.dynamicdrive.com/password` to generate your password hash and to get the proper `.htaccess` code. You must provide some information about your particular setup for it to provide you the necessary code.

Developing on a Desktop

The GNU/GPL tool called *WAMP* is a fully self-contained Windows desktop environment in which you can run Apache, MySQL, and PHP. For the most part, it will behave identically to a server.

This tool enables testing, provides a development location, offers a safe environment to explore patches before going live, and more. This tool enables you to develop without having to be constantly connected to the Internet.

Installation and configuration are very straightforward. This is a great way to safely explore and test extensions. If you use this method to develop, you can back up the finished site, and then upload it into production.

NOTE You can obtain the software at `www.wampserver.com`.

Performing CMS Installations

For the most part, the CMSs examined in this book all offer straightforward installations, and are well-documented. This section discusses generic installations, with special attention on security concerns. The first installation discussed is Joomla! 1.5, with a few notes about Joomla! 1.6. Next, you learn about installation of Drupal 6.xx, and see a few comments about Drupal 7.

Plone instructions follow, using the latest (as of this writing) version of Plone available. Finally, you'll learn about WordPress, which has the easiest installation of all.

For Joomla!, Drupal, and WordPress, you need the following before you get started:

- Working server (WAMP or Linux)
- Apache
- MySQL with a configured database
- PHP (5.xx)
- Your username, database name, and password for the database
- FTP or SSH account with credentials

In the case of Plone, you'll need access to the server via Putty or other means. You can do most (if not all) of the installation at the command line.

Installing Joomla! 1.5

Joomla! installations are usually straightforward and offer little trouble. The problems you may encounter will likely plague all the CMSs examined here, and that includes permissions, ownership issues, incorrect database settings, and so forth.

After you download the compressed installation file, you must unzip (uncompress) it and upload it to your server's web root directory (typically `public_html`).

To commence the process, open a browser and visit the domain where Joomla! will be installed, such as `http://www.YourDomain.com`. This kicks off the installation routine.

Like the other CMSs, Joomla! has the capability to support multiple languages. In the first screen, you choose the language the site will default to, as shown in Figure 3-2.

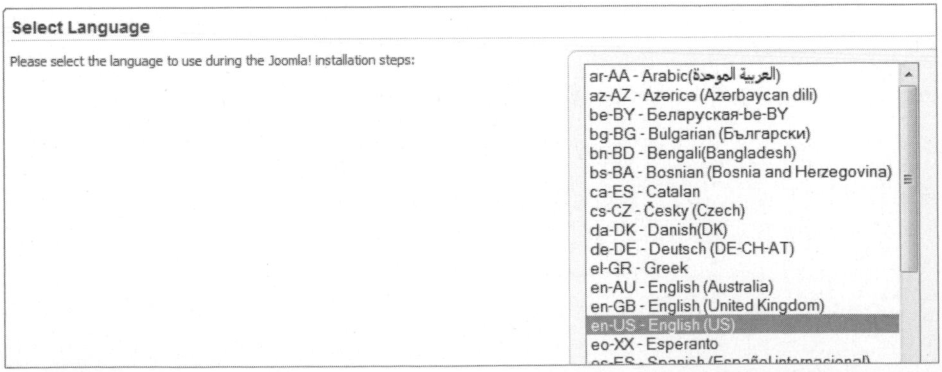

Select Language

Please select the language to use during the Joomla! installation steps:

ar-AA - Arabic(العربية الموحدة)
az-AZ - Azerice (Azərbaycan dili)
be-BY - Беларуская-be-BY
bg-BG - Bulgarian (Български)
bn-BD - Bengali(Bangladesh)
bs-BA - Bosnian (Bosnia and Herzegovina)
ca-ES - Catalan
cs-CZ - Česky (Czech)
da-DK - Danish(DK)
de-DE - Deutsch (DE-CH-AT)
el-GR - Greek
en-AU - English (Australia)
en-GB - English (United Kingdom)
en-US - English (US)
eo-XX - Esperanto
es-ES - Spanish (Español internacional)

Figure 3-2: Language choice

The installation script will check the environment where you are attempting to install. If an issue exists, you will see the problem displayed in the confirmation screen shown in Figure 3-3, the next screen in the installation process.

PHP Version >= 4.3.10	Yes
- Zlib Compression Support	Yes
- XML Support	Yes
- MySQL Support	Yes
MB Language is Default	Yes
MB String Overload Off	Yes
configuration.php Writable	Yes

Directive	Recommended	Actual
Safe Mode:	Off	Off
Display Errors:	Off	On
File Uploads:	On	On
Magic Quotes Runtime:	Off	Off
Register Globals:	Off	Off
Output Buffering:	Off	Off
Session Auto Start:	Off	Off

Figure 3-3: Pre-installation check

As you can see in Figure 3-3, the `Display Errors` setting is actually On, but the recommended setting is that it be turned off. You can remedy this situation in your `php.ini` file. After you review this page, write down anything that needs correction (such as the `Display Errors` setting in this example) for later remediation.

Click Next and the Joomla! license page appears. After you review the license terms, click Next to proceed to the Database Configuration screen shown in Figure 3-4.

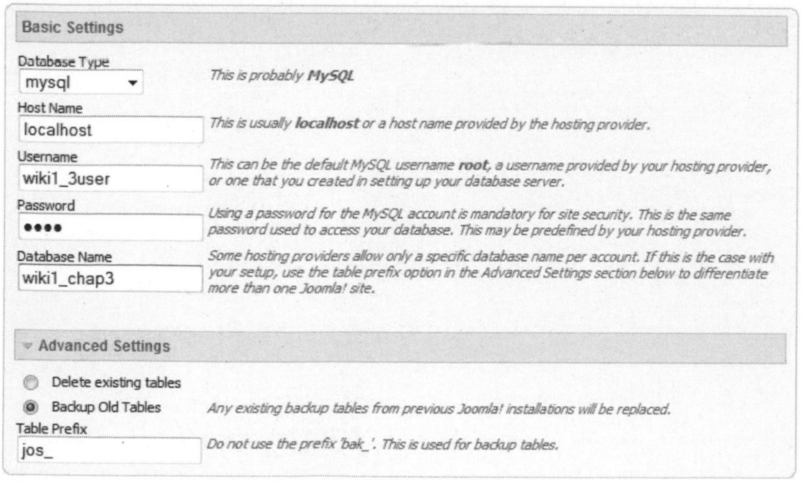

Basic Settings

Database Type
`mysql`
This is probably **MySQL**

Host Name
`localhost`
This is usually **localhost** or a host name provided by the hosting provider.

Username
`wiki1_3user`
This can be the default MySQL username **root**, a username provided by your hosting provider, or one that you created in setting up your database server.

Password
`••••`
Using a password for the MySQL account is mandatory for site security. This is the same password used to access your database. This may be predefined by your hosting provider.

Database Name
`wiki1_chap3`
Some hosting providers allow only a specific database name per account. If this is the case with your setup, use the table prefix option in the Advanced Settings section below to differentiate more than one Joomla! site.

▽ Advanced Settings

○ Delete existing tables
◉ Backup Old Tables   Any existing backup tables from previous Joomla! installations will be replaced.

Table Prefix
`jos_`
Do not use the prefix 'bak_'. This is used for backup tables.

Figure 3-4: Database Settings page

The settings here are categorized as Basic and Advanced. In the Basic settings, enter the database connectivity and other settings, using the following as a guide:

- *Database Type* — In this example, this is set for MySQL, which, for most people, will be the right choice.

- *Host Name* — Most of the time, this is `localhost`, but for some web hosts you will have a specific server name.

- *User Name* — This is the user specified for the database.

- *Password* — The password for the database.

- *Database Name* — This will be the name of the database you gave when you created it.

Under the Advanced Settings, you see two radio buttons and a text box. Selecting the "Delete existing tables" option will wipe your database clean of any previous entries. If you are reinstalling and have not backed up your database, then select the second option, "Backup Old Tables." This creates a database prefix of `bak_`.

The Table Prefix in your database defaults to `jos_`. You may want to change this for "security-by-obscurity" reasons. Changing the Table Prefix won't make you more secure, but it will lower the obvious profile. For now, leave it as the default of `jos_` and click Next to continue.

The built-in FTP layer allows specific File Transfer Protocol (FTP) functions within your Joomla! site, as shown in the next screen, displayed in Figure 3-5. Although opinions are mixed, the recommendation is to leave this disabled. If you want to enable it, you must provide the FTP authentication information. Click Next to continue.

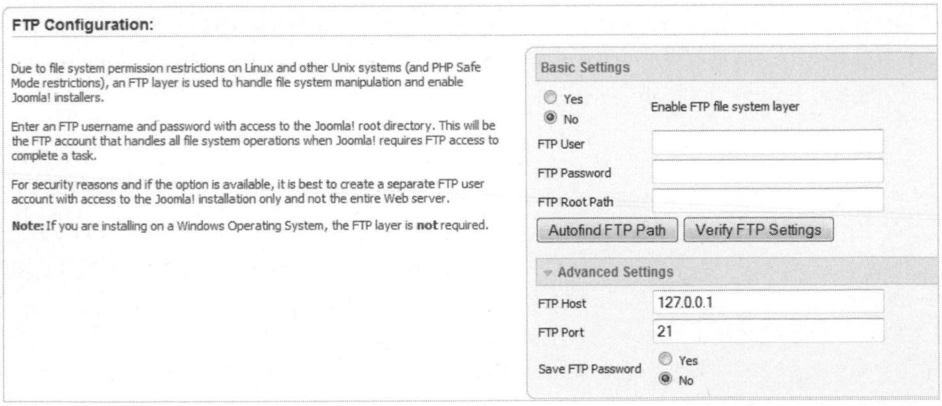

Figure 3-5: FTP Configuration page

The next screen you see enables you to enter information about your site, as shown in Figure 3-6. Here you fill in your site name, proper e-mail address, and choose a strong administrator password. Notice that the Your E-Mail option has the word `admin` in it. This is a default that appears in Joomla! 1.5. It does not change your actual superuser admin name.

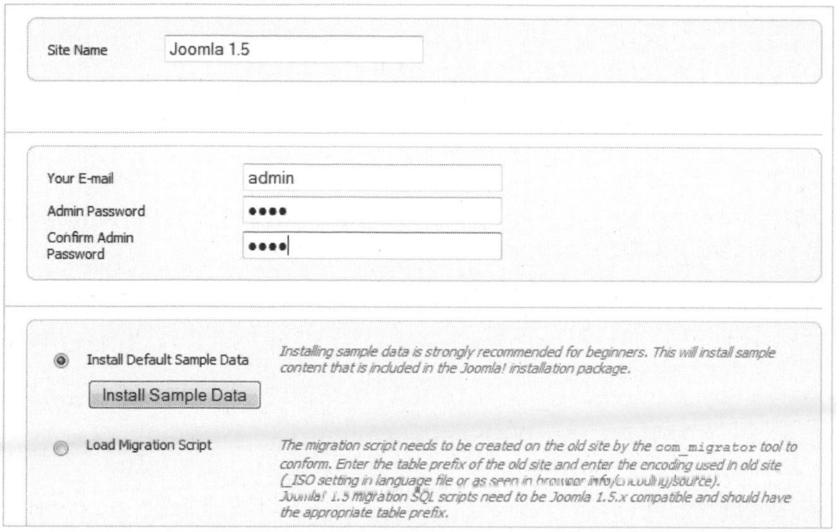

Site Name   Joomla 1.5

Your E-mail   admin

Admin Password   ••••

Confirm Admin
Password   ••••|

⦿ Install Default Sample Data   *Installing sample data is strongly recommended for beginners. This will install sample content that is included in the Joomla! installation package.*

    Install Sample Data

○ Load Migration Script   *The migration script needs to be created on the old site by the com_migrator tool to conform. Enter the table prefix of the old site and enter the encoding used in old site (ISO setting in language file or as seen in browser info/source). Joomla! 1.5 migration SQL scripts need to be Joomla 1.5.x compatible and should have the appropriate table prefix.*

Figure 3-6: Naming your site

In the lower portion of Figure 3-6, notice two other settings:

- *Install Sample Data* — Selecting this option will populate your site with all types of menus, content, sections, and categories. This is a great way to learn how the system works, but might get in your way for a production site.

- *Load Migration Scripts* — Select this option to migrate an old Joomla! 1.xx site to Joomla! 1.5. Migrations of 1.0 to 1.5 are beyond the scope of this book. Do not load the migration script.

Click Next to continue.

The final screen, shown in Figure 3-7, directs you to remove or rename the directory named `Installation`. You'll need to FTP or SSH into your server or website to take care of removing this directory. You should simply delete the folder.

From here, you can visit the site or log in as `admin`.

One detail that will improve your security is to get rid of the default `admin` user. Follow these steps:

1. Log in as `admin`.

2. Create a new user.

3. Escalate the privileges of the new user to super administrator.

4. Save the change and log out.

5. Log in again as the *new* super administrator you just created.

6. Lower the former `admin` user privileges to a registered user.

> **PLEASE REMEMBER TO COMPLETELY**
> **REMOVE THE INSTALLATION DIRECTORY.**
> **You will not be able to proceed beyond this point until the installation directory has been removed. This is a security feature of Joomla!.**
>
> **Administration Login Details**
>
> Username: admin
>
> **Joomla! in your own language?**
> Visit the Joomla! Help Site for more information and downloads.

Figure 3-7: Joomla! Installation complete

You've now removed the *default* `admin` user. What you have done is to remove the obvious `admin` as a target for a hacker. For example, changing it to `K39F028` as the username would make an attacker's attempt at a brute-force attack much more difficult, because the intruder wouldn't know the username.

Installing Joomla! 1.6

Joomla! 1.6 is the next generation of Joomla! For the most part, installation of version 1.6 is identical to version 1.5, except for the changes described in this section.

As shown in Figure 3-8, the FTP Configuration screen now indicates the FTP layer is Optional.

Figure 3-8: Joomla! 1.6 FTP Configuration screen

Another difference is at this point in the process where, in the 1.5 installation, you name your site. In the version 1.6 installation, you'll find a few new options.

Advanced Settings is now up near the top of the screen, as shown in Figure 3-9, and contains the Meta Description and Meta Keywords options. For search engine-related activities, this location is highly valuable.

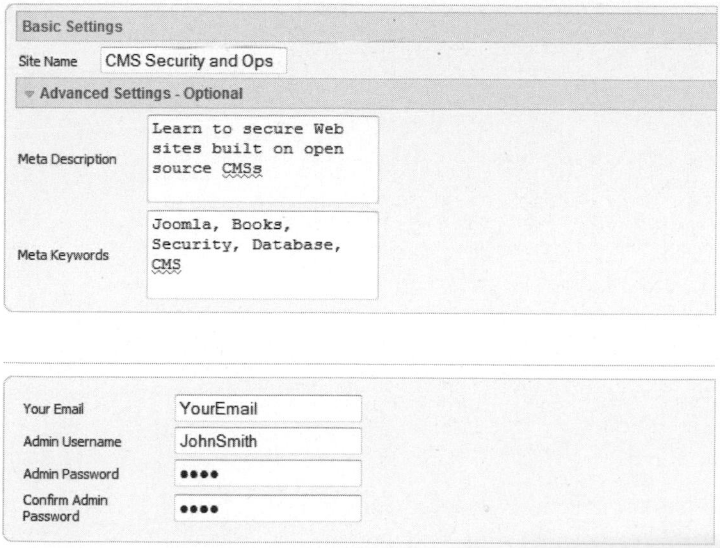

Basic Settings	
Site Name	CMS Security and Ops

▼ Advanced Settings - Optional

Meta Description	Learn to secure Web sites built on open source CMSs
Meta Keywords	Joomla, Books, Security, Database, CMS

Your Email	YourEmail
Admin Username	JohnSmith
Admin Password	••••
Confirm Admin Password	••••

Figure 3-9: Updated screen in Joomla! v1.6 installation

Another change is the capability to change the `admin` username at installation time. As you learned earlier in the description of the 1.5 installation, changing the default `admin` username is an important security step. However, version 1.5 installation does not offer a means to do so at the time of installation. Version 1.6 has remedied that. This important step in security has been made part of the default version 1.6 installation routine. Be sure to rename the `admin` user to something other than `admin`.

You will find the rest of the steps for installation are identical, or similar enough, to version 1.5 that you should not have any real surprises.

As a final note on security, version 1.6 offers a new ACL system that allows you to grant or revoke access to content and extensions in a very granular fashion. Be sure you spend time understanding the ACL so that you do not create an inadvertent security issue.

Installing Drupal

Drupal offers a mature and straightforward installation routine for the CMS. To begin, uncompress your Drupal installation files and copy them to the web root of your server using FTP or SSH. Browse to your domain and the installation should start automatically.

The first screen you see (see Figure 3-10) allows you to select your language. For purposes of this discussion, choose English, but note that Drupal has the capability to install other languages.

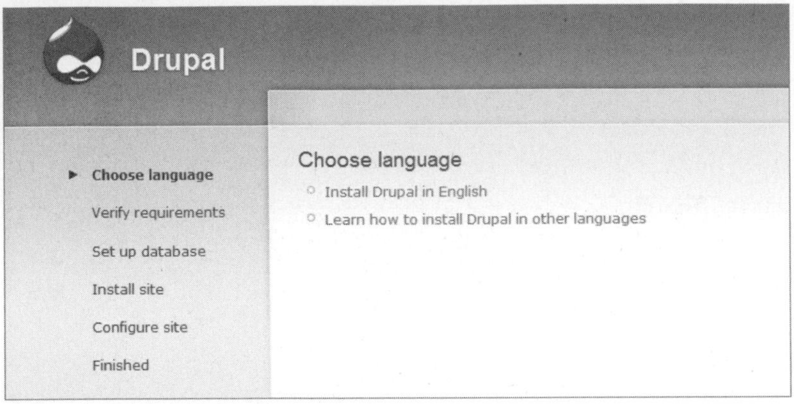

Figure 3-10: Choosing a language

Next up is the database configuration screen shown in Figure 3-11. Here you enter the database name, username, and password.

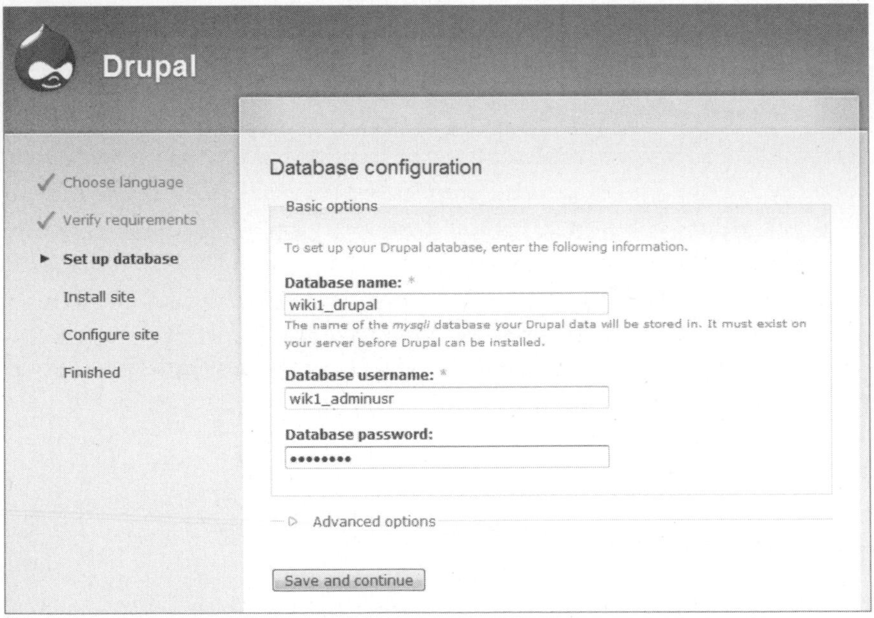

Figure 3-11: Database configuration screen

At the bottom of the screen is a link for "Advanced options." The advanced options shown in Figure 3-12 are necessary for some hosting situations. You may need to contact your host for information required in the advanced settings. Most users should not need to change these settings. However, if you do, following are some guidelines:

- *Database host* — This is almost always `localhost`, but for a host such as `GoDaddy.com`, you will receive an actual database server name. If you need to change the name from `localhost`, ask your host for the details.

- *Database port* — By default, MySQL uses port 3306. If you change this in your MySQL configuration, you'll need to provide the correct port number.

- *Table Prefix* — If you have more than one Drupal site installed on the same database host, you'll need to provide a different prefix to prevent your data from being overwritten.

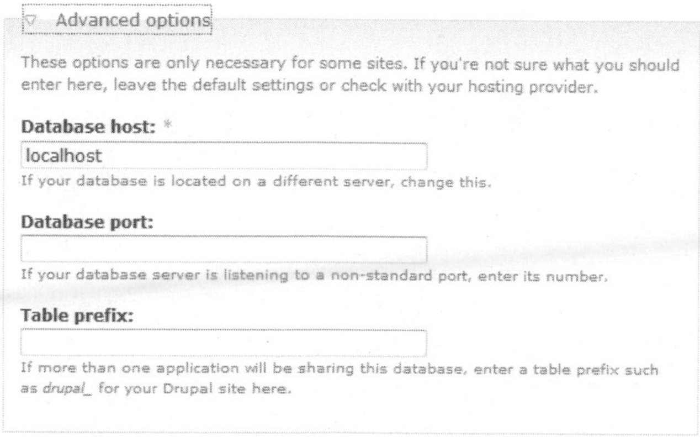

Figure 3-12: Advanced options

After you have finished filling in the options for database configuration, click Next to continue.

The details in the "Configure site" screen then appear, as shown in Figure 3-13. This is where your Drupal site gains its personality. Fill in the site name and site e-mail address. Next, choose your administrator username, e-mail address for the administrator, and a strong password.

Figure 3-13: "Configure site" screen

Note in Figure 3-14 that a weak password has been selected to demonstrate how Drupal will attempt to guide you on password security. Follow the recommendations from Drupal on the password strength.

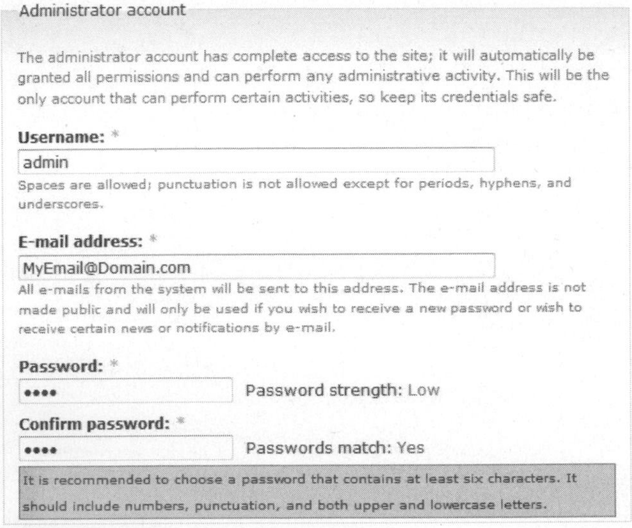

Figure 3-14: Administrator account

You can now log in to your new site by clicking the link that says, "You may now visit your new site."

Post Install

A module is available to assist you with your post-installation security. The module, called Security Review, will assist you in checking the site for issues and helping you correct your site's profile.

Figure 3-15 shows an example run on a test server.

In this example, it has identified two trouble spots. Clicking on details in the first error yields a lot of information and some actions you can take, as shown in Figure 3-16.

NOTE Currently, this module is available for Drupal 6.xx and 7.xx, and you can download it at `http://drupal.org/project/security_review`.

After you finish your installation, consider running this module to ensure that you have covered a number of the basics that are easy to miss. In addition to this module, several others security modules can be helpful to improve your security.

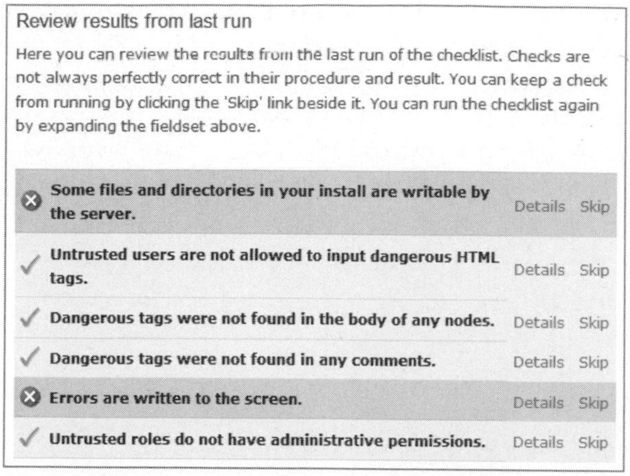

Review results from last run

Here you can review the results from the last run of the checklist. Checks are not always perfectly correct in their procedure and result. You can keep a check from running by clicking the 'Skip' link beside it. You can run the checklist again by expanding the fieldset above.

⊗ Some files and directories in your install are writable by the server.	Details	Skip
✓ Untrusted users are not allowed to input dangerous HTML tags.	Details	Skip
✓ Dangerous tags were not found in the body of any nodes.	Details	Skip
✓ Dangerous tags were not found in any comments.	Details	Skip
⊗ Errors are written to the screen.	Details	Skip
✓ Untrusted roles do not have administrative permissions.	Details	Skip

Figure 3-15: Drupal Security Review module

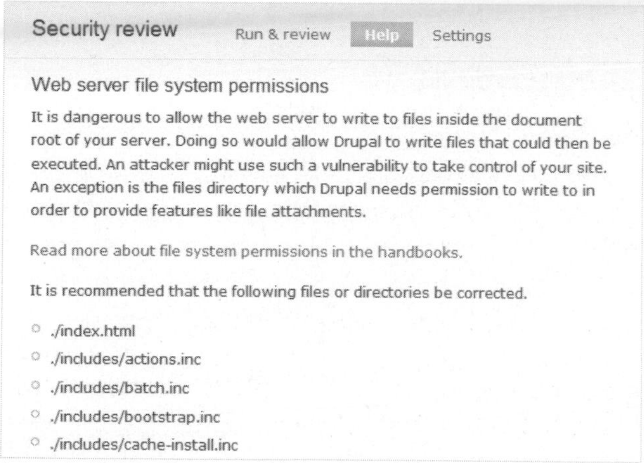

Security review Run & review **Help** Settings

Web server file system permissions

It is dangerous to allow the web server to write to files inside the document root of your server. Doing so would allow Drupal to write files that could then be executed. An attacker might use such a vulnerability to take control of your site. An exception is the files directory which Drupal needs permission to write to in order to provide features like file attachments.

Read more about file system permissions in the handbooks.

It is recommended that the following files or directories be corrected.

- ./index.html
- ./includes/actions.inc
- ./includes/batch.inc
- ./includes/bootstrap.inc
- ./includes/cache-install.inc

Figure 3-16: Detailed Actions needed

Permissions

Permissions in this context are associated with the user roles. In Drupal 6, two roles are created, `anonymous` and `authenticated`. Drupal 7 has a third default role, `administrator`.

However, you must observe some rules to maintain security. The Drupal roles are not difficult to understand. Following are a few basic rules:

- Any *right* granted to the `anonymous` role is not inherited by the `authenticated` role.

■ Any *right* granted to the `authenticated` role is automatically shared by every user who belongs to that group.

For example, if you assign a user `authenticated` backup duties (that is, you give that user permission to use the "Backup and Migrate" module), then everyone would automatically get the right to use that module. It's likely that you would not want everyone to have that right. A better way to assign specific roles is to create a role specifically for backup (or other functions). Let's walk through how to do this.

Figure 3-17 shows an example of the default view of roles.

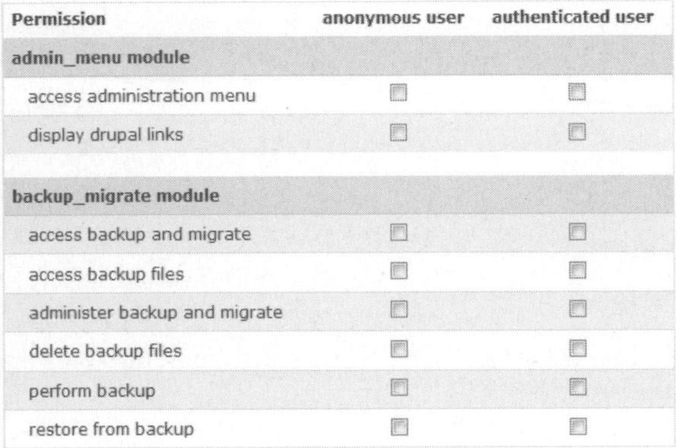

Permission	anonymous user	authenticated user
admin_menu module		
access administration menu	☐	☐
display drupal links	☑	☑
backup_migrate module		
access backup and migrate	☐	☐
access backup files	☐	☐
administer backup and migrate	☐	☐
delete backup files	☐	☐
perform backup	☐	☐
restore from backup	☐	☐

Figure 3-17: Default Drupal 6 roles

Suppose you want to add a role to handle the backup functions. To do this, go to the `www.YourSite/admin/user/roles` menu. Here, you click the "Add role" button, as shown in Figure 3-18.

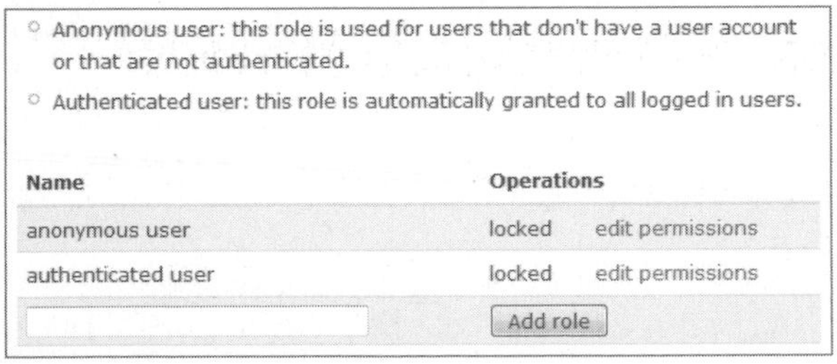

○ Anonymous user: this role is used for users that don't have a user account or that are not authenticated.	
○ Authenticated user: this role is automatically granted to all logged in users.	

Name	Operations	
anonymous user	locked	edit permissions
authenticated user	locked	edit permissions
	Add role	

Figure 3-18: Adding a role in Drupal 6

After you add the role, assign permissions to it by clicking the "edit permissions" option and assign the permissions, as shown in Figure 3-19.

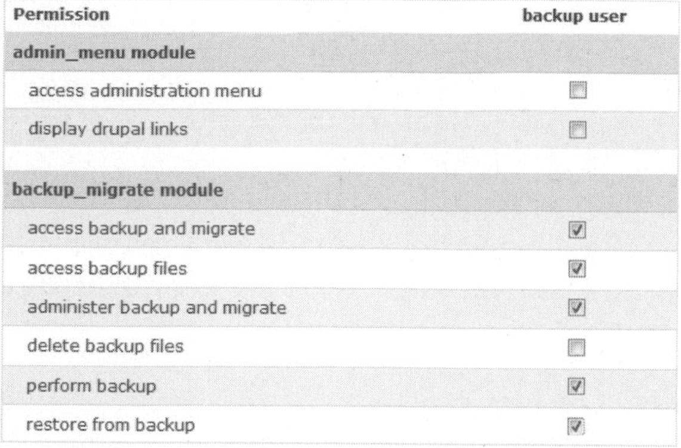

Permission	backup user
admin_menu module	
access administration menu	☐
display drupal links	☐
backup_migrate module	
access backup and migrate	☑
access backup files	☑
administer backup and migrate	☑
delete backup files	☐
perform backup	☑
restore from backup	☑

Figure 3-19: Assigning backup permissions

You may have noted that, in this example, the `backup user` role has been restricted from having "delete backup files" privileges. You can choose any level of granularity you need for any role.

The role of `backup user` is now the only one with the capability to run the backup and restore functions. Had you given the `authenticated user` role the rights to use the "Backup and Migrate" module, then everyone with login capability could do backups, restores, and delete old backup files. In other words, this would introduce *chaos*.

Drupal 7

Permissions are treated very similarly in Drupal 7, with the added benefit of an `administrator` role already being predefined, as shown in Figure 3-20. As you can see, with Drupal 7, you now have the capability to assign administrative tasks to an `administrator` role automatically.

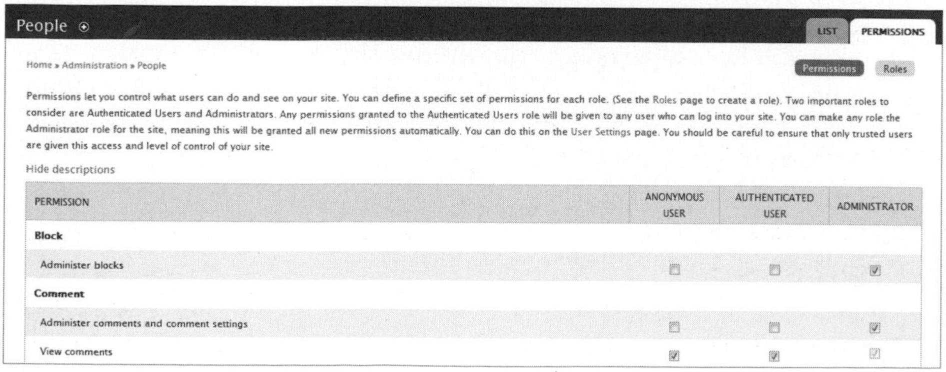

Figure 3-20: Default roles in Drupal 7

Installing Plone

Plone is very different in terms of design and setup than the other CMSs discussed in this book. However, Plone certainly entails what could be considered *technical heavy lifting*. If your technical skills are fairly basic, you should contract with someone to install Plone.

Plone is built on top of the Zope framework, and, as such, has different requirements than the CMS installations described thus far. Following are some of the requirements for Plone installation:

- The GNU Compiler Collection (GCC)
- The C++ extensions for GCC (G++)
- The GNU make-build control tool
- GNU `tar`
- `bzip2` and `gzip` decompression packages
- Python 2.4 or later
- Linux 2.6.xx or later

NOTE Other operating system requirements are described at `http://plone.org/documentation/kb/plone-system-requirements`.

Basic Zope Installation

Before you install Plone, you must decide whether you want to follow the Zope Enterprise Objects (ZEO) installation, or install Zope as a standalone. Consult the most current Plone documentation to help you decide on which installation to use. This discussion assumes the selection of the ZEO installation.

You first decompress the installation files as follows:

```
tar zxf Plone-VERSION-UnifiedInstaller.tar.gz
```

To start the ZEO installation, type the following:

```
./install.sh zeo
```

The installation routine commences. The installation will take some time, and will create the appropriate operating system user for you. After it completes, the "Installation Complete" message appears, accompanied by the administrative username and password you set up. You should use a very strong password.

What you have done thus far is set up the Plone/Zope environment, on top of which you build your websites. Now, at your browser, type **http://localhost:8080**, where *localhost* represents the domain this is installed on (or the host, if it's a WAMP environment).

This brings up the Zope Management Interface shown in Figure 3-21.

Figure 3-21: Create a new Plone site

NOTE If the Zope Management Interface does not come, up ensure that your Zope instance is running by typing **./bin/plonectl** at a shell (SSH) prompt.

Click "Create a new Plone site" and follow the prompts to quickly and easily set up your Plone website. To manage it, enter the following:

```
http://localhost:8080/manage
```

To add content, visit the domain where it's installed and log in. From there, you can add content and other code to make the site uniquely yours.

Other Resources

Chapter 6 of this book shows you how to back up and restore your Plone site. Plone is a very detailed topic and the best documentation is available online:

- For more details on Plone security, see `http://plone.org/documentation/kb/securing-plone`.
- Because Plone is supported on many different platforms, the instructions for each platform are beyond the scope of this book. For more information, see `http://plone.org/documentation/phc_topic_area?topic=Installation`.

Plone is a heavy-duty and secure CMS. It requires strong technical skills, and, thus, may be the wrong choice for a small business starting out that does not have access to technical resources.

Installing WordPress

Of the four CMSs discussed in this book, WordPress is by far the easiest to install. There is very little to go wrong during your everyday WordPress installation.

To begin, uncompress the WordPress installation files and upload them to the root of your website. After you complete this, browse to your site to commence the installation.

The first installation step (using WordPress version 3.0.3) is to create the configuration file, which WordPress can handle for you. As shown in Figure 3-22, simply click the "Create a Configuration File" button.

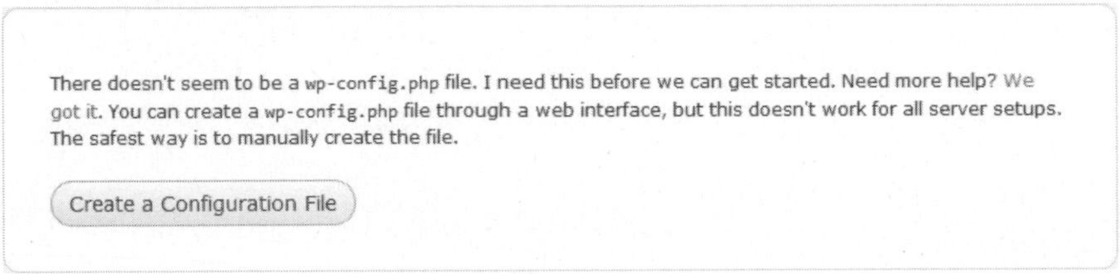

There doesn't seem to be a `wp-config.php` file. I need this before we can get started. Need more help? We got it. You can create a `wp-config.php` file through a web interface, but this doesn't work for all server setups. The safest way is to manually create the file.

Create a Configuration File

Figure 3-22: Automatic creation of `wp-config.php`

The configuration file contains all the pertinent information for your site to function.

The site itself stores its content in a database. The next screen you see provides you with the information you will need to get started. After you understand the information shown in Figure 3-23, click the "Let's go!" button.

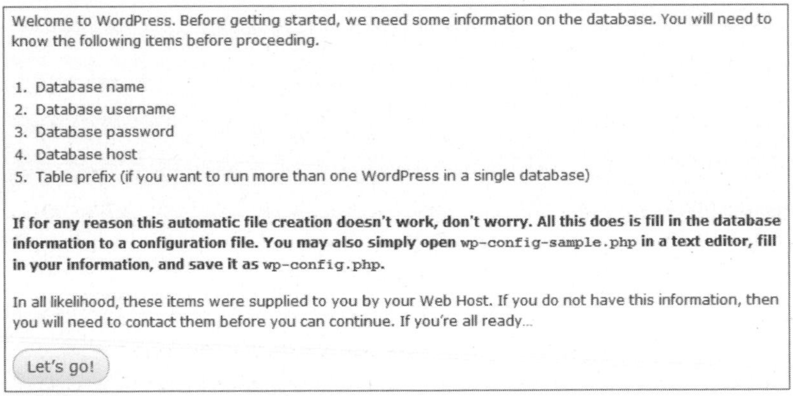

Welcome to WordPress. Before getting started, we need some information on the database. You will need to know the following items before proceeding.

1. Database name
2. Database username
3. Database password
4. Database host
5. Table prefix (if you want to run more than one WordPress in a single database)

If for any reason this automatic file creation doesn't work, don't worry. All this does is fill in the database information to a configuration file. You may also simply open `wp-config-sample.php` in a text editor, fill in your information, and save it as `wp-config.php`.

In all likelihood, these items were supplied to you by your Web Host. If you do not have this information, then you will need to contact them before you can continue. If you're all ready...

Let's go!

Figure 3-23: Pre-install checklist

On the ensuing database connectivity screen shown in Figure 3-24, you enter the details regarding the setup of your server. Enter the appropriate data for your setup. One particular point to note is that you can change the Table Prefix `wp_` setting to something else such as `mysite_`. This has the benefit of obscuring attack *bots* that look for the `wp_` and attempt to attack based on that. However, you can easily just install with the defaults.

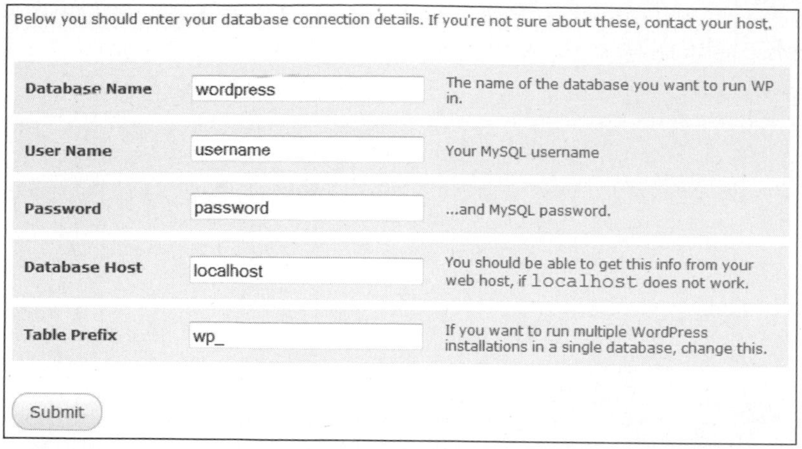

Below you should enter your database connection details. If you're not sure about these, contact your host.

Database Name	wordpress	The name of the database you want to run WP in.
User Name	username	Your MySQL username
Password	password	...and MySQL password.
Database Host	localhost	You should be able to get this info from your web host, if localhost does not work.
Table Prefix	wp_	If you want to run multiple WordPress installations in a single database, change this.

Submit

Figure 3-24: WP database setup

After you fill in the database details, WordPress will run a check to ensure that it can talk to the database. If all is well, it shows the message shown in Figure 3-25. When you see this screen, it means that the WordPress installation script was able to successfully connect to the database and is ready to install.

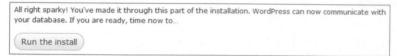

All right sparky! You've made it through this part of the installation. WordPress can now communicate with your database. If you are ready, time now to...

Run the install

Figure 3-25: Running actual installation

Click the "Run the install" button to continue.

You've now reached the part of the installation where you name your site and provide all the personal information, as shown in Figure 3-26. You should rename your username to something other than admin. This helps protect against bots that try a brute-force attack based on the admin username.

WARNING   Note that brute-force attacks are not limited to the word admin, but will try typical usernames. Choose a name that is semi-difficult to find, or choose a random selection of numbers and letters.

Click "Install WordPress" to complete your installation.

Optional Security Plug-in for WordPress

In the WordPress plug-in directory (www.wordpress.org) is a *security scan* tool that does a quick check of some basic items. Though very basic, it runs through a checklist of a few items that may be easy to miss. Visit `http://wordpress.org/extend/plugins/wp-security-scan` to obtain the plug-in. To install the plug-in, use the normal installation routine.

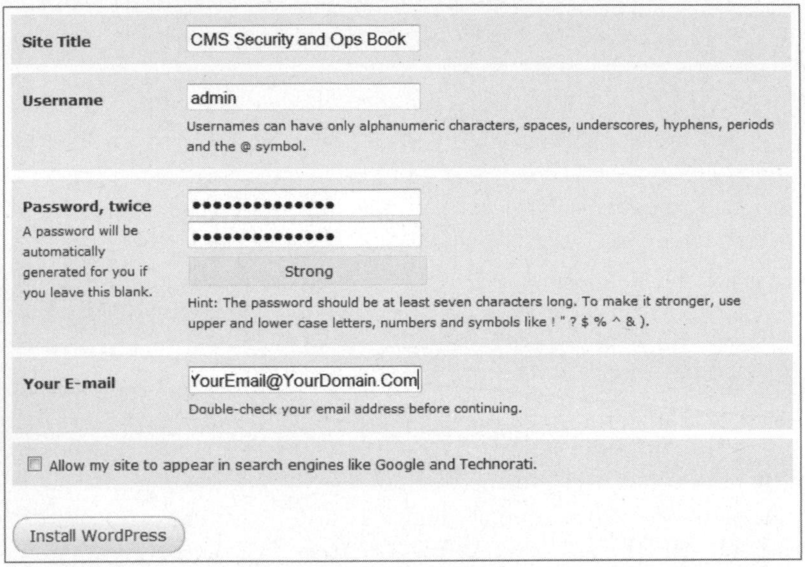

Site Title	CMS Security and Ops Book
Username	admin
	Usernames can have only alphanumeric characters, spaces, underscores, hyphens, periods and the @ symbol.
Password, twice A password will be automatically generated for you if you leave this blank.	●●●●●●●●●●●●●●
	●●●●●●●●●●●●●●
	Strong
	Hint: The password should be at least seven characters long. To make it stronger, use upper and lower case letters, numbers and symbols like ! " ? $ % ^ &).
Your E-mail	YourEmail@YourDomain.Com
	Double-check your email address before continuing.
	☐ Allow my site to appear in search engines like Google and Technorati.

[Install WordPress]

Figure 3-26: Personalizing the WordPress site

In a test server example, the tool provided a few tips such as no `.htaccess` file being found. Additionally, it said the defaults were still enabled, such as the user `admin` still being present.

You should install this tool and review the report to see what your security is like.

Shared Hosting

If you are running on a shared hosting server, consider running the following command on your configuration file. This locks out prying eyes from reading your database settings. You need to run this at the command prompt of your server (if available). If you are unable to do that, ask your host to set your permissions.

```
chmod 750 wp-config.php
```

NOTE With your WordPress site, you can force SSL logins and SSL administration, meaning that all your usernames and passwords are sent encrypted to the server. For more information, see `http://codex.wordpress.org/Administration_Over_SSL`

Advanced Security After Installation

As you have seen, many of the open source CMSs have a number of security add-ons available. Take the time to review all the tools available for your particular CMS to ensure you are safe.

On the commercial front, one tool that does a good job of protecting the PHP-based CMSs against most attacks is *SecureLive* from `Securelive.net`. It works with Joomla!, Drupal, and WordPress. It offers a number of very strong security features to help defend against hackers, and has a site report card to help you isolate other issues that could result in successful attacks.

Other good security measures to consider deploying are `mod_security` and another open source product, *ConfigServer Firewall* (available from `www.configserver.com`).

The key is to look at all your options (both Open Source and commercial) to ensure that you are not dependent on a *single* product, but rather can layer your defenses.

Cleanup and Verification Before Going Live

As a general rule, you should ensure that any installation files have been removed, temporary accesses have been changed, and so on, before you go live. Following is a checklist of things to do before you go live:

- Remove administrative access to any non-administrative personnel.
- Make a clean backup of the new and pristine site.
- Remove installation files (where appropriate).
- Ensure that any temporary files are removed.
- Double-check file and directory permissions.
- Verify that your design specifications have been met before making a final payment to a third-party developer.
- Record passwords (after you have changed them all) in a safe place.
- Copy the database to a separate location.
- Make a list of all third-party add-ons (that is, plug-ins, extensions, add-ons (Plone), themes, templates, and modules).
- Double-check to ensure your CMS application is at the latest version before you launch.

Summary

In this chapter, you learned about some of the business decisions involved with CMS selection that are often overlooked, decisions such as cost, supportability, and complexity. You learned about two different methods to set up a development environment, and how to do some planning on paper before you start.

You learned about installation for all four CMSs covered in this book in the context of security, including a generic setup and some post-installation tips. You learned about some security tools (both free and commercial), and how to clean things up before you go live.

Chapter 4 takes a look at how to review the security on your *existing* site, a process known as *baselining*.

Baselining Your Existing Website

In any business operation, you certainly want to consider both man-made and natural disasters that could impact your IT functions. You should create a matrix to identify what threats exist in your operation, the level of impact they could have, and what the plan of action is. This is known as the *baseline*.

In a phrase, this is an analysis of the impact statement to your business — that is, what the loss or reduction of availability of an IT system would have on your business. Out of this, you'll be able to the mix the risk management into your planning.

A very simple example of a baseline report could involve the server environment for your office. You would be concerned about power, backups, and cooling. You should also be concerned about the uninterruptable power supply (UPS), whether you keep backups onsite or take them away, and the capability to cool the server in the summer if you lost air conditioning. Table 4-1 shows what the baseline report for these concerns would look like.

Table 4-1: Sample Baseline Report

SERVER	CONCERNS	THREAT LEVEL AND RECOMMENDED ACTIONS
Primary server	Power	*Medium* — In the event of a power outage, the systems can run about 20 minutes on the battery-powered UPS. Ensure that the shutdown script runs properly when UPS switches to battery.

Continued

Table 4-1 *(continued)*

SERVER	CONCERNS	THREAT LEVEL AND RECOMMENDED ACTIONS
Server Room	Cooling	*Critical* — In the event that air conditioning is not available in the summer, when it's required, the server must be monitored for overheating. Future plans should include installing a spot cooler in the server room.
Recovery	Backup tapes	*Low* — The tapes are stored in the server room. The new plan will be to keep a rotating set of tapes offsite for security.

This very simple example shows where some of the operational threats are for a system.

This chapter shows you how to review the server and the CMS to make a determination of what threats exist in your site, and what mitigating factors you should employ.

For example, you may find that you are running an older version of a CMS and cannot upgrade because your site's CMS has some custom hacks (changes) made to it. The upgrade would cause those changes to go away. Yet, the version you are on is vulnerable, and you must update. In that situation, your mitigation would be a plan to move those changes to the new version of the CMS, test, document, and deploy. This might be an expensive solution, and would be time-consuming. By building your baseline, you'll be able to see everything that must be updated.

Starting Your Baseline

Baselining your site can yield quite a bit of valuable information. Some of that information will be useful to you on a regular basis. Following are some baseline items that are general to most sites:

- *Inventory* — What is installed on your site and your server?
- *Version control* — What are the versions of the installed extensions?
- *Patches* — What needs to be updated?
- *Security holes* — Do you have any software or settings (such as open ports) that may be a cause for security concern?
- *Improvement of workflow* — In going through your site, do you see anything that is causing poor performance, such as an older (but not insecure) package installed on your CMS? Or do you have users with too much access?

Determining this baseline gives you a good handle on what you are specifically dealing with in your site. You may have other questions and responses you want to add, depending on your site.

The following sections take a closer look at a couple of items on that list.

Taking Inventory

When you review your website, you may easily find third-party add-ons that you *forgot* about. Although they may be disabled on the site, they could be a point of attack. Alternatively, the add-on may have been installed with a valid software installation, but it is simply out of date and vulnerable. Either way, it's during this inventory period that you can begin the baseline process by capturing all the data in a spreadsheet.

At a minimum, you should capture the following information:

- The version of the CMS you are currently running
- Each third-party add-on that is installed on the system
- Special configurations or setup instructions unique to your website
- Distribution and version of the server's operating system
- Installed operating system modules such as PHP, MySQL, and so on
- The version of Apache Server that is installed and running
- Specifics about the *skin* of the CMS (themes, templates, portlets, and so on), including the version, the URL from where you obtained it, and so on

Figure 4-1 shows a sample spreadsheet representing one means to input this type of data. By doing this, you can quickly check what should be updated or removed. Of course, you would add columns or rows to fit your particular environment.

Software	Installed
CMS Version	Joomla 1.5.22
Ext 1	1.5
Ext 2	2
Ext 3	2.1.2
Ext 4	3
Ext 5	1
Template	Zappy - Version 2.1
Server OS	CentOS release 5.5 (Final)
PHP Version	PHP 5.2.11
Apache	Server version: Apache/2.2.14 (Unix)
MySQL Version	Server version: 5.0.91-community

Figure 4-1: Sample inventory sheet

Documentation

Documentation is very valuable. Having it will make your job easier.

Use whatever tool works best for you when you create your baseline documentation. Define the format or tool you will use to capture documentation and stick with it. In other words, don't change from one to another to another without good reasons.

Your system has many areas to document. Based on your particular needs, you'll know what those are. The following sections take a look at four areas that are fairly common to look at for your baseline.

CMS

As mentioned, for your CMS, you should capture and record the installed components, extensions, modules, plug-ins, or add-ons. Capture the core CMS version information. Don't forget that there are likely many settings that, if lost, would cause you concern. Document those settings in this report.

Your last update should be noted as follows:

- The name of the software or script
- The installed version
- The current version (the installed and current versions should be the same)
- The date you updated it

This information can help you when reaching out for technical assistance, planning upgrades to new versions, and in recovery.

Network

Network documentation might include information for something as simple as a Wi-Fi router or cable modem provided by your ISP. It could be as complex as a router and switches.

Although the following list will vary depending on your setup, these are some typical data points to capture:

- Manufacturer of device
- Firmware (BIOS) version
- Software versions used to manage it
- Telnet settings to connect to it
- IP settings (internally facing and externally facing)
- Subnet mask

- DHCP settings
- Various security settings
- Port configurations
- Power-up sequence
- Network map (how it all hooks together)
- SSID (for wireless)
- Settings specific to your wireless installation
- Voice over IP (VoIP) settings
- Remote connectivity settings

Networks are extremely complex, and the more you can document them, the easier you can troubleshoot them.

Server

Your server requires a number of data points. Again, depending on where it is, documenting your server will require more or less data to be captured.

The following points are considered both from a shared host and a co-location situation:

- The manufacturer
- Model number
- Physical configuration (memory, CPU, network cards)
- Firmware (BIOS) version
- The version of control software
- The RAID (Redundant Array of Inexpensive Disks) settings
- The operating system and its version
- Installed software and versions
- The startup sequence
- Passwords
- Physical location (office, rack number, address, and so on)
- Network settings (IP, remote access, and so on)
- The procedures to connect to it
- The process to obtain repair of the machine
- The version and make of the installed virus scanner

Likely you have other items to capture in your situation as well.

Desktops

The data to capture for a desktop, notebook, mobile device, or other client-side machines is similar to what you would capture for a server.

Ensure that the desktops and other machines have the latest updates and that virus scanners are enabled.

Compile all your documentation into one system and then keep it updated. All this information will be something you will refer to in the other processes described in this book (such as disaster recovery). Make every effort to gather this data.

Knowing When to Run Your Baseline

You'll conduct your baseline review at two times or events:

- The first is your initial baseline run, when you gather your data and get the site to a minimum safe standard. Doing a baseline at this time provides you with an initial starting snapshot.

- The second is when any changes occur to your site. These may be updates via patching, installs (or removals) of third-party software, or recovery after you've been hacked. Doing a baseline after changes enables you to see their effects when compared to the initial baseline.

Identifying Areas of Trouble

Trouble on your website and systems can occur in many forms. In this part of your baseline report, you identify weaknesses and correct them. This may be in an out-of-date extension or a misconfigured setting. The goal is to get the information captured and the problems removed.

The areas of concern are the operating system (and add-ons), the CMS (and its add-ons), the server/hardware, and the network.

Checking the Operating System and Add-ons

By and large, next to your CMS, the operating system is an area where you should focus a large amount of attention. If you are not managing the updates, or if your host is not, then chances are good your system will have some vulnerability that could affect you.

Document the various installed applications and modules of your operating system, and record the information in your baseline report.

The following commands will enable you to determine the version numbers of the installed server modules MySQL, Apache, Java, PHP, Python, and the Linux Kernel:

- *MySQL* — `mysql -v`
- *Apache* — `httpd -v`
- *Java* — `java - version`
- *PHP* — `php - v`
- *Python* — `python -v`
- *Linux* — `cat /etc/*-rel*`

NOTE **Note that all of these commands require you to log in to the shell (SSH) on your server.**

The Linux command should work on many distributions. However, if it doesn't work, the following commands will likely provide you the information you seek. These commands are broken down by Linux distribution:

- *Red Hat* — `cat /etc/redhat-release` or `cat /etc/redhat_version`
- *Fedora* — `cat /etc/fedora-release`
- *CentOS* — `cat /etc/redhat-release`
- *Slackware* — `cat /etc/slackware-release` or `cat /etc/slackware-version`
- *Debian* — `cat /etc/debian_release` or `cat /etc/debian_version`
- *Mandrake* — `cat /etc/mandrake-release`
- *Sun JDS* — `cat /etc/sun-release`
- *Solaris/Sparc* — `cat /etc/release`
- *Gentoo* — `cat /etc/gentoo-release`
- *ubuntu* — `cat /etc/lsb-release`
- *SUSE* — `cat /etc/SUSE-release`

Again, after you obtain all of this version information, record it in your report, and install the current revisions of the software. Update accordingly.

Checking Third-Party Add-ons for Your CMS

In terms of updating the internal components, the CMS itself may very well be the largest consumer of your time, after you are up and running. This section briefly examines each CMS spotlighted in this book to enable you to review installed third-party add-ons.

Your first important step is to remove any *unneeded* software from your CMS or server. This not only lowers the threat surface of your site, but will make maintaining it much easier.

The following discussions examine some built-in tools for each CMS to identify what's installed, and to verify whether it's vulnerable or should be updated, starting with Joomla!.

Joomla!

The Joomla! components, modules, and plug-ins all work the same way, as you can see in Figure 4-2. In most cases, the tool lists who the author is and the name of the author's website. You can determine the core (that is, the native CMS) extensions versus those from a third party. The Author column contains "Joomla! Project" for the core extensions. These will be updated when you update Joomla! itself.

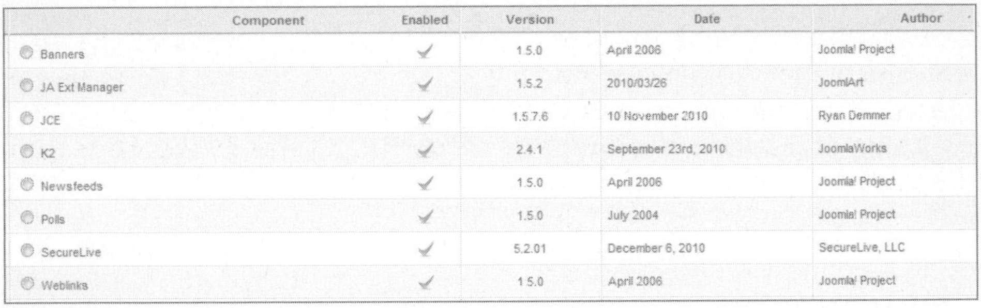

Component	Enabled	Version	Date	Author
Banners	✓	1.5.0	April 2006	Joomla! Project
JA Ext Manager	✓	1.5.2	2010/03/26	JoomlArt
JCE	✓	1.5.7.6	10 November 2010	Ryan Demmer
K2	✓	2.4.1	September 23rd, 2010	JoomlaWorks
Newsfeeds	✓	1.5.0	April 2006	Joomla! Project
Polls	✓	1.5.0	July 2004	Joomla! Project
SecureLive	✓	5.2.01	December 6, 2010	SecureLive, LLC
Weblinks	✓	1.5.0	April 2006	Joomla! Project

Figure 4-2: Joomla extension versions

In your baseline report, list all the extensions and indicate what they are (plug-in, modules, components), as well as where the developer's website is.

> **NOTE** Some developers (such as Akeeba) offer an in-place upgrade, allowing you to update with ease. Noting these in your baseline report is important.

The newest version of Joomla! (v1.6) has some features that allow for easy updating. For example, v1.6 allows for multiple extension installations in one package. This provides the capability to update a number of extensions with a single click.

Drupal

Drupal has a great system for notification of updates. When a new core module or a contributed (that is, third-party) module is in need of an update for any reason, then the Drupal administrator report will let you know.

On the Drupal site, shown in Figure 4-3, you see that Webform 6.x–3.4 is out of date. In fact, it states, "Security update required!"

Views 6.x-2.12		Up to date ✓
Also available:	6.x-3.0-alpha3 (2010-Apr-07)	Download Release notes
Includes: *Views*		
Voting API 6.x-2.3		Up to date ✓
Includes: *Voting API*		
Webform 6.x-3.4		Security update required! ⊗
Recommended version:	6.x-3.6 (2011-Jan-12)	Download Release notes
Security update:	6.x-3.5 (2011-Jan-10)	Download Release notes
Includes: *Webform*		

Figure 4-3: Drupal update report

To begin your baseline, first review the updates report and ensure that, at a minimum, you are up to the latest version. If you are not, take the time to update and record your findings in your baseline report.

To find this report, log in to Drupal as the admin and visit the reports section at the following URL:

```
http://Example.Com/admin/reports/updates
```

This provides you with a report of modules needing updating, as well as their version levels. Again, document your installed modules and their versions.

The next step is to determine which of the installed modules you can remove because you are not using them or do not need them. To see the list, log in as the administrative user for your site, and visit the modules link as follows:

```
http://www.Example.com/admin/build/modules
```

Remove any modules that are not in use.

Put this information into your baseline review spreadsheet. As you find updates or install new modules, update your baseline list accordingly.

Plone

In the context of security, Plone is very solid. It has very few bug or security reports. However, performing a baseline on your Plone site add-ons and your version of Plone is important.

To discover all the Plone add-ons you have, log in to your Plone as the admin. In the admin control panel (in the upper right), select Admin ➤ Site Setup. Here is an example of a shortcut:

```
http://Example.com:8080/plone/prefs_install_products_form
```

In the setup screen that appears, you can select "Add-ons," as shown in Figure 4-4.

Figure 4-4: Plone add-ons

Record your list of add-ons in your spreadsheet, and then visit `http://plone .org/products` to verify that you are running the latest for your version of Plone. If you find that your add-ons are out of date, follow the developer's instructions to update the add-on.

Remove any unneeded add-ons and document the remaining packages.

WordPress

Of all the CMSs examined in this book, WordPress is the easiest of all to use to identify and update your plug-ins.

Log in into your WordPress site as the administrator, and locate Plugin on the toolbar on the left side. Click the Upgrade Available link and a list of plug-ins that need updating appears, as shown in Figure 4-5. Additionally, you'll see a number (in this case, the number 2) showing the quantity available for updating. You can then proceed to update the add-ins by following the instructions.

After updating your plug-ins, record in your spreadsheet a list of your current (active and deactivated) plug-ins on the site. You can find that information by clicking the "All (*number*)" button in the Plugin section, as shown in Figure 4-6.

Remove any unneeded plug-ins and document your remaining ones in your baseline report.

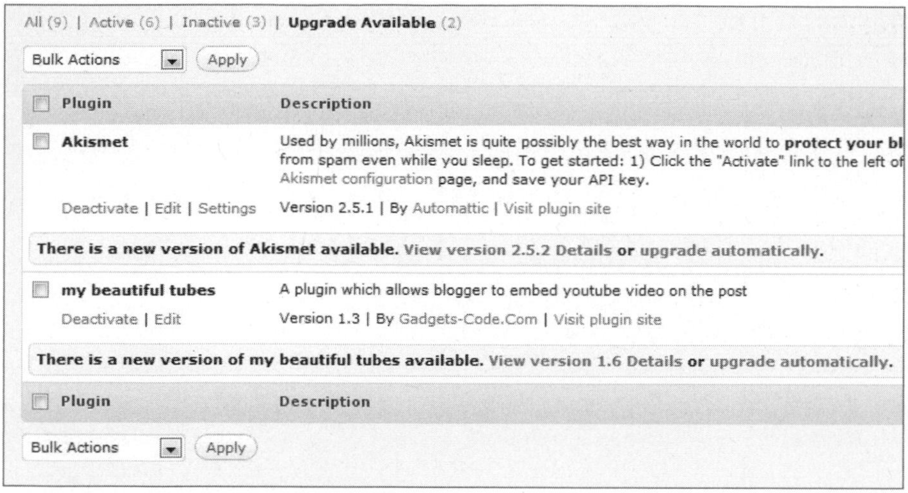

Figure 4-5: WordPress plug-in updates

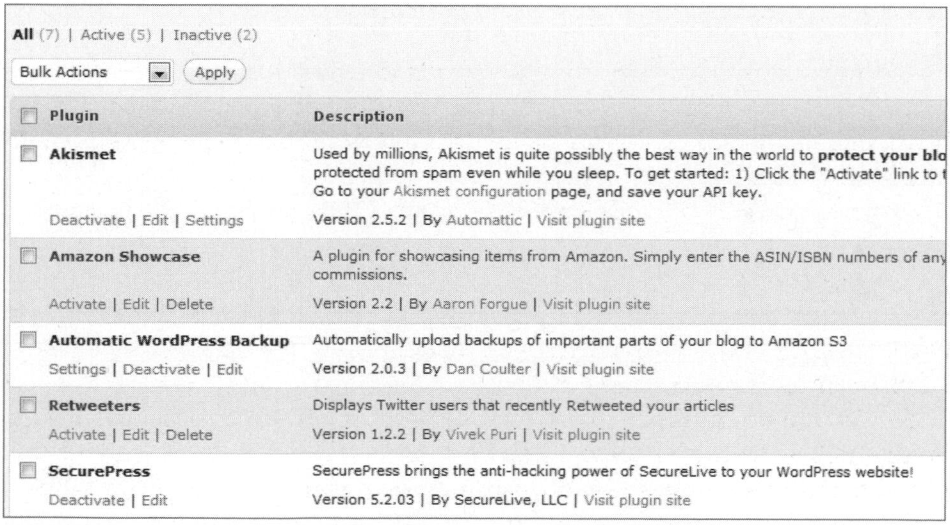

Figure 4-6: List of WordPress plug-ins

Understanding Hardware Vulnerabilities

Hardware has vulnerabilities just as software does. The biggest difference is that hardware vulnerabilities are less frequent. The most important vulnerabilities are often in the firmware or BIOS of the hardware, and the control systems (software) that ship with the hardware.

With that in mind, the big hardware areas are networking gear (such as routers), Wi-Fi systems (and switches), and printers (of all types and all capabilities). Although you may not have access to some of these items (especially in a hosting situation), you may have printers or networking gear in your office.

Network Gear

Networks deserve special consideration because they consist of hardware devices, usually have some form of software and firmware, and live at the heart of your system. They represent a prized target to a hacker.

Check the networking devices such as Wi-Fi routers, switches, and so on, for default passwords and exposed settings. Record the correct settings in your baseline report.

NOTE Be sure to visit the manufacturer's site to ensure that your drivers and firmware are up to date.

Collect all the settings for your baseline spreadsheet, and check them from time to time. It's difficult to provide a specific *frequency* for checking developer websites because vulnerabilities show up all the time. Two suggestions are either to set up a weekly time on your calendar to check all the websites, or subscribe to `SalvusAlerting.com`.

Printers

Today, many printer manufacturers include convenience options (such as mini-web servers) in the actual hardware. In fact, many printers today feature *wireless* connectivity.

What a treasure-trove of fun this feature could be for a bored hacker. Browsing for printers, copiers, and other print devices is simple. Using Google, locating a string to identify printers that are open to the Internet is easy. After hackers find a printer, connecting to it is often just as easy.

The problem is obvious — this wireless connectivity provides a way into your network. This is especially true if the software becomes vulnerable on the printer, and a hacker finds his or her way in.

As a test, the author performed a Google search using a Google *dork* (a search string built to look for vulnerabilities) for a specific model of printer. This search resulted in 25 entries listed in Google that were exposed to the open Internet. A dedicated hacker could potentially gain access through those, and run wild in the network.

Your baseline should determine the following information about any network-attached printers (including wireless systems):

■ Is it set up with the default username and password?

- Can it be seen from the open Internet? (A means to determine this is to attempt to browse to it from the outside world by using, for example, `http://ipaddress`.)

- Did you contact the manufacturer and determine whether updates are available?

- Is the printer running the latest drivers?

- Have you checked all the settings on the site?

Ensure that you review all of your network-enabled and wireless printers. Record these printers in your baseline spreadsheet, and check the preceding information for them periodically.

Uncovering Hidden Dangers Through Vulnerability Scanning

The server your site lives on is a very dynamic device, and the software on it ages. As this aging process happens, vulnerabilities might be discovered, new exploits might be written to attack it, or you may simply discover bugs in the code.

All these issues can add up to hidden dangers in your site. Many tools are available to the administrator (and to the hackers) to help identify vulnerabilities. Following are some of the tools you may want to become familiar with.

WARNING   Be sure you have permission of the owner of the server *before* using any of these tools.

- *MetaSploit* (`http://www.metasploit.com`) is one of the most popular and most powerful tools available. This open source tool is used by *penetration testers*, who are security professionals hired to *break into* sites or discover weaknesses.

- *Nikto2* (`http://cirt.net/nikto2`) is a web scanner that looks for weaknesses, outdated files, known vulnerabilities, and more. This is a quick and "noisy" tool. In other words, it's not stealthy, but is powerful.

- *Acunetix* (`http://www.acunetix.com`) is a commercial vulnerability scanner that checks the applications on your site for Cross-Site Scripting (XSS) errors. It checks for legal compliance, makes comparisons against the Google Hacking Database, tests for password-protected areas, and more.

- *BURP* (`http://portswigger.net`) offers a free and commercial version of a web-scanning tool. One powerful feature is that it can sniff the traffic between the application and browser. This offers you a wealth of information about how the application is working.

- *Nmap* (http://nmap.org) is not technically a vulnerability scanner. It is actually a network exploration or security auditing tool. It is included in this list because of its wide array of uses and its features. If you have a network of any size, this tool is strongly recommended.

- *Nessus* (http://nessus.org) is a tool that you should obtain and learn how to use. Nessus can help you identify problems such as out-of-date elements on your server, potentially dangerous holes, and more. In most cases, it offers you a path to remedy the issue.

WARNING   *Do not* use these to break into any server, because that may constitute a crime in most (if not all) parts of the world.

The following sections take a closer look at a couple of tools on that list.

Using the Nmap Tool

Nmap (or Network Mapper) is a popular open source tool that is very well maintained. It's one of those Swiss Army knife–type tools that you should have in your toolbox. In fact, a person skilled with Nmap can potentially make a map of an entire network.

Nmap can identify which ports are open, closed, or filtered on your server. It can identify your operating system and other hardware on your network. Nmap has the capability to map a network all the way down to the routers, firewalls, and switches, all the while *evading* an Intrusion Detection System (IDS).

For purposes of the baseline, you want to use Nmap to detect the port configuration and potentially other issues that may be uncovered.

One example use for Nmap is the identification of specific malware. One nasty worm that still makes the rounds on the Internet is the *Confiker worm* (it's primarily an exploit against Microsoft Windows servers). Nmap has the capability to detect it and provides the capability for you to take action.

WARNING   *Do not* attempt to run Nmap without reading the documentation at **http://nmap.org/nsedoc/scripts/smb-check-vulns.html**.

Nmap could identify that you have been hacked with a back-door Trojan, allowing the attackers to run an Internet relay chat (IRC) server from your machine. If you see ports 6665, 6666, 6667, 6668, and others, then you are likely the victim of one of the following Trojan attacks:

- Dark Connection Inside
- NetBus
- TCPShell.c

- LameRemote
- ProjectMayhem
- Backdoor.IRC.flood
- Backdoor.Hacarmy.E
- W32.Spybot, W32.Cissi.W
- W32.Linkbot.M
- W32.Zotob.D

Those open ports identified through an Nmap scan indicate trouble.

Installing Nmap

Nmap is available for Linux and Windows. Installation on your Linux server can be run from the command line with one of the two following commands:

```
# rpm Manager : rpm -vhU http://www.nmap.org/dist/<version>
Yum install nmap
```

NOTE You should be sure to run an update if you install from any source except directly from **nmap.org**.

For full installation instructions, review the documentation at `http://nmap.org/book/inst-linux.html#inst-rpm`.

Another method to install and run Nmap is from a Windows desktop. Download the latest version from `nmap.org` and install as you would any other Windows application.

WARNING Before reviewing some of Nmap's more useful commands, be sure you understand that legal restrictions may vary by the location the server is in. In other words, scanning a server in a particular country or state *may* be a crime. Therefore, never use Nmap to scan a server you do not expressly have permissions to scan. It's simply not a good idea, and could land you in trouble.

Using Nmap

The version of Nmap discussed here is running with a graphical user interface (GUI), but the commands are identical for other setups. The GUI for Nmap looks like Figure 4-7 on startup.

Here are some of the main features of this screen:

- *Target* — This is the *target server*. It can be a domain name or IP address.
- *Profile* — These are preconfigured settings that change the way Nmap scans the target.

- *Command* — These are the actual commands that instruct Nmap how to scan. They follow (by default) the Profile. You can change these to fit your needs.

- *Hosts and Services* — These are buttons that will show the results of the post-scan findings.

- *Nmap Output* — The results are shown here in detail.

- *Ports/Hosts* — This is a summary of the ports found, and their status, as well as a listing of the Hosts.

- *Topology* — This is a visual representation of the hops to the target.

- *Host Details* — This gives you a wealth of information about the host operating system.

- *Scans* — This shows the historical scans you have run.

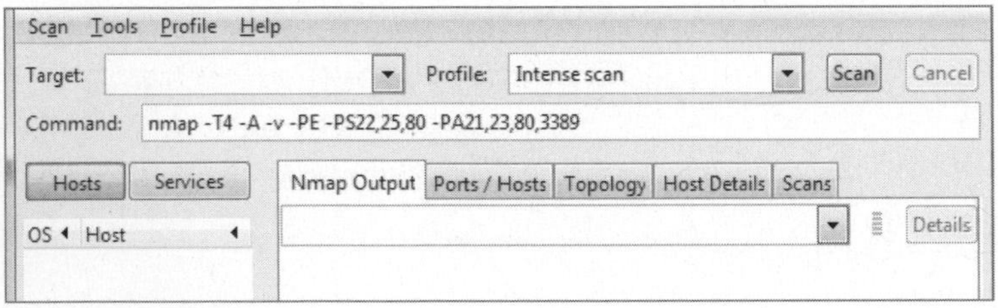

Figure 4-7: Nmap GUI

Figure 4-8 shows an example of a scan run on a server. It is a partial screen-shot of the Nmap output, which indicates that this target server has a number of ports open, and that it is running Apache and CentOS. More interesting, it has clearly identified (and is correct) that Plone is installed and is running. You may also note that Nmap found some hardware devices along the way, and again, you can confirm the existence of the hardware.

```
80/tcp    open    http     Apache httpd 2.2.3 ((CentOS))
|_html-title: Apache HTTP Server Test Page powered by CentOS
443/tcp   open    ssl/http Apache httpd 2.2.3 ((CentOS))
|_html-title: Apache HTTP Server Test Page powered by CentOS
3306/tcp open    mysql    MySQL (unauthorized)
8080/tcp open    http     Zope 2.12.13 (python 2.6.5, linux2; ZServer/1.1)
|_html-title: Plone
|_http-favicon: Unknown favicon MD5: 3905C0D2E530753B4C54A18C554B0B42
Device type: WAP|general purpose|broadband router|storage-misc|print server|specialized|remote manai
Running (JUST GUESSING) : Linux 2.4.X|2.6.X (95%), Actiontec embedded (92%), D-Link embedded (92%),
Google embedded (91%)
Aggressive OS guesses: DD-WRT v23 (Linux 2.4.34) (95%), Linux 2.6.20 (Ubuntu 7.04 server, x86) (95%
Linux 2.6.15 - 2.6.26 (92%), Linux 2.6.9 - 2.6.27 (92%), Actiontec GT701 DSL modem (92%), D-Link DN:
(92%), HP 4200 PSA (Print Server Appliance) model J4117A (92%), Linux 2.4.21 (embedded) (92%)
No exact OS matches for host (test conditions non-ideal).
Uptime guess: 40.315 days (since Tue Dec 07 15:06:51 2010)
Network Distance: 14 hops
TCP Sequence Prediction: Difficulty=190 (Good luck!)
IP ID Sequence Generation: All zeros
```

Figure 4-8: Partial Nmap output

Figure 4-9 shows the ports that Nmap found on the system.

◀ Port ◀	Protocol ◀	State ◀	Service ◀	Version
22	tcp	open	ssh	OpenSSH 4.3 (protocol 2.0)
25	tcp	filtered	smtp	
80	tcp	open	http	Apache httpd 2.2.3 ((CentOS))
443	tcp	open	http	Apache httpd 2.2.3 ((CentOS))
3306	tcp	open	mysql	MySQL (unauthorized)
8080	tcp	open	http	Zope 2.12.13 (python 2.6.5, linux2; ZServer/1.1)

Figure 4-9: Ports found in scan

As far as ports are concerned, all in all, this configuration is very safe. From Figure 4-9, you can confirm that Apache, CentOS, MySQL, and Zope (Plone) are running. However, this would be a shopping list for a bad guy.

If your server were to have many open ports, as shown in Figure 4-10, then you would have a really big problem. Although the figure shows quite a few ports open, this is a very small sampling of all the ports that were actually open. Real-life situations such as misconfigured firewalls, hackers opening ports, or other potential misconfigurations could lead to a situation similar to what is shown in Figure 4-10. Nmap would help you identify such an issue very quickly.

```
Discovered open port 8500/tcp on
Discovered open port 3031/tcp on
Discovered open port 7007/tcp on
Discovered open port 16993/tcp on
Discovered open port 34571/tcp on
Discovered open port 31038/tcp on
Discovered open port 1092/tcp on
Discovered open port 1097/tcp on
Discovered open port 1010/tcp on
Discovered open port 1052/tcp on
Discovered open port 1011/tcp on
Discovered open port 25734/tcp on
Discovered open port 7/tcp on
Discovered open port 5999/tcp on
Discovered open port 2605/tcp on
Discovered open port 1123/tcp on
Discovered open port 8649/tcp on
Discovered open port 783/tcp on :
Discovered open port 1000/tcp on
Discovered open port 3013/tcp on
Discovered open port 7999/tcp on
Discovered open port 5815/tcp on
Discovered open port 1058/tcp on
Discovered open port 5061/tcp on
Discovered open port 7937/tcp on
Discovered open port 6881/tcp on
```

Figure 4-10: Too many ports open

As mentioned previously, the purpose of the baseline is to identify where you have trouble and enable you to take care of it. Using Nmap to identify holes in the network will help you plug them.

You should use Nmap regularly just as a check on your server. However, running a slow-comprehensive scan from the preconfigured Profile settings will net a wealth of information.

Specifically, you want to see that you have no unexpected ports open, and, in fact, as few ports open as possible. Seeing what software is running is helpful, but later in this chapter, you'll learn about using Nessus for that purpose.

Although every configuration will vary, the following ports are what you typically see open on a properly configured server:

- *21* — FTP (File Transfer Protocol)
- *22* — SSH (the optional SecureShell client)
- *25* — SMTP (usually shown as Filtered)
- *53* — DOMAIN (DNS) (open or closed, depending on the host)
- *80* — World Wide Web (WWW) services
- *443* — SSL for your website
- *3306* — MySQL (varies depending on host)

If you determine what you have at the start, then checking them as you run future baselines is easier. In the future, you'll be able to check to be sure the port settings are all the same.

Using the Nessus Tool

Nessus is one of the most popular tools for vulnerability scanning. It's a well-built product that is maintained with the latest vulnerability data.

Nessus tests your website and server for several different vulnerabilities. It looks at the server-side software, looks for open ports, checks for backdoor applications, and much more. Some consider it to be one of the best tools in its class.

NOTE Nessus offers a free (home) version and a professional version. For the free version, you'll need to register and get a key. Visit `http://nessus.org/download/` for more information.

Setting Up and Running Nessus

For the purposes of this discussion, suppose that Nessus is installed and running as a Windows desktop application. It has two components to it — a Server and a Client. The Nessus Server manager must be started before you run the Client. Additionally, you must update the plug-ins, which can be done automatically. These plug-ins are definitions of new threats and vulnerabilities that you need Nessus to check for.

To start the Nessus console, click Start ≻ Nessus Client from your Windows machine.

WARNING The Nessus Client uses your default browser to display. Your browser may identify the client as an untrusted website. This is not a problem. Simply accept the site into your browser and use it.

Following are the options in the Client toolbar:

- *Reports* — This displays a collection of past vulnerability scans, allowing you to compare, review, and take action.

- *Scans* — You conduct the actual work of launching and checking for vulnerabilities here. You click Add Scan to start the process. Thereafter, you select Add Scan and you'll see a variety of vulnerability scans you can select to test your server.

- *Policies* — You will define your test sets here. Click Add to set up the tests you want to run. These will be run from Scans.

- *Users* — This is where you add/change/delete users and update passwords.

Interpreting the Results

After Nessus runs a scan, it will provide you with a list of any vulnerability found and a suggested remedy. After running it against the example test server, several vulnerabilities were discovered. The scan provided the following important information:

- The IP in question (192.168.2.200) was correct, because that was the IP tested.

- A total of 53 vulnerabilities were found (2 High, 5 Medium, and 41 Low).

- A total of five open ports were discovered.

A review of the High risk vulnerabilities showed that the host was in need of an update. In this test case, the OpenSSL component on the server needed to be updated.

Nessus provided enough detail to take action; in this case, to update the server, as shown in Figure 4-11. This update confirms that, indeed, Nessus correctly identified the OpenSSL as vulnerability.

```
Package                          Arch              Version

Updating:
 apr-util                        i386              1.2.7-11.el5_5.2
 apr-util                        x86_64            1.2.7-11.el5_5.2
 openssl                         i686              0.9.8e-12.el5_5.7
 openssl                         x86_64            0.9.8e-12.el5_5.7
 openssl-devel                   x86_64            0.9.8e-12.el5_5.7

Transaction Summary

Install          0 Package(s)
Upgrade          5 Package(s)

Total download size: 4.9 M
Is this ok [y/N]:
```

Figure 4-11: Updating the server to patch a vulnerability

The baseline of the server is simple to determine through a tool such as Nessus. You can quickly identify threats and mitigate them. You can identify areas where you might not have a fix, and need a workaround. You can also keep a running record of past scans, allowing you to measure the security of the host.

Take the time to learn more about Nessus and remember to ask for permission before scanning your servers.

Using Virus Scanning Tools

Without a doubt, you should check the status of your system files using a quality virus scanner. Chapter 9 provides more detail on using a virus scanner to remove viruses from a hacked site.

In the baseline, running the scanner will provide you with a clean bill of health. You'll want to check the site files in the following directories:

- `Public_html` (typically the name for the web directory)
- `Mail`
- Server files

Additionally, you'll want to ensure that you scan all your desktops or notebook computers that may connect to the site. This guarantees that you don't have a virus hiding in the midst of your systems.

Remediating Problems

The entire process of baselining is meant to find and eliminate issues that can and will impact your security. Remediation of any problems is very straightforward. In this step of the baselining process, you list and prioritize your issues, document the proposed fix, and lastly deploy it.

Categorizing and Prioritizing Issues

As issues are identified through the baselining process, try to define them by criticality. This can provide a proper road map to correcting the issues.

If you were to take the issues found by Nessus as described earlier, you might construct a spreadsheet like the one shown in Figure 4-12 to track and remedy the issues. Here, you can see that the spreadsheet is segmented by columns, allowing you to track the vulnerability, the risk factor, description of the vulnerability, and the recommended fix.

You can quickly review your list of items and focus your time on the problems that matter most, and spend less time on those that matter least. As shown by the final entry in Figure 4-12, some issues are described by "No fix required." You will want to track those anyway as part of the baseline. Although it's not likely, a Low risk factor could become a Medium or High if a new exploit is discovered that can take advantage of it.

Date	Jan-11		
Baseline Report	Server:200389		
Vulnerability	Risk Factor	Description	Recommended fix
		CentOS system s missing a security update which has been	
Svr: CentOS: RHSA-2010-0978	HIGH	documented in Red Hat advisory RHSA-2010-0978.	
Svr: Linux Daemons with Broken links to Executables	HIGH	missing Daemon link to executable.	
Svr: SSL Certificate name doesn't match host	Medium	The SSL certificate for this service is for a different host.	Purchase new SSL or Correct name
Svr: http trace/track methods allowed	Medium	Debugging functions are enabled on the remote web server.	Disable these methods.
Svr: Remote Listeners Enumeration	Low	Using netstat, it is possible to identify daemons listening on the remote port.	No fix required

Figure 4-12: Sample baseline report for Nessus scan

After you take care of all the issues, be sure to document the updated status of the site. In the previous example, you would note the new version of OpenSSL, the date of the fix, and any other issues.

Patching Security Holes

Generally speaking, after you identify where your system is weak, then patching or removing the suspect code is the first step. The next step, of course, is to check to see that your settings have not changed from your last review. Your baseline report is a document you may refer to fairly often for this purpose.

This is also a very good time for you to review your administrative users and remove any who may no longer need access.

Reporting Problems to the Hosting Company

There are correct ways to report to issues to your hosting company, and, of course, there are wrong ways. The wrong way is to give a weak explanation of the issues, such as "it doesn't work."

You won't get far with that method. The right way of communicating to a hosting company about remediating issues is to compile your data and follow the host's procedures for submission.

For example, suppose you suddenly see a set of ports open that previously were not. You would want to report this issue to the host as soon as possible. Your report should be something along this line:

"Dear <host>

We noted in our recent check on our server (date) that new ports (xxxx, yyyy, and zzzz) have been opened. Our last check (date) showed these to be closed. The configuration we need should have these closed.

Please review our server and advise."

In this example, you can show the host dates with results, proving something has changed. This type of information helps the host track down the changes that occurred in your configuration fairly easily.

The key to dealing with technical support is to be as detailed as possible. This helps the technical support staff help you. If you have a specific issue, provide the staff with a means to duplicate it. If you receive a specific error message, include it.

Summary

This chapter discussed the concept of a baseline report. This report helps you identify where threats exist in your operation, and should contain a plan to mitigate them.

The strength of the baseline report is in the use of it. In other words, if you use it once and forget about it, then it has no value.

You were introduced to a number of tools to help you identify security issues on your site, and you learned how to identify the add-ons for your CMS.

In Chapter 5, you will continue with the next step in the baselining process, which is hardening your server against attack. This process involves a more in-depth look at the systems, software, and processes used in your business.

Hardening the Server Against Attack

"Hardening a server," in generic terms, means "closing up vulnerabilities and holes in the server." Weaknesses exist in all software and hardware platforms, and new weaknesses are discovered on a very regular basis.

Servers are an asset both to you and to the bad guys. If the bad guys can gain control of your server, they can use it for their purposes. If that is an illegal purpose such as launching an attack against someone, then when the chips fall, you may be left holding the bag.

According to the *2010 Verizon Data Breach Investigations Report*, research conducted in conjunction with the United States Secret Service uncovered the following:

> *"Verizon Business investigative experts found, as they did in the company's prior data breach reports, that most breaches were considered avoidable if security basics had been followed. Only 4 percent of breaches assessed required difficult and expensive protective measures."*

Note that only 4 percent of all the cases they reviewed needed difficult and expensive measures to break into the websites. That means that 96 percent of the cyber breaches could have been avoided by taking proper steps.

The report further stated that "98 percent of all data breached came from servers." This is a major source of banking phishing scams, identity theft, and other criminal activity.

> **NOTE** You should spend some time reading the Verizon report because it's very insightful. It has a lot of information to help you keep apprised of the state of security. You can learn more by downloading the whitepaper from verizonbusiness.com/go/2010databreachreport.

This chapter provides a great deal of information about the process to secure your server, thus helping you to be in that 4 percent category, rather than the 96 percent category. Many of the settings or features discussed in this chapter will not be available to you on a shared server. The host can confirm whether the steps described in this chapter have been taken. If you are running your own machine or have responsibility for a managed machine, then you'll benefit greatly from reading this chapter.

In this chapter, you'll also learn about default passwords and how to spot them, how to secure your Linux operating system, how to deal with permissions on your server, how to secure Apache and PHP, and how to deal with Secure Sockets Layer (SSL).

The first weak point to examine is the passwords on your system and software.

Ensuring Secure Passwords

Passwords are the literal keys to your system. Break-ins occur for a variety reasons, but topping that list is weak passwords.

Weak passwords are easy to guess or break, and malware and botnets frequently target passwords to gain access. They often use a brute-force method, which means they try password after password to find one that's in a password dictionary or words in common use.

You must perform a few important tasks to harden your server with regard to passwords. First, ensure that there are not any accounts with empty passwords — in other words, accounts without passwords. The following command can identify whether any exist.

```
# awk -F: '($2 == "") {print}' /etc/shadow
```

Figure 5-1 shows the result of running the command with an account on a server that does not have a password. A *hash* of the password should appear next to the user tom.

```
[root@Booktest ~]# awk -F: '($2=="") {print}' /etc/shadow
tom::::  ←
[root@Booktest ~]#
```

Figure 5-1: Empty password found

If you find any of these accounts, either assign a password to the user, or delete the user.

Shadow Password File

A *shadow password* file stores the encrypted password (technically it's encoded, not encrypted) for users. This file can only be read by the root user, which prevents the dictionary attack from being successful.

The original implementation was built in 1987, after its author experienced a cyber break-in on a SCO XENIX operating system. It was ported over the years to various distributions of UNIX and Linux.

This software suite is meant to store the passwords and not allow them to be stored in the passwd file. After a password is shadowed, then you'll typically see an x or an * in the password field.

Use the following command to scan your system and ensure that all the passwords themselves are in the shadow file and not in passwd:

```
# awk -F: '($2 != "x") {print}' /etc/passwd
```

When you run this command, it should not return any results. You should take the corrective action of manually removing passwords that appear in this file. The hashes for all user account passwords should be stored in the file /etc/shadow and never in /etc/passwd. The passwd file is readable by all users. If you find a user with a password (hash) showing in the results of this command, then removing and re-creating that user may be best.

For the most part, you should not log in as *root*. You should log in as a normal user and then elevate your privileges to the root or super user. With that practice in mind, you want to ensure that root (the user) is the only user in the system with root privileges. To do this, issue the following command:

```
# awk -F: '($3 == "0") {print}' /etc/passwd
```

This command should only return one account, as follows:

```
foot:x:0:0:root:/root:/bin/bash
```

If you note other users in this output, lower their administrative privileges.

Expiring Passwords

In terms of managing security for your passwords, changing your passwords on a regular basis is a good practice. The frequency is solely your call, but a good frequency is every 30 to 60 days.

With Linux, you can set passwords to automatically expire. Doing so forces users to change their passwords.

Within your information security policy, define the time limit and complexity for passwords. After you do, change them by following a simple process.

Using WinSCP (or other application), connect to your server and navigate to the /etc directory. Once there, locate a file called login.defs, as shown in Figure 5-2.

```
# Password aging controls:
#
#       PASS_MAX_DAYS   Maximum number of days a password may be used.
#       PASS_MIN_DAYS   Minimum number of days allowed between password changes.
#       PASS_MIN_LEN    Minimum acceptable password length.
#       PASS_WARN_AGE   Number of days warning given before a password expires.
#
PASS_MAX_DAYS   99999
PASS_MIN_DAYS   0
PASS_MIN_LEN    5
PASS_WARN_AGE   7
```

Figure 5-2: Password aging default settings

The settings are as follow:

- PASS_MAX_DAYS — This sets the maximum number of days a password can live before changing it is required.

- PASS_MIN_DAYS (-m) — This prevents the passwords from being changed for "x" days. This important measure is to prevent passwords from being changed frequently.

- PASS_MIN_LEN — This assigns a minimum length to passwords.

- PASS_WARN_AGE (-W) — This gives the user "x" days (as defined in this setting) to change his or her password. In other words, a value of 5 would give the user five days to change. After that, the password is expired, and the user will not be allowed to log back in.

Change the settings in that file according to your particular information security policy. For example, if you want passwords changed every 60 days, then change PASS_MAX_DAYS 9999 to PASS_MAX_DAYS 60.

If this server has been in use for a while, you'll want to update your current users, using the following command:

```
# Chage -M 60 -m 7 -W 7 user.
```

Replace the numbers with your values, and user with the actual username.

Spotting Default Passwords

Default passwords are basically a password that can be applied to a machine or to software in the manufacturing process. With software, this means you may buy some package that has a default password to a database. In hardware, this means that (typically) the administrative interface ships in the box with the same password over and over.

Hardware manufacturers and software development firms are in a bad situation when it comes to default passwords. They must produce a product that is consumer-friendly and fairly easy to use. Yet, they must balance production costs with *servicing it* at the lowest possible expense. And one of the highest expenses any support organization incurs is the resetting of passwords.

If the manufacturer were to ship a unique password on every widget it made, the manufacturer's support costs would quickly eat up any profit. And, quite frankly, 99 percent of the passwords shipped out would be lost or stolen.

Hence, the best method to deal with this dilemma from the manufacturer's point of view is to use the default password — one that is set from the start and is not changed until the end-user customer changes it.

The challenge to this method is that people generally take the path of least resistance when it comes to passwords. End users get in a hurry and do not read the documentation and procedures. They do not account for the need to change default passwords across the board.

In fact, this problem is so widespread that entire websites are devoted to the tracking and publication of default passwords. Tracking down and recording default passwords is big business. Following are some examples of such websites:

- www.defaultpassword.com
- phenelit-us.org/dpl/dpl/html
- passwordsdatabase.com
- cirt.net/passwords
- default-password.info
- virus.org/default-password

Using these websites to find default passwords merely involves a couple of simple steps.

1. List your hardware and software systems.
2. Check them against the default password sites.

In reality, most anything that is electronic has a default password. Devices such as a wireless router will have a default password that is very often not changed. Many software packages are set up with either no password or a default password.

Take some time to identify all the devices, hardware systems, and software packages in your business. If they touch your network or your website, then they can be a means for hackers to penetrate.

Table 5-1 shows some examples to get you started.

Table 5-1: Identifying System Hardware and Software

NETWORKING DEVICES AND COMPONENTS	SOFTWARE SYSTEMS	HARDWARE SYSTEMS
Routers	Operating systems	Printers
Wireless routers	FTP	BIOS/Firmware (on servers, desktops, and notebooks)
Managed network switches	Telnet (which should be disabled)	Netcams/Webcams
PBX (telephony systems)	E-mail systems	Web-monitored security cameras
VoIP (telephony systems)	Database servers	Copy machines (in many cases, they retain copies of documents)
Voice mail	Web-facing applications and administrative interfaces	RAID cards (disk controllers)
		Remote access cards in servers
		USB devices (Bluetooth devices)
		Smart phones
		Cable modems
		Modems

Also, take the time to read and understand the documentation that came with the hardware and software products. If it says something to the effect of "here's *the current password*," then you can be sure the password is a default. Be sure to check the *database, administrative interface,* and any other passwords that give you control over the CMS site. If they are not difficult to guess, then change them.

One common factor in all the websites discussed in this book is that they run on the Linux operating system. The following section takes a closer look at the security of Linux.

Securely Configuring the Linux Operating System

As you are aware, the primary focus of this book is to help small and medium-sized business owners who are running a CMS-enabled website to be more secure. Although entire books are written on this subject, the discussion in this section addresses only those areas that require the attention of those website owners. The aim here is to give you a good framework, while addressing some common issues to help protect you.

Securing your server entails more than making technical changes. It also involves taking into consideration a bit of strategy.

Think about the value of your information. Is the information pertinent to an industrial company secret? Or is your company's site dedicated to selling quilting supplies? Both are important. However, one may be a hacker's target because of the value of the information contained on the server and potential credit card information, whereas the other may contain information of value to a competitor.

Consider employing every possible measure to protect all of your company's valuable information, including strong cryptography to protect the data. A hacker may be after credit card information you have or may want to use your server for disseminating spam. They may want to lurk on your site and sell their own wares.

Identify for yourself where your company falls on that spectrum and keep it in mind as this discussion examines how to protect the Linux operating system. You can take some preventative measures that may be described as "low-hanging fruit." These involve little effort, but pay off very well.

Let's begin with the login banner.

Changing the Login Banner

The *login banner* is the message that the user sees upon a successful login. Often, by default, this message can tell you a lot about the underlying system, such as the version of the operating system and possibly more. A dedicated attacker can use this information to build a *map* of the systems to be used for an attack.

Following are some ways to change the default login banner:

- Dilute any information that could allow a malicious user to learn the details of the operating system and its version.

- Change the technical message to a warning banner that this system is for authorized users only. This is to ward off any weak defense of someone saying, "I didn't know I couldn't log in because it didn't say I couldn't." Although changing the login banner in this way offers no legal benefit, making the change is better than not.

- Display the resources the person is allowed to use, or even news of the day, to help to reduce potential technical support calls.

Let's take a look at how to change that login banner message to something else. In effect, this produces the benefit of neutralizing any chance of a threat to you via information leakage.

You'll need a few things to get you started on this task:

■ Root access

■ A desk-side editor such as WinSCP (optional)

■ The message you want to use to replace the default login banner message

NOTE For the desk-side tool, if you are comfortable with one of the many editing tools such as *VI* in Linux, then feel free to use it. However, throughout this book, WinSCP is used in the examples because it is a highly valuable (and free) tool. You can download a copy from `WinSCP.net`.

To change the login banner:

1. Open your site with WinSCP (or your SFTP tool of choice) and navigate to the `/etc/issue` file. Right-click this file. An image similar to that shown in Figure 5-3 appears.

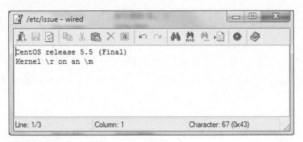

Figure 5-3: Default issue file

In this example, you see that the banner advertises at login the CentOS release 5.5 final version of Linux. In addition, you can see the phrase `Kernel \r on an \m`. This indicates the release (`\r`) and the machine (`\m`).

2. Determine what you want to display at login, and replace the default banner with it.

3. After you make the change, save it and copy it back onto the machine.

After you handle these preliminary tasks, you should ensure that you are running the latest versions of software. The utility called *yum* is what you can use for any required updates.

Using yum

To update a Linux server, you can either upload the patches yourself, or pull them from a trusted source, known as a *repository*.

In Red Hat Linux and other Red Hat distributions (such as CentOS and Fedora), the update command is `yum`. Another facility is called RPM. `yum` installs the software package you pick *and* other software that it may depend on. RPM installs only the *software package* you pick. For example, if you use `yum` to install Apache, you can be sure that you have pulled in the appropriate supporting files. Other versions of Linux will use different commands for updating.

First take a more detailed look at `yum`, followed by some commands for Debian Linux.

Basic yum Commands

This discussion will familiarize you with some commands that you will need as you work your way through this section. Note that the # (pound or hash sign) indicates the administrator prompts. You don't need to include it in the use of the commands.

Following are some commands you can use to install, remove, and update software packages with `yum`:

```
# yum install package name
# yum remove package name
# yum update package name
```

If you ever see a package running and are not sure what it is, you can use `yum` to help you identify the package in question, as shown here:

```
#yum provides name of package
```

Use the GROUP command appended to `yum` as shown here to get a list of items to be installed together:

```
# yum grouplist list
```

Type out the command **yum grouplist** to see all the groups that are installed and that are able to be installed. Table 5-2 shows an example of information returned by using this command.

Table 5-2: Results of Using `yum grouplist`

INSTALLED GROUPS	AVAILABLE GROUPS
DNS Name Server	Administration Tools
Development Libraries	Authoring and Publishing
GNOME Software Development	Base
Graphics	Beagle

Continued

Table 5-2 *(continued)*

INSTALLED GROUPS	AVAILABLE GROUPS
Legacy Network Server	Cluster Storage
Legacy Software Support	Clustering
Mail Server	Development Tools
Network Servers	Dialup Networking Support
OpenFabrics Enterprise Distribution	Editors
System Tools	Emacs
Text-based Internet	Engineering and Scientific
Yum Utilities	FTP Server

yum is a quick way to find and install a package. Using the returned list shown in Table 5-2, you could install a new FTP server quite easily by using the following command:

```
# yum groupinstall "FTP SERVER"
```

You can cluster on one line a set of commands to install, as shown here:

```
#yum install php-mysql php-devel php-gd php-mcrypt php-pecl-memcache
php-pspell php-snmp php-xmlrpc php-xml
```

This command can install several items, such as MySQL Server and the PHP development tools. It is handy for setup purposes.

Updating the Server Using yum

After you have updated your server, you are ready to begin the hardening process. You'll need to log on as the super user. Remember, you'll see the # prompt after you are logged in. Seeing $ means you are logged in as a regular user. The following examples involve using CentOS to demonstrate the use of yum.

Suppose you wanted to check the system for potential updates. The quickest way to do this is to use the yum update command. This checks that your installed applications are up to date and issues a report. Figure 5-4 shows an example of a server needing an update.

However, if you ran that command and no updates were needed, you would see something similar to Figure 5-5.

```
rpm-libs                          x86_64              4.4.2.3-20.el5_5.1
rpm-python                        x86_64              4.4.2.3-20.el5_5.1
selinux-policy                    noarch              2.4.6-279.el5_5.2
selinux-policy-targeted           noarch              2.4.6-279.el5_5.2
sudo                              x86_64              1.7.2p1-9.el5_5
tzdata                            x86_64              20101-1.el5
udev                              x86_64              095-14.21.el5_5.1
Installing for dependencies:
cpio                              x86_64              2.6-23.el5_4.1
device-mapper-multipath           x86_64              0.4.7-34.el5_5.6
dmraid                            x86_64              1.0.0.rc13-63.el5
dmraid-events                     x86_64              1.0.0.rc13-63.el5
kpartx                            x86_64              0.4.7-34.el5_5.6
mkinitrd                          x86_64              5.1.19.6-61.el5_5.2

Transaction Summary
=============================================================================
Install      6 Package(s)
Upgrade     46 Package(s)

Total download size: 75 M
Is this ok [y/N]:
```

Figure 5-4: Server needs updates

```
root@host:~
[root@host ~]# yum update
Loaded plugins: fastestmirror
Determining fastest mirrors
addons
base
extras
updates
wiredtree
Excluding Packages in global exclude list
Finished
Setting up Update Process
No Packages marked for Update
[root@host ~]#
```

Figure 5-5: Server is up-to-date

The Debian Distribution

Another popular distribution is *Debian Linux*, and its update/install/removal
tool is called aptitude.

This command works similarly to yum. Following are a few examples:

```
# aptitude install package name
# aptitude reinstall package name
# aptitude remove package name
# aptitude remove -- purge package name
```

Note that the last command in that list has -- purge appended to it. This
command removes the software package(s) and the installed files, essentially
cleaning up the server.

You can check the versions of all your installed software packages using the
-v command option, as shown here:

```
#aptitude - V install package name
```

To update an extension, you have a few options.

Sometimes you may want to simply download, but not install a file. The aptitude command provides a switch for that as well, as shown here:

```
# aptitude -d install package name
```

Patching and updating your server and your CMS is important. If you're running Debian, then you have different options:

```
# aptitude update
# aptitude upgrade
# aptitude dist-upgrade
```

These three commands differ as follows:

- update refreshes the cache (that is, the local list of packages and their repositories).
- upgrade installs a *new* version of the application. This is similar to RPM.
- dist-upgrade installs the most current version of packages, and may install additional packages. This is similar to yum.

The files you update and the files you store are all governed by *permissions*. That is, they have specific permissions dictating who can do what with them. The next hardening task is to examine *file permissions*.

Setting File Permissions

Files in Linux are given several attributes that correspond to specific groups, including the following:

- Owner of the file
- Groups (of people)
- Public (that is, anyone who accesses the system from the outside)

Each of these groups is allowed to do specific tasks or activities based on their permissions.

Permissions Represented as Octal Numbers

Misconfigured file permissions are one of the biggest threats to a web server or to a CMS website. In fact, early on in the Joomla! world, permissions were a huge problem, but that problem has been reined in a bit over the last couple of years.

The numerical notation for permissions is counted in the base 8 system known as *octal*. You would see octal counted in the following form:

```
0 1 2 3 4 5 6 7 10 11 12 13 14 15 16 17 20 21 22 23 24 25 26 ...
```

This is because, in the octal system, there are only the numbers 0 through 7.

Permissions look like `644 filename.ext`. Following is what the three numbers mean:

- The first number (in this case 6) represents the *owner* of the file. It states what he or she can do.

- The second number (4) represents the *group* (users are members of groups) and what they can do.

- The third number (4) represents the *public*, also known as world or global.

You might see permissions represented in binary form as well. The following will help you cross reference:

- Binary `000` — Octal 0
- Binary `001` — Octal 1
- Binary `010` — Octal 2
- Binary `011` — Octal 3
- Binary `100` — Octal 4
- Binary `101` — Octal 5
- Binary `110` — Octal 6
- Binary `111` — Octal 7

Following is how the permissions actually break down:

- `0` — No permission
- `1` — Execute (`x`)
- `2` — Write (`w`)
- `3` — Write and execute (`wx`)
- `4` — Read (`r`)
- `5` — Read and execute (`rx`)
- `6` — Read and write (`rw`)
- `7` — Read, write, and execute (`rwx`)

Thus, if you see a file with `400` (or, in binary notation, `100 000 000`), that means only the owner (*root*) can *read* the file, and no one else has rights to read or execute it.

NOTE Seeing a file with `777` means the file has been (most likely incorrectly) granted full read, write, and execute permissions to everyone. This is a very bad security risk, and if your site has changed from normal settings to that setting, you have a problem.

Now, take a look at the critical files for your passwords.

Critical Password Files

The files in question are passwd, shadow, group, and gshadow. These files are owned by the root user (super user) and contain the passwords for various parts of the system.

You must ensure that they are set up properly. In this case, work at the command line using the tool *Putty*. (You may download it from http://www.chiark.greenend.org.uk/~sgtatham/putty.)

1. Log in as super user (you'll see the # prompt) and change directory to the /etc directory. Use the following command:

```
# cd / etc
```

2. Type **ls passwd -l**, and you should a screen similar to Figure 5-6 appear.

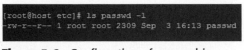

```
[root@host etc]# ls passwd -l
-rw-r--r-- 1 root root 2309 Sep  3 16:13 passwd
```

Figure 5-6: Confirmation of ownership

Note that the file is root and group is root. This is exactly what you want.

3. Repeat these steps for the shadow, group, and gshadow files.

NOTE You may not have gshadow on your system.

If you find that a file is owned by *anyone else*, then you most likely need to change it back to root. To do so, you use the chown command. chown instructs the Linux operating system to change ownership (thus, the name chown).

Consider the following example:

```
# chown root:root passwd
```

This command changes the ownership of the passwd file to root. Note, however, that the likelihood is slim that you'll find the password files incorrectly set unless you've been hacked.

NOTE It's worth noting that a better administrative position is to use groups to restrict access to your server's resources. With groups, you can contain your users and what they do, and not worry about the files (as much). This same concept applies to your Joomla!, Drupal, Plone, or WordPress site. Restrict the access to the areas that the person actually needs.

World-Writeable

The next task for hardening the server is to locate all the *world-writeable* files. As you have likely surmised, this term means that anyone can write to a file, if they have access to the machine. This access is not a good thing, and should be curtailed. Finding all the world-writable files is a snap, and doing so can help you eliminate that particular attack surface.

While logged in as the super user, execute the following command:

```
# find disk-part -xdev -xtype f -perm -0002 -print
```

This command provides a list of *files* that are world-writable. You should not see any output after you enter this command. If you have output from this command, a good possibility exists that you have something set wrong. Take the time to investigate the problem and take corrective action.

If you find files that need correction, then use the following command to correct the situation:

```
# chmod +t /dir (where /dir is the directory).
```

Using the chmod command, you can change the permissions to what you need. Generally, setting files to 644 (octal) or to 444 (octal) on any CMS running on Linux is a good idea.

> **NOTE** If you are running Linux on a Windows server, consult a guide from Microsoft for specific steps to set permission and other security needs located at **http://technet.microsoft.com/en-us/library/cc524539.aspx.**

Unauthorized SUID/SGID System Executable Files

If you have ever logged in as the super user (root) using the Secure Shell (SSH) protocol and uploaded files, you may have discovered that the files won't run from your browser in most cases. This situation is caused by the file(s) being uploaded and *owned* by the root user. Thus, they carry a level of power within the system. Logging in as root can be a dangerous activity if the file is something that could wreak havoc on the machine.

As the root or super user, systems such as Apache should not run files owned by root.

Close cousins to this scenario are the SetUID and SetGID bits. These bits can cause some odd and hard-to-track-down security holes in your site. In essence, when these bits are set, they *run* or execute under the privileges of the owner of the file. Thus, if an ordinary user or a user in group executes a file owned by root user, it will run *as if* the root user were logged in — again, not a scenario you want to see happen.

Checking for these bits is essential, especially if you are not sure what the status of the server is.

To check for them, execute the following command:

```
# find disk-part -xdev \( -perm -40000 -o -perm -2000 \) -type f - print
```

This command *may* provide you a number of files that need to be reset. If they have either of these bits set, these files will allow anyone to run the files as if he or she were the owner.

Find and correct any you find. If you are not sure, consult with your administrator.

Orphan Files

For many reasons, files can occasionally become *orphaned*, meaning that the file is no longer owned by a user. This may or may not represent a threat, but does indicate some kind of trouble is present. An orphan file may indicate that something has been installed improperly, or possibly that an attacker has been there.

Use the following command to locate any orphan files:

```
# find disk-part -xdev  \( -nouser -o -nogroup \) -print
```

If you find any orphan files, take the appropriate actions to assign it to a group or user. If the orphaned file is not needed, then delete it.

Reviewing Disk Access

In most cases, disk access should not be a real issue, especially if you're running on a managed host that has been properly configured. However, if you have set up your own server, consider the following tips:

- Set up a partition for your users' files. This practice keeps them separate from the rest of the files.

- Set up a separate disk partition for the /tmp directory, which is the place to store large files such as cache, installation files, and other transient data.

- Set up a separate logical volume (think c:>) or partition for logging. This action keeps users from accidentally writing into the logs, or deleting them.

Disabling Unneeded Services

In a stock system, you can probably turn off several services because they are not likely to be needed. In fact, these services can, in many cases, represent a significant threat.

One of those common services is Telnet, which is a very old protocol. It has had several revisions that have helped shore up its security. However, it still represents a viable threat to your CMS and server. A review of the document at `www.ietf.org/rfc/rfc3986.txt` can give you a list of bad things that are associated with this protocol.

Following are some services that you should remove:

- Telnet
- RSH Server
- TFTP

You can use the now-familiar `yum` command to easily deal with these services as follows:

```
# yum erase telnet
# yum erase rsh-server
# yum erase rsh
# yum erase tftp-server
```

WARNING Remember, although removing these services is important, be sure you aren't using them. For example, removing Telnet may cause your FTP server to stop working.

Securing an Apache Server

One area that all people who interact with your CMS website will touch is your web server software. The Apache `httpd` web server is the most popular of the web servers on the market, with more than 50 percent of the market share.

Apache is a very well-maintained and developed system; generally it's secure out of the box. However, this robust system offers many different configuration options and, hence, many opportunities to leave something amiss.

Obviously, one of the first steps to securing an Apache server is to ensure that you use the latest version of Apache.

Log in to your server via SSH using Putty and issue the command `httpd -v`. A screen similar to that shown in Figure 5-7 should appear. Consult the `Apache.org` website to determine whether you need to update your version of Apache.

```
[root@host /]# httpd -v
Server version: Apache/2.2.16 (Unix)
Server built:   Sep  4 2010 10:22:08
Cpanel::Easy::Apache v3.2.0 rev5186
```

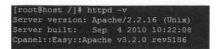

Figure 5-7: Apache version information

The rest of this section examines how to configure Apache for secure use and operation.

Configuring Apache for Secure Operation

An attacker who is more than a kiddie-scripter wants to gather as much information as possible. Given the likelihood you're running Apache, that part of the hacker's information gathering is out of the way. In that case, the next item the attacker wants to get is the version information about Apache, which means that you must restrict the information Apache gives out. Knowing your Apache version is a key source of information for an attacker.

Open your Apache configuration on file located at `/etc/httpd/conf/httd`
`.conf`. Scroll through the directives and locate the information shown in Figure 5-8.

```
# These can be set in WHM under 'Apache Global Configuration'
TraceEnable Off
ServerSignature Off   ◄──────────────
ServerTokens Prod
```

Figure 5-8: Restricting Apache information leakage

In your configuration file, either modify those lines to match what is shown in Figure 5-8, or add them if they don't exist. As you can see, this server is running Web Host Manager (WHM) and, thus, you can set these lines from the graphical user interface (GUI).

The first line, `ServerSignature Off`, prevents Apache from displaying its version on error pages. The second line, `ServerTokens Prod`, causes any page headers to display the word *Apache* only. To be fair, this doesn't really help security directly, but it does hide those critical version details.

Search through your configuration file for the `HTTP Digest Authentication` module. It provides for encrypted authentication sessions. You might not have this entry in your configuration file, but if you do, you should remove it. The use of SSL is preferred.

Look for the following line:

```
Load auth_digest_module modules/mod_auth_digest.so.
```

If you find it in your configuration file, comment it out by putting a # (pound sign) in front of it and save the file back to the server.

Lightweight Directory Access Protocol (*LDAP*) support is provided through the use of a module from Apache. If you are using LDAP for authentication, then skip this step. Otherwise, look for the following two lines in your configuration file and comment them out:

```
LoadModule ldap_module modules/mod_ldap.so
LoadModule authnz_ldap_module modules/mod_authnz_ldap.so
```

Server Side Includes (*SSI*) is a means to dynamically generate web pages through insertion of server-side code. This is a very big security concern, and likely it's not needed with your configuration.

If the server is not configured properly, some of the concerns are that arbitrary code could be inserted and run on it. Additionally, it would be vulnerable in some instances to Cross-Site Scripting (XSS) vulnerabilities.

Review your configuration file, comment out the following line, save to your server, and test your website:

```
LoadModule include_module modules/mod_include.so
```

If commenting out this line breaks your website or causes strange behavior, then uncomment it and review the Apache documentation regarding this module at http://httpd.apache.org/docs/2.2/mod/mod_include.html.

MIME Types are a system of definitions of non-ASCII characters. Originally, this system was used to enable mail systems to receive non-text input. It has been expanded to browsers, among other systems.

When a graphics element or other non-ASCII (non-HTML) element is sent to a browser, the browser attempts to identify and render the element. If the element cannot be rendered, then the `mime_magic_module` modules for Apache are a secondary line of defense to guard against opening restricted files. However, actual cases have been reported where `mime_magic_module` has been used, and it would not render information on one browser, but would on another. Removing it fixed this problem.

Your setup will likely not need this. Find the following file reference, comment it out, and save the configuration file:

```
LoadModule mime_magic_module modules/mod_mime_magic.so
```

WebDAV is the extension to the HTTP protocol that provides the capability for collaboration of web content. However, this extension allows one too many people to edit and update documents on a website. You can think of WebDAV as an Internet-enabled file system much like your desktop has a file system.

If your CMS does not need WebDAV, then you should disable it for security reasons. In the event that your server or CMS needs WebDAV functionality, take the necessary precautions to secure the server.

Review the configuration file and comment out the following:

```
LoadModule dav_module modules/mod_dav.so
LoadModule dav_fs_module modules/mod_dav_fs.so
```

Apache can provide *server activity status*, but this module introduces a number of vulnerabilities that would be valuable to an attacker. If this module is installed, but not needed, then comment it out as shown here:

```
LoadModule status_module modules/mod_status.so
```

If loaded, the *Web Server Configuration Display* (mod_info) module will make all configuration files available, even down to the directory level (think .htaccess). The security threat to your site is that this module will "leak" information about configuration directives to other parts of Apache. This could include such things as system paths, usernames and passwords, databases installed, and more. Not running this module in a production environment such as an Internet-facing server is strongly recommended.

Comment out the following line if it is found in the configuration file:

```
LoadModule info_module modules/mod_info.so
```

Part of a dedicated hacker's effort will be to *enumerate* your website. In essence, that means the hacker will attempt to find and name everything to map out the network and server. If installed, the speling_module module will attempt to find a *document* (that is, a resource such as a file) by comparing each document name in the requested directory against the requested document name without regard to case, and allowing up to one misspelling.

This scenario is perfect for continuing to ping a site with requests and see what files show up. Disabling this module (if it's installed) is recommended. Comment out the following line in your configuration file if found:

```
LoadModule speling_module modules/mod_speling.so
```

Using the capability of the directory translations module, an attacker could easily enumerate the web server's users. Disable the following if it is found in your configuration file, unless it is absolutely needed:

```
LoadModule userdir_module modules/mod_userdir.so
```

If you are not using your Apache server as a *proxy server* (gateway) to other servers, then ensure that the following lines (if they exist) are commented out:

```
LoadModule proxy_module modules/mod_proxy.so
LoadModule proxy_balance_module modules/mod_proxy_balancer.so
LoadModule proxy_ftp_module modules/mod_proxy_ftp.so
LoadModule proxy_http_module modules/mod_proxy_http.so
LoadModule proxy_connect_module modules/mod_proxy_connect.so
```

If you do not know what the proxy server is for, you likely do not need it. Having it on is very dangerous if the server is not fully secured.

NOTE For more information about directives in Apache configuration files, see http://httpd.apache.org/docs/2.2/mod/quickreference.html.

Disabling or Setting Up Proper Services

Although each Apache configuration is very different, understanding what programs start at boot time is important. This knowledge can give you a very good picture of what programs you should enable or disable. You'll likely have services similar to those shown in Figure 5-9, which shows the services that start up on this particular server.

```
[root@host /]# chkconfig --list | grep :on
bandmin          0:off  1:off  2:on   3:on   4:on   5:on   6:off
courier-authlib  0:off  1:off  2:on   3:on   4:on   5:on   6:off
courier-imap     0:off  1:off  2:on   3:on   4:on   5:on   6:off
cpanel           0:off  1:off  2:off  3:on   4:on   5:on   6:off
crond            0:off  1:off  2:on   3:on   4:on   5:on   6:off
csf              0:off  1:off  2:on   3:on   4:on   5:on   6:off
dcc              0:off  1:off  2:on   3:on   4:on   5:on   6:off
exim             0:off  1:off  2:on   3:on   4:on   5:on   6:off
fastmail         0:off  1:off  2:on   3:on   4:on   5:on   6:off
filelimits       0:off  1:off  2:on   3:on   4:on   5:on   6:off
funcd            0:off  1:off  2:off  3:on   4:on   5:on   6:off
haldaemon        0:off  1:off  2:off  3:on   4:on   5:on   6:off
httpd            0:off  1:off  2:off  3:on   4:off  5:on   6:off
ipaliases        0:off  1:off  2:on   3:on   4:on   5:on   6:off
iptables         0:off  1:off  2:on   3:on   4:on   5:on   6:off
lfd              0:off  1:off  2:on   3:on   4:on   5:on   6:off
lm_sensors       0:off  1:off  2:on   3:on   4:on   5:on   6:off
lvm2-monitor     0:off  1:on   2:on   3:on   4:on   5:on   6:off
mcstrans         0:off  1:off  2:on   3:off  4:off  5:off  6:off
messagebus       0:off  1:off  2:off  3:on   4:on   5:on   6:off
mysql            0:off  1:off  2:on   3:on   4:on   5:on   6:off
named            0:off  1:off  2:off  3:on   4:on   5:on   6:off
network          0:off  1:off  2:on   3:on   4:on   5:on   6:off
openibd          0:off  1:off  2:on   3:off  4:on   5:on   6:off
portsentry       0:off  1:off  2:off  3:on   4:on   5:on   6:off
pure-ftpd        0:off  1:off  2:off  3:on   4:off  5:on   6:off
rawdevices       0:off  1:off  2:off  3:on   4:on   5:on   6:off
restorecond      0:off  1:off  2:on   3:on   4:on   5:on   6:off
ror              0:off  1:off  2:on   3:on   4:on   5:on   6:off
securetmp        0:off  1:off  2:on   3:on   4:on   5:on   6:off
sendmail         0:off  1:off  2:on   3:on   4:on   5:on   6:off
sshd             0:off  1:off  2:on   3:on   4:on   5:on   6:off
syslog           0:off  1:off  2:on   3:on   4:on   5:on   6:off
sysstat          0:off  1:off  2:on   3:on   4:off  5:on   6:off
```

Figure 5-9: Services enabled at startup

Take the time to check your server with the following command:

```
# chkconfig --list | grep :on
```

Investigate the services and, if you determine that you do not need one or more of them, disable the service using the following command:

```
# chkconfig service off
```

Replace the word `service` in that command with the service name, as shown here:

```
# chkconfig pure-ftpd off
```

This command disables the FTP server from running at the next restart.

WHAT IS THAT SERVICE?

Occasionally, you may see a service running that you are unsure of. This is not a cause for alarm, but you may want to investigate further. To learn what RPM package (installation package) the service came from, run the following command:

```
$ rpm - qf /etc/init.d/servicename
```

This reveals what package installed it. It could easily be a dependency for another service.

You can also get a brief description of what the RPM package does by typing in the following command:

```
$ rpm - qi rpmname
```

Note that this command may not work on all distributions of Linux.

The one service you should have turned on is ModSecurity. Let's take a closer look at this very important module.

ModSecurity

ModSecurity (available from www.modsecurity.org) is an open source Web Application Firewall (WAF). Its job is to protect the web application layer against a variety of attacks that target weaknesses in a CMS and other web applications. It does this with a variety of defenses, including monitoring of the HTTP (web) traffic, a flexible rules engine, and real-time analysis of your traffic.

ModSecurity (or mod_security) works as a reverse proxy, and provides a virtual patch against attacks. Using this or another type of WAF is highly recommended.

The installation of mod_security is quite simple using yum:

```
#yum install mod_security
```

The default configuration likely will work for you, but given its flexible rules engine, you have the option of deploying highly customized configurations on it.

The deeper details are beyond the scope of this book. The following sources can provide more information:

- *Mod Security Handbook* (London, Feisty Duck, Ltd., 2010), written by the principal developer of ModSecurity, Ivan Ristic. For more information, see www.feistyduck.com/books/modsecurity-handbook/index.html.

- Another reference is a fairly well-documented guide to the installation of ModSecurity on Ubuntu, located at: www.thebitsource.com/infrastructure-operations/web-application/securing-apache-web-servers-modsecurity.

Securing SNMP

Simple Network Management Protocol (*SNMP*) allows a machine (such as a server) to communicate its status to an application. Things that can be communicated from servers typically include temperature of the machine, the speed and operation of cooling fans, the output of the power supplies, and more.

An administrator can remotely manage the server using SNMP. This is a typical setup in many hosting situations where the administrators are physically present in the data center. Many hardware manufacturers such as Dell, Hewlett-Packard, IBM, and others support this protocol, and offer tools to monitor and manage servers.

Overall, SNMP can be considered a weakness, and should be shut off *if* it's not in use. However, if you are renting a server from a hosting company or a co-location facility, you likely won't be able to shut this protocol off on your own. What you want to be sure of, however, is that if in use, it's configured as securely as possible.

One classic weakness is that the Community *string* is often left at public. In essence, the Community string is the password to the system. With it, you can read and write to the machine in question, and because default passwords are prevalent in the computer industry, chances are good that the SNMP password is set to public on many machines out there today.

SNMP has two parts that you'll interact with:

- The *Management Information Base* (*MIB*) contains the description and controls for various devices in the server, networking gear, and other SNMP-enabled machines.

- A *trap* is the name of the message it sends out to you with information.

SNMP can be a wonderful tool for an administrator, and you should certainly use it, as long as it's properly set up. The following sections take a look at how to achieve the proper setup.

Configuration

If you manage your own server physically, and you want to use SNMP, be sure you follow these simple guidelines:

- Change the default password (public).

- Use SNMP Version 3 or greater (most modern systems do).

- Disable write access to the MIB unless allowing it is absolutely necessary. In other words, make it read-only. This can prevent all kinds of nonsense.

- Practice the principle of *least privilege* when assigning access to the MIB. This means that whoever is allowed to access it should only be given the amount of privilege needed to do his or her job.

- If possible, restrict any access to the SNMP console to your private network.

- Ensure that traps are sent to authorized management systems or stations only. These tools are typically the software tools that the manufacturers ship, or open source tools such as *Cacti*.

- Set permissions on the /etc/snmp/snmpd.conf file to 640 or even 440.

- Because the MIB contains the vital machine information, set the permission level to a minimum of 640. For added safety, set it to be even more restrictive.

Disabling

If you are running your *own* server (not one owned by a hosting company or a co-location company), then you may want to disable SNMP.

To disable SNMP from the Linux operating system, use the following two instructions while logged in as the super user:

```
# chkconfig snmp off
# yum erase net-snmpd
```

The previous example may not apply if you use any of the manufacturer tools such as Dell OpenManage, HP OpenView, or IBM Tivoli. Consult the documentation for proper setup instructions for your specific configuration.

Turning SNMP off *if* you are not using it is very important. If you are using it, then be sure you take the precautions to secure it.

Configuring PHP for Secure Operation

PHP is the language of three of the four CMSs spotlighted in this book. Joomla!, Drupal, and WordPress are written in PHP.

PHP is an *interpreted* language, meaning that the commands are acted upon by a command-line processor added to the web server. This PHP processor module will generate a traditional web page from the commands. PHP has been around since 1994 and has a very actively maintained code base.

Securing PHP is important not only for your server and data, but also for others on the Internet. Running an older, insecure version of PHP is just the same as running a vulnerable server. Fortunately, you can secure PHP fairly easily.

This section covers various security tools and processes, as well as a little about the php.ini configuration file.

suPHP

One of the first items of business is to determine (if you do not know) what the baseline of your PHP software is. Ideally, you want to be running *suPHP*, which is a tool that forces PHP scripts (like your CMS) to be executed with the permissions of their owners.

suPHP is a great tool to use to ensure that you are running PHP in a very secure fashion. If you are using a managed virtual private server (VPS) or dedicated server at a hosting company, a quick telephone call to the support staff can help you establish if you are running it.

The next method is to try to set folder permissions to 777. If you're running suPHP, you'll get a `500 Internal Error` when you browse.

phpinfo

PHP has a great method for examining the entirety of the settings. Using the `phpinfo` function provides a useful tool to have in your toolkit.

The steps listed here to execute the `phpinfo` function are very easy to follow, and the end results are invaluable:

1. Create a text file in the root directory and name it `phpinfo.php`. In that file, insert the following:

```
<?php phpinfo(); ?>
```

2. Save the file and ensure that the permissions are set for 644.

3. From your browser type the following:

```
http://www.yourdomain.com/phpinfo.php
```

A lot of information about your server and its environmental settings appears. Near the top of the screen, you should see an entry that resembles Figure 5-10.

Server API	CGI/FastCGI

Figure 5-10: suPHP installed

If you see `Apache` in place of the words `CGI/FastCGI`, then you likely do not have suPHP installed.

PHP has many settings that can be tricky to catch. Fortunately, a free and open source tool is available that will give you a good evaluation of your settings, as discussed in the following section.

PhpSecInfo

The PhpSecInfo tool, from a group of international experts in PHP security, the PHP Security Consortium (PHPSC), is built to evaluate your servers' setup and ensure that you have all the PHP holes closed. You can get the tool by visiting `http://phpsec.org/projects/phpsecinfo/`.

When run on your server, this tool will test for a number of issues that could affect your security. Figure 5-11 shows an example of one such warning.

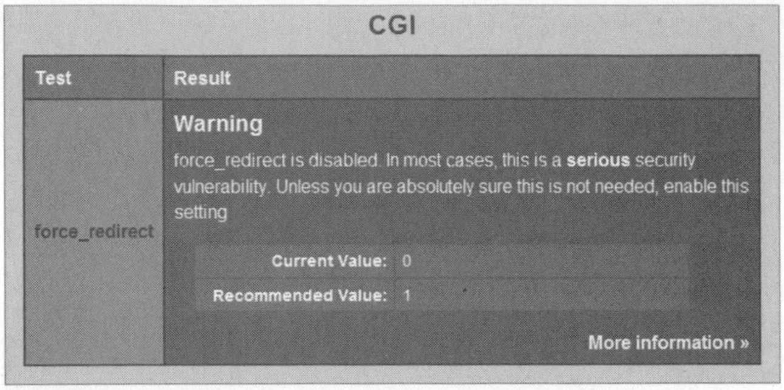

Figure 5-11: Warning produced by PhpSecInfo tool

This warning appears in red. The various warnings and errors are color-coded.

This particular error is telling you that the `force_redirect` directive is disabled. Note the "More information" link on the lower right, which provides you with a detailed explanation of this warning.

At the bottom of the report is the Test Results Summary, as shown in Figure 5-12. It states that 18 tests were run and 10 notices, meaning they need attention. It produced 2 items marked as severe.

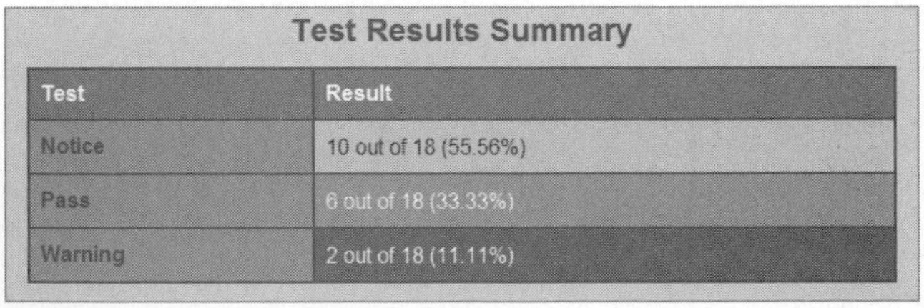

Figure 5-12: Test Results Summary

You should run this tool regardless of how long your server has been in production. You might find that you have a number of holes. Be sure to run it after any upgrade, or after any incidents that occur.

php.ini

When you're using suPHP, you can find a file in the root of most websites called `php.ini`. This file allows you to issue commands to the PHP Interpreter. As was previously stated, you can use this file in place of the `/etc/php.ini` file. Check with your host to ensure the server is running suPHP.

Using WinSCP, locate the `/etc/php.ini` file. If this file does not exist in this directory, it can and may exist in your `public_html` website directory.

Read through the `phpinfo.php` file and determine whether you need to update or change any settings for your particular situation. Items that may need to be adjusted are things like memory size, because the default in modern implementations of PHP is 128MB. This means that a script could ask for and use that much memory. Other settings, such as execution time, can help prevent your server from crashing if a PHP script has a bug and runs too long.

In essence, you can fine-tune your PHP server through this helpful file. Make the following changes:

- Turn off PHP error messages to external users. This prevents malicious users from exploiting possible vulnerabilities in code on your website. Add the following entry to your `php.ini` file:

```
display_errors = Off
```

- Prevent PHP scripts from running shells and other evils by inserting the following:

```
safe_mode = On
```

- Only allow access to executable files in an isolated directory by using the following:

```
safe_mode_exec_dir = php-required-executables-path
```

- Limit external access to PHP environment by inserting the following:

```
safe_mode_allowed_env_vars = PHP_
```

- PHP can provide a great deal of information to hackers through information leakage. Restricting PHP from giving out too much information is important, so insert this:

```
expose_php = Off
```

- Because you have suppressed the errors, you should log all errors with the following entry:

```
log_errors = On
```

- The `Register_Globals` directive has been rendered useless as of PHP 5.3.0. However, if you are running anything less than that version, you are should set it as follows:

```
register_globals = Off
```

- POST is used to gather inputs from a form and submit them to the application. By minimizing the size of POST, you are lowering the risk of an evil payload being uploaded. This recommendation is just that, a recommendation. You should test it with your data set and needs. If you find it to be too restrictive, raise the size of the POST upload size and repeat the test. Minimize the allowed PHP POST size with the following:

```
post_max_size = 2M
```

- Ensure PHP redirects appropriately by inserting the following:

```
cgi.force_redirect = 0
```

- If you allow file uploading to your site, consider the maximum size of files you'll accept. For example, if you are going to allow very large or very small files, you'll need to adjust the directive. The default is 2MB. To change this size, set the following directive:

```
upload_max_filesize memory -
```

Change *memory* to a number in megabytes to match your needs. Remember that the larger the upload, the larger the evil payload that potentially could be uploaded.

- Change the following to prevent uploads to your site:

```
file_uploads = Off
```

- Prevent file requests (such as attempts to open files) with the following:

```
allow_url_fopen = Off
```

> **NOTE** For a full list of all the directives of `php.ini`, see `http://php.net/manual/en/ini.core.php`.

Checking for Open Ports

Ports in the vernacular of computing can refer to hardware ports such as serial or USB ports. It also can refer to software ports, which is the context used for this discussion.

Figure 5-13 shows an example of a system with many ports open to the outside world. This screen indicates not only what ports are open, but also what services are being offered, as listed in the right-hand column.

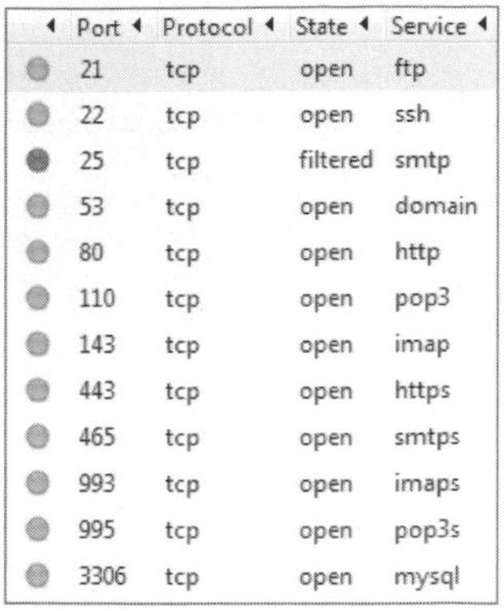

◄ Port ◄	Protocol ◄	State ◄	Service ◄
21	tcp	open	ftp
22	tcp	open	ssh
25	tcp	filtered	smtp
53	tcp	open	domain
80	tcp	open	http
110	tcp	open	pop3
143	tcp	open	imap
443	tcp	open	https
465	tcp	open	smtps
993	tcp	open	imaps
995	tcp	open	pop3s
3306	tcp	open	mysql

Figure 5-13: Ports open to the outside world

This information has been generated by the NMAP network mapping tool. As designated by NMAP, the term *Open* means that the application or service on this machine is listening for requests, and the term *Filtered* means that something (such as a firewall) is blocking the port. Note how the SMTP port is designated as *Filtered*, which means this server is blocking requests to it. Note that FTP is *Open*, meaning that it is ready to accept a connection.

Closed (not shown) means that the port has no services running on it or it's specifically closed. You can open closed ports at any time as needed.

As you learned in Chapter 4, NMAP is a good tool to use to discover security holes in your website. The action here is to check whether any ports are open that should not be. Multiple reasons exist for ports to be open that are not necessarily the sign of hackers. However, at the end of the day, if ports are open that should not be, then you should investigate why and perhaps close them.

Specific ports that are open can indicate that you've been hacked. Table 5-3 shows a short list of some ports that, if open, may be running one of the hacker tools listed next to it.

Table 5-3: Correlation Between Open Ports and Hacker Tools

PORT	HACKER TOOLS
6666	Dark Connection Inside, NetBus worm
6667	ScheduleAgent, Trinity, WinSatan
6669	Host Control, Vampire
6670	BackWeb Server, Deep Throat, Foreplay or Reduced Foreplay, WinNuke eXtreame
6711	BackDoor-G, SubSeven , VP Killer
6712	Funny Trojan, SubSeven

Continued

Table 5-3 *(continued)*

PORT	HACKER TOOLS
6713	SubSeven
6723	Mstream
6771	Deep Throat, Foreplay or Reduced Foreplay
6776 2000	Cracks, BackDoor-G, SubSeven , VP Killer

NOTE Appendix A provides a good list of hacker tools and their associated ports.

Using `iptables` or a firewall such as ConfigServer Security Firewall (`www.configserver.com`), you can close off or open up ports. As a general rule, you should use `iptables` to block everything, and then individually open ports you need (such as port 80 for Internet access). This ensures that you don't have a port open that you didn't know about.

If you find a port such as 6776 open, this could be one of many backdoor applications used by attackers. Use the NetStat tool to find out who is logged in and running applications. Additionally, be sure to *kill* the process for the backdoor. After that, go about cleaning it up — after you close the port.

Securing FTP Communications Ports

File Transfer Protocol (*FTP*) is an old protocol. It was first drafted in April 1971, well before web servers were even dreamed of. In fact, FTP is one of the most popular means to connect to web servers. It's easy to use and simple to set up. FTP is also a least-favorite communications protocol among security experts.

Many of the readers of this book most likely weren't born yet when the FTP standard was drafted. And yet, many users depend on this protocol daily.

The challenge with FTP is that everything is transmitted in *clear text*, meaning that anyone *listening* on the wire could easily gain your username and password. A Trojan horse on a PC could easily gain this information.

As this chapter was written, one of the more popular FTP server software packages was discovered to have a nasty bug. The bug report from ProFTPD (`http://bugs.proftpd.org/show_bug.cgi?id=3521` November 7, 2010) stated the following:

> *"This vulnerability allows remote attackers to execute arbitrary code on vulnerable installations of ProFTPD. Authentication is not required to exploit this vulnerability."*

Further, the bug advisory also stated the following:

"The flaw exists within the ProFTPD server component which listens by default on TCP port 21. When reading user input if a TELNET_IAC escape sequence is encountered the process miscalculates a buffer length counter value allowing a user controlled copy of data to a stack buffer. A remote attacker can exploit this vulnerability to execute arbitrary code under the context of the ProFTPD process."

In general terms, what this says is that a dedicated attacker, without having authenticated access, could attack an FTP server with the goal of running his or her malicious (listed as "arbitrary") code on the server. That means that this fairly modern version of software suffers from a *buffer overflow*. Version 1.3.3c fixes it.

WARNING If you are running version 1.3.3b or earlier of the software, you are vulnerable. Be sure to note it and update the software. If you are running this program, and you want to disable it and install a different one, a couple of others (among many) are actively supported. *Pure-FTPd* from `pureftpd.org` is a very popular FTP application with many hosting companies choosing it. Very Secure FTP (*VSFTP*) ships with Red Hat. Both of these are examined later in this chapter.

Hazards of FTP

If you are using FTP, you should be aware of several hazards. This section offers a look at a few of the most common ones.

Firewalls

FTP has many security issues surrounding its use, and one of the biggest is that you must make allowances in your firewall settings for it. FTP requires two connections for it to work, which are known as *channels*. A hacker may use this avenue to issue commands to your server (over the command channel), or may use a weakness in the FTP software to gain access.

Remote Command Execution

An optional FTP extension, "SITE EXEC," allows clients to execute arbitrary commands on the server. Because FTP has a *command* channel, many documented cases exist where attackers have used it to issue commands.

Bounce Attack

Many versions of FTP servers are susceptible to an interesting attack known as the *bounce attack*. This well-known attack works quite well, all the while giving the perpetrators a high degree of anonymity. Tracking down the attackers is nearly impossible.

How it works is the attacker sends an FTP PORT command to an FTP server that contains the IP address and port number of the machine (and service) being attacked. This file contains commands relevant to the service being attacked (SMTP, NNTP, and so on), instructing a third party to connect to the service. Hence, rather than connecting directly to the machine, it makes tracking down the perpetrator difficult, and can circumvent network address–based access restrictions.

As an example, suppose that a client uploads a file containing SMTP commands to an FTP server. Then, using an appropriate PORT command, the client instructs the server to open a connection to a third machine's SMTP port. Finally, the client instructs the server to transfer the uploaded file containing SMTP commands to the third machine. This may allow the client to forge mail on the third machine without making a direct connection.

Privacy

FTP essentially sends everything unencrypted across a network. If you need to send information such as confidential files to a server, then you should use encryption.

While the subject of encryption is beyond the scope of this book, you may wish to review www.pgp.com or www.file-encryption.net for examples of tools used for encryption. There are several different software packages and encryption methods available. It's wise to carefully review the packages you choose before use. The first one listed here is a well-known commercial package.

Protecting Usernames

One simple method to determine what usernames work, and what usernames do not work, is to simply deploy a bot. Standard FTP will return error code 530 after an attempt to provide a bad username. The rejection is what the bot will look for.

When it receives that error code, the bot then obviously knows that the username is bad. If the username is good, the FTP server gives a response code of 331. If the bot gets a good username, then the attacker could try a brute force attack until it finds a password.

Another strategy is to disable logins after "x" tries and block the IP address. Explore the options included with your FTP software to determine the best course for closing up this vulnerability.

Common FTP Mistakes

Now take a look at a few common mistakes experienced with the use of FTP.

Anonymous FTP

One type of situation that has the potential to be abused is the *anonymous* login. What this means is that an FTP server set up in this fashion will accept any legitimate FTP connection with no or minimal authentication.

An anonymous user can upload, download, or read any files available to it. Although FTP typically won't allow you access above a specific level, it will more than likely allow you access to the website itself.

This would give the hacker the capability to upload a shell program, backdoor application, or viruses. Attackers often set up listeners on the server, which will allow them to eavesdrop on your activity. All in all, you should never allow an anonymous user on your FTP server.

Ensure that you do not have anonymous users. Additionally, make sure each person authorized to use FTP has his or her own login credentials. This enables auditing of activity.

Weak Passwords

Many FTP systems do not restrict the retrying of a connection multiple times. In that scenario, a malicious user could simply keep trying username and password combinations until a good one is found.

Your action here is to ensure that your password is very difficult to guess. Although there's no solid rule, here are a few tips:

- Use a combination of uppercase and lowercase letters, as well as allowable punctuation.

- If your password (no matter if it is uppercase or lowercase) is in a dictionary, or could be similar in spelling, do not use it.

- Change your FTP passwords regularly. On a site with lots of FTP users and activity, you should change it every 30 days.

Misconception of Security

Many people believe that FTP is safe and secure. One issue is the sharing of FTP credentials to upload files. This is less of a technical issue and more of a trust issue. That is, in trusting the person to whom you are giving the credentials, you are giving that person and that person's machine access to your server. If the machine is compromised, that person could easily expose you to the malware.

There was once a case where a site was severely hacked. The attacker came through the FTP server with legitimate credentials. After reviewing the logs and a lot of detective work, it turned out that a subcontractor had hired another subcontractor to assist him.

The sub-subcontractor was running a Mac and believed (erroneously) that Macs would not get infected. It turned out that his Mac was indeed infected, and the hacker was listening via a backdoor application and simply obtained the credentials.

After that, the hacker simply logged into the site. The security systems in place had no idea he was a bad guy because he had proper credentials. This is covered in greater detail in Chapter 8.

The problems here were trust and lack of education. The trust was that the subcontractor shared the login, but should have obtained a specific login for himself and the sub-subcontractor. The sub-subcontractor was not up to speed on his knowledge of malware and backdoors as they related to the operating system he was using.

This entire situation could have been averted.

Another misconception is that the upload folder is secure. The misconception is that even if someone were to load something, the intruder could not get it to do anything.

This is highly foolish in that even if the intruders couldn't execute the uploaded material directly, they could entice someone else to. Even more disturbing, improperly set-up folders (directories) could allow the intruders access.

FTP is a very old and very insecure protocol. It should never be turned on for any public-facing machine. In essence, if a server is on the Internet, it should not have FTP on it.

> **NOTE** For a very detailed tutorial on FTP, see the guide to VSFTP (very secure FTP, included with Fedora) at `www.linuxhomenetworking.com/wiki /index.php/Quick_HOWTO_:_Ch15_:_Linux_FTP_Server_Setup`.

Exploring Alternative Versions of FTP

Red Hat and Fedora are a couple of the more popular Linux platforms in use today. Red Hat and Fedora currently ship with a fairly secure FTP platform called VSFTP. Overall, if you are going to use an FTP application, then VSFTP is one of the better ones to use. Another reasonably secure (and popular) FTP server is Pure-FTPd.

Both VSFTP and Pure-FTPd allow the use of SSL for passwords and user-names, thus helping to protect your sessions. SSL is used by many reputable firms, and is considered very strong.

> **NOTE** If you are on a shared server, then you have no choice but to use FTP. If security is a concern, do not use a shared hosting situation.

Using VSFTP

Fortunately, VSFTP has been written by a security researcher. Therefore, much of the normal concerns are gone, because it has been coded with the idea of eliminating many security issues.

To install VSFTP (in Red Hat and Red Hat distributions of Linux), log in as root and enter this command:

```
# yum install vsftpd
```

To shut off VSFTP, log in as the root user, and, after ensuring that you have a recent backup, run the following commands to disable or remove VSTFP from your server:

```
# chconfig vsftp off
# yum erase vsftp
```

While still in the VSFTP configuration file, update the banner located at /etc/banners/vsftpd. Be sure to add the appropriate warnings to the FTP user about your information security policy.

Figure 5-14 shows an example from the guide for the Community Enterprise Operating System (CentOS), which is a Red Hat-derived distribution of Linux.

```
220-Hello, %c
220-All activity on ftp.example.com is logged.
220-Inappropriate use will result in your access privileges being removed.
```

Figure 5-14: Example banner in VSFTP

Note the %c in the banner. When a user logs in, he or she will see the user information, including username, host, IP address, and potentially other information about the connection in place of that %c. The purpose of changing the banner is to help remind users that their actions are being recorded, and thus ward off potential harm.

VSFTP defaults to allow anonymous access. Thus, if you do install it, you must edit the configuration file to remove anonymous access.

NOTE A complete guide for CentOS on securing and configuring VSFTP is available at www.centos.org/docs/5/html/Deployment_Guide-en-US/ch-server.html.

Using Pure-FTPd

Pure-FTPd is another good choice if you need to offer FTP servers.

Installing Pure-FTPd includes many steps and a good number of options. Visit http://download.pureftpd.org/pub/pure-ftpd/doc/README to get the full instruction set.

To uninstall Pure-FTPd, log in as root, and execute the following commands. (Be sure you have a recent backup.)

```
# ./configure
# make uninstall
```

WARNING Not that you should only take these actions if you are on your own server. These instructions will not work on a shared server. If your server is managed by a host, then you can ask the host to remove Pure-FTPd.

Another option for security is enabling SSL (TLS) with Pure-FTPd. For more information on this topic, see `http://forums.theplanet.com/lofiversion/index.php/t45824.html`.

The better protocol to use in place of FTP is SFTP, as discussed in the following section.

Securing SFTP Communications Ports

As you have seen, FTP generally is a very insecure and easily compromised application. Simply too many cases exist where weak passwords allowed a hacker to gain access and cause damage.

The alternative is SFTP, which has no direct relationship with the FTP protocol. Rather, this protocol depends on the Secure Shell (SSH) protocol for encryption and authentication of the connection.

SSH is the best method currently available to connect to a server. You may hear about several tools that allow you to connect to SSH. Following are some examples of open source tools that support the current version of SSH (SSH-2):

- Putty
- Terminal (Mac)
- WinSCP
- FileZilla

NOTE SSH-1 is a vulnerable application and should never be used. Although this note is somewhat dated, it's important to keep in mind.

The most common software stack for SSH is OpenSSH. This GNU/GPL licensed code is widely available on many web servers. According to the Internet Engineering Task Force (IETF), the organization that ratifies Internet standards, "The SSH File Transfer Protocol provides secure file transfer functionality over any reliable, bidirectional octet stream. It is the standard file transfer protocol for use with the SSH2 protocol." In other words, SSH sets up a secure communications channel between your machine (the client) and the server.

A key difference between FTP and SFTP is that SFTP maintains the date and time stamp of files, whereas FTP traditionally does not.

The downside with SFTP is speed. It can be very slow (it is dependent on connection speed) because of the encryption of the SSH traffic. However, speed is a small price to pay for security.

SFTP is supported by many clients for both Windows and Mac platforms. A personal favorite is WinSCP, a GNU/GPL client shown in Figure 5-15. It is a very well-maintained application. The left side of Figure 5-15 shows your local client, and the right side is the target server. The SFTP client allows editing, uploading, and full navigation of the server (within your login area).

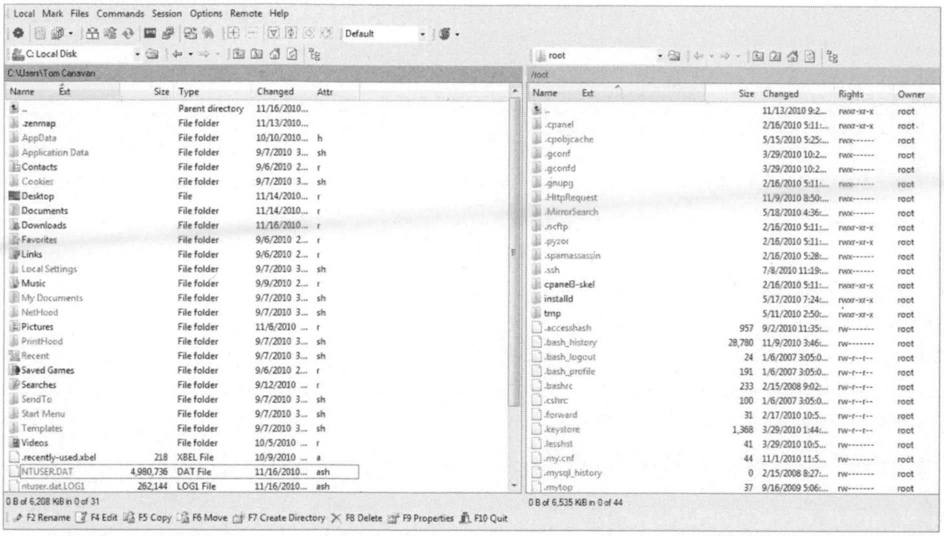

Figure 5-15: WinSCP SFTP client

For the most part, configuration of SSH is a *checkbox*–type thing. While it's wise to check the SSH settings, you will very likely find that the SSH will be set up appropriately.

One file in particular that you should look at is located at /etc/ssh/sshd_config. In this configuration file, you can restrict access to specific users very easily.

As the root, open the configuration file and locate the following:

■ DENY — Use this option to implicitly *deny* specific users from logging in. The format is as follows:

```
DenyUsers Username1 Username2
```

The situation where this may apply is dependent on your needs.

■ ALLOW — The implicit ALLOW allows login privileges to the users you specify. This is more than likely a realistic scenario for you. Now that you know logging in with SSH is better than with FTP, you'll want to add your users here. As a root, log in to the configuration file and add the usernames as follows:

```
AllowUsers Username1 Username2
```

This command tells SSH to only allow those users on the list to connect with proper credentials.

When administering a machine, you should take care of business and then log off. Leaving an open connection is a bad idea. However, getting distracted by a co-worker or a phone call is simply part of life. Rather than living with the possibility of leaving a connection open for a long time, setting a time out is best.

To limit the time a logged-in connection can remain idle, open the configuration file and locate the following files:

```
ClientAliveInterval interval
ClientAliveCountMax 3
```

In the first line, `ClientAliveInterval` refers to the time (in seconds) that SSH will wait after not receiving any data before disconnection. Depending on your situation, replace the word `Interval` with a number (in seconds).

The second line, which defaults to 3, is the number of messages or attempts it will try before disconnecting. Thus, if you have the interval set to 15 seconds, a non-response from the SSH client (WinSCP, Putty, and so on) will disconnect in 45 seconds (15 times 3). Set these for the times appropriate to your needs.

SSH (via Putty) can allow you to log in directly as the super user. However, you should not do this as a matter of course. Rather, log in as your normal (non-super user username) and then escalate your privileges once in there. What that means is that once you log in with Putty, you should see a $ sign versus a # sign.

Edit your configuration file as follows to disable root login (super user) on SSH:

```
PermitRootLogin no
```

This ensures that you cannot log in as root from SSH.

The default is to not allow a username only. Rather, you must have a username and password. Check to ensure that the following line is set to `no`:

```
PermitEmptyPasswords no
```

SSH (and SFTP) by default runs on port 22. You can change this to almost any other port. In fact, although it's not anywhere near foolproof, changing your port is a good idea. To do so edit the field in your configuration as follows:

```
Port X
```

Change *X* to the port number of choice.

> **NOTE** A great many more configuration options are available to you for SSH. For a complete list, see `http://unixhelp.ed.ac.uk/CGI/man-cgi?sshd_config+5`.

Ensuring Secure Logging

Logging is very important to security. In fact, logs are a nearly flawless view of history of your server, and while exceptions do apply, logging is simply the right thing to do.

You'll learn about logging in greater detail in Chapter 8. However, because logging is an important part of hardening your server, the following sections touch on it briefly.

VSFTP Logging

When using VSFTP, ensure that you are logging all transactions. Open the `vsftpd.conf` configuration file in either the `/etc/` directory, or the `etc/vsftpd/` directory. Check whether the following lines are in the configuration file, or you'll need to add them:

```
xferlog_std_format=NO
log_ftp_protocol=YES
```

These lines ensure that all commands sent to the FTP server are logged using the verbose `vsftpd log` format. The log file located at `/var/log/vsftpd.log` is the default log to which VSFTP will write.

Syslog

Syslog is the function that writes your log files out. Platforms such as Apache will write messages to it. In turn, it places the message (the log entry) into the appropriate log file.

Access Logs

Your access log lists all requests for individual files made from your website. This file can become very large, very quickly. It includes the HTML files, any graphic files, and other files that are associated with them. Thus, a single request for a page may encompass several lines in a log file.

Access logs provide vital information such as the visitors to the IP address, potentially who referred them there, times, dates, what they requested, and a bit more.

Security Logs

The security logs located at `/var/log/secure` contain any error messages from security events. These can include failed logins or abuse attempts. Reviewing these logs on a regular basis is important, because they will tell you about potential abuse.

Using cPanel

cPanel is one of the most popular programs available for basic web server hosting control. Typically, most web hosts will keep logging off by default. In order to activate logging, you must log into your web hosting account by clicking the cPanel icon, shown in Figure 5-16. After you click the Raw Log Manager icon, you'll see two checkboxes, as shown in Figure 5-17.

Figure 5-16: cPanel Log Manager settings

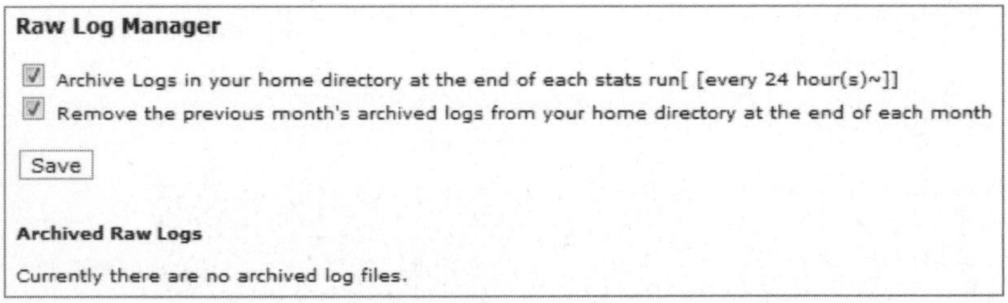

Raw Log Manager

☑ Archive Logs in your home directory at the end of each stats run[[every 24 hour(s)~]]

☑ Remove the previous month's archived logs from your home directory at the end of each month

[Save]

Archived Raw Logs

Currently there are no archived log files.

Figure 5-17: Raw Log Manager settings

Click the two boxes if they are not selected. The first one will maintain a daily log for you. If it's not selected, then it will wipe out log information from the previous 24 hours. This can be a tough situation if you're tracking down an issue. The second checkbox will remove the previous 30 days of logs (for disk space conservation). If you must keep your logs intact, either uncheck the second checkbox, or copy the log files before they are erased.

Using logrotate

As you'll see in Chapter 8, you must *rotate* your log files, or in other words, archive them. This practice helps prevent the disk from filling up. Log information collects very quickly, and the files can get very large.

Fortunately, as you just saw, with cPanel, you have a means to remove and archive them. Although cPanel offers you an automated means, those who are not using it will need another method.

The software responsible for this task is `logrotate`, and it should be part of most Linux distributions. Figure 5-18 shows an example of a typical `logrotate` file.

```
/var/log/messages /var/log/secure /var/log/maillog /var/log/spooler /var/log/boot.log /var/log/cron {
    sharedscripts
    postrotate
        /bin/kill -HUP `cat /var/run/syslogd.pid 2> /dev/null` 2> /dev/null || true
        /bin/kill -HUP `cat /var/run/rsyslogd.pid 2> /dev/null` 2> /dev/null || true
    endscript
}
```

Figure 5-18: logrotate script

By default, this file should be set up properly. However, to check it, open the file `/etc/logrotate.d/syslog`. After it opens, you'll see something that resembles the following:

```
/var/log/messages /var/log/secure /var/log/maillog /var/log/spooler
/var/log/boot.log   /var/log/cron {
```

(This will likely be a continuous line.)

What that file says is to rotate the `messages`, `secure`, `maillog`, `spooler`, `boot`, and `cron` logs. By default, the logs are rotated (copied) weekly. The system will store four archived copies of each log.

Figure 5-19 shows an example of the `syslog.conf` file itself.

```
# Log all kernel messages to the console.
# Logging much else clutters up the screen.
#kern.*                                                 /dev/console

# Log anything (except mail) of level info or higher.
# Don't log private authentication messages!
*.info;mail.none;authpriv.none;cron.none               -/var/log/messages

# The authpriv file has restricted access.
authpriv.*                                             -/var/log/secure

# Log all the mail messages in one place.
local0.notice;local0.debug;mail.*;mail.none;mail.info;local0.info -/var/log/maillog


# Log cron stuff
cron.*                                                 -/var/log/cron

# Everybody gets emergency messages
*.emerg                                                *

# Save news errors of level crit and higher in a special file.
uucp,news.crit                                         -/var/log/spooler

# Save boot messages also to boot.log
local7.*                                               -/var/log/boot.log
```

Figure 5-19: syslog.conf

Your action here is to check either your cPanel setting or review your log rotate configuration to ensure you are properly capturing logs.

Security of the Log Files

Log files should all be owned by root and have a permission of either `644` or `600`. Anything else is unacceptable.

For each log file, enter the following. (Change the `logfile` in each case to match your log filename.)

- ▪ `# touch logfile` — This ensures that the file actually exists by attempting to write to it.

- ▪ `# chown root:root logfile` — This assigns the ownership of that file to root.

- ▪ `# chmod 0600 logfile` — This changes the permissions to `600`. (Again, it can be `644` to fit your needs if `600` doesn't work.)

Using SSL

Given that the Internet is nothing more than a group of networks tied together, you should have no reasonable expectation of privacy when traversing the World Wide Web. Rather, you should expect that somewhere along the way, prying eyes are looking at your data.

Secure Sockets Layer (*SSL*) is essential in an e-commerce society. Without it, you could not conduct Internet financial transactions. In fact, current law requires SSL for online financial transactions. This provides a solid layer of protection for the transmission of the files. However, this does not guarantee that the files are safe after they are on the server.

SSL lives in terms of the technology above the wire (your network connection) and below the application (think shopping cart). This gives it the capability to be the gatekeeper of the data that is being sent. In a perfect world, the application will entrust the data to the SSL *envelope*. This will be taken directly to the recipient, who is the only one who can unlock it.

If you conduct any type of financial transactions (such as acceptance of credit cards) on your CMS, you must install SSL on your website. In fact, if you collect any type of information that could be gathered by eavesdropping on the network connection and used against someone, then you need to consider SSL.

In this section, you'll learn how SSL works, and see some use cases. How to purchase and install your certificate (from a high level) rounds out this topic discussion.

NOTE For more information about SSL, see `www.nurdletech.com/` `https.html, http://isc.sans.edu/diary.html?storyid=2163,` `www` `.hermann-uwe.de/security/articles/securing-apache-checklist,` `www.linuxplanet.com/linuxplanet/tutorials/6660/1/,` and `http://` `articles.slicehost.com/tags/security.`

Understanding How SSL Works

SSL is essentially a private conversation in an open environment. The entire SSL protocol (also known as TLS) uses what is known as a *shared secret* to establish a cryptographic tunnel between the client and the server.

When a client requests a connection over port 443 (the SSL port), it sends the server some information about itself and its *public key*. Part of that information is the cryptographic methods it will support. The server and client each have a public key, which they exchange. After this happens, the server sends the client a copy of its password, encrypted with its *private key* and the customer's public key. The client decrypts this and continues the transaction. This establishes a two-way trust with the server.

That is not to say that a bad guy can't have SSL. A hacker can indeed. What it means is that the certificate, if bad, should not verify if checked. And if the SSL certificate is not issued by a third party, the certificate will generate an error.

Understanding When to Use SSL

As mentioned, you must use SSL for financial transactions. If you are a PCI-compliant merchant (meaning that you accept credit or debit cards for payment), then you are required to secure your website with an *SSL certificate* (among other requirements).

NOTE If you only accept PayPal you *may not* need SSL. Review the PayPal requirements for up-to-date information and requirements. However, if you're handling payments of any type, then running SSL is simply a good idea.

If the user of your website (the client) has sensitive information to transmit, then sending it in the clear is a very bad idea. Enter SSL.

Let's use e-mail as an example to illustrate this point.

When Alice wants to send Bob an e-mail, she crafts the note and sends it via her favorite e-mail client. Bob receives it when it reaches his e-mail server. This transaction occurs millions of times a day.

What *really* happens is that Alice's e-mail, which is text, is broken up into pieces and sent in *packets* to Bob. Then Bob's e-mail server reassembles the packets in the proper order and sends them to his e-mail client.

In order to get there reliably and in a timely fashion, the Internet may choose to send the packets over various routes.

Now, suppose that Eve is a bad person who wants to gather information about Alice and Bob. She eavesdrops on their connection, and literally will be able to read every packet, thus enabling her to read the e-mail.

If Alice and Bob were using SSL, however, the connection and data would be encrypted as it's sent from Alice to Bob. So, although Eve may have other means of getting the data, this particular avenue would be removed.

The same process applies if you are receiving information such as social security numbers, medical information, or even corporate trade secrets. If you connect to a server on the Internet without SSL, then someone, somewhere can read it. Thus, if you are really concerned about security, turn on SSL encryption.

Following is a brief list of areas that would benefit from being protected from prying eyes. Indeed, some of these *do* require SSL.

- E-commerce transactions
- Medical records
- Personal information such as social security numbers
- Company trade secrets
- Confidential communications
- Job applications
- Home mortgage applications
- Credit card applications
- Banking transactions

Now that you have a good idea of the how SSL works, and why you need it, let's look at how you obtain an SSL certificate.

Obtaining a Certificate

Certificates come in various strengths and flavors. Each has its own benefits, but they all share the same purpose — that is, to secure data through encryption.

The certificates can be obtained in a 128-bit or 256-bit strength. They can be a General (read, easy to get), or they can be the high-strength, extended validation type.

Although both provide solid encryption, the 256-bit version is stronger because of its higher bit rate (the more bits, the stronger the encryption). There are more underlying technical tidbits that can make one certificate better than another, but overall, encryption is encryption.

The extended validation certificate provides a green bar in the address bar of your browser's website. In actuality, this is not doing anything for your security. This is a marketing effort to raise the visual awareness of the consumer.

The *padlock icon* in the lower right of your browser tells you that you are in a secure session. However, people weren't looking for the padlock, plus a malicious site could "fake" that icon. However, if you don't see HTTPS: in the address, then no matter what, you're not secure.

> **NOTE** You can learn more about extended validation by visiting http://thegreenaddressbar.com.

The key thing to remember about the extended validation certificate is that it requires a detailed background check, and it can take a number of days to receive it. Additionally, these certificates do cost more than the basic certificate.

Overall, you should buy the "most" certificate you can afford. The higher-priced ones typically offer some type of monetary guarantee in the event of a break-in. You'll have to read all the fine print to see what is right for your situation.

Visiting any number of hosting companies such as GoDaddy, VeriSign, and others will enable you to purchase your SSL certificate quite easily.

After you process all the requirements, you'll be issued a certificate, which you can then install and activate on your website.

Creating Self-Sign Certificates

The point of having a third-party issue a certificate is they have no vested interest (financial or otherwise) in your business. They stand to vouch for you digitally. They verify that the certificate being requested (its identity) is coming from the server they issued the certificate for. The rest is handled on your server.

Installing and having a certificate on your server without paying for it to be issued is possible. Creating your own certificate and installing it on your server is known as *self-signing*. This practice is never recommended, except for testing situations.

Installing a Certificate

For the most part, if you are in a hosting situation where you can take advantage of your host's technical skills to install the certificate, then you may want to do that. Typically, you'll depend on your host in 95 percent of the cases, and, quite frankly, it's easier. If, however, you are managing your own hosting or want to go through the process, it's fairly straightforward.

The certificate installation comes in two parts. The first is the portion that lives at the issuer's home, the person from whom you purchased the third-party certificate. The third party will issue you a certificate that, after you install it, becomes the *root certificate* to your site. Figure 5-20 shows an example of a root certificate.

You can validate a site's authenticity by right-clicking on the padlock icon. The information shown here is being pulled from the certificate issuer. The issuer is stating that the URL https://www.salvusalerting.com is indeed a secured site, and that the information matches the issuer's records. This helps eliminate phishing scams.

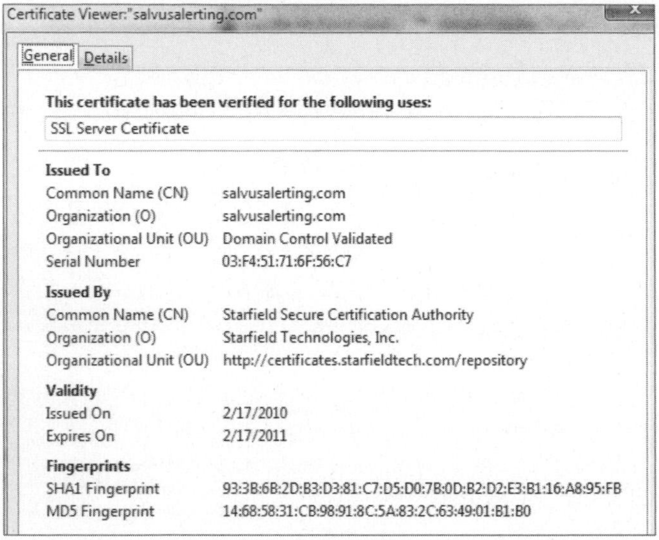

Figure 5-20: SSL root certificate

The second portion of the certificate is information you generate on your server, which is a combination of some software and some credential information.

These two combined parts make up your SSL certificate.

Working with Your Hosting Company

If you have managed support or a VPS situation, your host more than likely handles the certificate setup for you. Check whether the host requires that you purchase certificates from it, or allows you to shop around. In many cases, hosts will allow a third party to issue a certificate. That gives you a lot of options for choosing the best certificate for your budget and needs.

Installing an SSL Certificate Yourself

If you are not using a host, you need to generate a SSL certificate for your server. Locate the method in your server setup that allows you to generate a certificate. Figure 5-21 shows an example using WHM.

After it's filled out, this particular form generates three different pieces of information, as shown in Figure 5-22. The resulting generated text file contains several sections. You'll provide portions of that to the SSL certificate issuer.

From this point, follow the specific directions provided by your certificate provider to complete the setup.

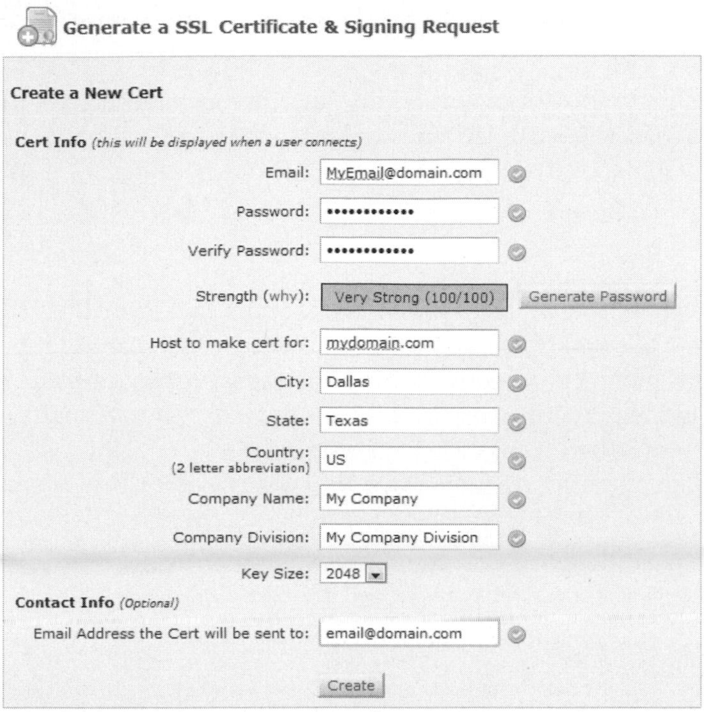

Generate a SSL Certificate & Signing Request

Create a New Cert

Cert Info *(this will be displayed when a user connects)*

Email: `MyEmail@domain.com`

Password: `••••••••••••`

Verify Password: `••••••••••••`

Strength (why): `Very Strong (100/100)`   `Generate Password`

Host to make cert for: `mydomain.com`

City: `Dallas`

State: `Texas`

Country: `US`
(2 letter abbreviation)

Company Name: `My Company`

Company Division: `My Company Division`

Key Size: `2048`

Contact Info *(Optional)*

Email Address the Cert will be sent to: `email@domain.com`

`Create`

Figure 5-21: SSL certificate creation

Signing Request

```
-----BEGIN CERTIFICATE REQUEST-----
MIIC/jCCAeYCAQAwgZsxCzAJBgNVBAYTAlVTMQ4wDAYDVQQIEwVUZXh
hczEPMA0G
A1UEBxMGRGFsbGFzMRMwEQYDVQQKEwpNeSBDb21wYW55MRwwGgYD
VQQLExNNeSBD
b21wYW55IERpdmlzaW9uMRUwEwYDVQQDEwxteWRvbWFpbi5jb20xITAf
BgkqhkiG
9w0BCQEWEk15RW1haWxAZG9tYWluLmNvbTCCASIwDQYJKoZIhvcNAQ
EBBQADggEP
```

Certificate

```
-----BEGIN CERTIFICATE-----
MIIEwTCCA6mgAwIBAgIJAIqbf+hr5/qGMA0GCSqGSIb3DQEBBQUAMIGb
MQswCQYD
VQQGEwJVUzEOMAwGA1UECBMFVGV4YXMxDzANBgNVBAcTBkRhbGxhcz
ETMBEGA1UE
ChMKTXkgQ29tcGFueTEcMBoGA1UECxMTTXkgQ29tcGFueSBEaXZpc2lvbj
EVMBMG
A1UEAxMMbXlkb21haW4uY29tMSEwHwYJKoZIhvcNAQkBFhJNeUVtYWlsQ
GRvbWFp
hi5ib20wHhcNMTAyMiAzMTcyNzU5WhcNMTEyMiAzMTcyNzU5WiCBmzELM
```

Key

```
-----BEGIN RSA PRIVATE KEY-----
MIIEpQIBAAKCAQEAx+Y0uhgCHgd7hs3xuva05w+QhPO+pDZFrhXZ6sgB
LijSifZ9
IcrSO2XnJvMb3sOJ54VpDsPdBSgEJOXQDMiAIFcfMUJScpuOKatzepLZJ1uZ
wn5p
Zm7frcdnjaw1uZ8fFkr/4cgOIITFTsDZ09TAm9gLLo2uTAz3gwMSoQgXYhb3
tpi4
77cXPm3VfxNmnROah3s2AkDSyfz+SmjJAI+LT0GU2pDvPwB2zOd3w9/Lls
cdbxt0
kX56CFNBsSo4Pu1y35+7kUKnP73MsFFphhanvS0XnM2SPiKQK5SQ1KlIIC
```

Figure 5-22: Generated SSL certificate information

Miscellaneous Hardening Tasks

Although this chapter provides information in many different areas about how to harden your server, some miscellaneous tasks still need attention, as discussed in the following sections.

Packet Sniffing

The term *sniffing* means to collect all the traffic (known as packets, as you learned earlier) going through a network interface card (NIC). Many tools can do this, and legitimate reasons exist for doing so. However, if a server in a production environment for which you have not authorized the use of a tool such as *WireShark* has a sniffer on it, bad things are happening.

Using WireShark, a person can access passwords, sensitive data, and more. Basically, anything that is travelling on the wire can be obtained. Figure 5-23 shows a sample capture (obtained from the WireShark website) that is decoding the traffic.

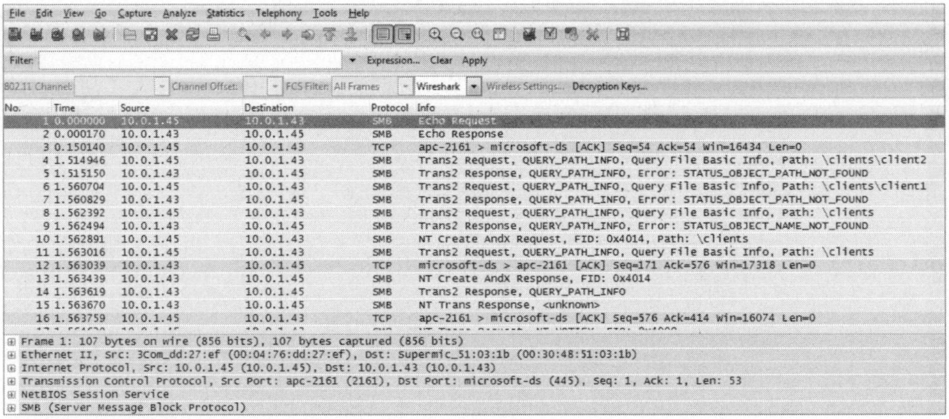

Figure 5-23: WireShark packet capture

In a capture such as this one, the traffic will allow the user sessions to be reconstructed, enabling a person with the right tools to learn what is being done. It will yield passwords, usernames, and more.

To check for sniffers, log in as the super user on your server and navigate to the following folder:

```
/proc/net/packet
```

You should see one header line looking something like this:

```
SK     RefCnt     Type     Proto     Iface     R     Rmem     User     Inode
```

If you see numbers appearing below this line, then you have a sniffer running. You might look for the following services running:

- TCPDUMP
- WireShark
- TShark

Finding and shutting down the sniffer is vital.

WARNING   Be sure you understand the implications and legal ramifications of using WireShark in any PCI environment.

Securing SMTP

Simple Mail Transfer Protocol (*SMTP*) is part of your solution for sending and receiving mail on your server. Many servers have an *open-relay* that allows bad guys to send spam through those servers to millions of people. If you are running an open-relay system, you may be delivering spam mail. If so, it won't take you long to get blacklisted and in trouble.

You can check whether you are in this situation by using a variety of methods. Take a look at a simple method to test your server.

If you're using a Windows machine, click Start ➢ Run, and then type **CMD**. A black box appears in which you can issue commands at the c:> prompt. Enter the following:

```
telnet domain.com 25
```

If port 25 is open, you'll see the mail server greet you with something like this:

```
220 domain.com ESMTP SendMail 8.x.x.x/8.x.x.x.x; Dec, 4, 2010 15:00:00
```

This is a good thing if you want to send *forged* (fake) mail through your server. Even a basic kiddie scripter could take it from here by simply asking the mail server for help by typing "?".

At this point, if you were able to get the mail server to prompt you as shown, you're already in bad shape. Filter port 25 (or whatever port your mail is on). Keep in mind that closing a port will stop mail flow.

In the event that you absolutely do not need mail service on your server (that is, you have it elsewhere), then can remove the service by using yum. Two popular packages are available, and depending on the one you're using, here are the commands:

```
#yum erase sendmail
# rpm --erase postfix
```

If you intend to leave mail on your server, PostFix is a very good choice for the mail server to run. It's well-documented and maintained. One other suggestion is to move mail to port 587. Although it's not a perfect fix, it keeps down some automated bots from attempting to connect and send mail.

Zone Transfers

The scope of zone transfers and DNS can and do fill entire volumes. The security point pertinent to this chapter is that you must ensure that your Domain name servers are not set to allow zone transfers. Information derived from zone transfers is very important and can give a dedicated attacker a map of your network.

The steps to take are to contact your host or your administrator and verify you are running the latest version of Bind 9. Also, ensure that your site will not allow the zone information (transfer) out.

NOTE Chapter 2 provides more information about zone transfers as a security threat.

Physically Securing Equipment

Guarding your server from external assault is simple if it is in a locked cage at a co-location facility. However, if you have your server located on your premises, following are a few tips for physical security of the hardware:

- If economically possible, put your server in a locking cage and restrict access to it.
- If no cage is available, then place your server in a locked room (with proper cooling and fire safety protection).
- Use a locking bezel (front cover), if available, on your hardware.
- Use password protection for the console or startup if the server's BIOS (firmware) offers it.
- Disable unnecessary ports. These include things like unused serial or parallel ports, any FireWire ports, or unused NICs. Use caution when disabling USB ports, however, because they are often needed for mice and keyboards.

For the most part, if a server is in a locked room, with access control for that room, then you should be fine.

Summary

This chapter has covered a lot of ground. Reading through this chapter a couple of times to ensure that you have a full understanding of the information presented is a good idea.

You learned about why and how you harden a server against attacks, which includes securing your Linux operating system and Apache web server. Other tasks that are often overlooked, but can be sources of trouble, include the open or closed ports, changing default passwords, and proper setup of FTP.

You learned about the importance of reviewing your logs, and how to establish a method to archive them. You also learned how to set up SSL, as well as how to review and test your mail servers to be sure they are not sending spam.

In Chapter 6, you'll work through the concept of developing a disaster recovery plan for when things go wrong with your website. The chapter will take you through the planning, writing, and testing phases. You'll finish up with a good framework to use when developing your own plan.

Establishing a Workable Disaster Recovery Plan

As you read the title of this chapter you might have thought, *"Oh no. I don't care about writing out a disaster recovery plan. After all, I am just a small business — not one with a large budget and lots of staff. Besides nothing has ever gone wrong."*

If you don't have a large budget, how will you pay for restoration of your site after a hacker breaks in? If the media rings your phone requesting a statement about your outage, what will you say? If you experience a significant problem like a fire, weather disaster, or earthquake, how will you be able to stay in business *without* a disaster recovery plan? If your hosting company has a severe outage, how will you take care of your clients?

This chapter includes a mix of practical knowledge about how to back up various content management systems (CMSs). Also mixed in is some practical knowledge on how to build out a framework and documentation to *manage* the disaster.

When you see a fire truck rushing to a scene of a fire, you don't think about all the hours of drilling and training and preparing the firefighters put in. If you're driving, you think about getting out of their way, and you're glad it's not you they are coming to see. To have a successful disaster recovery plan you need to drill, train, and learn with the same intensity as the firemen do for their jobs. When a disaster visits, you want to be able to respond.

As a business owner, you have a moral responsibility to your employees, shareholders, families, and customers (and possibly your banker) to have as good of a disaster plan as possible. In this chapter, you'll learn about building your team, installing the proper backup software, and testing and improving your disaster plan. You'll also learn about the additional odds and ends that tend to be missed, like e-mail systems, telephones, DNS, new equipment, and more. However, you must realize this single chapter is not meant to cover the entire gamut of *disaster planning*. It's written as a guide to help you build a framework to respond to events.

The chapter begins with a discussion of site and systems disaster planning.

Understanding Site and Systems Disaster Planning

During a disaster, people tend to lose their ability to reason and process complex tasks. You can see this phenomenon in the behavior of most people during a severe tragedy or event. They generally have trouble understanding commands. Keep this principle in mind for your plan, and tailor your instructions so that they can be understood simply and easily.

After a crisis passes the average person's ability to think returns to the normal level and, thus, the person is able to mentally process. For more information on this topic, conduct an Internet search for Dr. Robert Chandler and review his work on emergency notification during a crisis. He has done extensive work on the subject, and you will find it valuable.

The purpose of your plan is to prepare for what will be done during a crisis. To be fair, you cannot (nor should not) try to plan for every conceivable event. That's a waste of time and energy. Rather, this plan should be one that covers *outages* and what you will do to restore service. This plan should be broken down into manageable categories.

You may be a very small business with just a handful of people. Given that, understanding the *effective* (not *perceived*) capabilities of your staff is even more important. Operationally, be prepared to test your plan through drills. Using cloud solutions available today from many vendors, setting up a test scenario that will help prevent any interruption to your production systems is easy. Planning, training, and testing for you and your staff will help eliminate or mitigate many severe issues.

To understand and develop a plan that will work, you must understand your business — the various technologies that are in it, and how they interact.

While designing and developing your recovery plan, consider that you or your staff may not have worked through a major disaster or large-scale outage. The staff may very well regard the idea of a test or plan with some apprehension that could become a road block. Because of a lack of experience, a tendency may exist to underestimate the time or money needed to recover. Clearly, items will be missed if they are not documented in advance.

As an example, you would need the following, at a minimum, to recover a basic Joomla! website:

- The FTP (or SSH, SFTP) username and password
- cPanel or Control systems login
- Super user administrator control
- Copies of extensions and the correct versions
- An up-to-date copy of the database
- Login for phpMyAdmin (if so equipped)
- Access to the server (remote access)
- Possibly `htaccess` passwords
- Any settings for the server such as `php.ini`
- Settings particular to the site

This list is just for a Joomla! site. Think about a small business operation that has much more going on in addition to its Joomla! site.

Asking employees to *remember* all these critical items is bad management. Assuming that the right person with all the required knowledge will be available on the day of disaster is foolish. Disasters have a tendency to not schedule themselves around your timeframe, or the presence of a specific staff member.

Defining a Disaster

For the purposes of this discussion, a *disaster* will be considered anything that interrupts the IT systems in your business. What that can mean is that your site may be up, but perhaps a backhoe cuts the Internet connection coming into the building where your server is housed. Effectively, you are cut off from the world of the Internet. Following are some possible disasters that could plague your IT systems and operations:

- Weather (such as tornados, hurricanes, snow, floods, extreme heat)
- Hackers, viruses, Trojan horses, disgruntled employees
- Hardware failures
- Backhoes (as just described)
- Legal actions that cause an immediate outage
- Failure of supporting infrastructure such as e-mail, Domain Naming Service (DNS), Voice over IP (VoIP), or other telephony products
- Distributed Denial of Service (DDOS)
- Vulnerabilities that have yet to show themselves

- Upgrades gone bad
- Fire
- Electrical outage
- Sewage or plumbing problems

As a small or medium-sized business owner, you may face any of these scenarios, or even a combination of them. Although you may be a single-person shop, you are not immune from any of these disasters. Your risk might be lower, but nonetheless the risk still exists.

Time Considerations

In 1978, the University of Minnesota conducted a study to determine how long a business would survive if it experienced an outage. The results of the study were published in the "An Evaluation of Data Processing 'Machine Room' Loss and Recovery Strategies" working papers by D.O. Aasgard (et al) from the Management Information Systems Research Center (MISRC) (University of Minnesota: Minneapolis, 1978). What that study found is that the average survival period was two to six days. If a company suffered an outage and couldn't recover in a week or more, then, in all likelihood, it would be out of business within a year.

Clients of this author who have been hacked often ask, "When will it be up and running?" Or "How long will it take?" They need to be back online making money. In many cases, they did not have a recent backup, and in some cases, they had no backup at all. Of course, the sad news to those unfortunate clients is that it will take more time than they would like — to which, without fail, they groan and complain that this event is costing them *money* in terms of time.

You should seriously consider *how long* it will be before you can activate your plan. For example, you would not activate your disaster recovery plan if your site momentarily went offline for, say, 5 minutes. Inversely, you would be foolish to not take action of some sort after, say, an hour. In this part of your plan, you'll want an *escalation plan*. Consider in your plan *what* constitutes the need to activate it, who can activate it, and when.

To expand on that idea, let's use the example of a patched server that requires rebooting. That reboot is technically an outage or downtime. However, this event is one that is tolerable. You might consider this a business interruption, really an annoyance at best.

Other business interruptions are not so tolerable. A client of this author recently experienced a long outage (about three hours). The root cause was a faulty circuit breaker at the client's hosting facility. The result was a series of events that caused an outage at most of that hosting facility. Because this happened at a peak time, it was very unfortunate for the hosting company.

The reason this is highlighted is to put into your mind the idea of a pre-determined time that you set before you declare a disaster. This is a solid time that cannot be moved. In your planning, if you have determined that three hours is the absolute longest time you can be out of service before you start emergency restorations, then that's your time frame. When you have reached that time limit, no matter what, you must initiate your plan.

Determining that time limit is a matter of conducting serious analysis of your infrastructure, systems, and operations. Review each piece and see what the impact would be financially and in terms of recovery time.

Table 6-1 shows a few important areas from a fictional online company that conducts 100 percent of its business online. The purpose of examining the areas in this way would be to help you evaluate where you could be impacted, as well as the financial costs associated with each. Using this as a metric, you will be able to see where you are vulnerable. Assign to each area a predetermined time that you can reasonably be down before you activate your plan.

Table 6-1: Sample Business Impact Evaluation

SYSTEM	IMPACT	AREAS IMPACTED
Web server	Critical	Order entry, online presence, customer service
ISP	Critical	Online customer service
DNS	Critical	ISP has a fully redundant DNS
Telephone systems	Medium	Customer service operations
E-mail	Medium	High impact on operations, but an outside e-mail provider
Printers	High	Packing slips (affects shipping and requires a backup to be in place)

As you will learn throughout this chapter, you must be conscious of what assets are important to your business, and what disasters can trigger implementation of the disaster recovery plan. If e-mail is vital because you deliver something electronic through it, then it is mission-critical. If e-mail is merely a secondary communications channel, then the trigger to activate an emergency plan would occur much later in the life of a disaster.

Cost Considerations

Your disaster planning process (and possibly the activation of the plan) will have a financial component to it. Often, company management won't approve the costs of a plan mainly because of not understanding the financial impact an outage will have.

If you are the senior management, take the time to understand the legal and financial impacts that a serious outage could have. If you are tasked with selling this plan to the senior management, then your first step will be to build a case to justify it.

When investigating the costs in terms of people, systems, software, and time, be as honest as you can. Don't provide a lower number hoping to sell it. Do not put in a cushion and state in the plan that you have added "x" dollars to cover unforeseen costs. Past experience has shown that playing aboveboard beats begging for forgiveness later.

If you are working with a third-party firm for disaster assistance, be sure to review all fees carefully. Ask whether there is a fee to activate your disaster plan (known as a *declaration fee*). Add in any potential overtime or shift-differential pay that your employees may be paid.

Formulating Your Contingency Plan

As you begin building your plan, realize that no specific style or method is *right*. What is *right* is what matters to you.

For example, if you only have a small operation, having a solid and documented backup and recovery plan may be perfect. If you're a medium-sized business that potentially has several servers, some switches, and possibly a dedicated Internet connection, you'll have a larger and different plan.

You might look around and find some templates to get you started on a disaster plan. However, keep in mind that really, no tools are out there that will fit your scenarios exactly.

Determining Responsibilities

Table 6-2 provides a list of resources that may or may not apply to your situation. The people and departments you involve are based strictly on your company. Again, if you're a small one- or two-person business, that's a simple decision — you and the other person are the team. At a larger business, you may want to involve people from both internal and external groups.

Table 6-2: Groups and Responsibilities

GROUP	RESPONSIBILITIES
IT group	First and foremost, the IT group's task is to work through the restoration of services. If you have four to five people in this group, then someone will need to be tasked to develop the plan and lead this group. *Do not* attempt to lead by consensus. Put someone in charge, and give that person the responsibility and the authority to execute the plans.

GROUP	RESPONSIBILITIES
HR department	If you have an HR department, its involvement will be vital. That department may need to be involved in the hiring of the right person(s) to be brought in. The department may be responsible for providing employee telephone numbers, e-mail addresses, and so on.
Senior management	If senior management is only you, then great! If not, then be sure you involve the senior management team at the inception of the plan. Buy-in by the team will make or break your plan. To some degree, senior management will have say in the recovery plan. They will need to sign off on the development road map of this plan, as well as set priorities for recovery. Of course, funding will likely come from the senior management team.
Legal department	Consulting with your attorney or corporate legal department is also vital. They may know of specific considerations for your business or industry regarding compliance issues. The Legal department will be able to guide you on these matters. You may have a situation where outside counsel must be enlisted. Either way, legal considerations are part of the initial planning process.
Outside vendors or partners	This can be hardware or software vendors. In some situations, it might even be a food vendor. If you have a medium-sized staff and find yourself in a long outage, have the names of some 24-hour restaurants handy, because food is important during a crisis. Other vendors could be your hosting partner or co-location facility.
Law enforcement	In today's society, you may be faced with a disaster scenario that includes a bomb threat, a cyber-threat, or even a person or persons who could take your data center hostage. Although you hope this will never happen, being prepared for it is best.
Local utilities	This could be as simple documenting the various utilities that you may need to contact, such as water, gas, electrical, or telephony providers. Where appropriate, consider contacting them regarding emergency procedures as they relate to your company's needs.
Your customer or user community	Because this book is all about Internet sites, you're going to have customers one way or another. Involve them where appropriate. However, you do not need to give them your disaster recovery plans. What is needed is a plan for communicating with them during a disaster.
State and local government emergency agencies	This will really have more value to a medium-sized business than a very small business. Where appropriate, coordinate what to do about evacuations, local emergencies, and other potential disasters. The level of coordination will ensure that you know who to call for what.

Continued

Table 6-2 *(continued)*

GROUP	RESPONSIBILITIES
Your insurance agent	If you are a business of any size, then you'll have an insurance company. If you are a small business, then consider the local disaster of a stolen laptop, or a laptop that has water spilled on it. How will you replace that equipment? Review your policy with your agent and, if possible, add coverage for your business machines. As a medium-sized business, you'll have different insurance needs. In either case, involve your insurance agent in the initial planning process to determine whether the agent can help. Be sure you have documented what you will need to provide the insurance company.
Media and bloggers	Today, CMS projects get a lot of media coverage. However, the media may not know the specifics of your CMS site beyond the fact that you are running, say, Drupal. They will, however, know whether your Drupal site fails (for whatever reason). They may write an article about it based on what they know. As part of your plan, prepare some type of media response. Remember that "the media" can be as simple as a single blogger with a large audience. One bad blog will stay cached on a lot of servers forever. Make sure you are guiding the reporter or blogger. The action item here is to be sure to find out who the reporters and bloggers in *your* industry are. Document how to contact them. Prepare a media kit in advance on a few different topics, and have a plan to discuss the issue of an outage as appropriate. Remember, probably nothing these days is considered "off the record." What you say or send out will likely get out. Think carefully before the disaster. Dedicate a person to discuss the situation with the media. Then make sure everyone knows to point people in that point person's direction.
Your landlord or building facilities people	If you are renting office space (as so many of you may be), be sure you have contacted your landlord and/or building maintenance people. In the event that there's a fire and you have all your office or server assets in the building, what will you do? How will you gain access again? What if a floor floods from a leaky toilet and gets into your data closet? The bottom line is to be sure to talk to landlords about their plans for the building. Also, be sure to ask about the proper emergency contact information.

Mapping Your IT Assets

As a small business, you obviously won't face the myriad of challenges a larger business would face in the event of a disaster. A medium business with more moving parts and departments that are affected will have a greater challenge.

With both models of business, you should develop a questionnaire to discover information you don't know. For example, in a medium-sized business, the IT department may deem that the website itself has a higher priority for service restoration than the accounting services. Your Accounting department and senior management may disagree. Obviously, these situations are when senior management becomes part of the decision-making process. If a disaster happens on the same day that payroll is being run, the priority for the time spent restoring those systems will be much higher than the priority to restore your website.

Start by determining all the players impacted by an outage, including your HR department, Accounting department, software developers (if you have them), your factory, your legal folks, your customer service folks, and so on. Draft a map against the IT services each department or business function (Accounts Payable, Customer Service, Ordering, and so on) has, and prioritize restoration of services to those departments. In other words, if you have a total loss of IT, which person or group gets attention first?

If you are a small business, then prioritizing is a simpler task, but the decision will have higher impact because your website business may easily be your *only* access to you that your clients have. For the small business, your plan most likely will revolve more around restoration of your website and your merchant account services. The need to sell, provide services to customers, and receive money is your lifeblood.

First and foremost, in all cases of all businesses, your people are *not* expendable assets. They are your number one disaster priority. Map out how you will get your people (even if that's just you) out of harm's way. Make sure you have an egress and escape plan.

Include in your IT assets any external locations for backups. This could be a home, another office, or a bank safety deposit box. Your mapping and questionnaire effort must discover all the settings, passwords, database names, and so on that would be involved in restoring operations.

Table 6-3 shows some items to consider as you develop a questionnaire.

Table 6-3: Questionnaire Items

ITEM	DESCRIPTION	NOTES AND EXAMPLES
Technical Items	These include settings, passwords, copies of software, licenses, and so forth.	DNS settings.
		E-mail server settings and passwords.
		SSL Certificate vendor, password, or other information.
		Database names, passwords, paths, and version information.
		CMS version information, including a list of plug-in, add-ons, modules, or extensions.

Continued

Table 6-3 *(continued)*

ITEM	DESCRIPTION	NOTES AND EXAMPLES
		Software vendor names and telephone/Skype/ e-mail or Instant Messaging (IM) contact information.
		Operating system inventory, version, and source to obtain.
		Software licenses.
		FTP/SSH authentication information.
		Restoration information, such as your Amazon S3 or other cloud services authentication information.
		Any sort of cryptographic information, including PCI (merchant), cryptographic tokens (RSA, VeriSign, and so on).
People	Think about how you would reach your staff in the event of a disaster. During 9/11, a call list was very valuable to many, many companies to identify those who may have been in the New York City area.	Home addresses, telephone numbers, and next of kin for staff.
		A breakdown of skill sets for staff.
		A list of outside vendors or consultants (for example, if you don't have anyone on staff who could assist with virus outbreak research, or if you have a vendor who does). Make sure you know and have rates upfront (so that "emergency rates" don't kick in all of a sudden).
Vacations	Ensure that you have a plan for vacation or leave time for critical staff members. In other words, if one staff member is the only person who can perform "x," you want to be sure to cross train someone else.	In your discovery questions, ask alternate staff members about their abilities to deal with your infrastructure.

ITEM	DESCRIPTION	NOTES AND EXAMPLES
Costs	Determine what financial items are to be included.	Costs include time and money. Find out during your discovery how much time is involved in various efforts to restore the site and services. Find out whether any financial costs are involved.
Risks	What risks exist in your business? Detail the risks that you may face, and, if possible, the methods to mitigate or transfer risk to someone else (for example, insurance).	If you depend on your website for income, then the risk is weighted very heavily toward external factors such as hackers. Do a lot of digging into this scenario. Doing so can help you eliminate or mitigate a lot of the risk involved.
Downtime	Closely aligned with risk is how much downtime you can afford. This is a factor of time, money, recovery time, loss of business, and so on. The one key point that drives your recovery objectives is the order in which you bring things back up.	Referring to Table 6-1, downtime should be gauged against the impact on your business. If you can stand to have e-mail down for only an one hour, that's the downtime you can take. If another system can be unavailable (down) for, say, eight hours. that's the time you can be down.
Post-event	Collecting information after an event is essential.	This could be after a test was run and found to be not successful, or could be after a hacking event. In any case, your questionnaire should include the questions of "who, what, when, where, why, and how" in relation to the event. If something goes wrong during the test, look first at the plan. Do not immediately lay blame on the employees. Fix the problems, identify the holes, update the plan, and carry on.
Procedures	You will capture specific items here such as login procedures and other task-oriented processes.	Specific technologies will have specific procedures. These could be any number of systems, such as DNS, web servers, e-mail, VoIP, Instant Message, chat, or other IT-related systems. Be sure you look carefully around your environment because you might be surprised as to what you see. Make sure you capture those in your plan.

Assessing Risks

As part of your plan development, spend time looking at the risks associated with your specific technology. For example, if you do not run a virus prevention tool on your desktops (you should no matter what), a risk factor would be that you could easily transfer a virus to your website.

Take into account all your critical systems, their inherent risks, and how they touch each other. Consider the impact to your business if your customer service staff is unable to assist clients. This non-tangible item can have a material effect on your finances.

After you identify as many of the risks as you can, list the costs associated with removing each risk. For example, if you have six desktops, but none have virus scanning, what's the "cost" to acquire and maintain virus scanning tools? If you have an e-mail server and do not protect it, what are the costs of adding protection to it?

In the event that you have risks that cannot be eliminated, determine how you will *lower* the impact the risk will have. This might include using spare equipment, onsite backups, and more.

Another threat is the business processes. An example mentioned previously was a vacationing critical staff member. Suppose that the staff member has left the country for that dream of visiting Australia. During that time, the staff member is unavailable, and your site crashes. Could you restore it? If not, that's a risk, and should be mitigated with a properly documented and tested plan for site restoration.

After you have identified the risks and eliminated the ones you can, your next step is to draft the objectives of your plan.

Establishing Plan Objectives

Your objectives will become the cornerstone of your disaster recovery plan. The plan will define what will be done, by whom, and the standards by which you want it conducted. That is, if you want it documented for auditing or legal means, then have the documentation drafted ahead of time. After your e-commerce site is hacked, don't say in the midst of the crisis, "Did you collect the logs?"

Define upfront what you need to have happen for a given scenario. Remember, though, "boiling the ocean" is a waste time. The true secret to a good disaster recovery plan is to *keep it simple*.

Lastly, your objectives should include a means and time (that is, a plan within a plan) to keep the disaster recovery guide up to date. Pick a time that's appropriate for your business.

Determining Data Value

One final piece of information you should gather is determining what the value of your data is — not overall, but specifically. Take the time to identify what parts of your data sets are of a critical nature as opposed to nice to have (for example, frequently asked questions versus customer transactions).

Classifying the value of your data drives your recovery objectives. In a small business, the value of the data will likely be in a monolithic stack, such as your entire website and data. In a medium business, value could take any number of directions.

Having gathered all that information, it's time to move to drafting your initial plan.

Drafting the Initial Plan

As you have probably noted, the entire purpose of a disaster recovery plan is to shorten the time from when recovery starts to when it ends. As noted at the beginning of this chapter, a business that cannot recover in less than a week will likely be gone within a few years.

To recap, the plan should include the following elements:

- The first vital decision is "who" to not call. In other words, while the idea is to make the plan simple in terms of implementation, you don't want the janitor or mailroom clerk to activate it. Make sure you know the entire list of people who can (or might have to) operate the plan. Build your notification list accordingly.

- What are the objectives for this plan? Will it be simply to conduct a restore, or will it involve getting the staff to a temporary work location? Do you need to plan for an offsite or alternate location?

- What situations will you declare to be a disaster and commence the operation? This can be a power outage, hardware crash, hackers attacking, and more.

- Who is the person (or persons) who can declare a disaster?

- What is the role of each staff member, and what are their skills? That is, if a specific person is in charge of database administration, that person must be part of the plan.

- What actions will you take first? What actions will you take second, third, and so on? What specific actions do you take for each specific critical technology in your operation? This will guide you in your tactical actions.

- How will staff be notified? Will you use Skype? Is it a phone call? Is it a text message? Define this in the plan, and define the order in phone calling (cell, home, work, and so on). Make a call list and indicate alternative numbers to be used. Define in your call plan what to do if the person cannot be reached. The purpose of a call list is to notify members of your company about the issue who are not directly involved in the recovery. They are, however, to be considered stakeholders, and thus will be impacted by any outage.

- What information does the staff need to collect during this time? This can be log files, record of actions taken, and so on.

- With what method will usernames and passwords be stored and retrieved? The idea here is that you do not necessarily want to store usernames and passwords in your disaster recovery plan. They should be cycled regularly, and, thus, you would have to update the written plan more frequently. Also, if the plan were lost or stolen, then you would be risking a breach.

- How will the plan itself be validated? The plan needs a plan for testing.

Next, consider what form this "plan" will physically assume. This can be whatever physical form best suits your needs. For example, it can be a spreadsheet or Word document.

You should not keep an *electronic only* version of your plan for the simple reason that, if you cannot get to it because of an outage, then it's no good to you. Preferably, you should print and place it in a binder so that it can be easily retrieved. Make sure it's indexed and easy to navigate. Consider the use of screenshots and simple-to-follow work instructions as part of the plan.

No matter what form it takes, the plan should be kept up to date because the team will need the "latest and greatest" at the time it needs to use it.

Involving the Team

Your team supports the disaster recovery plan. The written plan is, for all intents and purposes, just that — a plan. It's not foolproof, and will only work as well as it's written. At disaster recovery time, you'll be relying on your team. Their wisdom (or lack thereof), experience, and willingness to support the effort will dictate its success.

The team should be trained thoroughly on the operations of the plan. Keep the core team as tight and small as possible for the development of the plan. As you involve other members in the preparation and planning, keep your training focused on the elements of recovery that they will respond to.

When training, keep in mind that the members in training might find this useless, and they may mentally check out. They may find it exciting and be engaged. It really falls on the back of the trainer. Make sure the training objectives are clearly defined ahead of time.

Training falls into the standards for good presentations and education. Here are a few tips:

- Start *on time* and end *on time*. It's alright to stray slightly over time for questions, but planning for those questions is better.

- Have a specific training plan (better known as an *agenda*).

- Avoid the "death by PowerPoint" syndrome where you plow into your audience with 8 million slides. You should use as few slides as possible, and keep the training more interactive with real-world examples or hands-on time.

- Define any specific technical terms that may be unfamiliar to your audience. If possible, keep your language in layman's terms.

- If you don't feel comfortable with the material, find someone who can speak to it authoritatively.

Remember, not everyone can manage well under stress. The effect of the drills will reveal some of this. But in a real disaster, keep an eye on the mental states of both yourself and others. Most of the disasters your business may face won't likely trigger anything other than annoyance, but preparing is good nonetheless.

Defining Team Roles

Roles help people know what they are supposed to do. In real life, we all have roles — father, mother, son, daughter, friend, wife, husband, boss, employee, and so on. Those roles help us define what we do, and how we react to various situations. They guide us in determining what level of respect and involvement we give to various situations.

Who is in charge could be multiple people or only one. Defining this role ahead of time and making the team aware of who is in charge of what will eliminate a lot of confusion.

Define clearly in writing who can activate the disaster plan. Make sure that person's contact information is well published in the documentation your team will use.

Define clearly in writing as well who has what leadership roles, and who has individual contributor roles. This latter role could be a webmaster or a database expert, or a server hardware technician.

The leadership sets the tone of the entire event. A weak, unprepared leader will cause his or her team to fail. An effective and prepared leader will ensure success through preparation and guidance.

It's critical to remember that, when a disaster occurs, jumping the chain of command or the hierarchy during a disaster will result in going from bad to worse. Jumping the hierarchy may even result in you not being able to recover.

Each person on your team should have a defined role and scope of authority. This prevents people from stepping on each other, and will ensure a smoother and faster recovery.

For example, you may want to assign a specific team member to update a blog site during a disaster to keep the customer or user community well informed. This person should have a defined update window (for example, every 15 minutes, every hour, and so on). This person will need the latitude to ask what the status is and so on. This person may also be the central point of communications for the company or press.

Testing Your Plan

Now that you have written your plan, and believe you have captured everything you need, take a deep breath. Your plan is about to break. It's guaranteed that it will not withstand the first few run-throughs. Don't let this concern you or even dissuade you. It's simply how things work.

Testing the plan in advance of really needing to implement it is obviously better. In the context of your personnel, make sure you let them follow the written plan during the test, and encourage them to make notes on where it failed.

This section lays out three steps of the test cycle:

1. Do what is basically a desktop or paper exercise.

2. Test various portions of your plan to make sure they work individually.

3. Conduct a real test where you either simulate a failure, or you run the test live on a backup system.

Performing a Desktop Test

The desktop test is in essence a paper exercise. What you should do is conduct this test *as if* you were really doing the drill. However, this will just be verbalizing the actions. Talk each step through. Ask a lot of questions, such as "Is this right?" or "Is there an alternative approach?"

The intent is to ensure that the approach works, the roles are understood by everyone, and minor (or major) steps are not missed.

Using a Phased Approach

In the second step of your testing, you use a phased approach to do the hands-on testing of various components of your system. For example, one phase might be obtaining a backup tape or CD/DVD from an offsite locker, and restoring it to a test server. Another part of the plan may actually be bringing up your spare e-mail server, or activating a new web server in place of the old.

The phases should also include any non-technical tasks, such as contacting everyone on a call list. This call list should be tested as part of either the phased approach or dry runs. Like any other business process, this should be monitored for updates and changes. Establishing a central repository for the results may be the function of the HR department. The HR representative could provide regular updates of key players.

During this phased approach, any findings that differ from the expected results should be documented and the action retested.

Conducting a Live Test

The final step is an end-to-end test of your plan. If you have a very complex system, you may choose to test individual portions of your IT services separately.

In this step, you may schedule an outage to test the real capacities of your plan. Or, as an alternative, set up an identical environment using one of the public cloud services. The results you are looking for ensure that you have met your recovery objectives in your plan and that you have minimized downtime as much as possible.

Perform your drills for this step until you are satisfied with the responses. Then look at a regular (6 months or so) test of the plan.

Again, a safe bet is that you'll have some issues and hiccups. Don't sweat it. Learn from it, modify your plan, and move on.

If you have any major changes to your infrastructure, you will need to revisit and adjust the plan. And, of course, retest.

Performing a Post-Test Review

At the end of the event, all team members should gather and review the event. This report (the *After Action Report*) is designed to capture information while it is fresh — what went right, what went wrong, what the root cause of the failure was, and so on.

Consider all the information in the After Action Report. You should reformulate your plan if there are (and there will be) errors and issues with the plan. This should not be a punitive event. If it's seen as such, you're guaranteed to have less cooperation next time.

Following are some sample questions for the post-disaster meeting:

- Why did the event happen? Be sure to look at mundane things such as patching or updates that were missed.
- What risk was not mitigated or eliminated (if any)?
- Where did the plan have holes that need to be closed?
- What can the leader(s) do better next time?
- What can the staff do better next time?
- What went right?
- What feedback from the user community did you receive?
- Have you addressed all stakeholders' concerns (including customers, both internal and external) in a timely fashion?
- Is there any bad press that must be dealt with?

Incorporate these things into your plan, and schedule a disaster drill soon after to ensure that the plan has successfully been updated.

The post-test review is where you formulate your After Action Report. Chances are good that if you have convinced the senior management team to spend the money on developing a disaster recovery plan, they're going to want to know the results. If the test doesn't go well, the impression might be that it was a waste of money and time. It's only a waste, however, if no improvements are made as a result of the tests.

As part of your test, you should have a trusted and neutral person monitor and observe. That person's role will be to gauge reactions, check on progress, and, basically, just see how the test goes.

After the test is done, schedule a follow-up for just the leadership within a few days. Ask the person monitoring for a candid review of the leadership's performance. You may hear some things you don't want to hear, but your finding them out now is better than finding them out in a real emergency. Gather feedback on the staff's performance — good, bad, and ugly. You can use this information to improve performance on all fronts.

Technical glitches that are found should be brought up in a staff meeting dedicated to gathering impressions, facts, ideas, and changes. If you trust your staff, then trust their impressions. Update your materials and redistribute the changes to the plan.

What you may find is that some procedures that were documented don't actually work. For example, in one a real-life situation the documentation from a hardware manufacturer was inaccurate for a large uninterruptable power supply (UPS). This huge piece of equipment had a particular stop and startup procedure. The documentation was wrong, and the test discovered it. Had this discovery been made during an active disaster, the company's time to recover would have been much longer.

You should consider retesting your plan within 90 to 120 days.

Anticipating the Unexpected

You should always expect to find the unexpected, whether that be during a test or during any real disaster. Do not expect your well-oiled plans to work every time. Expect failures. Expect resistance from the websites and technologies. Because disasters are typically chaotic moments, expect some of that chaos to rub off on your process. The phenomenon touches people, processes, technology, missed shipments, and more. These are simply part of the event.

Identifying a Basic Backup Policy

Your backup policy is a guide that you will write that dictates the how, when, and the frequency with which you back up your sites and systems.

Your specific backup policy is something that you will determine on an individual basis. You have the choice of doing a full backup every time, which has the advantage of maintaining a complete backup of all data. It has the downside of getting very unwieldy to manage. Your earlier discovery phase should have identified what is to be backed up, and how often.

One factor to determine is the *rate of change* of the data. This is the amount of data that changes within a given timeframe. This will guide you to the frequency of backup — that is, hourly, daily, weekly, monthly, or some other schedule. If you have a very busy site with lots of traffic, you may opt for a daily backup. If you have a very static site, then monthly or even less is probably okay.

The other choices in your policy include which system or systems you need to back up. If you have a single site, then that's simple. However, if you are backing up multiple CMSs and other server data, you'll have to decide which systems to back up.

When you back up means *what time of the day or night* you will conduct a backup. This may or may not be a big factor in your situation. The idea is to avoid performance issues for your users. As you will see later in this chapter, you can take a Drupal site offline temporarily while you make the backup. This is preferable *if* the backup activity can impact production.

How you backup means primarily the method. When writing your policy, you must determine and document the process to remove the data from the server and take it to an off-site location (such as a fireproof safe). Inversely, the policy should clearly document the process for retrieving the data. If you are taking it home, and you leave for vacation in Hawaii, and your staff cannot get the data, then you might as well not even have a backup.

Data retention should be considered in your policy. If you need to keep data for ten years, then state that in your policy. Also consider that if you needed to retrieve it nine years from now, will it be in a form that's readable? If you only need a month or two of backups, then draft a destruction process into your policy that lists how to dispose of the data.

If you are retaining on tape, server storage, or remote storage, any identifiable personal information (such as credit card numbers) should be encrypted. Encryption strategies themselves should be considered in your plan — specifically, the management of the encryption/decryption keys. In essence, ensure that you have documented the location of the keys, who can access them, logging of that access, verification, and more. As part of your plan, ensure that you have captured the process for obtaining the keys and who is authorized to use them.

NOTE For more information, see the National Institute of Standards guide for Key Management at `http://csrc.nist.gov/publications/nistpubs/800-57/SP800-57-Part2.pdf`.

Finally, you want some form of logging. Logging systems or software should include the date and time of the backup, who conducted it, what issues (if any) were encountered, what was backed up, and where the backup is located. Many other data points could be captured in this log that enable you to make that determination. As you draft your policy, be sure you don't forget things such as e-mail that may be on your server as well. Don't forget to review your discovery questions to ensure that you didn't miss anything.

In essence, your backup policy is to guide you and your staff in the handling and disposition of the data. It should be clear, concise, and easy to follow.

In regard to specific hardware solutions, it all depends on your need and your budget.

For a small business, a local Linear Tape Open (LTO) tape taken nightly or weekly and stored offsite might be sufficient. For example, you might want to review the BackupExec software for small business: (`www.symantec.com/business/products/family.jsp?familyid=backupexec`). This would provide you with the logging needed and the capability to recover.

When you grow into a medium-sized business, you want to "break the tape habit" by moving into an offsite replication or data-duplication solution. You might consider using a product such as the Dell Equallogic storage system (`www.equallogic.com`) to create a local snapshot, and then replicate that to an offsite Equallogic box. The replicated storage machine would then do a snapshot in the remote machine. This gives multiple backups and a means of recovery.

Additionally, in a medium-sized environment, you will likely be deploying some form of virtual computing (such as VMware) in that environment. Using a mix of the Equallogic and the Quantum solution for virtual backups (`www.quantum.com/Solutions/Virtualization/Index.aspx`) would enable the logging and protection you need.

> **NOTE** For more detailed information on the entirety of planning and implementing backups, see the book, *Implementing Backup and Recovery: The Readiness Guide for the Enterprise* by David Little and David Chapa (Indianapolis: Wiley, 2003).

Server-Side Backup and Restoration Methods

The cPanel utility includes a great facility for backing up your web server. Incorporating this method into your plans is easy to do, and provides a full backup of your website. The downside to this tool is that it does a full backup, and the file can quickly grow in size. If that's what you need, however, then there should be no problem. The size of the files could be large and take a little time to deal with during a download.

Another manual backup method is to use the command line (via Putty) to pull a copy of the database and the files separately. This has the advantage of speed and size, but the disadvantage of managing multiple file sets.

First take a closer look at the cPanel method.

Using cPanel

In many hosting situations the commercially available application cPanel is in use. This is one of the best website management tools around. It's highly stable and easy to learn.

The steps outlined here assume that cPanel is installed on your web host. The purpose of this discussion is to show you how to back up and restore using the cPanel system.

To use cPanel, follow these steps:

1. In cPanel, find the phpMyAdmin button and click it to open the phpMy-Admin administrator interface.

2. Locate the database you want to export. In the example shown in Figure 6-1, the chosen database is called `watcher_cookbook`. Click the Export button at the top of the screen to start the process.

Figure 6-1: Selecting the database

3. On the left side of the screen, click Select All to export the entire database. On the right side of the screen, click the checkboxes shown in Figure 6-2.

The Comments checkbox under the heading, "Add custom comment into header (\n splits lines)" inserts the date and time information into all your table entries, as shown here. This is good for reviewing the correct database for a future restoration.

```
--
-- Table structure for table 'backup_jos_sobi2_categories'
--
-- Creation: Dec 06, 2010 at 05:20 PM
-- Last update: Dec 06, 2010 at 05:20 PM
```

```
--

CREATE TABLE IF NOT EXISTS 'backup_jos_sobi2_categories'
```

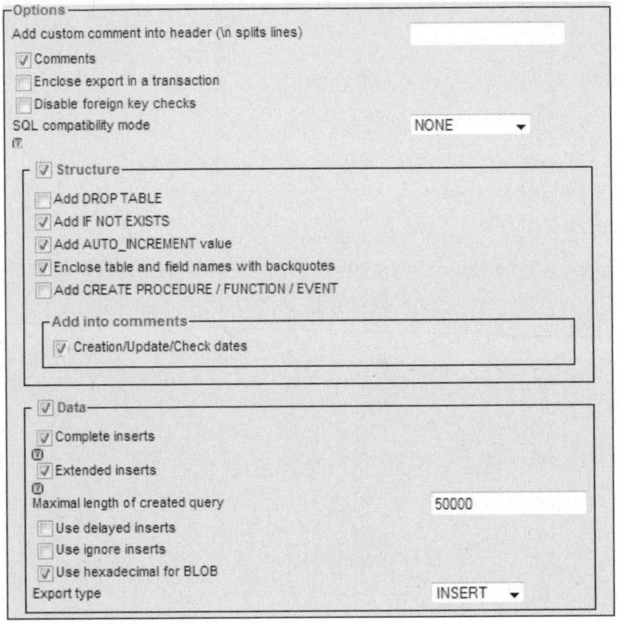

Figure 6-2: Export settings

4. Choose the "Add IF NOT EXISTS" checkbox in the Structure category to allow you to *insert* (load where no table exists) a database using the `create table if not exists` command, as shown here. The other checkboxes in this category support the basic *import* of your data.

```
--
-- Table structure for table 'backup_jos_sobi2_categories'
--

CREATE TABLE IF NOT EXISTS 'backup_jos_sobi2_categories'
```

5. At the bottom of this screen, fill in the name of your export file and choose your compression method. Most of the time, you will select either "zipped" or "gzipped" for the compression method. Selecting None as the compression method will open up your database in a text editor. If your database is very large, selecting None could cause a long delay as you wait for it to open.

6. After you fill out the required information, click Go in the lower-right of the screen to perform the export.

Backing up your data and tables is only half the battle. The other half is getting them back into your database for use, which is known as *restoration*. Let's take a look at how to manually restore the database tables.

This example uses an empty database called `wiki1_CMS_SecBook`. Follow these steps to restore the database tables:

1. With the aforementioned database selected from the phpMyAdmin login page, shown in Figure 6-3, click the Import button.

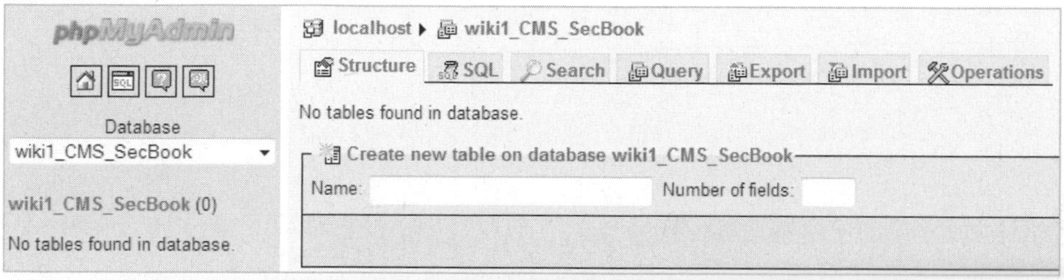

Figure 6-3: Empty database needing to be restored

2. Click the Browse button located at the bottom of your screen (not shown in Figure 6-3) to locate your SQL backup file. Remember, it may be a `.sql` (text) file, a `.zip`, or a `.gz` file. Select the rest of the settings (search criteria) as shown in Figure 6-4.

3. After you locate the backup file, click Go in the lower-right corner of the screen to begin the import. The time needed will vary based on the amount of information you need to import.

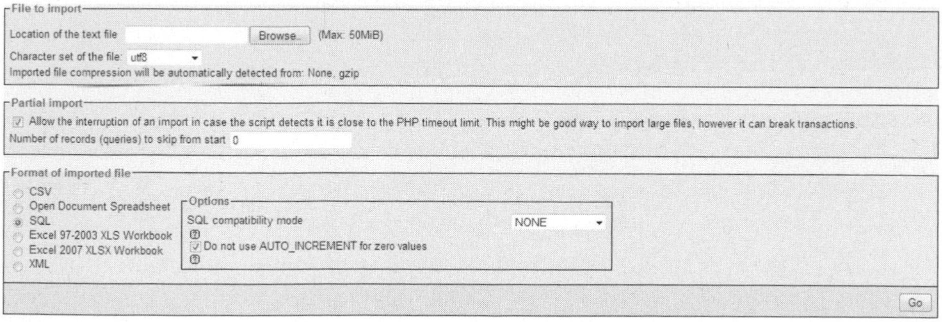

Figure 6-4: Import selection

When the process completes you'll see the tables on the left have been restored, as shown in Figure 6-5.

Sometimes you may need to simply replace or update a single table. This is very simple to do by selecting the entire table out of your `.sql` backup file. You can copy it out of the database dump using your favorite text editor. Then, click the SQL button in the phpMyAdmin page and paste in the database dump. Click Go and it should quickly reinsert that table into the database.

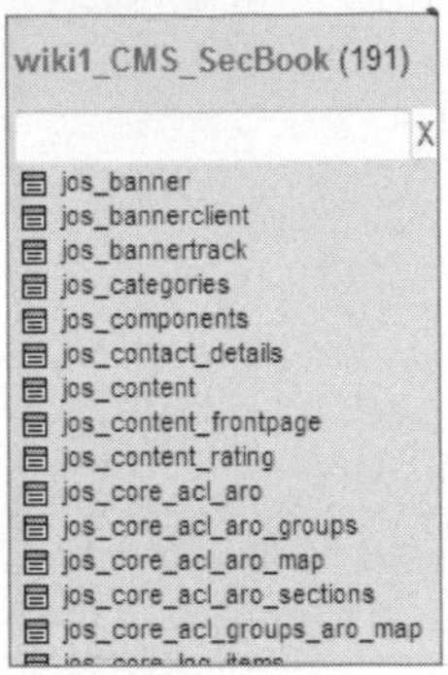

Figure 6-5: Fully populated database

Using the Command Line Method

Backing up the database using the command line is an advanced method, but is included here to ensure complete coverage.

> **NOTE** The steps described here are for conducting the actual backup. Be sure that you write them into your particular process if you decide to use this method.

In this example, you interact with the MySQL server and use a tool built into Linux known as `tar` to compress. The next few sections outline the steps you take in relation to the tasks they are performing.

Backing Up the Database

You can manually back up the database, which in technical terms is known as *dumping* the database. You'll need the MySQL username and password. Log in to your server using Putty or another command-line SSH tool.

Next, log in to MySQL using the following command:

```
[root@Chpter6-Centos ~]# mysql -u YourUserName -pYourPassword
```

After you are logged on to the server, you use a command at the pound prompt (#) to dump your database. You will need to know the name of the database and you must choose a name for the backup file.

In this example, suppose you have a database for your CMS called `productiondb` and you want to dump it out to `backupdb.sql`. The `-p` parameter in the following command specifies a password. However, because it is not included in the command, you will be prompted for it, as shown here:

```
[root@Chpter6-Centos ~] mysqldump -u root -p productiondb > backupdb.sql
Enter password:
```

If the database is very large, you can compress it using the `tar` command as follows:

```
[root@Chpter6-Centos ~]# tar cvzf Dec2010.tar.gz backupdb.sql
backupdb.sql
[root@Chpter6-Centos ~]# ls -l
total 208
-rw-r--r-- 1 root root 87287 Dec 8 01:01 backupdb.sql
-rw-r--r-- 1 root root 22983 Dec 8 01:14 Dec2010.tar.gz
```

In the first part, you can see that `tar` was used to create a compressed archive file called `Dec2010.tar.gz`. Also, as you can see, the size is dramatically smaller, with the original weighing in at 87KB and the archived version only 22KB.

Depending on the rate of change in your data, you may need to run this command daily or weekly. With *cron,* automating this task is possible.

NOTE See `http://dbperf.wordpress.com/2010/06/11/automate-mysql-dumps-using-linux-cron-job/` **for an easy method to set up your cron job.**

Restoring the Database

When it comes time to restore a database (also known as *importing*), use the following command:

```
mysql -u root -ppassword database < backupname.sql
```

In this example, notice the caret (<) is pointing to the left. This indicates import. A right-pointing caret indicates export. Following is an example of the command in use with the username of `tom`:

```
[root@Chpter6-Centos ~]# mysql -u root -ptom productiondb < backupdb.sql
```

WARNING **This method is very advanced. If you are at all uncomfortable, do not use it. You can cause the accidental erasure of data. Additionally, be aware of the file you're writing *into*. You may need to re-create a database and import your `.sql` file if you are not sure of the contents.**

Compressing the Files

After you have dumped your database files, you want to compress the directory or directories that hold your CMS website. Figure 6-6 shows a basic Joomla! website.

```
drwxr-xr-x 11  503 games     4096 Nov  3 18:15 administrator
drwxr-xr-x  2  503 games     4096 Nov  3 18:15 cache
-rw-r--r--  1  503 games    76539 Nov  3 15:00 CHANGELOG.php
drwxr-xr-x 13  503 games     4096 Nov  3 18:15 components
-rw-r--r--  1  503 games     3411 Jan 26 2010 configuration.php-dist
-rw-r--r--  1  503 games     1172 Jan 26 2010 COPYRIGHT.php
-rw-r--r--  1  503 games    14918 Nov  2 13:49 CREDITS.php
-rw-r--r--  1  503 games     2773 Jan 26 2010 htaccess.txt
drwxr-xr-x  6  503 games     4096 Nov  3 18:15 images
drwxr-xr-x  8  503 games     4096 Nov  3 18:15 includes
-rw-r--r--  1  503 games      588 Jan 26 2010 index2.php
-rw-r--r--  1  503 games     2049 Jan 26 2010 index.php
drwxr-xr-x  7  503 games     4096 Nov  3 18:15 installation
-rw-r--r--  1  503 games     4344 Jan 26 2010 INSTALL.php
-rw-r--r--  1 root root   4893246 Nov  3 19:20 Joomla.tar.gz
drwxr-xr-x  4  503 games     4096 Nov  3 18:15 language
drwxr-xr-x 16  503 games     4096 Nov  3 18:15 libraries
-rw-r--r--  1  503 games    17816 Jan 17 2009 LICENSE.php
-rw-r--r--  1  503 games    27986 Jan 26 2010 LICENSES.php
drwxr-xr-x  2  503 games     4096 Nov  3 18:15 logs
drwxr-xr-x  3  503 games     4096 Nov  3 18:15 media
drwxr-xr-x 22  503 games     4096 Nov  3 18:15 modules
drwxr-xr-x 11  503 games     4096 Nov  3 18:15 plugins
drwxr-xr-x  2 root root      4096 Dec  8 02:15 public_html
-rw-r--r--  1  503 games      304 Aug  8 2006 robots.txt
drwxr-xr-x  6  503 games     4096 Nov  3 18:15 templates
drwxr-xr-x  2  503 games     4096 Nov  3 18:15 tmp
drwxr-xr-x  4  503 games     4096 Nov  3 18:15 xmlrpc
[root@Chpter6-Centos joomla]# pwd
/root/CMSWebSite/joomla
```

Figure 6-6: Joomla! website directory listing

You can see from the `pwd` (print working directory) command that the path to this site is `/root/CMSWebSite/Joomla`. If you wanted to compress this entire folder, you would use the following command:

```
tar -cvf Dec-07-2010-backup.tar.gz /root/CMSWebSite/joomla/*
```

The following response shows that the command has done its job by creating an archive of the files:

```
Dec  8 02:32 Dec-07-2010-backup.tar.gz
```

One of the most common errors is not allowing for enough space. If this happens, simply change the directory up to a folder that has room, and run the command again as follows:

```
/root/ -tar cvf archivename.tar.gz /path/to/your/site/
```

This causes the archive to reside in the *root* folder.

After both the database dump and the normal CMS files have been compressed, you can take one of two paths:

- Simply copy both the files archive and the database backup archive (or file) down using FTP or an SSH connection, and keep them in a safe place.

- Add the database `.sql` file to the files archive, thus keeping them together.

You are strongly encouraged to follow the second path. Be sure to make a copy and store it offline.

You can copy or move (mv) the database .sql file you dumped to the same directory as your files' backup. The copy command works as follows:

```
cp file /path/to/newlocation/
```

As a simple example, suppose you wanted to copy a robots.txt file to a TMP directory. You would use the following command:

```
cp robots.txt tmp
```

After you copy the database backup file to the desired location, use the following command to *add* it to the archive:

```
# tar -rvf Dec-07-2010-backup.tar.gz backupdb.sql
```

The -r in rvf means to append.

Next, execute the tar command to ensure that the files are intact and that the database file was added:

```
# tar -tvf  Dec-07-2010-backup.tar.gz | more
```

The -t in tvf means to list.

The more command at the end will display the results on a screen-by-screen basis.

This completes the capture and compression of the database and CMS files. This will work for all PHP-based CMSs discussed in this book running on Linux. The backing up of Plone is covered later in this chapter.

Restoring the Files

If you must restore, you can do a full restore by using the database import instructions outlined previously in the "Using cPanel" section. Use tar to restore the files from the archives. You may have to copy or move them back into place.

Following are commands that will assist you during restoration. To perform a full uncompressing of all files, use the following:

```
# tar -xvfz archive.tar.gz
```

To extract only a specific file, use the following:

```
# tar -xvf archive.tar /path/to/file
```

To extract a directory, use the following:

```
# tar -xvf archive.tar /path/to/dir/
```

CMS Backup and Restoration Methods

As you have just seen, manually backing up and restoring is no walk in the park. So, now take a look at backup and restore methods that are some of the best of the class in their respective open source projects.

The first section covers Joomla! and the tool Akeeba Backup.

Joomla! Backup and Restoration

The Akeeba Backup backup utility for Joomla! v1.5 and Joomla! v1.6 is available from www.akeebabackup.com. Formally known as *JoomlaPack,* this utility is offered in two versions — a free version and a professional version. They both work identically. The professional version offers a wealth of additional features such as offsite backups to Amazon, Rackspace, and more.

Akeeba is capable of running a full restoration using its special .jpa format without your having to first install Joomla!. That means that you can restore or move a site simply using the archived .jpa file(s) and the utility known as *Kickstart.*

The extension installs using the normal Joomla! installer, so let's move on to configuration and operation. This section starts by describing features common to both versions, and then highlights the differences in the professional version.

Requirements

Following are server-side requirements:

- Joomla! 1.5.xx or later in the 1.5.x or 1.6.x range. As of this writing, the latest version of Joomla! 1.5 is 1.5.22, and Joomla! 1.6.

- PHP 5.1.3 or greater; 5.2.1 or later highly recommended.

- Akeeba Backup will not work on PHP 4. PHP 5.2.4 and 5.2.5 are not supported because they contain grave bugs that will not allow Akeeba Backup to function properly.

- MySQL 5.0 or greater is recommended for optimal performance. Even though Akeeba Backup may run on MySQL 4.1 or later, restoring the backup generated on such a host may be impossible. Thus, move to MySQL 5.0 or greater.

- Minimum 16MB of PHP memory. However, 32MB to 64MB is recommended for optimal performance on large sites.

- The PHP function opendir must be available.

- Available free space or quota limit at about 75 percent to 80 percent of your site's size.

■ The cURL PHP module must be installed on your server for FTP and cloud backup to work.

Following are the supported browsers:

■ Internet Explorer 7 or greater

■ Firefox 2.0 or greater

■ Safari 3 or greater

■ Opera 9 or greater (Opera 10 highly recommended)

■ Google Chrome 3 or greater

■ Konqueror 3.5.9 or greater

Configuration

Akeeba has a considerable number of options. It is one of the best documented open source packages available. As such, this discussion focuses on a subset of the application. For more information, you should read through the user's guide.

Follow the normal Joomla! process to install Akeeba. After installing it, click Components ➢ AkeebaBackup to begin configuration. The first time you use Akeeba, click the Configuration Wizard button to begin the wizard.

The wizard examines your particular server settings and capabilities, and then, as shown in Figure 6-7, reports a best guess as to the settings.

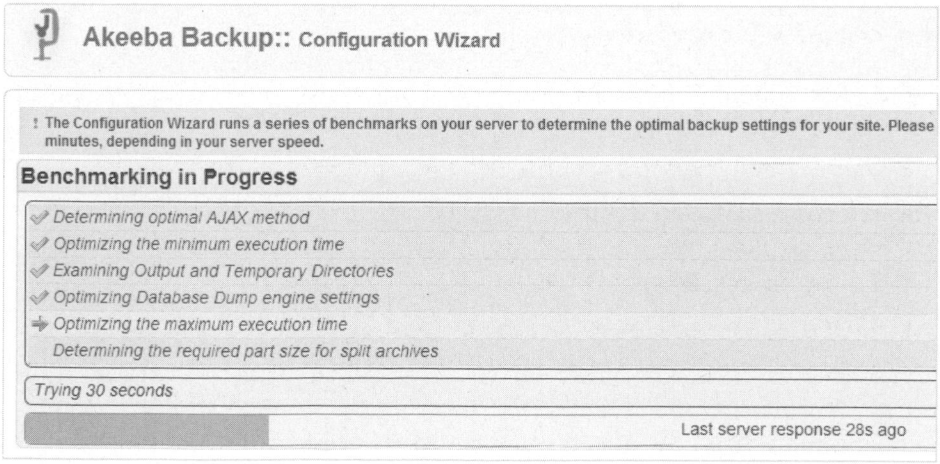

Figure 6-7: Akeeba Configuration Wizard

Although the guess may not be the *best* match, it will be very close. If you need to manually adjust the settings for your particular situation, use the Configuration button, as shown in Figure 6-8.

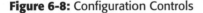

Figure 6-8: Configuration Controls

Optionally, you may set up different *profiles* for your backups. Use the Profiles Management button as shown in Figure 6-8 to set up profiles for your needs. This is helpful for designing various types of backups such as "Fulls," "Incremental," or any other configuration that matches your needs. To set up a profile, click the Profiles button and click New. From there you can adjust the settings.

In the configuration of both the free version and the professional version, you can exclude files and directories from being backed up. The professional version offers a wider array of options, including the following:

- Files and Directories Exclusion
- Database Tables Exclusions
- Extension Filters
- RegEx files and Directories Exclusion
- RegEx Database Tables Exclusion

The free version is limited to the following exclusion choices:

- Files and Directories Exclusion
- Database Tables Exclusion

To select any exclusions click the icon representing the type of exclusions you want to invoke.

During regular use of Akeeba, you complete your configuration by selecting what you want it to do after you create the .jpa files, which is known as *post processing*. The professional version offers several options to choose from. As you can see in Figure 6-9, many of the large cloud storage providers are represented. The free version only offers "Send by Email" and "No post-processing" options.

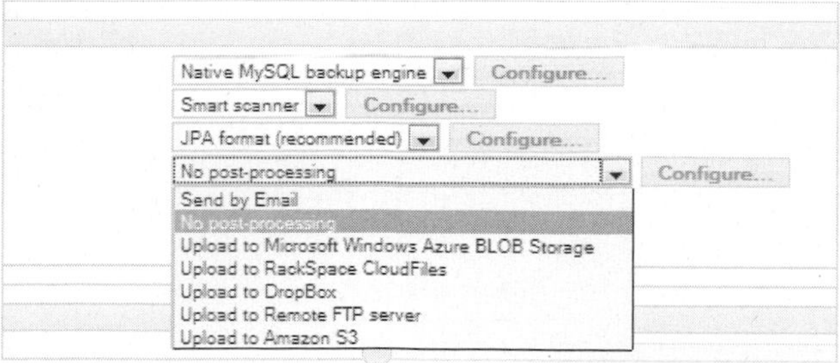

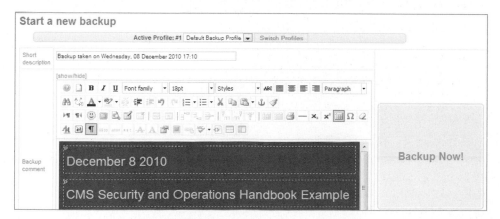

Figure 6-9: Professional version post-processing options

You should read the Akeeba documentation thoroughly before changing the other settings in the Configuration folder. You'll need to determine what is important to your situation and data set.

You should try the free version of Akeeba to get a feel for its use, and then perhaps buy the professional version. It's a solid extension, and the support is very good.

Backups

Akeeba is a very point-and-click type application, which means that it is very easy to use and you can easily understand what is going on. To demonstrate this ease of use, let's walk through the steps to conduct a new backup.

Log in as the Super Administrator to your site and select Components ➢ Akeeba Backup. Click the Backup Now button.

Part of your backup process (no matter what process you choose) should be to document the backup. As shown in Figure 6-10, Akeeba offers an editor window with each backup. Enter the relevant information such as date, time, and so on. Other options include administrative information or possibly the operator. All this will help identify the proper file to restore.

Figure 6-10: Starting a new backup

Akeeba will keep you well-informed of the progress of the backup by displaying the Backup Progress window. It's important that you do not close this browser or browse away until the backup is complete. Otherwise, your backup will fail.

When the backup completes, you should see a success message. If there are any issues, Akeeba will present a very visible error message. Consult the Akeeba documentation for the solution. If you cannot find the solution, visit the Akeeba website (www.akeebabackup.com) for assistance options.

After resolving any issues, copy the backup files from your server for security and safety reasons. To do so, click the Administer Backup Files button. A dialog appears that shows all the backups on your server.

Akeeba offers an option to download your files via the browser (HTTP protocol). The challenge with HTTP is that it can time out or lose part of the download. You'll receive the following message to warn you:

```
Downloading backup files through your browser can result
under certain circumstances to corrupt or partial downloads
and subsequent restoration failure

Are you sure you want to continue?
```

Instead, you should log in via SSH (or FTP) and download your files.

For example, suppose you have set up an incremental profile. This profile has some directories you want to exclude. So, as shown in Figure 6-11, you can select the profile and start a backup. By using this profile, only specific directories that you choose will be backed up and saved.

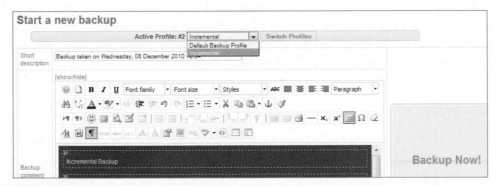

Figure 6-11: Using the Incremental profile

Cloud Storage

As mentioned previously, Akeeba supports most of the current cloud storage providers. For example, suppose you want to select the Amazon S3 Data Processing engine. You can find that option by clicking the Configurations button in the Akeeba control Panel, as shown in Figure 6-8.

WARNING   As with any third-party service, be sure to read and understand the Service Level Agreement (SLA) that is offered. You may review Amazon's at `http://aws.amazon.com/s3-sla`.

On the ensuing screen, you may select from the following checkboxes and fields:

- *Process each part immediately* — Select this option to send each backup part immediately to Amazon S3 as it's written. The downside to this approach is that, in the event of a failure, the entire backup fails. If you do not use this option, the upload to the cloud will happen after the backup is complete. If the full part fails, then there is a valid backup left on your server, which you can manually upload to the cloud.

- *Delete archive after processing* — If this option is enabled, the archive files will be removed from your server after they are uploaded to Amazon S3.

- *Access Key* — This is your Amazon S3 access key.

- *Secret Key* — This is your Amazon S3 secret key.

- *Use SSL* — Uses SSL to transfer (which will take longer).

- *Bucket* — This is your Amazon S3 bucket name.

- *Directory* — This is the directory name in your bucket.

After completing your selections, you can browse your Amazon S3 bucket to see the upload. Using this approach, you can easily restore in an emergency, or you can move to a new server. Either way, the entire site is included and ready for installation.

Akeeba has a built-in Joomla! installer that restores the original site back to normal. You don't need to install Joomla! beforehand, because this *bare-metal* (that is, only the operating system, web server, and MySQL are installed) process can handle it quickly and easily.

Restoration

To demonstrate a Joomla! restore, take a look at the following two separate scenarios:

- The first scenario is that you have experienced a loss of data, such as through accidental deletion, or perhaps a hacker has broken in and defaced the site. In this scenario, you will need the professional version of Akeeba to perform the restore.

- The second scenario is that you want to perform a server move or an upgrade. This entails using the *bare-metal process*, meaning a server that has nothing on it and must have the operating system, web server, database, data, and so on, reinstalled.

Scenario One: Loss of Data

To restore lost data using the professional version of Akeeba, follow these steps:

1. Log in to your super user account in Joomla! and navigate to your Akeeba menus. Click the Restore icon.

2. To initiate a restoration of a site, you must upload the .jpa file (or files) to your server. Choose the version of backup you want to restore, and then click the Start Restoration option, as shown in Figure 6-12. If you want to use the FTP Layer Options, see the specific instructions available in the Akeeba documentation.

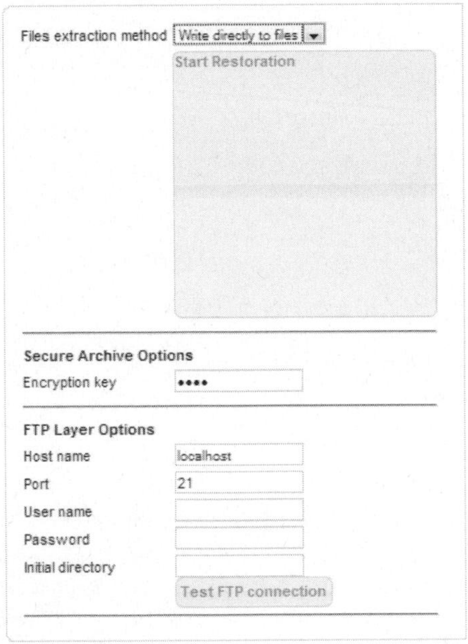

Figure 6-12: Start Restoration

As the restoration continues, you'll see the archive being extracted with a screen showing a progress bar. *Do not* close this window.

3. When the extraction completes, click the "Run the site restoration script" button, which launches the installer. The screen shown in Figure 6-13 appears, which confirms everything is ready to go.

4. Click the Next button in the upper-right portion of the dialog. The installer then opens a dialog where you confirm that all the settings are correct.

5. Click Next in the upper right of this screen after you verify the settings. You will see an "OK" after it completes its run.

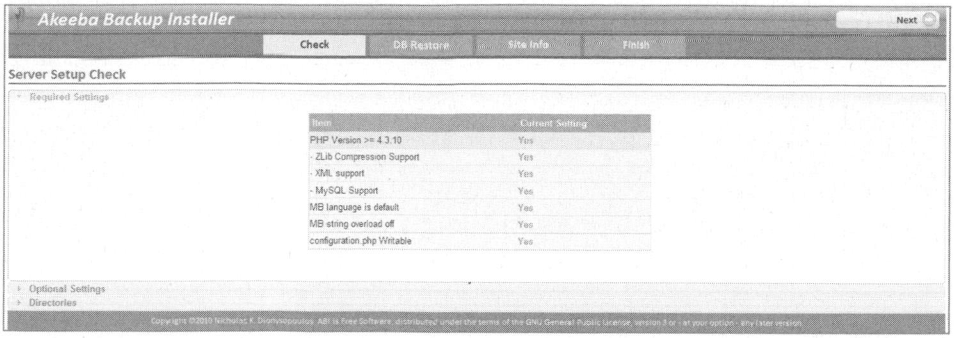

Figure 6-13: Akeeba Backup Installer

6. Click through the next screen. The Site Parameters dialog appears. Here you can set the site name, the e-mail address, the URL of the site, and additional instructions. Fill in the details and click Next.

7. Remove the `installation` directory that was temporarily added. Click OK and Next. The following message appears:

```
The installation directory has been deleted. Pressing OK will
redirect you to your site's home page.

Thank you for trusting Akeeba Backup installer for your site's
restoration!
```

8. Click OK; the restoration process is complete.

The next restoration method is very similar in nature, but is used if you have a new server, you are moving hosts, you have lost your site entirely, or you otherwise require a full install on a new server.

Scenario Two: Moving or Upgrading a Server

The developers at Akeeba have crafted a tool known as *Kickstart*. This tool unarchives a `.jpa` file after it's loaded up on a server.

The process to use Kickstart is very similar to the previous method. Follow these easy steps:

1. Upload the `.jpa` file (or files) to your `public_html` (or your web root) directory.

2. Upload `kickstart.php` to your web root directory.

3. From your browser, open your website as follows:

```
domain.com/kickstart.php
```

This identifies the file and presents you with the screen shown in Figure 6-14.

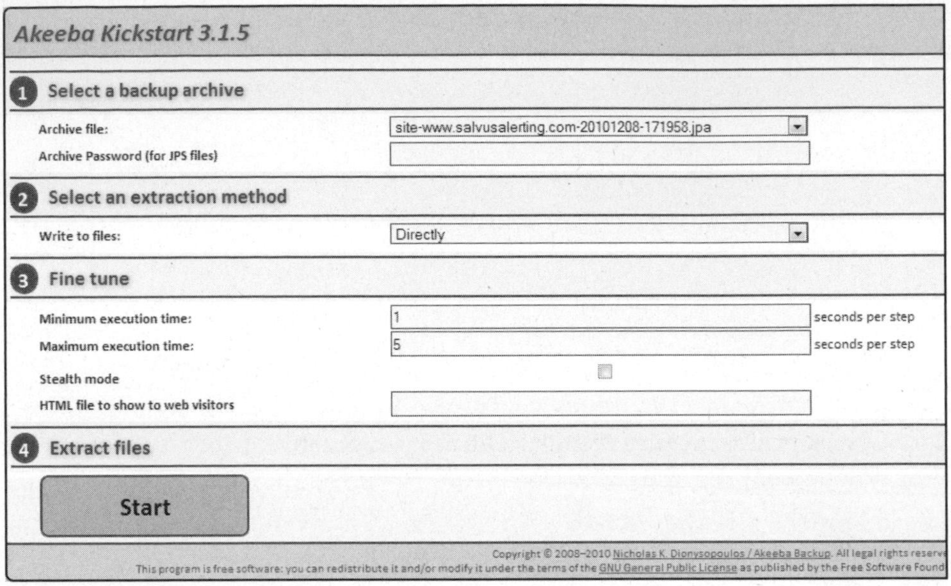

Figure 6-14: Starting Kickstart

4. Choose the proper archive file, if you have more than one, and click the Start button to continue the installation.

5. You will see the application extract the files from the archive. Follow the prompts to get to the installer. (The installer process is identical to the one described in step 3 of the first scenario.)

After you go through these steps, your site should be fully restored.

WordPress Backup and Restoration

A convenient plug-in for WordPress backup and restoration is the Automatic WordPress Backup tool, which is available for download at `www.webdesign company.net/automatic-wordpress-backup`. This tool features easy installation and use.

Requirements

Following are the system requirements for this tool:

- Linux
- PHP version 5 (or greater)
- An upload folder (`wp-content`) with write permissions

This plug-in tests your server setup for required and optional needs automatically. After the plug-in determines that all the required software is either enabled or installed, you are ready to go.

Configuration

This tool has a number of available configuration options, including the following:

- *AWS Access Key* — This is your Amazon S3 access key.
- *AWS Secret Key* — This is your Amazon S3 secret key.
- *S3 Bucket Name* — This is your storage folder on Amazon S3.
- *Backup schedule* — Your options here are None, Daily, Weekly, or Monthly. This handles the automated scheduled backups for you.
- *Parts of your blog to back up* — You can select all the checkboxes here for a full backup, or only some for a partial backup. The partial backup could be treated as an incremental backup.
- *Delete backups older than one month* — You have a few options here to mix and match. These will be checked based on your needs and your available storage.

Backups

After you have selected all the desired options, you can save your changes and return to blogging, or you can save changes and back up now. The latter choice will conduct a manual backup.

Restoration

To conduct a restore, log in to `wp-admin` and locate the plug-in from the menu. Scroll down until you see the "Restore from a backup" tab. Click the tab.

Your only choices are from which database to restore, and whether or not to change the database settings. After making your choices, click "Restore from backup" and you're done.

By early 2011, the next release of this tool will be available. According to the developers, it will have an updated interface and a file-by-file upload for very large sites.

Plone Backup and Restoration

On the whole, Plone is a very different system than the other CMSs discussed in this book. The only commonality among the four CMSs is that they can all run on Linux or Windows.

There the similarities end. Plone is a very robust and powerful CMS. It also requires a higher degree of technical skill for administration versus the other CMSs in this book. The user side for content management is very friendly and easy to use. However, administration is not as simple.

Requirements

Overall, if Zope is running after your install, then you have met all the requirements you need to for doing a basic Plone backup. Scripts are available to automate the backup and make it much easier than doing it manually.

The main requirement you will need is the capability to log in to your server via SSH and use the `tar` and `mv` commands.

Configuration

No configuration is required for the simple backup method described here.

Backups

Plone stores its essential data in a few files. The idea is to back up the following files:

```
/var/filestorage/Data.fs
/var/blobstorage
/products
```

In essence, you can probably just back up the `/var/filestorage/Data.fs` file, because it should contain everything. The following steps describe the simplest method for backing up Plone:

1. Log in to your management console as follows:

   ```
   http://localhost:8080/manage
   ```

2. A login screen appears; enter your username and password.

3. After you are logged in, open the Zope Management Console shown in Figure 6-15. This will allow you to view the database status and other elements of your Plone site.

4. To reach the Database, click Control_Panel ➢ Database. The Database Manager allows you to view database status information. It also allows you to perform maintenance tasks, such as database packing and cache management. For example, you might see database information is as follows:

- *Database Location* — `/usr/local/Plone/zinstance/var/filestorage/Data.fs`

- *Database Size* — 1.2M

Your database size will differ and your file location *may differ*.

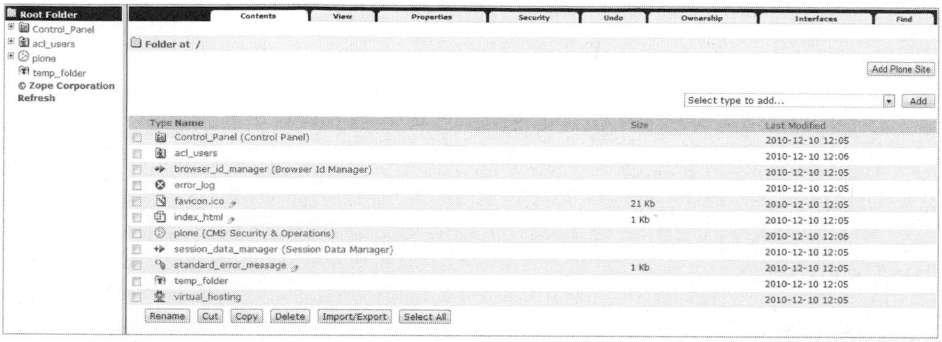

Figure 6-15: Zope Management Console

5. Select the database from the Zope Console. Click the database to bring up the `pack` menu.

6. The next step is to pack the database. Select the number of days back from today that you wish to back up. For today, leave it at zero. Once you have the number of days back to back up, click `pack`.

   Note that, when complete, this function will not provide you much in the way of a completion message. Rather, this function creates the `Data.fs.old` file, which is your packed and safe-to-use file. If you try to back up the `Data.fs` file while the site is running, you may encounter problems. If you need to back up the `Data.fs` file, shut down the site using the following command:

   ```
   ./bin/plonectl stop
   ```

7. Copy the `Data.fs.old` file. Use the following command to archive (compress) the database file:

   ```
   tar -cvf Data.fs.old.tar.gz Data.fs.old
   ```

   After you complete this, you must capture the two directories previously mentioned, `blobstorage` and `products`.

8. To reach the directory on an example server, you would use the following:

   ```
   CD /usr/local/Plone/zinstance/var
   ```

Run the following command:

```
tar -cvf blobstorage.tar.gz blobstorage/.
```

This archives the contents and directory structure of `blobstorage`.

9. Change the directory to `/usr/local/Plone/zinstance`.

10. Using the `tar` command, archive the `Products` directory as follows:

```
Tar -cvf products.tar.gz products/.
```

Suppose you have already copied all the `tar` files and the `Data.fs.old` to a directory called `PloneBackup`. Next, you `tar` all that into one file and copy it from your server by using the following command:

```
tar -cvf  BackupNameDate.tar.gz PloneBackup/
```

This creates a full backup of the Plone site. Your final step for safety would be to copy that down using FTP or SSH (whichever is appropriate to your setup). Store that archive off of the server for restoration purposes.

Restoration

If you need to restore, first shut down Plone using the following command to stop Plone from running:

```
./bin/plonectl stop
```

Next, run the `tar -xvf archive.tar` file to extract the files. Overwrite the respective file locations with the backup data. You need to rename `Data.fs.old` to `Data.fs` for it to work on the live site.

Following are some advanced resources to assist you in developing a more robust backup and restore process. Some of these address the capability to do incremental, full, and snapshot backups.

- `http://plone.org/documentation/kb/backup-plone`
- `http://pypi.python.org/pypi/collective.recipe.`
  `backup#easy-zope-backup-restore-recipe-for-buildout`
- `http://ingeniweb.sourceforge.net/Products/PloneMaintenance/`

Drupal Backup and Restoration

The Backup and Migrate module is an excellent choice for backup and restoration in Drupal. You can find it at `drupal.org/project/backup_migrate`.

This particular module is very powerful and feature-rich. It was contributed to the Drupal community by Ronan Dowling of Gorton Studios. Using this module in combination with Drupal's Backup and Migrate Files option will provide you with a complete solution. With it, you can back up and restore an entire Drupal site. You can store the backup on a remote FTP server or Amazon S3, or e-mail your backup.

One particular feature that is especially useful is the capability to use AES encryption to protect your backup files.

Requirements

The requirements for backup and restoration depend on the Drupal version you are using. The Files module requires the server to have PEAR and Archive_Tar installed.

This method has been tested with MySQL and Apache. Other environments are not covered in this book.

Configuration

Follow the normal Drupal procedure for installing and enabling the modules.

NOTE If you are not familiar with Drupal module installation, see `http://drupal.org/documentation/install/modules-themes`.

Portions of this module require cron to be run. Log in to cPanel and locate the Cron Job button. Click it and select Standard. The Standard Cron Manager page opens, as shown in Figure 6-16.

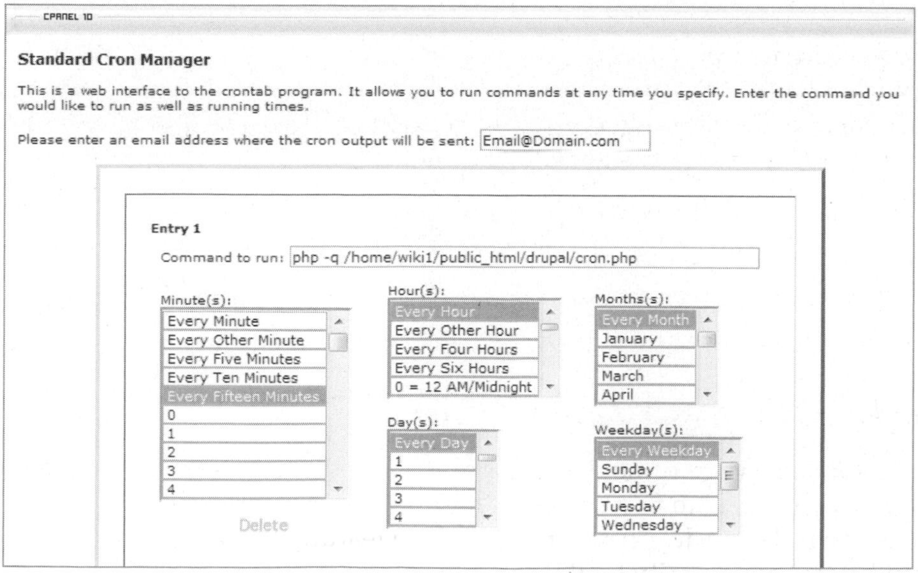

Figure 6-16: Standard Cron Manager

In "Entry 1," enter the following command:

```
php -q /home/site_directory/public_html/drupal/cron.php
```

The path you enter is specific to your setup.

This allows the scheduler in the Backup and Migrate module to run. Set the options you want for your particular system, and then click Save.

Next, log in to your administrator console in Drupal. For the purposes of this walkthrough, let's say the Admin Menu module has been installed, so you will be starting there:

1. Open the Admin Menu and select Content Management ➢ Backup and Migrate. The module opens, as shown in Figure 6-17.

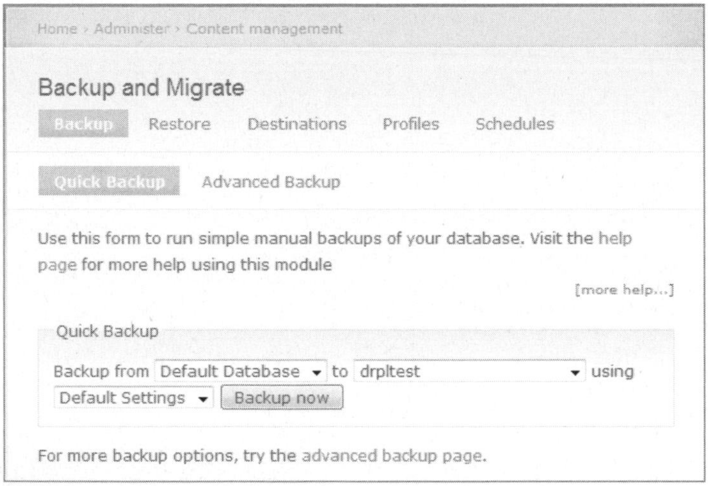

Figure 6-17: Backup and Migrate module

2. Click Profiles to set up your specific needs. For the List Profiles option, you will see listed the Default Settings, which is standard. For the purposes of this walkthrough, a profile called `files` has been created. From this screen, click "Create a new profile"; the Create Profile screen appears, as shown in Figure 6-18.

3. Fill in the Profile Name and "Backup file name" fields. Select any additional timestamp, compression, and file encryption options that fit your needs.

4. Scroll down the page to see the following categories of options:

   ▪ *Database Options* — These allow you to include or exclude tables from a database, and/or the data in tables.

   ▪ *File Backup Options* — These allow you to exclude specific files or directories from your backup.

■ *Advanced Options* — This is where you can enter your e-mail notification for successful or failed backups, as well as take the site offline during the backup.

Select your options, and then click the "Save profile" button.

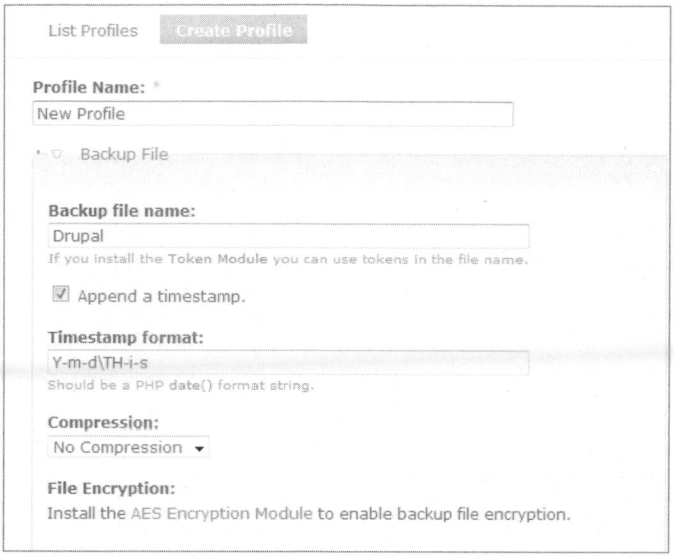

Figure 6-18: Create Profile options

5. Click the Schedules tab, on which you can set up a schedule for your backups. Under the Operations heading, select "edit" to modify a schedule, or "delete" to remove it. You want to add a new schedule, so click "Create new schedule." The screen shown in Figure 6-19 appears.

6. Choose a name for the new schedule, what it should back up (database or files), the profile it's attached to, and the backup frequency. The number of backup files to keep is strictly up to you.

7. Note that the Destination in the sample shown is set for Scheduled Backups Directory. This could be a security risk if someone were able to browse your directories. Choose a different destination, or click the "Create new destination" button, which opens the screen shown in Figure 6-20.

If you click the List Destinations tab, you will see all the locations on this site. If you click the Create Destination tab, you will see the options shown in Figure 6-20.

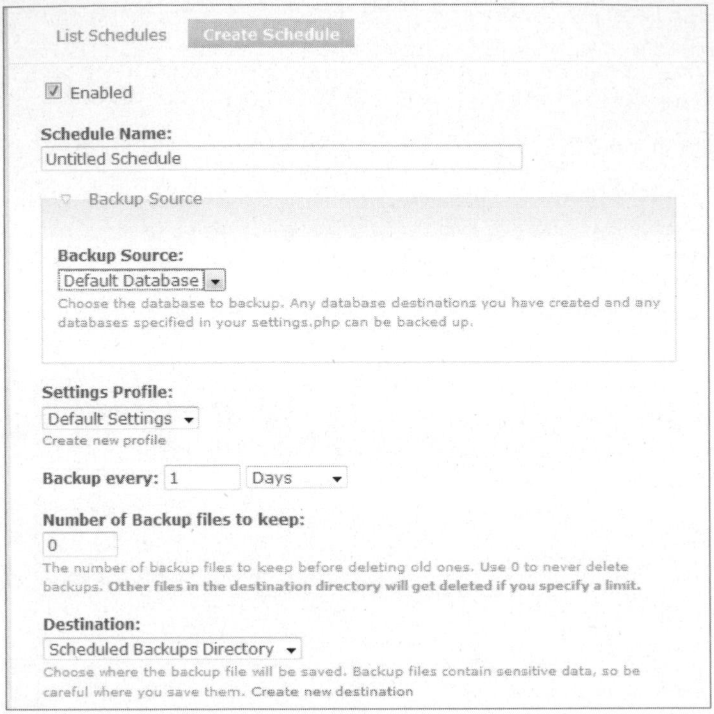

List Schedules   Create Schedule

☑ Enabled

Schedule Name:

Untitled Schedule

▽   Backup Source

Backup Source:

Default Database ▾

Choose the database to backup. Any database destinations you have created and any databases specified in your settings.php can be backed up.

Settings Profile:

Default Settings ▾

Create new profile

Backup every: 1   Days ▾

Number of Backup files to keep:

0

The number of backup files to keep before deleting old ones. Use 0 to never delete backups. **Other files in the destination directory will get deleted if you specify a limit.**

Destination:

Scheduled Backups Directory ▾

Choose where the backup file will be saved. Backup files contain sensitive data, so be careful where you save them. Create new destination

Figure 6-19: Creating a new schedule

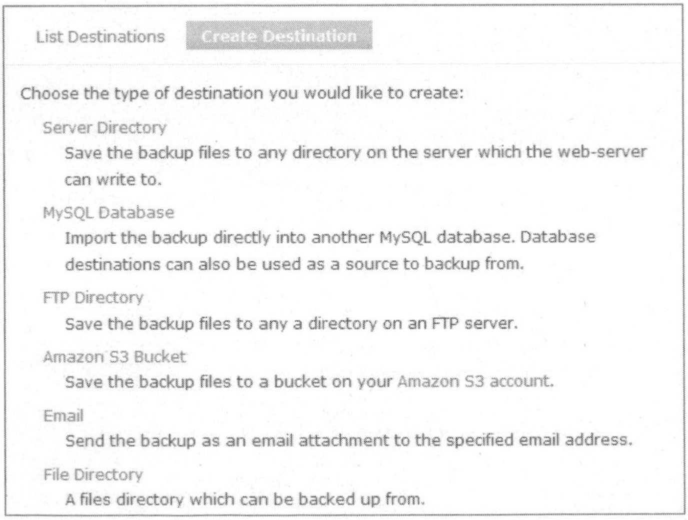

List Destinations   Create Destination

Choose the type of destination you would like to create:

Server Directory

    Save the backup files to any directory on the server which the web-server can write to.

MySQL Database

    Import the backup directly into another MySQL database. Database destinations can also be used as a source to backup from.

FTP Directory

    Save the backup files to any a directory on an FTP server.

Amazon S3 Bucket

    Save the backup files to a bucket on your Amazon S3 account.

Email

    Send the backup as an email attachment to the specified email address.

File Directory

    A files directory which can be backed up from.

Figure 6-20: Create Destination

Backups

After you work through your configuration options, you have a wealth of options for backing up as well. From the Backup and Migrate page, click the Backup tab. On the ensuing screen, you see the following two tabs:

- *Quick Backup* — Clicking this tab allows you to make an immediate backup. When the backup completes, the following message appears:

```
Default Database backed up successfully to Drupal-Files-
2010-12-09T14-11-35 in the destination drpltest in 805.26 ms.
(download, restore, delete)
```

- *Advanced Backup* — Clicking this tab enables you to select the Load Settings, profile to use, the backup source, the backup filename, the timestamp format, the compression to use, and file encryption (including AES for greater security).

If you click the Database Options, you can exclude specific database tables and/or data from those tables, as shown in Figure 6-21. You'll note when you scroll down that the cache data tables are excluded by default.

Figure 6-21: Advanced Backup Database Options

There might be directories and files you do not want to back up. Click File Backup Options to exclude them.

To keep up with the success or failure of your backups, click Advanced Options and enter the appropriate e-mail addresses, as shown in Figure 6-22. You'll note that you can have two *different* e-mail addresses. Additionally, you can take the site offline during the backup.

Finally, click Backup Destination to choose a *destination* for your backup.

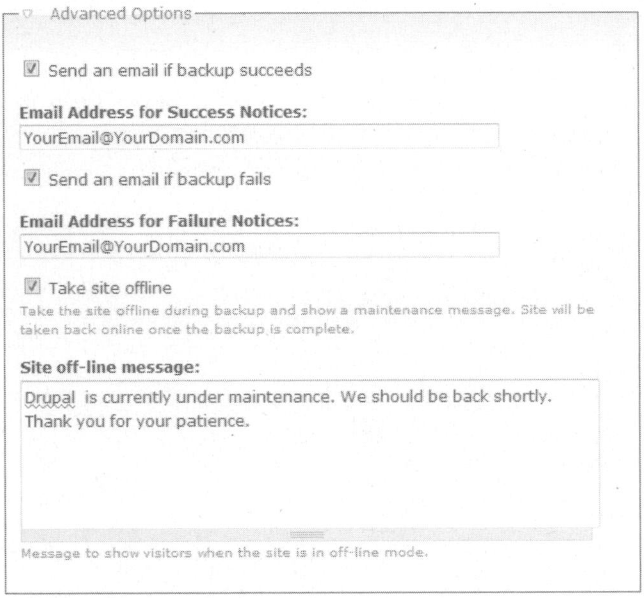

Figure 6-22: Advanced Backup e-mail options

After selecting all of your options, click the "Backup now" button to complete the backup process.

Restoration

When it comes time to restore, you will find the operation to be very easy. Begin by clicking the Restore tab from the Backup and Migrate screen.

To restore, in the "Restore to" drop-down list, choose restore to the database *or* restore the files of your site. The Advanced options allow you to take the site offline during a restoration. Using this method you can quickly recover from most any issue.

WARNING   Restoring will overwrite some or all of your data. Do not do it indiscriminately.

After you complete the restoration a success message appears. In Figure 6-23, the message indicates a successful restoration to an earlier version of the database.

Snapshots in Drupal

You can *snapshot* your Drupal site in order to roll back to an earlier version. This method is good for development or demo sites. It can be a backup method, as long as you copy down the files. The module is known as the Demo module. For more information and a short instructional video, see `http://cmsquickstart` `.com/blog/backing-your-drupal-site`.

Figure 6-23: Restoration of drupal.sql

Considerations for Setting Up Alternative Web Hosts

Today, the low cost of hosting providers enables you to have a "hot" standby available. As part of your disaster recovery plan, you may want to mirror your content over to an alternative site. Another use could be a development platform separate from your production site.

Although many good reasons exist for having an alternative host, you should consider a number of things. Here are a few items to think through regarding the use of an alternative provider:

- Does your business need to justify the added cost of pursuing an alternate provider? This will be not only a monthly or annual cost, but there is a hidden "people cost" as well.

- Do you need the added or unnecessary complexity in your disaster plan?

- Are you familiar with the different procedures between hosting companies?

- Have you thought through the DNS or IP considerations (such as the added time) for an alternate site?

- When using mail services from your host, have you considered moving them over? Processes such as FTP or SSH should be clearly documented and tested to ensure they work.

These are just a few of the things that you will need to think about, but there are many more.

Additional Considerations

Before wrapping up this chapter, you must consider some loose ends that your disaster recovery plan should take into account. These are items that you may not think about, but are vital to your success.

E-mail System

E-mail is the lifeblood of many companies today. In fact, it's sometimes the only method you have to reach your clients. You might consider using an e-mail provider (such as Google Apps) to support your e-mail.

In any case, be sure that you have a good, solid — that means tested — plan to migrate your e-mail and systems in the event your host goes dark.

Where Does Your DNS Live?

While writing this chapter, the author received a phone call from a client whose hosting company literally shut its doors without warning. The customer service phone was gone, the primary site was gone, and the client was dead in the water. To make matters worse, the client did not have a backup of multiple sites, and the client's e-mail was gone.

This client had few options. On the encouraging side, however, the client's DNS is at a very large hosting company. With that, she could quickly get e-mail flowing again at a minimum. The client was able to point her DNS to a new host, set up e-mail, and start the journey of rebuilding her sites.

The moral of this story is that if her DNS had been living with the *super low-cost* hosting company, she would have been completely lost.

Where does your DNS live? You should park your domains with a large and healthy *registrar*. This step, combined with your backups, will keep you safe from the nightmare of the hosting company going dark, and eliminating the phone lines issue that this client experienced.

In your disaster plan, include an option for documenting your DNS, and some tested plans to move it if need be.

Planning for Lost, Damaged, or Dated Equipment

Loss of equipment is typically an issue for any size of business. The loss of a system or mobile device with sensitive data on it can represent a form of a disaster. For example, if passwords and other authentication information are on the lost media, a malicious person could compromise your systems.

Theft represents another avenue of loss that could be used to get your data.

Loss of service to your systems can occur through a failed server component, loss of a hard drive (or drives), or through any other network systems, among other things.

Dated equipment that has reached its end of life is a serious issue. If a problem or vulnerability is discovered in the BIOS (firmware) or the software drivers, for example, they may not be supported. That would mean you would have to buy new equipment. If you do not have it in your budget, you may be stuck using vulnerable equipment.

Local Equipment

Your plan needs to account for the loss of data on equipment such as a notebook computer or mobile devices (such as smart phones). You must account for both backing up the data and protecting the equipment with either locking devices or disk-encryption (for mobile devices).

Be sure you review what you would do if your building suffered from the *smoking hole syndrome*, which is a disaster that completely wipes out the building because of any number of horrific causes. Would your employees have a place to work? If so, would they have equipment to work with?

These hard questions cannot be answered simply by saying that you would buy new equipment. Following are a few data points about local equipment you should keep in mind:

- Operating systems license keys
- Application source (installation disks) and licenses
- Data on the drives
- Replacement cost of equipment
- Potential liabilities for specific industries

Be sure you look around at your everyday IT equipment and include a plan for its disaster recovery.

Summary

This information-packed chapter discussed the need for a disaster recovery plan, no matter what the size of your business. All businesses are at risk if they cannot recover from a serious outage within a week.

Developing a plan and a team, and testing your plan are tasks that will sharpen your skills and raise the likelihood you'll recover from a disaster or serious outage.

In this chapter, you learned about backup and restoration processes and tools for each CMS. You also learned about some loose-end items such as e-mail, local equipment, and DNS systems.

You should spend considerable time on the disaster recovery topic and formulate your own plan to protect your business.

With disaster recovery planning out of the way, Chapter 7 dives into a methodology for developing and running a successful patching process for your websites and systems.

Patching Process

If you have used a Windows desktop, then you are already familiar with the idea of patching, which Microsoft refers to as an *update*. These updates download automatically (assuming you have set it up to do so) on a regular basis and then are applied. This helps keep the operating system at its safest level. The patching process is built into modern versions of Windows, giving Microsoft a great method to help all Windows users stay safe.

Likewise, a similar process is built into distributions of Linux. For example, in CentOS, you use the yum command, which checks predetermined *repositories* for updates. If it finds them, it will ask you whether you want to download and apply them. Although this process can be automated, it's often done manually.

As you'll see in this chapter, the process of patching a CMS does not necessarily work in the same manner. In fact, most of the time (with rare exception), you must conduct this process manually. The patching process consists of a methodology to monitor, test, apply, and document. The actual application of the patch is nearly the last step in the process.

Understanding the Patching Process

If your business consists of more than one person, and you have the luxury of an IT staff, then equipping that team with a process like the one described in this chapter can make for smooth upgrades.

This team should be organized around a process, rather than around a person. By doing so, you can quickly substitute for a person who is on vacation or who may not be available. The process described in this chapter is called the *patching process*. It follows seven general steps:

1. Monitor information sources for patches, vulnerabilities, and updates.

2. Back up your site and your database

3. Download the patch. (If one does not exist, you must provide a workaround.)

4. Test the patch to determine that it works and that it does not break anything in the process.

5. Deploy the patch following the instructions specific to your operating system, CMS, or hardware device.

6. Run another backup of the site and database after you patch.

7. Document the work you conducted and then return to Step 1.

As you can see, the patching process involves much more than just grabbing a patch from a website, applying it, and moving on to the next task.

Another factor that may be pertinent in the patching process is what takes place after a successful patch application. Returning to the Microsoft Windows desktop example, if you download a patch and apply it to your desktop, it might require a reboot, which is not really a big deal for your basic user. However, a reboot of a server operating system can be a real problem, because rebooting a server is an event that can affect many, many people. A rebooted machine may have services that need to be manually restarted, or have specific settings that may change. So many things are involved with a reboot. Part of your process should be to document the server settings before reboot.

Understanding the Need for the Patching Process

You may be thinking that you don't necessarily need to patch, or that you don't really have the time to go through the process. That is definitely the mindset of many site owners today. However, if you ignore patching, you are doing so at your own peril. That is not a lighthearted statement; it's backed up by research.

For example, in 2003, a worm was released on the Internet that swept literally around the world in a few short hours. Its target was Microsoft SQL servers. It attacked any SQL Server instance that did not have a specific patch. The issue was that the patch had been available for several months. Applying it would have neutralized the attack. The cost was incalculable, and the downtime was embarrassing. Companies (both large and small) were hit by this attack, crippling infrastructures, and stopping worldwide commerce. Numerous studies have been conducted using publicly available information that shows the act of patching would have stopped the bulk of attacks. One study published in

2000 written by Hilary K. Browne and William A. Arbaugh of the University of Maryland, and John McHugh and William L. Fithen of the Software Engineering Institute, was entitled, "A Trend Analysis of Exploitations." In that study, the authors proposed a theory that states after a patch is released, users who do not apply it are exposed to an excessive window of opportunity for attacks. Specifically, they noted the following:

> *"The data we extracted confirms the hypothesis in which the vast majority of exploits occur long after patches that would thwart them are available — demonstrating that poor administrative procedures are an enabling factor."*

Note the part that says, *"exploits occur long after patches that would thwart them are available."* In other words, most of the time, you could have prevented being hacked.

Thus, you should patch to protect your site from exploits and attacks. This won't remove the attempts, but it will lower the threat surface that enables the kiddie scripters and professional hackers from launching a successful attack against your site.

Financially speaking, if you are hacked, then you are exposing yourself to undue burden of costs such as cleanup, loss of customer goodwill, as well as potential fines and levies. In some states in this country, certain types of data loss could be considered a crime.

What about respect and credibility of your site? Today, a trust with your clients may *only* be established through your website. A publicized hack will likely become bigger in the eyes of the public than it really is. In other words, it could easily be blown out of proportion. The loss of customer respect could be great. That is not something you can simply buy back. Consumers are unlikely to share personal or financial details (such as credit card information) with a website that had been hacked and had information stolen. Keep this in mind as you read through the remainder of this book.

Patching can prevent attacks on your systems and sites. It is part of a good set of administrative practices, and it can have a positive material and direct effect on your financial bottom line.

Either the site administrator or an IT group is typically responsible for patching. The organizational requirements for this responsibility are straightforward, but are often ignored. The following sections take a look at organizational requirements and how you can implement them.

Organizational Requirements

No matter the size of your company or your support staff, you will have specific requirements for the staff to ensure a smooth operation. This section looks at requirements for the medium to large organization, as well as the small one-person shop.

Medium to Large Organization

In medium to larger organizations, organizational requirements for the patching process may involve outside parties (such as other company divisions) or clients (such as a telecom group). If a change occurs in the way things work, then your client base will be a downstream recipient of the changes. The changes applied might require a marketing person or training group in the event of a workflow change or new training requirements. Generally speaking, situations that require the interaction of marketing or training and patching are rare.

The patching group should be given the task and authority to conduct the following activities:

- Track down and document a system-wide inventory that includes servers, desktops, mobile computers, network equipment, firewalls, your CMS, and other corporate information resources.

- While collecting the inventory, the group should have the skill to identify the operating system version and settings, drivers installed, firmware of machines, and any physical configurations.

- The person or group should be required to track down and monitor for updates, patches, workarounds, and other issues that could impact your security. The members of this organization should be able to make some intuitive leaps in judgment to essentially connect the dots. This means that the organization should have a very good working knowledge of the infrastructure.

- Optionally, your group should have a person or persons (either on staff, or perhaps a third party) to work with who understands and has coding skills for the programming language in your CMS.

Your organization should have strong technical skills, good communication skills, and good documentation that is available to the team responsible for patching. As the manager, you should establish a well-defined escalation path within this organization to take care of issues and have someone the team can reach out to in the event of trouble.

Creating a Team

This discussion assumes you have in place some form of a team. The idea of team creation could be one of staffing, but in this discussion, it's more about organizing a team around the patching methodology.

This team could be an ad hoc team that comes together for the purpose of upgrades and patching, or the team could be dedicated to the task. Unless you are a large enterprise company, your team will fall under the ad hoc umbrella. The team will adopt the patching process as a means to monitor and mitigate threats and vulnerabilities.

Creating Patching Standards

The first task that this team should do is to develop a patch standard. No standard is being proposed in this chapter, because each company's implementation will vary in design. However, at a minimum, the standard should include the following:

- A list of sites to monitor for patches
- A method for testing the updates
- A documented procedure to follow for backing up
- A developed standard for documenting fixes

The idea is to create a standardized workflow and procedure to facilitate updating and repairing your code. This does not have to be a long and wordy effort. It could be something as easy as a spreadsheet based on the template shown in Figure 7-1.

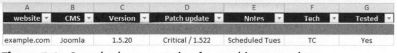

	A	B	C	D	E	F	G
	website	CMS	Version	Patch update	Notes	Tech	Tested
	example.com	Joomla	1.5.20	Critical / 1.522	Scheduled Tues	TC	Yes

Figure 7-1: Sample documentation for patching procedure

In this very simple spreadsheet, you see the technician has captured the domain, the current version of the CMS, and notes about the update.

Assessing Threats

The team should take on the task of assigning priorities to incoming threats measured against the impact of the threats to the organization. For example, if you have a very important WordPress blog, and a vulnerability is found that would allow a successful attack to yield admin control, then that's a critical priority.

Even if you have a single website, it usually contains enough software that you should assign a threat level to the points of vulnerability that may affect your site. If you have a number of vulnerabilities, or a number of sites, assigning a priority to each vulnerability is the best approach to ensure that you work on solving the problems in order of priority.

One good tool is to use a *threat matrix* for such situations.

Using a Threat Matrix

The idea of the threat matrix is to give you a quick visual of where you might encounter security trouble. Your team should be in charge of preparing this matrix and should cross-train to ensure all members can use it.

Table 7-1 shows a sample to help you understand the concept.

Table 7-1: Sample Threat Matrix for yoursite.com

VULNERABILITY	TARGET	THREAT	VIABILITY	PATCH AVAILABLE	ACTION
Buffer overflow	Operating system	Critical	High	Yes	Patch as soon as possible
SQL injection	Contact form	High	High	No	Edit code
Information disclosure	CMS	Low	Low	No	Monitor until a patch is available

This matrix helps the team discover and prioritize what really matters in its setup. In this example, the operating system would be the first choice on which to focus attention. Following that would be the "Contact form." As you see, there is not a patch for the "Contact form," only vulnerability. In this example, the team could either disable the "Contact form," or edit the code to fix it. As you can see in this example, the code correction would require a member of your team to have some coding skills.

Developing this matrix can also help you to identify where you are weak in terms of resources. You may discover that you need a better developer, or other areas that need attention. You may find you're very out of date on patching. And you'll see where you could be hit by the bad guys, and the impact such an attack might have.

Single-Person Business

As a sole proprietor or a small business, you clearly have other issues on your mind (such as cash flow, revenue, marketing, and other business needs). You may be limited on resources, and, thus, you can greatly benefit from a patching process.

The challenge is that if you ignore the technical needs of your site, one hack getting through could easily disrupt your cash flow. Thus, the time and cost you put into developing this process will pay off in the long run. If you are hacked, the costs of recovering from the hack would greatly exceed the cost of prevention.

On the flip side, as a small business, you likely do not have a great deal of the equipment and various software packages to keep track of. This makes your baseline report much easier to do and your threat matrix smaller than one used for a larger company.

If you are a small business, the following is a quick list of the tasks and functions that can help you be a team of one:

- Ensure that you have a complete (and frequent) backup.

- Ensure that you remove all unneeded software from your website.

- Apply all the available and necessary patches to your CMS and third-party add-ons. (If you have not done this in a while, you may have a long list of items.)

- Create a spreadsheet to track your version and update information.

- Contact your host to ensure that the server is properly updated.

The last bullet point could be difficult if you do not know the right questions to ask. This is not an indictment of any hosting companies, but rather an observation about technical people in general. Typically, when asked, a technical person will provide a straightforward answer to a technology question. Suppose the question is, "Is my server safe?" The answer will likely be "yes." That doesn't make it so, but rather is the *answer* to the question you asked. The better question to ask is, "Does my CentOS operating system have all the most up-to-date patches applied?"

Following are some areas that you want to address with your host to be sure you're up to date:

- If you're running an Apache web server, your server may be running any number of versions. Take the time to find the version of your current system. After you do, review the change logs available from `http://projects.apache.org/projects/http_server.html`.

- Find out whether operating system patches have been applied. (The distributions of Linux you might hear are Red Hat, CentOS, Gentoo, Debian, Ubuntu, mandrake, and others.)

- What is the host's policy on updates and patches?

- Is MySQL Server up to date and running the most current patches?

- Check with the host and find out the BIND (Berkeley Internet Domain Services) version that you're on. It should be at a minimum of the 9.xx series and be patched.

- Ensure that PHP is running version 5.xx. Note that version 4.xx has reached its end of life and should be updated. Many hosts are still running the 4.xx version. Note that some older PHP applications may fail on 5.xx. Test before upgrading.

- Verify that your version of Python (for Plone users) is up to date and patched.

Starting with a reputable host will ensure that many of these issues are already taken care of. Hosts such as `GoDaddy.com`, `Rochen.com`, `WiredTree`

`.com` and `Rackspace.com` are some examples of hosts that are considered reputable, though this list is by no means exhaustive.

Security Metrics

Author W. Edwards Deming has been considered by many to be the father of modern quality. He was an advocate of *processes* versus *quotas*.

His background was in manufacturing quality, but his principles still apply. He advocated crafting a process and the proper measurement, and then fine-tuning the process to achieve better numbers. He was against the ideas of "mass inspection" and "quotas." In this sense, a *quota* is pieces built per hour, or number of units inspected per hour.

Deming pointed out that, in manufacturing, you cannot put quality into a product through the process of mass inspection. It must be designed from the start, and that includes a process to create it. Including metrics for the sake of having metrics might be impressive to upper management, but they mean nothing if they are not applied in an effort to improve. In his extensive work in the manufacturing space, Deming advocated consistency and improvement within statistical boundaries, not just the inclusion of numbers.

Your infrastructure should be measured against a metric to determine the quality of your security. It should be a gauge of how safe your site is against attack. Note that the last sentence did not say "impervious to attack," because that site doesn't exist. Rather, there are degrees of safety, and the metrics examined next should help you reach a higher degree of safety.

Deming advocated *"constantly and forever"* improving quality. With that goal in mind, take a look at security metrics you can use to make a difference in the security of your site.

Determining What to Measure

Your first task is to decide what to measure. Will it be how quick a technical person answers a telephone? Or will it be how many days, weeks, or months it's been since your site was hacked? Whatever the measurement is, defining it and measuring it will be your first task.

Business leaders often think (correctly) that measuring everything you do is a great thing. Where they falter is in the idea of using this information as a punitive measure.

For an example, consider the telephone technical support world. A typical technical telephone representative is required to answer calls in "x" seconds, and only spend a specific amount of time on the phone. However, putting technical support in the firing line of a poorly designed product with bad documentation is wrong. Why not ask why you are getting a certain volume of calls and what you can improve to reduce that situation? What typically happens is that the technical support reps will miss statistical goals because they are buried or trying to help.

What's wrong with this picture is the technical support person is being held responsible for product design and education.

In your security metrics, as you measure both employee performance and things such as uptime, review the process in detail by tracing through the steps. Discover the *root cause* for the issues. Don't automatically accept the *"numbers are bad so the people are bad"* conclusion.

A few things that are important to measure in security can be tied directly to processes. These may include response time to patches, number of times your site is hacked (hopefully never), costs such as license fees, and, of course, uptime. For the purposes of this discussion, you want to measure and record the metrics surrounding the following:

- How susceptible is your system to attack?
- What is your response time from the notification of an available patch to the fix?
- What are the costs associated with each patch?

The idea behind this is to find out whether you are vulnerable, how long you will be vulnerable on average (after patch release), and what each of the patches cost you. The following sections examine each of these facets in a bit more detail.

Susceptibility to Attack

All sites are vulnerable to attack — some more, and some less. The idea behind measuring your susceptibility to attack is to lower your number. For the sake of this discussion, suppose a higher number means that you are more vulnerable, and that taking the steps to lower that number would make you safer.

This number could actually be represented numerically in two ways. For example, you could simply state, "I have four critical patches to apply." Or this number could be represented as a ratio, such as "I have 30 extensions (add-ons) on my site, and 15 are vulnerable to attack." In that case, 15 divided by 30 gives you a 50 percent ratio.

This example is a demonstration to help you calculate or devise your own metric. Determining how much of your software is vulnerable in your site can provide a metric to measure.

Response Time

Today, metrics are used for "response time," such as the foolish metric for on-time arrivals in the airline industry, or doctors being timed by insurance companies on how long they sit with patients. The issue with these metrics is they are punitive in nature; they do not provide a means for quality improvement.

In the response time category, you are interested in *reducing* the time from the notification to the fix. If you discover that many days are going by from the notification to the fix, then you have a problem in your process. Naturally, you want to design a process that guides the team in checking for and applying updates.

For example, suppose that on Monday at 9:00 a.m. local time, your team becomes aware of a critical patch that, if not applied and a hacker were later to exploit the vulnerability, could cause you great harm. The proper course of action is naturally to take care of this task as soon as possible.

A real-world example is the 2003 *Slammer* outbreak that impacted Windows Servers worldwide (see `http://en.wikipedia.org/wiki/SQL_Slammer` and `www.cseweb.ucsd.edu/~savage/papers/IEEESP03.pdf`) as well as airlines and ATM machines all over the globe. In fact, this particular virus spread itself worldwide within a few hours. The patch for it had been available from Microsoft for quite a while. Systems run by administrators who applied the patch before the outbreak were not infected. That's the kind of response-time metric you don't want to explain to your boss.

The response time metric needs to measure the time of notification to the time of either patching or remediation of the fix. You want the time that elapses between notifications to fixes to be as short as possible.

Include in the response time a period of time for emergency workarounds. Emergencies will happen, but not often. Tracking them is best so that you can either eliminate the emergencies as much as possible, or work to reduce the time.

Costs Associated with Each Patch

Normally, costs associated with each patch are not tracked, except in cases of license fees or other costs associated with an upgrade. However, you may want to track this metric to capture the cost per patch. Following are some suggestions of things to track:

- The amount of time spent to find the patch (in hours).
- The amount of time spent by each employee to apply a patch. Include after-hours costs or overtime, because this is a real financial figure.
- If the patch results in downtime, record the cost per hour.

One example might be where a development firm does a shoddy job, and then charges for "fixes" in the name of updates to the code. Real-world cases have also existed where development firms charge for several hours for applying patches that should only take 15 to 30 minutes to apply. This practice artificially drives up the cost. Even reputable technology services people or firms have spent and charged excessive time because the systems were not documented. You should track the time needed for all these tasks because they drive up cost.

A final example would be a hosting company that does not proactively update and allows you to get hacked. You should measure this in terms of the costs of hosting (that is, not taking care of you), or the cost to mitigate the damage and loss of your time.

Capture all the hard and soft costs, and measure the value your systems are providing you against the cost.

Eliminating Known Vulnerabilities from the Start

As you begin your initial patching, refer to the baseline you created in Chapter 4 and research your installation to ensure that your server and applications are up to current levels. If you have not patched in some time, you might be surprised at the amount of work you have ahead of you. You might even discover that your site has been hacked.

The goal is to eliminate all the known vulnerabilities and start with a very secure infrastructure. Key areas to focus on are the applications, the CMS, the operating system, and, of course, your desktops. Don't forget about those, because they will interact with and connect at some point to your website.

Monitoring for New Vulnerabilities

The earlier-mentioned study conducted by Browne, Arbaugh, McHugh, and Fithen concluded that *after* a patch is released, the number of attacks continue to rise at a very measurable level. The frequency of attack doesn't follow a nice, safe bell curve; rather, they are on a linear track upward.

The reason for that the longer a patch (or vulnerability) is published, the more hackers find out about it, and the more attempts are made against sites, with hackers using the vulnerability as a launching point to attack. They gamble that you have not patched your gear, and they are usually right. Their attacks are very successful because of the sheer number of available targets. Remember, if you *apply* a patch, you have likely foiled the attacker's efforts of launching a successful attack against you.

Because new vulnerabilities are discovered every day by developers, researchers, and criminals, tracking and monitoring the vulnerabilities is important. This seemingly easy task can quickly become burdensome as the number of vulnerabilities you must keep up with increases.

Making a list of the developer's websites and other *validated* resources is your step here.

Sources of Information Regarding Patches

Literally hundreds of sources are available for patch and vulnerability information. As mentioned previously, keeping a list of the ones that matter to you is a best practice. The following is a short list to get you started:

- The vendor of the software
- The project (CMS) website
- `http://nvd.nist.gov`
- `http://www.owasp.org`
- Commercially available services

Feel free to review other sources beyond these, but be sure you trust the content and any code they distribute.

Commercial Services

One service you may want to subscribe to is SalvusAlerting (`www.salvusalerting .com`). This service monitors and alerts subscribers about vulnerabilities, patches, and other security-related matters. (The author is a co-founder of SalvusAlerting.)

Another available commercial service is Qualys (`www.qualys.com`), which offers a host of vulnerability and security services.

Testing for Deployment

Testing is necessary to ensure that the patch you were given actually works in your environment. In enterprise businesses, patches are usually put through a rigorous set of tests to ensure that they comply with company information policies. The IT staff must be sure the patches work with the company applications.

Testing your patch may be as easy as merely determining whether it works, or it may be as complex as running a series of tests against it. The degree of testing depends on the patch and the environment.

Although laying out specific processes for your environment in this book is difficult, following are some questions you should consider:

- *Does the patch work?* — This is a yes/no question. Does it fix the issue in question? Does it break anything in your environment?

- *What are the monetary costs of the patch?* — This is strictly the cost to acquire the update. Normally, no cost should be involved.

- *What prerequisites are there for this patch*? — Find out whether you must uninstall the old code, reboot the machine, or have other code installed with it to make it work.

- *Do you have the expertise in-house to apply the patch*? — Some patches may include Apache Web Server upgrades, PHP updates, MySQL updates, and other compiled environments. This could be a situation where some coding must take place.

- *Will this patch result in procedural changes*? — Think about scenarios where backup/restores or other documented procedures will change.

- *Will this patch result in a reboot*? — Most of the time, this should be "no." However, if a patch requires the server to be rebooted before it can take effect, then a scheduled downtime is likely in order.

- *What downstream clients (internal or external) may be affected*? — What will the impact be to the user community? Will workflows, new login procedures, passwords, or other processes change?

- *What departments or organizations should you involve*? — This can include ancillary departments such as compliance, telecom, networking, or even outside vendors.

- *What systems may be impacted*? — For example, will your patch change your PCI compliance status?

- *Will this patch require a software developer or system administrator to update*? — This can be the case in instances such as PHP or Apache web server updates. Any time you have a compiled application, it involves more than just simply applying patches.

Other questions that may arise will be specific to your environment. After you add any additional questions to this list, set out to write a set of procedures to test and answer these questions before you deploy the patch.

Obtaining Safe Patches

Your methodology should take into account *where* the patches are coming from. A few cases have been documented in which a source was contaminated by a hacker, resulting in the distribution of hacked code.

Plenty of cases have also occurred where download sites have been hacked, which may leave you with the impression that the download may not be safe. Fortunately, this occurrence is rare, but be sure to scan everything with a virus-scanning program either during or after the download.

Some websites offer distribution of a patch that is not necessarily the vendor's or developer's site. These are referred to as *mirror* sites. They are usually very safe and should not present any problems.

Sites you should stay away from are sites that offer *free download* of commercially available products. These are known as *warez* (pronounced "wares") *sites*, and are often tainted with a virus. Avoid these for a variety of reasons, including the potential trouble they may bring on if they also serve up adult content. So, in short, stay away from them.

Always be certain that you are downloading the genuine article by visiting the developer's site.

Some developers offer a Message Digest 5 (MD5) hash that uniquely identifies that particular code. The *hash* is a string of alphanumeric characters that looks like `98d8ab5a01747009387c3f54db505e94`. Using any number of available MD5 tools, you can quickly check your version against its hash. If they don't match, don't use it. Download a new copy (and check again).

Deploying a Patch or Fix

Deployment of a patch hopefully should be an easy and straightforward process. Although several ways exist to conduct the actual installation of the patch, following are some of the more popular means you might encounter:

- Auto-update (as in Windows Update)
- Updaters (such as `yum` in Linux)
- Code with an install routine
- Updater scripts (such as `update.php` in Drupal)
- Recompilation of code (such as Apache)
- Editing code (typically through a text editor, and possibly done by a software developer)

You will find that the more mature products in the CMS space offer an installation-type routine. The less mature ones may offer code "fixes." Documenting your preferred method of setup ahead of time should be part of your process.

As an interesting example of software maturity, WordPress (3.0.x) offers the capability for a single-click update of the core CMS and the plug-ins. This makes a typical WordPress update very fast and painless. Get into the practice of conducting a backup before doing an auto-update of any code.

In the case of compiled code (for example, Apache), it's not a simple matter of updating the code with a patch. Updating Apache requires downloading the source and compiling the code on the machine. Take special care in these instances to preserve any configuration files, or you'll wind up doing a restore to gather them back up.

Distributing a Patch to Your Administrators

Plenty of small, medium, and large companies have more than one site or administrator. Your patch process should account for this situation if it exists in your environment.

Patches should be tested and distributed from a central group to the remote or other administrators. This practice ensures uniformity and, of course, system-wide security.

Establish as part of your process a means for the remote administrators to be notified of the patch, and how to report back on the application of it. This is a good example of how an online database could be used to collect the information.

When you distribute the patch, include a set of work instructions on how to implement the update.

In this organizational situation, you want everyone to follow a single set of instructions. Allowing remote admins to choose whether and when they patch is a recipe for trouble.

Documenting Your Patches

In the early days of the author's career, the PC "standard wars" were in full swing, and everyone was trying to make it to the top. His employer at the time had several wings of a massive industrial complex filled with mainframes and minicomputers. In the course of his job, whatever tasks he performed on the equipment in that environment were written down in a notebook. This note-book would stay with the equipment for others who came after him to know what he did.

In the same way, you should find a way for documenting your patches. You should make a complete list of what you did in some form. The following are items you should capture:

- *Date and time* — Always record the date and time the patch was deployed.

- *What patch version was applied?* — This may be a number, a notation, or other means to identify it.

- *What vulnerability or issue does this fix?* — This may be something along the lines of a SQL injection, XSS scripting error, or other non–security-related problems.

- *Who applied the patch?* — This is the developer, technician, company, and so on. You want to be able to reach out to the person responsible for its implementation.

- *What software or hardware system did you patch?* — This could be your CMS, a third-party add-on, a switch or router, and so on.

- *Where was the patch obtained from?* — This should include the source of the patch or the developer.

- *Any observations* — Did anything happen, such as errors or configuration changes?

- *Was a backup conducted post patch?* This is a yes/no question.

- *Dependencies* — This is a situation where you may need other patches or other software combined with this patch. Another dependency might be remembering if you must *back out* the patch. That is, if something breaks in the update, you'll need to know the process to roll it back.

- *Other* — Always provide a blank field for general use.

Once again, capture this information in a manner that works best for you.

Patching after a Security Breach

Chapter 9 discusses in detail the topic of being hacked. This brief discussion of the topic is meant to introduce you to a number of concerns should you need to apply a patch after being hacked. Here you will learn about some often-overlooked issues after a hack.

As mentioned earlier in this chapter, you are less likely to get hacked if you follow a timely patching routine, but it can still happen. There are times when you can do everything absolutely right and get hacked through an undisclosed vulnerability or a zero-day exploit. A *zero-day exploit* is an attack that seeks out an unpublished vulnerability. Usually, a hacker finds it and uses it for his or her gain to attack on wide scale. Often, the hacker will write an exploit and either sell it or deploy it. Fortunately, not many zero-day exploits and vulnerabilities occur. However, when they happen, they are devastating.

More than likely, you will be faced with patching after you were hacked, because you didn't patch, and thus were hacked. It's plain and simple: *Not patching is a poor administrative practice, and it will make you a target.*

Issues and Concerns

After you have been hacked, you must check a number of things. The list is long, but some areas of concern might be viruses, Trojan horses, Remote administration Trojan horse applications (RATs), ports open that should be closed, data copied off to unauthorized persons, tampered code, eavesdropping tools, and more.

Of course, the first step is to determine what damage has been done. One method to discover this is to look at the patches that have not been applied. You may be able to determine the exploit the bad guys used, hence what they changed/added. In this situation, patching is an emergency, and you may want to forgo testing of the patch and push it into deployment.

Even if it means backing up hacked and malware-infested software, the second step is to make a backup before you patch. Do this in the event you need to roll back the changes.

Rootkits

Rootkits are also known as *remote administration tools* or *trojans*. A number of them are available on the Internet, with varying degrees of features. Sadly, some of these could easily be very nice tools to manage a server, if they were not pressed into service for evil.

Following are some of the names of the files of the rootkits you may encounter:

- C99
- C100
- R57
- Stuxnet
- Zeus
- Bypass.txt
- Enlightenment
- SafeOver

Many of these give the hacker the capability to listen, record keystrokes (key logger), change files, mail out spam, and much more. The presence of any of these is a really bad problem.

You can find rootkits using tools such as `rkhunter` or a variety of others. Rootkits can and do evade detection very well. They fall into the *code-tampering* type of attack, where a process is hidden from normal view.

Also, be aware that many times, if a rootkit is embedded deep enough, simply moving the hosting, or reformatting and reinstalling the operating system, is the best solution.

Lastly, if you have a rootkit and you can see it in the files (via FTP or SSH), check the date. You might have had it for a while, and, as such, you may have backed it up many times. Your backups will no longer be viable from the current time back to when the rootkit was placed on there, unless you can remove it from your backups as well.

Viruses

Generically speaking, viruses fall into a number of classifications. The ones in the context of this discussion are the kind that attempt to download onto a visitor's computer via a browser.

This type of attack is known as a drive-by-download. If this happens, you may have been a victim of a cross-site scripting (XSS) attack, or you have an extension (third-party add-on) that is vulnerable to a *remote file injection*.

Clean up the virus code and patch. Then, check all your desktops because they are likely infected as well.

Code Tampering

One particular strategy a hacker may take is to tamper with code to maintain control over the system. This attack is slightly different than planting malware onto a system. In the Linux operating system, you have a number of ways to determine what *processes* are running. The idea is that if you are troubleshooting your server, you could look at the running processes and kill any you don't need, or start up ones you do need.

An example of code tampering might be if a hacker can gain enough access to your system, and then replace the utilities that provide the process status. The idea is that the hacker's version of the process monitor would *hide* any evil code the hacker may be running. Said a different way, run only what you need, and reduce the number of areas an attacker may seek out. A number of schools of thought exist on this topic. However, if a hacker has replaced key utilities on your server, then it's time to reformat the disk and reinstall.

Monitoring for Unauthorized Changes

If you want to monitor your system for unauthorized changes, install something like *TripWire* to the system (`http://sourceforge.net/projects/tripwire`), which will monitor your files and directories for changes. The best method is to start with a known good, clean system to ensure that no malware or replaced code is on it. TripWire (and other software packages that provide the same solution) will alert you to changes, allowing you to take a proactive stance.

Next, let's take a look at patching the various CMSs discussed in this book.

Patching a CMS

In the final section of this chapter, you learn about the particulars of each CMS in terms of updates. Each one does it differently than another.

NOTE Because technology is always changing, referring to the most current documentation before updating your CMS is best. As of this writing, what is presented here are the most current methods as documented by the CMS projects. Each CMS is in active development, meaning that updates are likely available for either your CMS or the add-ons for it.

Joomla!

Joomla! 1.5.xx does not offer a native means to update the CMS, but it's a very simple task to do. The CMS development team offers two versions of updates, and you can choose the one that works best for you.

Minor Version Patches

The minor version patch only updates the version from one dot release to the next.

NOTE To obtain the minor patch updates, visit `http://joomlacode.org/gf/project/joomla/frs`.

As you can see from Figure 7-2, the Joomla! code download is currently in development version 1.6, marked as beta. The figure also shows the Joomla! files.

Package Name	Latest Release	Maturity	Files	FileSize
Joomla1.6RC1	Joomla1.6.0RC1	4 - Beta	Joomla_1.6-RC1-Full_Package.zip	8.07 Mb
		4 - Beta	Joomla_1.6-RC1-Full_Package.tar.bz2	5.18 Mb
		4 - Beta	Joomla_1.6-RC1-Full_Package.tar.gz	5.97 Mb
Joomla1.5.22	Joomla1.5.22updates	6 - Mature	Joomla_1.5.15_to_1.5.22-Stable-Patch_Package.zip	1.53 Mb
		6 - Mature	Joomla_1.5.21_to_1.5.22-Stable-Patch_Package.tar.gz	91.15 Kb
		6 - Mature	Joomla_1.5.4_to_1.5.22-Stable-Patch_Package.tar.gz	2.04 Mb
		6 - Mature	Joomla_1.5.20_to_1.5.22-Stable-Patch_Package.zip	136.56 Kb
		6 - Mature	Joomla_1.5.21_to_1.5.22-Stable-Patch_Package.zip	131.24 Kb
		6 - Mature	Joomla_1.5.15_to_1.5.22-Stable-Patch_Package.tar.bz2	665.19 Kb

Figure 7-2: Joomla! minor version patch download

The packages are available as a ZIP format or a GZ format. The first of the 1.5 updates you see is for updating your version 1.5.15 site to version 1.5.22. If you notice further down, you could update from version 1.5.4 to 1.5.22. Each minor release always has an update like this to the current minor release.

Full Update Files

Another update method is to simply copy all the files from the full installation package. You can find this package on the home page of `Joomla.org`, as shown in Figure 7-3.

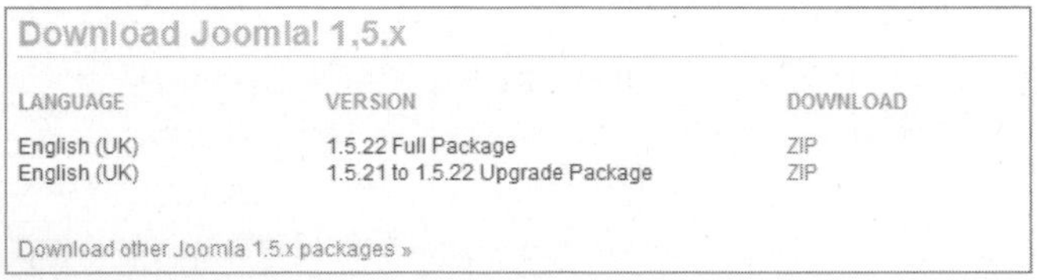

Download Joomla! 1.5.x

LANGUAGE	VERSION	DOWNLOAD
English (UK)	1.5.22 Full Package	ZIP
English (UK)	1.5.21 to 1.5.22 Upgrade Package	ZIP

Download other Joomla 1.5.x packages »

Figure 7-3: Download the latest Joomla!

WARNING Do not copy the `Installation` folder from the source file to your site for patching.

Conducting the Update

You upload and apply both minor and full updates in the same fashion, as follows:

1. Back up your site and database. For convenience, put the site into offline or maintenance mode, as shown in Figure 7-4.

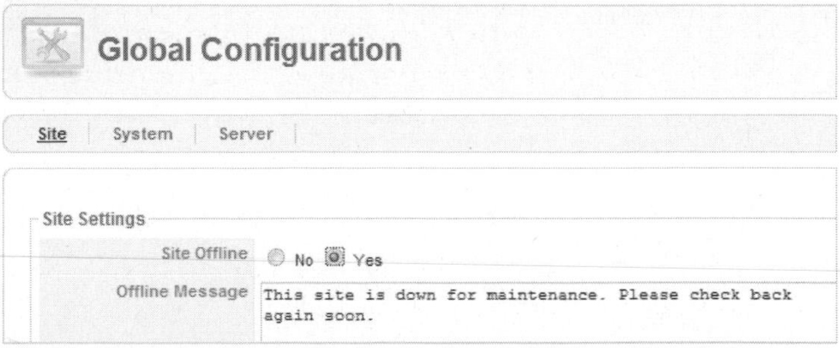

Global Configuration

Site | System | Server

Site Settings

Site Offline ○ No ◉ Yes

Offline Message `This site is down for maintenance. Please check back again soon.`

Figure 7-4: Putting Joomla! in maintenance mode

2. In the administrator console, navigate to Global Configuration and switch SITE OFFLINE to Yes. This step shuts off access to the outside world while you update.

3. Use FTP or SSH to upload all the files you unzip (except the `Installation` folder) to the root of your Joomla! site. This is typically `public_html`. However, you may have a different root directory.

4. When the upload completes, revisit the Global Configuration page and put the site back online.

5. In the administration screen, check the upper-right portion of the screen to see the version of your site. It should match what you just uploaded.

Updating Extensions

The term *extension* refers to a class of add-ons that are known as *plug-ins*, *modules*, and *components*, depending on your CMS. Each of these carries its own version and method. Let's take a look at one of the easiest ways to determine your version information for your extensions:

1. Log in to the administration screen and click Extensions ➢ Install/Uninstall, as shown in Figure 7-5.

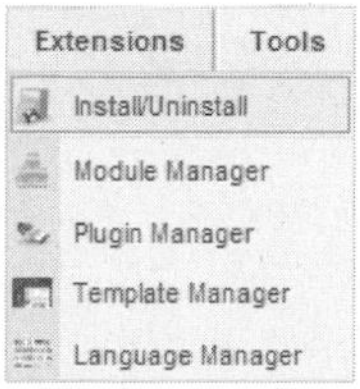

Extensions	Tools
Install/Uninstall	
Module Manager	
Plugin Manager	
Template Manager	
Language Manager	

Figure 7-5: Verifying extension version

2. Select Components to open and display the installed components. Figure 7-6 shows an example of the components of an installed system. In this example, you can see the various components, their enabled status, and the version. Each tab follows the same format, allowing you an easy method to get the version information.

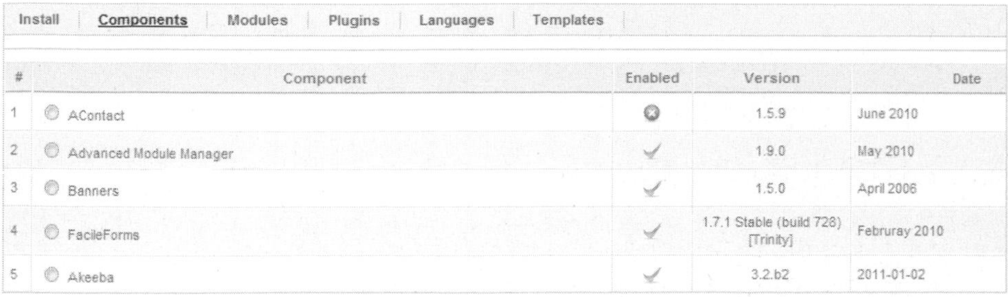

Install	Components	Modules	Plugins	Languages	Templates		
#	Component				Enabled	Version	Date
1	AContact				✕	1.5.9	June 2010
2	Advanced Module Manager				✓	1.9.0	May 2010
3	Banners				✓	1.5.0	April 2006
4	FacileForms				✓	1.7.1 Stable (build 728) [Trinity]	Februray 2010
5	Akeeba				✓	3.2.b2	2011-01-02

Figure 7-6: Components in a Joomla! site

3. Select the Install tab, as shown in Figure 7-7. Note the three methods: the Browse button and "Upload File & Install"; "Install from Directory"; and "Install from URL." Choose the one most appropriate to your extension (typically the Browse button or "Upload File & Install").

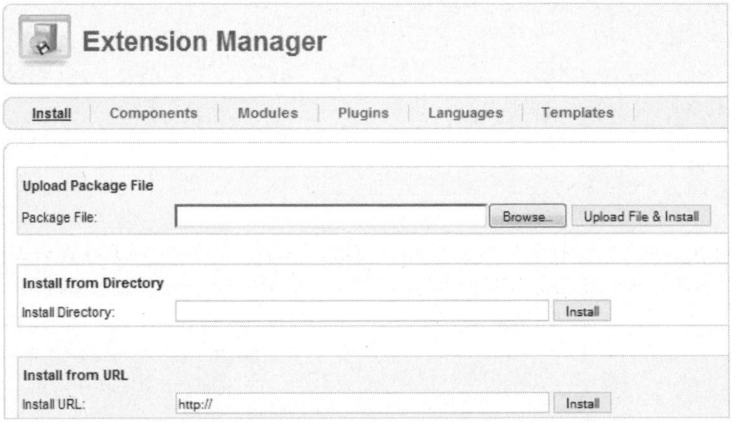

Figure 7-7: Installation of extensions and updates

You can find most Joomla! third-party developers under the Plugins tab by looking under the column titled Author, as shown in Figure 7-8. Here you see an actual URL, or you can hover over the name to get further information. You'll note some of the authors are listed as `Joomla! Project`. This is part of the core Joomla! installation, and that add-on would be updated by any CMS patch.

Figure 7-8: Joomla! author contact information

Some extensions (such as Akeeba Backup) provide a *phone home* type of feature where the extension will check in from time to time for an update. In the Joomla!

space, this is a very mature feature, and many of the third-party developers do not do this. Akeeba presents a button when you open the extension for use, letting you know a backup is available. Clicking the button quickly downloads and updates the extension.

Other extensions, however, allow you to go through the normal installation routine to update them. They will overwrite the old one.

Most Joomla! extensions require you to uninstall the old version before installing the updated or patched version. Consult with the developer on specific instructions for each extension.

WordPress and Its Plug-ins

Current versions of WordPress have a very mature means for updating your CMS and the plug-ins (that is, add-ons for WordPress). WordPress itself will tell you in the Dashboard when an update is available. If a new version becomes available, the message "You are using WordPress 3.0.4" indicates a new version out to the right of the message. To update, simply click the Update button and, within seconds, you have the latest version of WordPress.

Plug-in updates and patches work in a similar fashion. You reach them by visiting the Dashboard and scrolling down on the right until you see the Plugins control panel, as shown in Figure 7-9.

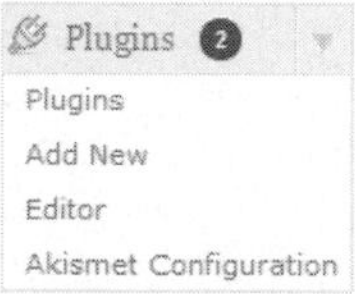

Figure 7-9: WordPress Plugins Control Panel

In this figure, notice the "2" in a shaded circle next to the word "Plugins," which indicates that two updates are available. Click Plugins to review and update, as shown in Figure 7-10.

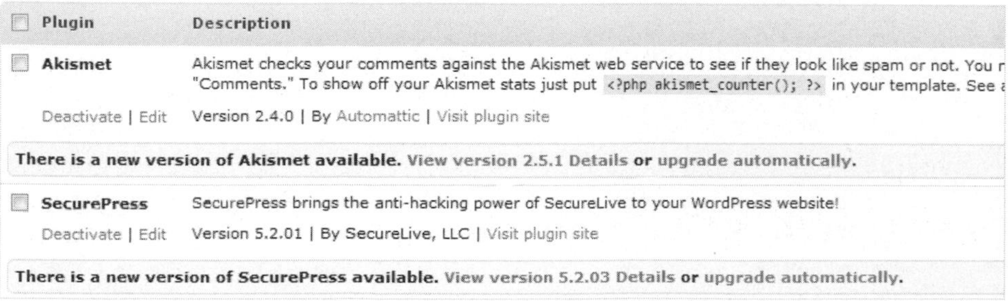

Plugin	Description
Akismet	Akismet checks your comments against the Akismet web service to see if they look like spam or not. You r "Comments." To show off your Akismet stats just put `<?php akismet_counter(); ?>` in your template. See a
Deactivate | Edit	Version 2.4.0 | By Automattic | Visit plugin site

There is a new version of Akismet available. View version 2.5.1 Details or upgrade automatically.

SecurePress	SecurePress brings the anti-hacking power of SecureLive to your WordPress website!
Deactivate | Edit	Version 5.2.01 | By SecureLive, LLC | Visit plugin site

There is a new version of SecurePress available. View version 5.2.03 Details or upgrade automatically.

Figure 7-10: Dashboard shows two updates

To update the plug-ins, click the "upgrade automatically" link to download and install the plug-in. Figure 7-11 shows the process, which only takes a few seconds in most cases.

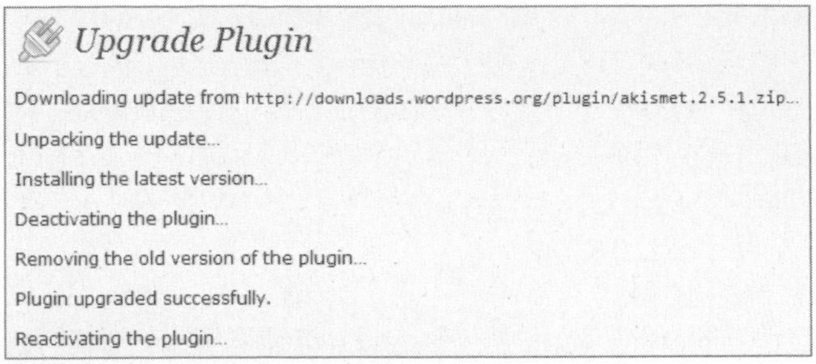

Upgrade Plugin

Downloading update from http://downloads.wordpress.org/plugin/akismet.2.5.1.zip…

Unpacking the update…

Installing the latest version…

Deactivating the plugin…

Removing the old version of the plugin…

Plugin upgraded successfully.

Reactivating the plugin…

Figure 7-11: Upgrading the WordPress plug-in

NOTE As with all CMSs, backing up your system before performing this procedure is best.

Drupal

On the difficulty scale, Drupal falls between Joomla! and WordPress as far as updates go. Like WordPress, Drupal offers a robust notification system that keeps you apprised of changes to the core, as well as changes to the modules (the add-ons for Drupal). For example, the module shown in Figure 7-12 indicates it has a security update when you review the updates available list.

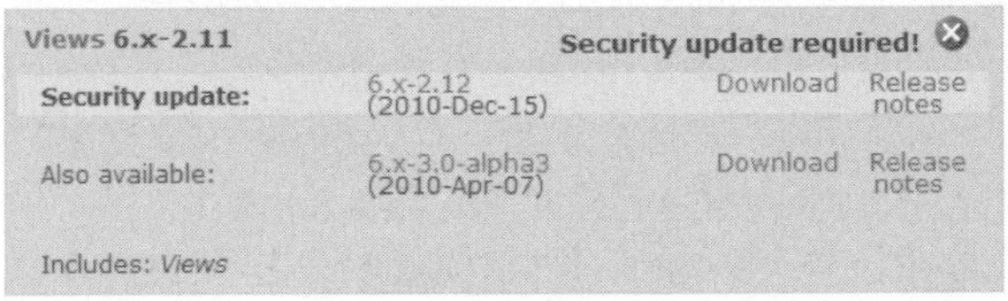

Views 6.x-2.11   Security update required! ⊗

Security update: 6.x-2.12   Download   Release
                      (2010-Dec-15)   notes

Also available: 6.x-3.0-alpha3   Download   Release
                      (2010-Apr-07)   notes

Includes: *Views*

Figure 7-12: Modules show security update available

This section examines the steps for Drupal 6.xx. For other versions, consult the documentation available at `Drupal.org`.

To begin, log in as User ID 1 (or, in other words, the super user).

There are two parts to updating Drupal: the core and the modules. The *core* refers to the Core Drupal code that makes up the CMS. The modules refer to the *contributed modules* developed by third-party developers. Each has different steps, and each is examined separately in this discussion.

Updating the Drupal Core

Drupal stores the pertinent parts of the site that make your Drupal installation uniquely yours in the database and the `Sites` folder. To update the Drupal core, follow these steps:

1. To begin, log in and visit the reports section of your site. You can navigate there, or you can simply type in the URL www.yoursite.com/admin/reports/updates. A screen similar to that in Figure 7-13 appears. In this example, the Drupal core is at version 6.19, and it's reporting that a 6.20 version is available.

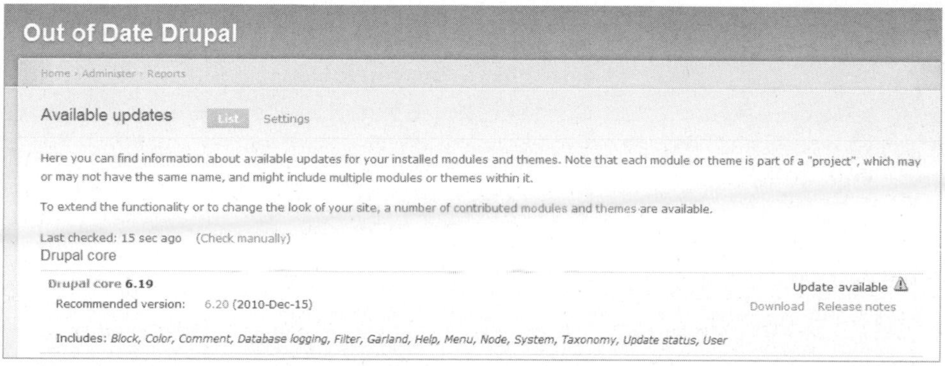

Out of Date Drupal

Home › Administer › Reports

Available updates   List   Settings

Here you can find information about available updates for your installed modules and themes. Note that each module or theme is part of a "project", which may or may not have the same name, and might include multiple modules or themes within it.

To extend the functionality or to change the look of your site, a number of contributed modules and themes are available.

Last checked: 15 sec ago   (Check manually)
Drupal core

Drupal core 6.19   Update available ⚠
Recommended version: 6.20 (2010-Dec-15)   Download   Release notes

Includes: *Block, Color, Comment, Database logging, Filter, Garland, Help, Menu, Node, System, Taxonomy, Update status, User*

Figure 7-13: Available updates screen

2. Click the Download button in the lower right of the screen, which will download the latest version for this release, and unzip the downloaded file onto your machine.

3. Navigate to `yoursite.com/admin/settings/site-maintenance`. Note that this is in Online mode. Switch your site to Offline mode, as shown in Figure 7-14. Place an appropriate message in the box, click the Off-Line radio button, and then click Save Configuration at the bottom of the screen.

4. Navigate over to `yoursite.com/admin/build/themes` and enable a default theme such as the Garland theme. You will reassign the theme after the upgrade.

5. The Drupal modules list will be the next area of focus. Navigate to `yoursite.com/admin/build/modules/list`. There you'll see listed all the installed modules, along with the core installed modules. Make a list of the *contributed modules*, which are any modules that are not part of the core.

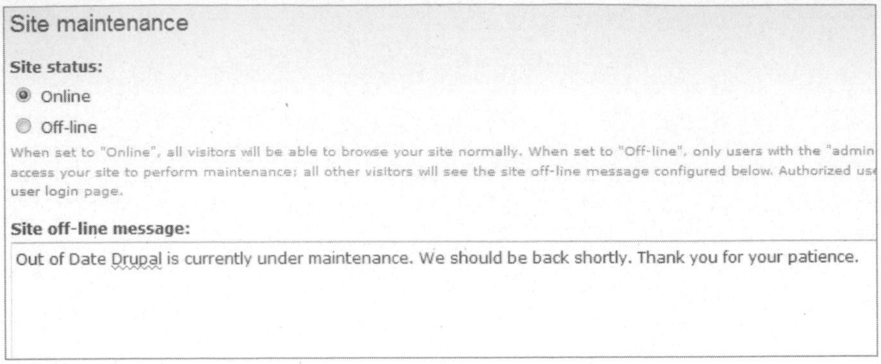

Figure 7-14: Turning on site maintenance

6. After recording the list of enabled modules, disable all modules *except* the "Core - Required" and "Core - Optional" modules. This will be necessary information to have when you complete the upgrade.

7. Log in with FTP or SSH and make a complete copy of the files for safety. The primary folders you are interested in are the Sites and Files folders that hold the site configuration data.

8. Delete all the old files and directories from the site and upload the new Drupal files and folders back to the site. After you complete copying the new Drupal files up, copy the old Sites and Files directories that you backed up.

9. Return once again to your website and run the update.php script to update the database, and then ensure that everything is in its proper order. To do so type the following:

```
yoursite.com/update.php
```

10. The update presents you with the screen shown in Figure 7-15. Because you've already followed these directions, simply click Continue.

    The database auto discovery runs next, presenting a screen similar to Figure 7-16.

11. Click Update to update the database for the newest version of Drupal. If you see any additional instructions for your version, follow them, because they will be unique to your environment.

The update should only take a few moments and, after it's finished, the screen shown in Figure 7-17 appears.

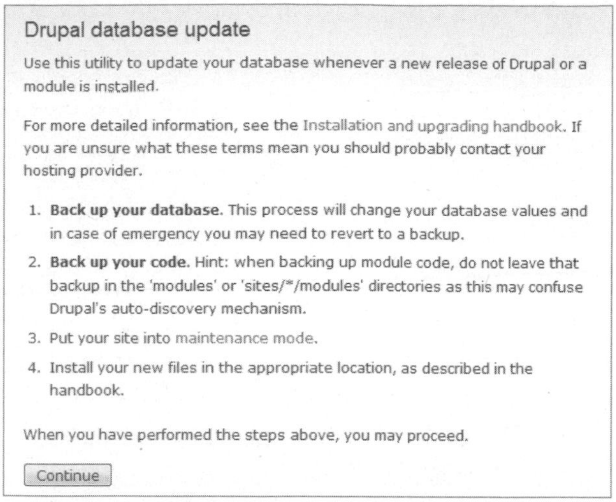

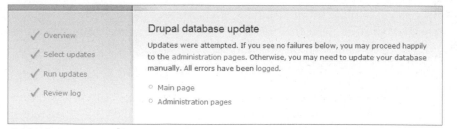

Drupal database update

Use this utility to update your database whenever a new release of Drupal or a module is installed.

For more detailed information, see the Installation and upgrading handbook. If you are unsure what these terms mean you should probably contact your hosting provider.

1. **Back up your database.** This process will change your database values and in case of emergency you may need to revert to a backup.

2. **Back up your code.** Hint: when backing up module code, do not leave that backup in the 'modules' or 'sites/*/modules' directories as this may confuse Drupal's auto-discovery mechanism.

3. Put your site into maintenance mode.

4. Install your new files in the appropriate location, as described in the handbook.

When you have performed the steps above, you may proceed.

Continue

Figure 7-15: Update script initial screen

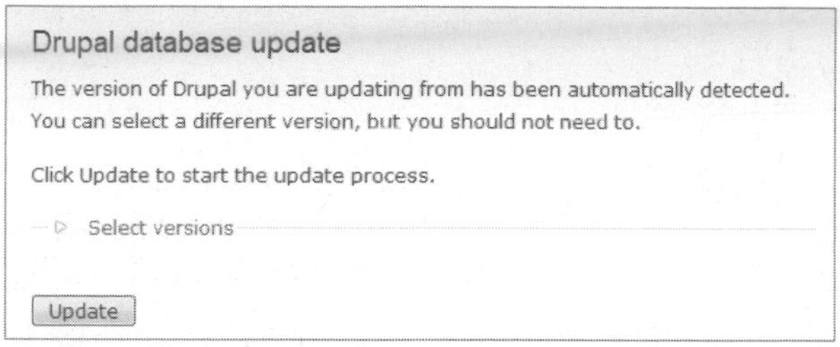

Drupal database update

The version of Drupal you are updating from has been automatically detected. You can select a different version, but you should not need to.

Click Update to start the update process.

▷ Select versions

Update

Figure 7-16: Update database

Drupal database update

✓ Overview
✓ Select updates
✓ Run updates
✓ Review log

Updates were attempted. If you see no failures below, you may proceed happily to the administration pages. Otherwise, you may need to update your database manually. All errors have been logged.

○ Main page
○ Administration pages

Figure 7-17: Finished database update

You have now updated the core, and you'll need to re-enable the core modules that you disabled, set the previous theme, and then put the site back online. For safety, rerun update.php after this to ensure that everything is back in the database properly.

> **NOTE** You should perform another full backup of the files and database after you complete any upgrades.

The download of Drupal contains a file called `Upgrade.txt` with the instructions for this process, should you get stuck.

Updating the Core with Drupal 7

With Drupal 7, although the procedures to update the core from a minor release are easy enough to do, going between major versions requires a different procedure. Take the time review the documentation and plan your upgrade (which will involve finding modules compatible with version 7.0). Read the most current documentation available before you start.

Updating Drupal Modules

Drupal modules are very easy to update; just follow these steps:

1. Download and unzip the module.

> **NOTE** Take time to read the instructions that *may* be with the module. The developer may have a different set of update instructions. If so, those will supersede the instructions presented here.

2. Run a full backup and copy the backup file off of the server. Switch the site to maintenance mode by visiting the administrative link at `yoursite.com/admin/settings/site-maintenance`.

3. Disable any dependent modules. When it comes to Drupal modules, keep in mind that modules can share dependences with other modules. Thus, you may encounter an issue when trying to disable a module. Don't worry; disabling a dependent module requires only a few additional steps.

   Figure 7-18 shows an example of a module that cannot be disabled until you remove the dependency on another module. Notice that the Content module is *grayed* out.

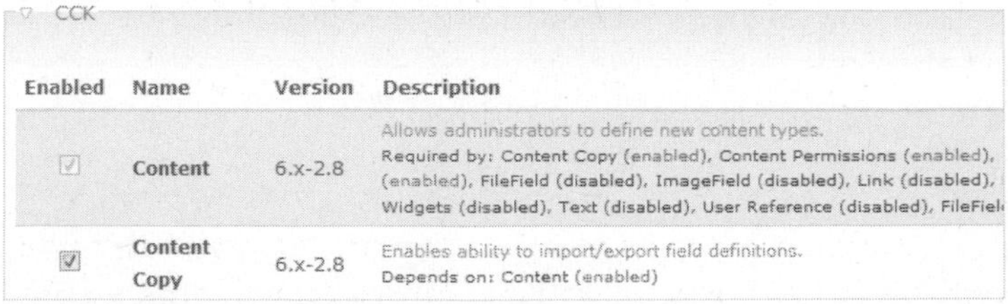

Figure 7-18: Drupal module dependency

To disable Content, you must first disable Content Copy (and others in this example), and then save the configuration. You then return to Content, disable it, and save the configuration. Make a list of all the modules you disable.

4. Navigate to the `updates` report to do the update. You may also go there directly by following `www.yoursite.com/admin/reports/updates` to download the updated code. Additionally, you can obtain the updates from `drupal.org`.

5. FTP or SSH into your site and remove the module's code from the `modules` folder. For the Backup and Migrate module, the URL would look something like `yoursite.com/modules/backup_migrate/`.

6. Delete all the files and folders from inside the folder, and then upload the new module code into the folder. In essence, you are simply replacing all the files in this folder with new ones.

7. Run the update script (`update.php`) to ensure that all is well. You can do so by logging in as the administrator and browsing to `www.yoursite.com/update.php`. Follow the update instructions. This is not an optional step, but rather is required.

8. Now you need to re-enable the modules that you previously disabled. Return to `yoursite.com/admin/build/modules/list`. Using your list of modules you disabled, re-enable and then save the configuration.

9. Run another backup and put the site back online.

NOTE People have mixed opinions on disabling modules *before* updating them. If you experience issues, you may want to reverse the process (that is, update and then disable).

Plone

The Plone CMS is built on top of a platform called Zope, which offers a mini-foundational *content management framework*. This makes Plone a unique platform in this book, and, as you can imagine, it has its own set of patching procedures.

This section provides a basic set of instructions for Plone updating. If you are adept and accomplished with Plone, you may choose to skip reading this section.

Before You Start

Because Plone is a very technical product, the instructions here for updating Plone are presented as a *guideline*. Always refer to the most current documentation available for your upgrade. When Plone is updated by the development community, it sometimes undergoes internal changes that can alter the procedures, based on that particular version. Look for the *CMFPlone Directory* of the Plone download for the pertinent instructions.

Research and review the add-ons for your site. Ensure that they are compatible with the version you are upgrading to. For example, if you are moving from a 2.xx site to a 4.xx site, then the possibility is very high that your add-ons won't work. Should you need upgraded add-ons, updating them before you start the actual Plone update is best.

Plone and Zope run on Python. Thus, you must ensure that your new version of Plone is compatible with the version of Python you are running. If it requires a new version, then you'll need to bring Python up to the correct level. Additionally, you may need some new or updated Python libraries.

Because Plone is built on Zope, and Zope runs on Python, you might see a pattern. The following is the order in which they should be upgraded:

- Python before Zope
- Zope before Plone
- Plone last

The good news is that *usually* Plone will update Zope using its installer.

Again, read all the current materials before you upgrade, specifically the `readme.txt` and other types of files that come with Plone.

NOTE The Plone version used throughout this book is v4.02, but the instructions for upgrading are general to almost all versions of Plone.

Updating the Core and Add-Ons

In regard to updating the core, each version presents a slightly different method to update. The following is a list of resources for Plone to guide you, depending on the version you're using:

- *Updating 2.5 to 3.0* — `http://plone.org/documentation/manual/upgrade-guide/version/2.5-3.0`

- *Updating 3.x to 3.2* — `http://plone.org/documentation/manual/upgrade-guide/version/upgrading-from-3-x-to-3.2`

- *Updating 3.2 to 3.3.x* — `http://plone.org/documentation/manual/upgrade-guide/version/3.2-3.3.x`

- *Updating 3.xx to 4.0.x* — `http://plone.org/documentation/manual/upgrade-guide/version/upgrading-plone-3-x-to-4.0`

Add-On Updates

The third-party code and extensions to Plone are called add-ons. Like the core, each has a version specific set of instructions. For more information, see the following:

- *Upgrading 2.5 to 3.0* — `http://plone.org/documentation/manual/upgrade-guide/version/2.5-3.0/products`

- *Upgrading 3.x to 4.x* — `http://plone.org/documentation/manual/upgrade-guide/version/upgrading-plone-3-x-to-4.0/updating-add-on-products-for-plone-4.0`

Summary

Now that you have completed this chapter, you are well versed on the process of patching.

You learned quite a bit in this chapter, starting with the basic seven steps of a patching process and moving into the organizational and team-building process. You learned about testing your patches for safety, developing work instructions, and downloading patches safely. Readers who have remote administrators were introduced to the concept of standardizing patch deployments to them. The mark of a good organization versus a great organization is having good processes, and good processes start with documentation. Learning about how to document your updates wrapped up the team discussion.

At some point, your site might be hacked, and, if so, you'll be able to better deal with it using the guidelines presented in this chapter for patching after a breach.

This chapter also provided some basic and general guidelines for patching each of the CMSs featured in this book.

Chapter 8 discusses the very important topic of log review. In that chapter, you'll learn about how to read logs for your site, server, and more. You will also learn how to use the logs to respond to various issues.

Log Review

Every day, millions of website owners read the newspaper, or get their news online. They watch the morning "talking heads" inform them about what happened in some part of the world. They consume the information that helps them feel informed. Sadly, 99.999 percent of the news they consume makes zero difference to them.

Many website owners rarely (if ever) look at their systems or website logs. If they would do so, they would get a lot more beneficial information that *could* impact their day. If they would review the log files, they could see things such as disk space usage, bandwidth consumption, attempts to break in, errors on their sites, and much more.

Log files are records of events for such software as operating systems, applications, content management systems, and blog software. Hardware systems such as servers also record logs. Logs are historical, and are critical to your site's safety. Information you should be interested in includes details about visitors to your site, your system's applications, and events that may be causing errors within the system.

There are plenty of state and federal regulations for log retention, and there are potentially industry-related laws. Another reason for log retention is, in the event of a lawsuit, you may have a requirement to produce months of data. In all cases, check with your lawyer, because this is not legal advice.

This chapter examines everything you need to know about these logs. That's not to say that you'll learn about everything you *can* know about them, but just the information you *need*.

The reason that you should care about logs is that they can warn you of impending problems, fraudulent activity, unauthorized activity, or hardware problems such as failing disk drives. If you manage a server, you'll want to monitor the machine logs. Logs provide a view of activity on your site, allowing you to tweak your site to reach your goals.

In short, logs are the history book for your servers and website.

Understanding the Need to Retain Logs

From a legal perspective, retaining logs is more and more important to many businesses. In fact, the Payment Card Industry (PCI) Data Security Standard (DSS) dictates the need for a business to "track and monitor all access to network resources and cardholder data." This means you must ensure that you track your visitors, as well as access to your servers and resources. You are required to ensure that the logs are safe from alteration. Consult with a PCI auditor for specific retention questions for log data.

One benefit of maintaining good logging is the capability to track down what happened after a server or website is hacked.

Here's a real-world example from an FTP server's log following an upload of an exploit via FTP on the server. (The source of the attack and some other data have been removed to protect the website's identity.)

```
Admin [17/Sep/2010:04:23:44]  "STOR exp_ingom0wnar.c"
Admin [17/Sep/2010:04:23:44]  "STOR pwnkernel.c"
Admin [17/Sep/2010:04:23:45]  "STOR exp_cheddarbay.c"
Admin [17/Sep/2010:04:23:46]  "STOR exp_wunderbar.c"
Admin [17/Sep/2010:04:23:47]  "STOR exp_therebel.c"
Admin [17/Sep/2010:04:23:48]  "STOR exp_moosecox.c"
Admin [17/Sep/2010:04:23:48]  "STOR exp_vmware.c"
Admin [17/Sep/2010:04:23:49]  "STOR exp_framework.h" 226
Admin [17/Sep/2010:04:23:49]  "STOR run_null_exploits.sh"
Admin [17/Sep/2010:04:23:50]  "STOR run_nonnull_exploits.sh"
Admin [17/Sep/2010:04:23:51]  "STOR exp_paokara.c"
Admin [17/Sep/2010:04:23:56]  "STOR exploit.c"
Admin [17/Sep/2010:04:23:56]  "STOR funny.jpg"
Admin [17/Sep/2010:04:23:57]  "STOR exp_powerglove.c"
Admin [17/Sep/2010:04:23:57]  "CWD /YourWebSite.com"
Admin [17/Sep/2010:04:23:37]  "STOR run_null_exploits.sh"
```

This log shows that on September 17, the Admin logged into the server at 4:23 AM (local to the server). The files loaded were exploit files meant to bypass several parts of Linux security. The problem is that the real administrator did not log in and upload these files.

The attacker actually had comprised a different machine — one owned by a contract developer who was working on this site. By gaining access to his machine, the attacker was able to grab the username and passwords, attack this website, and move on.

Had the logs not been kept, the administrator of the machine would not have been able to track down the source.

A common mistake is not validating the security of a third-party developer's machines or environment. In this case, the machine was a Mac, and the owner of the machine (the contractor) wrongly assumed the machine and environment were safe because the developer was not using a PC. The developer was not running anti-virus software on the Mac.

The best course of action in all cases is to set a minimum security standard that third parties must follow. Additionally, assignment of rights to the web server should be specific. That is, if you must provide a password and user-name, ensure that the information is unique to that individual. This practice will make tracking and auditing easier. Lastly, employ the principle of "least privileges" needed into your standard planning. If third parties don't need access to everything, then do not allow it.

Logs are important for many reasons, including the following:

- Ensuring legal compliance, such as e-discovery (that is, the process of providing electronic records in a legal discovery)
- Complying with Article 10 of the PCI DSS
- Monitoring the access and activity of third parties
- Ensuring that breaches have not occurred
- Keeping tabs on suspected hacks
- Watching your traffic for trends
- Learning about malfunctions with your site, operating system, or hardware

Throughout the remainder of this chapter, you will learn how to plan, manage, and act on information in your logs.

Planning for Your Logs

Planning for logs might sound about as fun as going to the dentist. And, yes, sadly, sometimes log management can be painful. However, doing some planning can ease that pain. One great thing is that planning can occur at any time, even if you've been running your site for some time.

Your plan should take into account such things as the retention time for logs, when to review (and who reviews) the logs, where you will store the logs, and, of course, how you respond to events.

Most of the time, you can put your logs on auto-pilot with a good plan.

Developing a Retention Policy

There probably isn't a good rule that says you must keep logs for "x" months. The amount of time you should keep logs around is very dependent on your business, industry, amount of traffic you receive, and other factors.

The best way to determine how long to retain logs is to consider the following guidelines:

- *Business and legal needs* — Your business may be one that has a legal requirement or a specific need for log retention. This could be that you're an e-commerce-type business, or perhaps a medically oriented business. It could be that you want to track long-term traffic trends for marketing and search engine optimization (SEO). You will want to define the process used to destroy and retain log data, as well as which logs are to be kept. In this category, your specific needs will outweigh other factors.

- *Size of logs* — Even an average site can quickly create very large access logs. According to `Apache.org`, 10,000 hits to a website can quickly write out a 1MB log file. This is okay, except when you are trying to review a large log file. If your logs are growing quickly every day, you may want to do a nightly archive, or set up a custom log rotation schedule directly on your server.

- *Time* — In terms of days, weeks, or months, "time" is based on several factors that will be unique to your situation. One thought on this is that logs are nothing more than text files, which compress very well, so storing is not an issue. It's more of a matter of do *you need* logs for more than three to six months? After a while, unless it's a legal requirement or interesting reading, then logs become a filing burden.

Who Does What and When?

Many of you probably have a small operation. If you only have a single-person company, then who does what is simple. It's you. If you happen to have a staff of sorts, then it's matter of delegation.

The following guidelines are primarily built around business requirements, and not so much around technical requirements:

- *Who* do you trust to copy your log files offline? Who do you trust to log in to your server? Determining who handles the logs is a matter of trust, because giving access to a server is 100 percent trust-based. This holds especially true if you are storing credit card data. The role of the log caretaker should be somewhat of an administrator's function. If you have a site administrator, then you'll likely assign this task to the administrator.

- *What* the caretaker does with the logs is, again, very dependent on your business. You may want to perform a review of your logs and just delete the archived (compressed) version. Your needs may include reviewing and archiving the log file, and then pulling it offline. If you have a policy of keeping only, say, the last three months of logs, your task would be to delete the fourth month. As you'll see later in this chapter, you can automate some of this by using log rotation.

■ *How often* you perform log maintenance is also based on the needs of your business. Your Drupal site may warrant a daily log archive because of the amount of web traffic. Or, having the logs archived weekly (using log rotation) because of low traffic may be fine. The key is the size of the logs. If they are too big, they are difficult to manage; if they're too small, then you're dealing with busy work.

Determining Where to Store Logs

Storage of your logs means two things: where and how.

Where are you going to *geographically* store them? Will this area be in a file cabinet at your office or at your home? You probably will not need quick and immediate access to your previous log files, so storing at the office or in a box in the closet shouldn't be a problem. Just consider when you would need the log files, and plan accordingly for retrieval. Be sure you take into account the media they are stored on and the environmental conditions.

The *how* in this equation introduces an electronic question. What type of media will you use? Your options include leaving the files on the server, or making an offline copy onto some type of media.

Although not likely to change, the media could be an issue. Media storage choices include CD-ROM, DVD, or USB key. You should not rely on paper copies.

If you really do have a valid reason to keep your log files for a very long term, consider burning them to CD-ROM or DVD. The prices for read-writeable DVD burners have dropped to near CD-ROM levels, so cost should not be a factor. Both of these types of media should be around for the duration of your lifetime.

If you're looking at short-term storage (three to four months), then an inexpensive USB key will suffice just fine. Long-term storage on a USB key is a big "no-no." Among the many reasons for not using a USB key for long-term storage is the prime concern that data may be lost because of the loss or failure of the key. The wash, spin, and dry cycle when laundering your pants (as well as dangers of other everyday events) is a real-world concern for loss of the data.

Responding to an Incident

The lines of the earlier FTP log file example showed an unauthorized upload of files, which resulted in a defaced Joomla! site. Fortunately, the only real damage was that these hackers replaced the `index.php` file, which was easy to fix.

The course of events following the telephone call from the client was to immediately download the logs and then remedy the damage.

The response to the event was enhanced by looking through the log files and determining the path the bad guys took.

The access logs did indeed show the bad guys were there, but nothing too odd showed up in the logs. However, activity in the FTP logs indicated that they had uploaded a lot of server-side attack code in addition to the defacement. The defacement was most likely meant as a distraction while the bad guys worked to launch the server-side code. However, the logs pointed to where they uploaded the code, so it was simple to remove the files and repair the damage.

The next action was to determine how the bad guys obtained the username and password. Three people had access to the credentials. Two of the three people were able to quickly prove they were not the source. As it turned out, the third person had his sites hacked by the same people, and he had the credentials on his machine for the hacked website.

You don't need to be Sherlock Holmes to figure out that this third person was the source. He installed a virus scanner on his Mac and found he had several infected files and three Trojan horse viruses. Cleaning up the damage was routine from that point on.

Thus, the response to this attack was simple:

1. Change all passwords system-wide.

2. Copy the log files.

3. Clean up damage.

4. Review the activity of the attackers in the logs.

5. Double-check to ensure it is all gone.

6. Find the original attack vector (in this case, the third-party contractor's desktop) and remove it.

7. Block the attackers' IP address (optional).

Had those logs been unavailable, the cleanup could have been accomplished, but how the bad guys got in would not have been revealed. This, of course, assumed that they didn't break in by using some vulnerability on the server. To all the security systems involved, there was a genuine user.

Logs are very valuable when responding to incidents. Note that in this real-world case, the review did not entail just a single log, but rather multiple log files.

Using Logs to Respond to Events

When you hear "responding to an event," it sounds like you're sending an RSVP to a party indicating that you'll be attending. In the context of this discussion, however, "responding to an event" could mean responding to a security event or an outage. In either case, you have a problem.

The steps outlined here represent a philosophy and not so much a hard-and-fast rule. However, they are built on the experience of dealing with hacked websites.

This section may seem out of place given this chapter's topic of hardening the server, but the inclusion is based on the fact that if there's a break-in, it's important to consider where you missed it.

Obtain the Evidence

The first order of business is to obtain the log files. These will be all the log files on hand, including archived logs.

Copy these to a USB key or to a separate system, such as a laptop. Be sure you have virus protection enabled to prevent anything from getting on to your machine.

Specifically, copy the directory `/var/log`. This will contain several log files, including the following:

- Boot logs
- Cron logs
- Mail Logs
- DMesg (for system start-up events)
- Security logs
- Xfer logs (which may be located elsewhere)

It's important to preserve these logs because they are a record of events.

Navigate to your access logs, typically (but not always) located at `/usr/local/apache/logs`. This will house the following very important information:

- Access logs for the server (not the website)
- Error logs
- SuExec logs
- Your archive directory

Once you have these, you should review them to see what is currently on the site.

Who Is Logged On

Before moving on to cleanup, determine if there is anyone logged in to the server who should not be.

Using the `netstat` command provides you with a great deal of information about the network subsystem. You're interested in who is connected and who is logged in. The connected users are likely okay, but it's good to make note of who they are.

At the root prompt, type **netstat -a**. This will provide you with a great deal of connection information.

Another (and simpler) method is to type the letter **w** at the command prompt as follows:

```
# w
```

This will display all *logged in* users. The difference between the two commands presented here is that `netstat` will show you vital information about other processes and services, where `w` shows you who is logged in and from where.

If you are responding to an event and *do not* recognize the users who are logged in, terminate the user's session using the `kill` command. You should then look at your user list and remove unauthorized users from it.

If these users are logged in as `root`, you must immediately change your password to prevent them from logging back in.

What Services Are Running

Another task is to determine *what* is running. For example, if you see a backdoor or virus programs running, you can terminate it.

To see all the running services, enter the following command:

```
# ps -All
```

This will provide you with a huge list of services that are running. Unless you spend a lot of time on the Linux console, you may not recognize all of them.

The purpose of running this command is to capture the resulting information for review. Use the following command to send the information to a text file:

```
ps -All >> filename.txt
```

This will write that information to the file you indicate in `filename.txt`. In this command, note that `All` is case-sensitive.

This command provides you with a snapshot. To monitor the services for an ongoing period, use the following command:

```
# top
```

Historical View

If you believe your server has been hacked, getting a list of historical logins is vital.

To do so, at the root (#) prompt, enter **last**. This will provide you with a list of who logged in, from where, and when. You'll be able to determine if anyone else is logged in as well.

A convenient way to do this is to use the following command:

```
last >> filename.txt
```

This will write that list to the file you indicate in `filename.txt`. This enables you to review the information offline with a standard text editor.

Next, enter the command **lastlog**. This lists all the service accounts on the system and when the service last logged in. Since all services have accounts, determining if the service logged in (or when) will tell you a lot. Again, you can use the following form to allow easy collection for review:

```
lastlog >> filename.txt
```

For example, if a hacker has loaded a service and it logged in and ran, you'll see this (in most cases) after running this command.

For a quick view of the *messages* log file that contains the last few events (including logins, logouts, sessions, cPanel connections, FTP events, and more), use the following command:

```
tail /var/log/messages
```

This provides information that is helpful in the short time after a break-in or an event.

Navigate to the `/home/domain-name/access-logs` folder on your server and make a copy of the `access_logs` file. This will help you determine what the perpetrator actually did while on the site.

Historical Attempts

As an ongoing security effort, or after a breach, review the failed log-in attempts using the `lastb` command as follows:

```
# lastb
```

This command can produce a very large file, so piping it with `>>` is preferred. Following is a sanitized example of failed logins of a server. This breakin attempt came from Venezuela and was conducted by an automated tool given the time.

```
smmsp ssh:notty 190-xx-xx-24.dy Wed Feb 20 21:54 - 21:54
gdm ssh:notty 190-xx-xx-24.dy Wed Feb 20 21:54 - 21:54
gdm ssh:notty 190-xx-xx-24.dy Wed Feb 20 21:54 - 21:54
webalize ssh:notty 190-xx-xx-24.dy Wed Feb 20 21:54 - 21:54
webalize ssh:notty 190-xx-xx-24.dy Wed Feb 20 21:54 - 21:54
named ssh:notty 190-xx-xx-24.dy Wed Feb 20 21:54 - 21:54
tomasi ssh:notty 190-xx-xx-24.dy Wed Feb 20 21:54 - 21:54
tomasi ssh:notty 190-76-xx-24.dy Wed Feb 20 21:54 - 21:54
candido ssh:notty 190-76-xx-24.dy Wed Feb 20 21:54 - 21:54
```

If you find a huge number of break-in attempts, the best response is to block that IP address at your firewall.

Response

Once you have collected this wealth of information about your system, it's time to go about the task of responding.

To start, try to determine what has happened. For example, if your Joomla! site was defaced, then review the date and time of the file change. With this information in hand, open the access log files and locate that data and time range. As a starting point, you should review the time before it occurred as well.

Following are proper responses:

- Block any IP addresses that are continuously trying to log in (using the `lastb` command).

- Review access logs for nefarious entries such as very odd URLs or scripts inserted in the URL.

- Review date and time stamps on files to ensure that they haven't changed without your knowledge.

- If you have been breached, run a virus scan on your website folders and files. Verify the date and time stamps.

- Run RKHunter at the command prompt to check for a rootkit virus using the command `# rkhunter -c`.

- Check to ensure that permissions are correct.

- Replace any code that has been compromised.

If your server is attacked, and has a rootkit inserted above the website, it's best to consider backing up data and re-imaging the machine instead of hunting for it. Some root kits will replace key files with their own. This makes it very difficult to tell without a code audit.

Other rootkits can hide themselves from detection, or will leave a backdoor open for the hackers. This alone is one of the many good reasons for frequent and complete backups.

Using Standard Log Files

Again, a log is a recording of historical events in a software application or hardware system. It tells you what has happened to your CMS or blog site, or what someone did while there.

Many logs are available to you, and the items they capture vary by what they monitor. Let's review a few of the common log types:

- *Apache access logs* — These are the primary files of record. They record all the activity for your website. Every time you browse a site such as www.google.com, you leave a wealth of information behind, and your site is no different. You can tell what their operating system was, what resources they wanted, how long they stayed, and more.

- *Error logs* — When something happens that should not happen to an application, to the CMS, or to other parts of the web server, an error is recorded. The error is recorded in the `error.log` file.

- *FTP logs* — The FTP logs record all activity that occurred when a person connects to the FTP service on the server. This shows who logged in, what he uploaded or downloaded, and his success rates. More information may be available based on the different FTP servers.

- *Application-specific logs* (*Drupal, Joomla!, WordPress, and Plone*) — Each of these has different means of recording information about what has happened.

- *Mail log* — This is a very generic term for the logs that apply to your e-mail services. They are good for troubleshooting to see whether mail is going out or coming in, whether bounces have occurred, and other mail-related issues. In the event of a compromised mail server, any nefarious activity will be recorded.

Most of these logs are common to every Linux, Apache, MySQL, and PHP (known as *LAMP*) server. The application-specific logs pertain directly to their own environments.

With those basics in mind, take a look at an example of how an Apache log is built.

Anatomy of an Apache Web Server Log File

Apache is an open source project dedicated to the development of a web server for UNIX, Linux, and Windows systems. In February 2010, Apache celebrated its fifteenth birthday. As of September 2010, according to `http://uptime.netscraft.com`, Apache had a commanding 57 percent share of the Internet market web server space. Apache has a wealth of features that make it one of the most popular web serving platforms on the market.

Although Apache serves a host of needs, of interest for this discussion is its capability for logging activity on web servers. So, let's learn a bit about the Apache log files.

When a single "hit" occurs on a web server, a *log entry* is written. When the visitor's web browser loads the requested page, it also requests and loads everything on that page.

If a page consists of images (for example, a video with text), all of it must be loaded to complete the request. If the page has 10 items on it, then you'll see 11 hits recorded for the request. After the web page and the 10 items it holds are loaded, the logging system records those 11 hits.

Keep in mind that the log entries on a busy site may be interspersed with other log entries.

Understanding Log Formats

Apache logs are very flexible, allowing you to configure the order of their entries. What they collect is extremely customizable, which gives you the power to collect log entry data in a manner that fits your needs. For most mere web server administrator mortals, the default logging settings will suffice.

Following are the three types of logging formats:

- *Common log format* — This is the default for Apache 2.2x. This format is very common and easy to read. You'll see shortly that it has the basic information about the transaction, such as IP address, date, time, and resource requested.

- *Combined log format* — This is identical to the common log format, but offers two additional fields that track where the client came from, and what the *agent* is. This could be the browser or a bot (such as Google bot).

- *Custom* — This entails building a custom log to meet your needs.

> **NOTE** The custom log is out of the scope of this book. See `http://httpd .apache.org/docs/current/mod/mod_log_config.html#customlog` to learn more about it.

Common Log Format

The common log format consists of the following elements:

```
LogFormat "%h %l %u %t \"%r\" %>s %b"
```

Each of these placeholders is populated with data. Following are descriptions of each of these placeholders:

- `%h` — This field represents the IP address of the client. For example, it could be the IP address of your visitors, or a bot. By turning on `HostnameLookups` in your Apache configuration, attempting to look up the name of the site (for example, `Google.com`) and populating it in place of the IP address is possible. Typically, this practice is *not* recommended because of the unnecessary load you'll place on your server.

> **NOTE** Should your business requirements dictate the need for this practice, consider using the `logresolve` directive instead. To learn more about `logresolve`, see `http://httpd.apache.org/docs/2.0/programs/ logresolve.html`.

■ %1 — This field commonly represents the RFC 1413 identity of the client, which is determined by `identd` on the client's machine.

NOTE Because this information is seldom reliable, the Apache log seldom includes it unless you've made a special configuration. If the information is not available, the field is populated with a hyphen. Thus, when you see a hyphen in the log entry, it means that the information requested is not available.

■ %u — This field shows the username if the login shows a `userID` of the person requesting the page (which, of course, requires a logged-in user). However, for the most part, you'll likely see another hyphen in this field.

■ %t — This field indicates the date and time, as shown here:

```
[17/Sep/2010:08:10:00 -0600]
```

The format is as follows:

```
[day/month/year:hour:minute:second zone]
day = 2*digit
month = 3*letter
year = 4*digit
hour = 2*digit
minute = 2*digit
second = 2*digit
zone = (`+' | `-') 4*digit
```

■ %r — This particular field in the log entry is very important. It gives you an idea as to what visitors are requesting from your site. Following is an example of information shown in this field:

```
"GET /filename.gif HTTP/1.0"
```

The information inside the double quotation marks is the client's request. This says that the client is using GET to connect to the website, and states that the client (the browser or the bot) is requesting the `filename.gif` file. It is using the `HTTP/1.0` protocol.

■ %s — This field shows a *status code*. For example, the entry 200 means that all is well. The server sends back a status code to the client to indicate what has happened. You will learn more about the specifics of status codes later in this chapter.

■ %b — The last part of the log entry, %b, indicates the size of the object returned to the client, not including the response headers. As mentioned, if no content was returned to the client, this value will be represented by a hyphen (-).

Following is an example of a log entry from an Apache server:

```
192.168.1.126 - - [09/Sep/2010:12:07:38 -0500]
"GET /components/com_ezautos/ezautos/truck.jpg
HTTP/1.1 200 9643 "http://domain.com.com/" Windows; U; Windows NT
5.1;en-US; rv:1.9.1.11) Gecko/20100701 Firefox/3.5.11 (.NET CLR 3.5.)"
```

Table 8-1 highlights some key areas found in the common log entry format and appearing in this example log entry.

Table 8.1: Apache Log Format Example

VALUE	DEFINITION
192.168.1.126	This is the IP address from where the visitor originated.
–	This entry is more or less deprecated. You will almost always see it as a blank. It will be represented by a hyphen in your log entry.
–	This entry can be the *remote login name* in some cases. Most of the time, it will be blank, and will be represented by a hyphen in the log entry.
09/Sep/2010:12:07:38 -0500	This is the time and date of the request. This server is in the -0500 time zone, which means that it is five hours away from the Greenwich Mean Time (GMT). In simple terms, that's Eastern Standard Time (EST) in the U.S.
GET /components/com_ezautos/ ezautos/truck.jpg HTTP/1.1	This entry represents the resource (files, programs, and so on) that the visitor requested. In this example, the resource is the EZ-Autos program, and the visitor has viewed a truck for sale. The HTTP/1.1 entry means that the protocol used to connect is HTTP 1.1.
200	This is the status code of the entry.
9643	This is the amount of data transferred, represented in bytes.

Combined Log Format

If you look closely at the original example log entry, you'll notice more data than what Table 8-1 describes. This is because the example entry was actually in a combined log format, which is the preferred format, because of the greater amount of information provided.

With the combined log format, you get the benefit of additional information such as including the *Referer* (and, yes, that's the way it is spelled). As shown in the following example, this HTTP request header gives the site the visitor came from (that is, it represents the source website):

```
"http://domain.com.com/"
```

Following is another piece of information to note in the earlier example:

```
"(Windows; U; Windows NT 5.1;en-US; rv:1.9.1.11) Gecko/20100701
Firefox/
    3.5.11  (.NET CLR 3.5.30729)"
```

This provides a boatload of identifying information from the browser, such as its version, brand of browser, and the operating system. This information can be very handy for troubleshooting browser incompatibility. In the example, you can see that the user has a Windows XP or higher machine, running Firefox 3.5.11.

Status Codes

Any time a web server serves up a request, it marks that request with a code to indicate what happened to that specific request. This is known as a *status code*.

Status codes fall into five major classes and sub-classes. The major classes are all specific to certain classes of activities.

Apache Status Codes

Table 8-2 can help you quickly read through your Apache logs and identify any issues you may be experiencing.

Table 8-2: Apache Web Server (httpd) Status Codes

CLASS/ SUBCLASS	DEFINITION
100 Series	Informational messages instructing the client that the server has received the information and is continuing to service the request
101	Continue
102	Switching protocols
200 Series	Success — all is well (meaning that the request was accepted and completed)
201	OK

Continued

Table 8-2 *(continued)*

CLASS/ SUBCLASS	DEFINITION
202	Created (resource, file, directory, and so on)
203	Accepted
204	No content
205	Reset content
206	Partial content
300 Series	Redirection information, meaning that the client (browser and user) must take additional steps to continue
301	Multiple choices
302	Moved permanently
303	See other
304	Not modified
305	Use proxy
306	Not in use
307	Temporary redirect
400 Series	Client errors, meaning that something in the request was formatted incorrectly, or was wrong (for example, bad links, attempts to do unauthorized or malicious activities, and so on)
401	Unauthorized/authorization required
402	Payment required
403	Forbidden
404	Page (resource) not found
405	Method not allowed
406	Not acceptable
407	Proxy authentication required
408	Request timeout
409	Conflict
410	Gone
411	Length required
412	Precondition failed
413	Request entity too large
414	Requested URI too long
415	Unsupported media type

CLASS/ SUBCLASS	DEFINITION
500 Series	Server errors
501	Internal server errors
502	Method not implemented
503	Bad gateway
504	Service temporarily unavailable
505	HTTP version not supported

NOTE For a complete and detailed list of status codes, see `http://www`
`.w3.org/Protocols/rfc2616/rfc2616-sec10.html`.

Error Logs

By far, error logs are your most important source for spotting trouble. The error log is where your web server will send all information such as diagnostic messages and error messages. If you're troubleshooting your server, this is the prime location to review for problems. The error log usually provides detailed information about the error and where the error is occurring.

If you're configuring a brand-new server, then reviewing the error logs will help you through any start-up errors. If a site is hacked, you might see the error log file filling up quickly with PHP or application errors. Reviewing those errors will lead you to the source of trouble in most cases.

The name and location of the error log file is set in the Apache configuration in the `ErrorLog` Directive. When running a Linux system, the name is typically `error_log`. This can vary by the distribution of Linux, but identifying it shouldn't be difficult.

Error logs are broken down into four parts as follows:

```
[Date] [Severity of error] [IP Address of client] [error message]
```

Following is an example:

```
[02-Sep-2010 21:27:01] PHP Warning:  PHP Startup: Unable to load dynamic
  library '/usr/local/lib/php/extensions/no-debug-non-zts-20090626
/pdo_sqlite.so' - /usr/local/lib/php/extensions/no-debug-non-zts-200926
/pdo_sqlite.so: undefined symbol:sqlite3_libversion in Unknown on line 0
```

This error indicates an issue with the `pdo_sqlite.so` service.

Access Logs

Access logs are highly useful for marketing, security, and general knowledge about your site. Access logs are typically located (by default) at `/usr/local/apache/domlogs`. (However, your location may vary.) If you take a look at that directory, you should see something like what is shown in Figure 8-1.

Figure 8-1: Directory listing of log files

The first entry shows the FTP log. The second entry shows the `accesslog` file, and the third entry is the SSL log. If you open the `accesslog` file, you would see several entries, as shown in Figure 8-2.

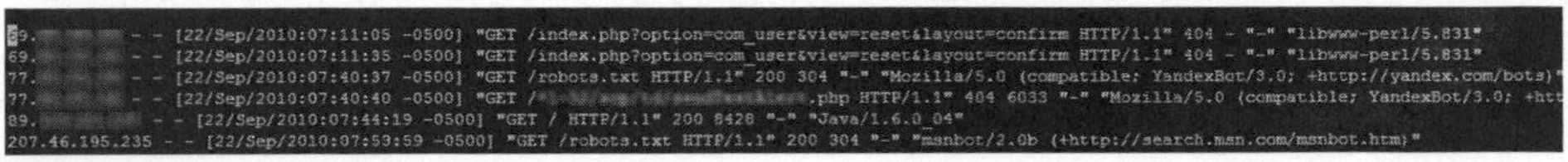

```
89.        - - [22/Sep/2010:07:11:05 -0500] "GET /index.php?option=com_user&view=reset&layout=confirm HTTP/1.1" 404 - "-" "libwww-perl/5.831"
69.        - - [22/Sep/2010:07:11:35 -0500] "GET /index.php?option=com_user&view=reset&layout=confirm HTTP/1.1" 404 - "-" "libwww-perl/5.831"
77.        - - [22/Sep/2010:07:40:37 -0500] "GET /robots.txt HTTP/1.1" 200 304 "-" "Mozilla/5.0 (compatible; YandexBot/3.0; +http://yandex.com/bots)"
77.        - - [22/Sep/2010:07:40:40 -0500] "GET /              .php HTTP/1.1" 404 6033 "-" "Mozilla/5.0 (compatible; YandexBot/3.0; +htt
89.        - - [22/Sep/2010:07:44:19 -0500] "GET / HTTP/1.1" 200 6428 "-" "Java/1.6.0_04"
207.46.195.235 - - [22/Sep/2010:07:53:59 -0500] "GET /robots.txt HTTP/1.1" 200 304 "-" "msnbot/2.0b (+http://search.msn.com/msnbot.htm)"
```

Figure 8-2: Accesslog entries

Check with your host if you are unsure where your log files are located on your server.

FTP Logs

FTP is a useful tool for uploading and downloading information to your website. As part of your security measures, you should change your FTP password frequently. If possible, switch over to *Secure FTP* (*SFTP*) using a tool like WinSCP (`www.winscp.com`).

FTP servers typically use the format known as XFERLOG. Although this is not universally true, it's a safe bet that this is the case.

A typical FTP log looks like this:

```
Mon Sep 20 09:26:13 2010 2 192.168.1.1 3191
/home/site/public_html/login.php a _ i r admin@domain.com ftp 1 * c
```

Table 8-3 shows a breakdown of the typical XFERLOG format.

Table 8-3: XFERLOG Format

EXAMPLE	DESCRIPTION	PARAMETERS
`Mon Sep 20 09:26:13 2010`	Current date and time when this occurred	
`2`	Transfer time showing how long it took (in whole seconds)	
`192.168.1.1`	IP address of remote host	
`3191`	File size in bytes	
`/home/site/public_ html/login.php`	Filename (including directory)	
`A`	Transfer type	A = ASCII; B = Binary

EXAMPLE	DESCRIPTION	PARAMETERS
`"_"`	Special action flag	C = Compressed; U = Uncompressed; T = TAR compression; "_" = No action was taken
`I`	Direction of transfer	I = Incoming (upload); O = Outgoing (download); I = Incomplete (didn't work)
`r`	Access mode	a = Anonymous; r = Real
`admin@domain.com`	Name of user who logged in	
`FTP`	Service name (typically FTP)	
`1`	Authentication method	0 = None, 1 = RFC931
`'*'`	Authenticated-user-ID	
`c`	Completion status	C = Complete; I = Incomplete

NOTE You should review your FTP log files weekly to ensure that you are aware of what is going on. If you find entries in your logs that you know should not be there, then it's time to take action. The type of entries you should look for are simple. If you know no one logged in, but some entries contradict that, then change passwords, and review your system for hacked or illegally uploaded files.

Using Tools to Assist in Log Analysis

Now that you have a basic understanding of what you can expect to find your log files, take a look at some tools that can help with the analysis of log files.

AWStats

In many web hosts, you'll find a handy application called AWStats. This GNU/ GPL tool is written in Perl. Following are a few of the things you can review with AWStats:

- Visitor data (such as number of visits, duration of visit, last visit, unique and authenticated visitors)
- Days of the week and rush hours with pages, hits, and so on
- Errors that have occurred

- IP addresses of visitors
- Browsers used by visitors

AWStats is one of the better tools to use for your SEO, and it supports several file types.

Take a look at a few features included with AWStats. Figure 8-3 shows a visual look at visitors to a website. In this case, 668 unknown (unresolved to domain) and 572 unique visitors have hit this website. You can also see the bandwidth the visitors consumed and their IP addresses.

Hosts				
Total : 0 Known, 668 Unknown (unresolved ip) - 572 Unique visitors	Pages	Hits	Bandwidth	Last visit
69.16.	3216	3284	38.20 MB	03 Sep 2010 - 11:59
69.16.	3206	3283	38.23 MB	01 Sep 2010 - 20:00
173.71.	1199	6077	22.55 MB	19 Sep 2010 - 21:36
173.74.	364	1073	4.20 MB	19 Sep 2010 - 21:34
72.14.	340	340	1.84 MB	20 Sep 2010 - 06:49

Figure 8-3: Visitor information delivered by AWStats

Month-over-month views are valuable in measuring traffic, gauging bandwidth, and counting pages/hits. This is important for your security because if you see a sudden jump in bandwidth as shown in Figure 8-4, but you do not see an equal jump in traffic, someone may have hacked your server.

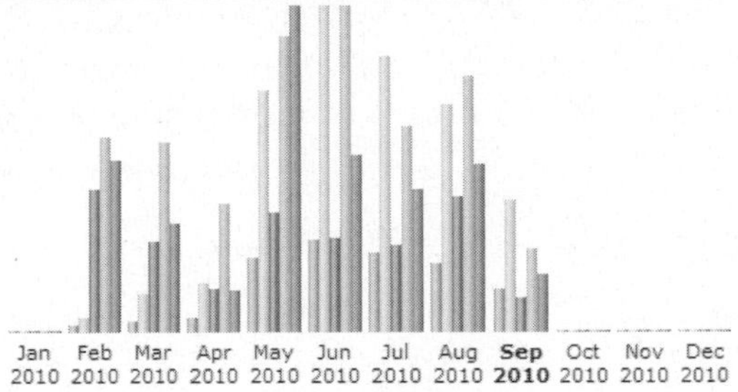

Month	Unique visitors	Number of visits	Pages	Hits	Bandwidth
Jan 2010	0	0	0	0	0
Feb 2010	91	192	45588	62627	678.76 MB
Mar 2010	143	499	28533	60810	430.98 MB
Apr 2010	195	641	13900	40908	161.35 MB
May 2010	994	3267	37869	94547	1.27 GB
Jun 2010	1232	4393	29799	104402	701.62 MB
Jul 2010	1064	3720	27597	66103	564.40 MB
Aug 2010	926	3052	43034	82060	667.33 MB
Sep 2010	572	1773	10451	26478	227.75 MB
Oct 2010	0	0	0	0	0
Nov 2010	0	0	0	0	0
Dec 2010	0	0	0	0	0
Total	5217	17537	236771	537935	4.62 GB

Figure 8-4: Month-over-month view of traffic

As shown in Figure 8-5, a large amount of hits (77.7 percent) reported "404 (Document Not Found)" errors. This could mean a damaged or missing link.

HTTP Status codes		Hits	Percent	Bandwidth
404	Document Not Found	66893	77.7 %	513.04 MB
302	Moved temporarily (redirect)	15550	18 %	2.66 MB
301	Moved permanently (redirect)	3393	3.9 %	48.07 KB
303	See other document	115	0.1 %	1.45 KB
400	Bad Request	43	0 %	205.69 KB
206	Partial Content	38	0 %	32.52 KB
500	Internal server Error	15	0 %	15.12 KB
417	Failed	6	0 %	2.36 KB

Figure 8-5: HTTP status codes

Figure 8-6 shows another view of your bandwidth in an easy-to-view summary.

Summary					
Reported period	Month Sep 2010				
First visit	01 Sep 2010 - 00:09				
Last visit	20 Sep 2010 - 07:07				
	Unique visitors	Number of visits	Pages	Hits	Bandwidth
Viewed traffic †	573	1773 (3.09 visits/visitor)	10451 (5.89 Pages/Visit)	26478 (14.93 Hits/Visit)	227.75 MB (131.53 KB/Visit)
Not viewed traffic *			89903	90574	545.29 MB

Figure 8-6: Summary view

Typically, AWStats is designed more for general traffic information and loads. However, you can use it to visually view where your clients are going. For example, if you are running a WordPress site and you see a high number of hits on your admin login page, this means that someone has been trying to break in. AWStats is a good tool to learn and use frequently.

SyHunt

The purpose of SyHunt is to give you a quick (and good) means to find out whether attacks have been occurring. Log analysis is vital after a hack, and this tool makes it easier. SyHunt is a tool that enables you to review your log files for potential and confirmed attacks. The tool runs on your Windows desktop, and is very easy to use.

NOTE You can download this tool at `www.syhunt.com/pub/downloads/`
`sandcat-loganalyzer-1.0.zip`.

You can use this tool by running `logcheck.exe`. This command opens the primary control screen for SyHunt, as shown in Figure 8-7.

Note the Log File Format drop-down menu located near the upper right of the screen. Clicking that menu provides the options shown in Figure 8-8.

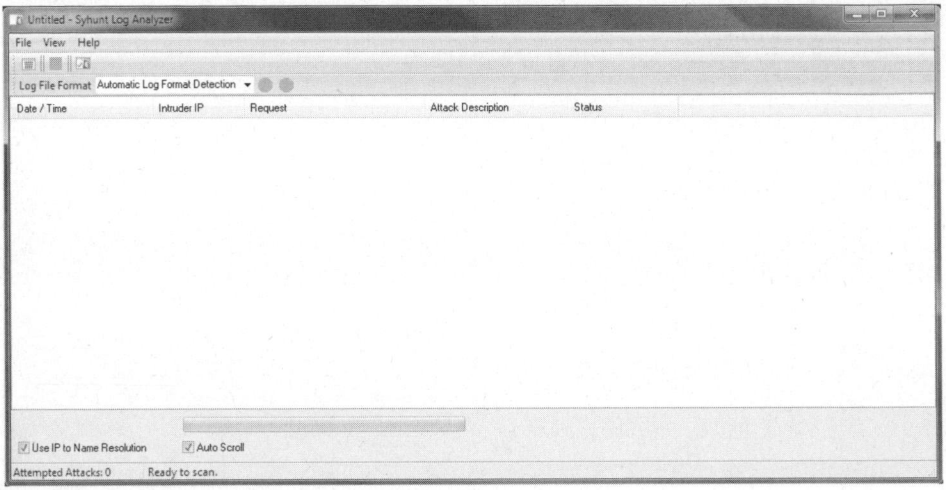

Figure 8-7: SyHunt main screen

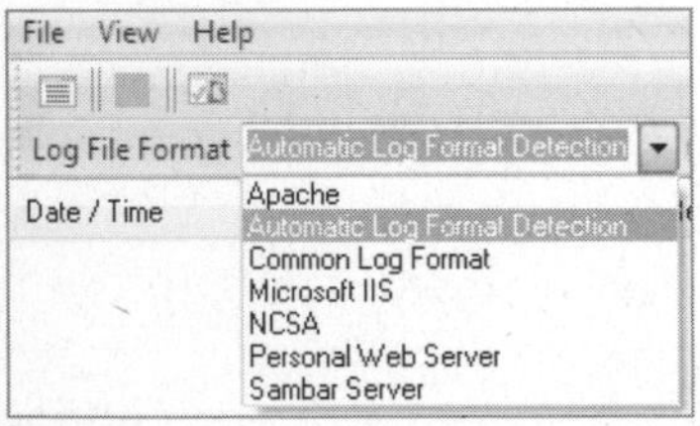

Figure 8-8: Choosing a log format

From this menu, you can select one of many different log types, or choose Automatic Log Format Detection. This makes parsing through the log types that may be set up on your web server simple.

To begin using SyHunt, follow these simple steps:

1. Click File ➢ Open and leave the Log File Format as Automatic Log Format Detection.

2. Navigate to a copy of your log file and open it.

3. You may receive an error such as `No items match your search`. In the "Files of type" drop-down, the default is a text file (log file) that ends the extension `.log`. Change the type to "All files," as shown in Figure 8-9.

As shown in Figure 8-9, this example opens a log file called `access.log.37.3` from a sample website. Let's review it for trouble.

Click the green arrow next to the Log File Format. This starts the parsing process, which takes some time. During the processing you'll see a progress bar similar to that shown in Figure 8-10.

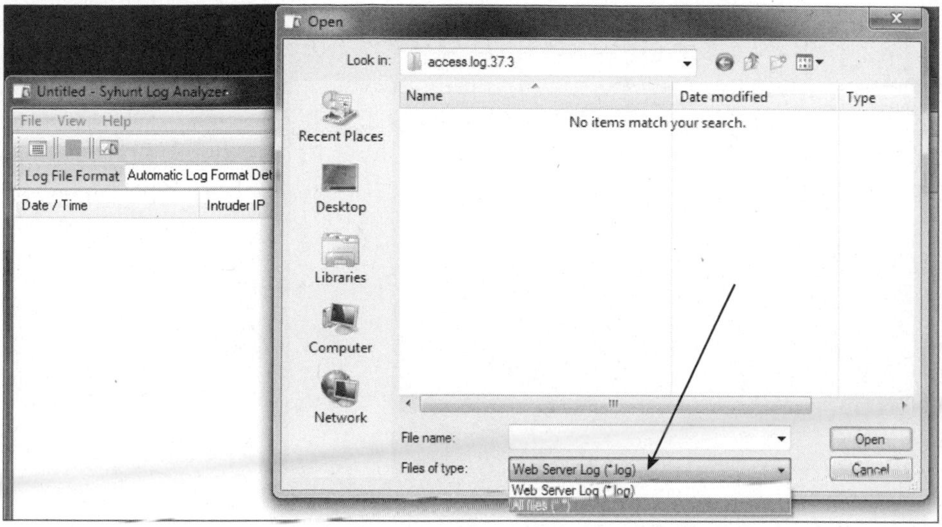

Figure 8-9: Opening SyHunt log files

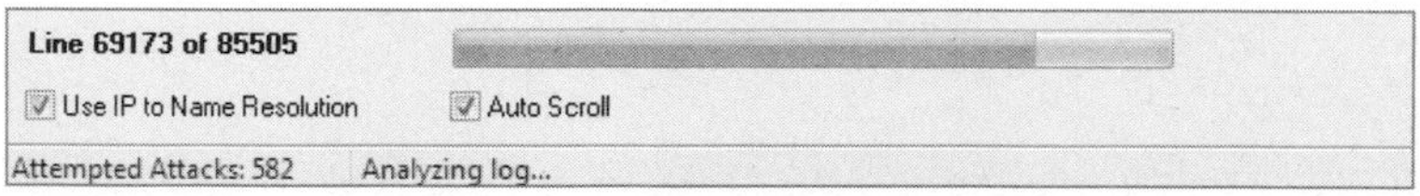

Figure 8-10: SyHunt parsing logs showing attacks

After SyHunt has finished processing, it notes 69,173 log entries out of 85,505 entries. This is a very small log file. Additionally, you would see that there were 582 Attempted Attacks. Figure 8-11 shows a few samples of these attacks that were reported after the tool has completed its run.

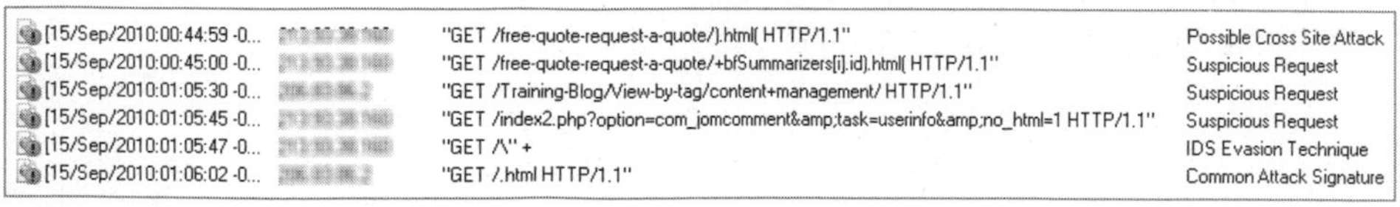

Figure 8-11: Potential attacks found

Figure 8-12 shows how SyHunt isolates lines that show potential attacks in the forms noted on the right-hand side.

```
"GET /components/com_portfolio/includes/phpthumb/phpThumb.php?w=220&src=../../../../images/stories/portfolio/item_original/4_1274150903.jpg HTTP/1.1"    Common Attack Signature
"GET /components/com_portfolio/includes/phpthumb/phpThumb.php?w=220&src=../../../../images/stories/portfolio/item_original/1_1274146448.jpg HTTP/1.1"    Common Attack Signature
"GET /components/com_portfolio/includes/phpthumb/phpThumb.php?w=220&src=../../../../images/stories/portfolio/item_original/2_1274149213.jpg HTTP/1.1"    Common Attack Signature
"GET /components/com_portfolio/includes/phpthumb/phpThumb.php?w=220&src=../../../../images/stories/portfolio/item_original/3_1274150081.jpg HTTP/1.1"    Common Attack Signature
```

Figure 8-12: Common attack signatures

Drilling into the logs further shows entries that SyHunt identified as Common Attack Signatures. This designation can sometimes represent a false positive.

After the tool has completed its run, it provides with you a list of IP addresses that are suspected as sources of attacks, as shown in Figure 8-13. The total list shows 111 IP addresses. This information now allows you to review each one.

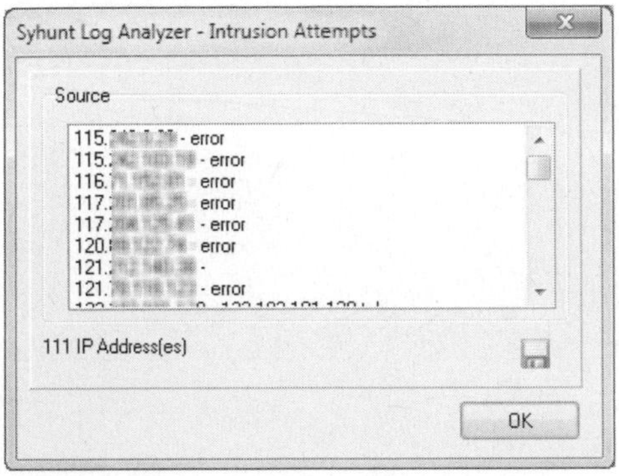

Figure 8-13: List of intrusion attempts

After you complete the run, you can save the list of intrusion attempts for further analysis using Notepad++.

Analyzing Your Logs with Notepad++

NotePad ++ (available from `http://notepad-plus-plus.org`) is a great open source tool that can be used on Windows desktops. It can open very large text files (such as logs), and it includes some features that make your log review much easier.

After you install Notepad++, open the raw access log and then open the list of intrusion attempts, as shown in Figure 8-14. In this example, you can see that both files are open so that you can easily work on them. The first tab provides access to raw access logs, and the second tab shows the potential attacks found by SyHunt.

Review each attack by searching for the IP addresses listed. You first want to eliminate known false positives out of the list of intrusion attempts and focus on the attacks. Figure 8-15 shows examples of two false positives.

In Notepad++, open the search box by clicking Search ➤ Find ➤ Current document. When you select the Find All in Current Document option, Notepad++ displays the results in a separate window for you to deal with, as shown in Figure 8-16.

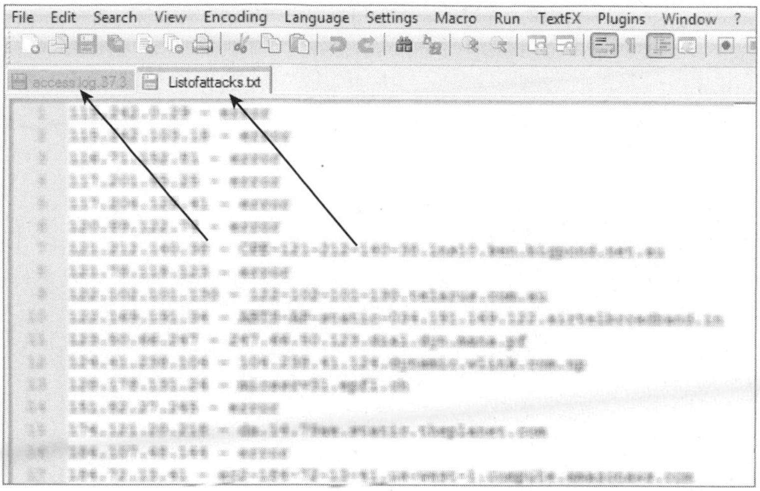

Figure 8-14: Notepad++ opened for analyzing files

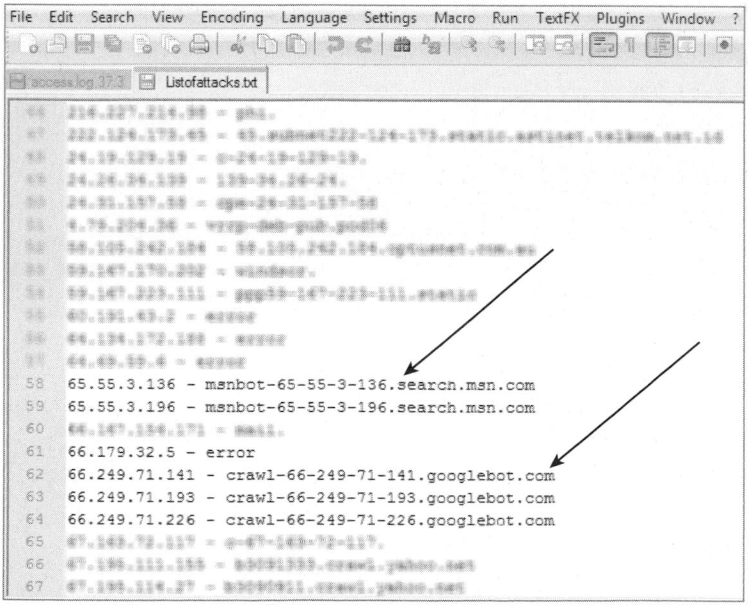

Figure 8-15: Notepad++ showing Google bot in logs

For this example, find `googlebot.com`. Notepad++ returns the lines shown in Figure 8-17 from the access log.

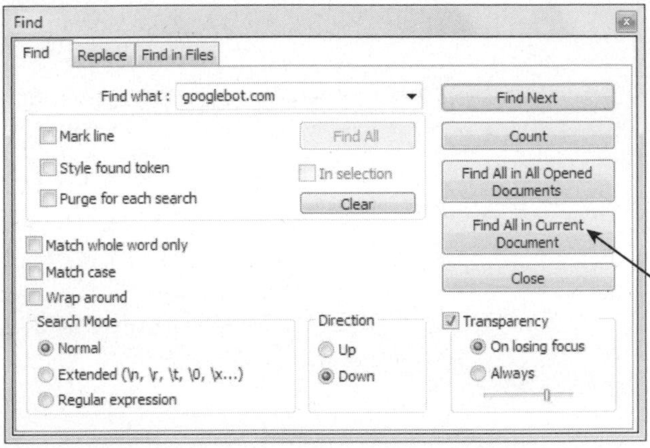

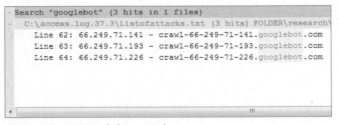

Figure 8-16: Finding all entries in the document

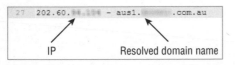

```
- Search "googlebot" (3 hits in 1 files)
- C:\access.log.37.3\Listofattacks.txt (3 hits) FOLDER\research\
     Line 62: 66.249.71.141 - crawl-66-249-71-141.googlebot.com
     Line 63: 66.249.71.193 - crawl-66-249-71-193.googlebot.com
     Line 64: 66.249.71.226 - crawl-66-249-71-226.googlebot.com
```

Figure 8-17: Search box results

The results of the search tell you which entries to remove from the list if you want. In this example, these would be lines 62, 63, and 64 in the raw log files. Highlight them and delete them. Repeat this process as needed.

Now, return to the list of attack items. Grab another IP address, which also yields results. The (sanitized) IP address shown in Figure 8-18 resolves to a host in Australia.

```
27  202.60.██.███ - aus1.██████.com.au
```
          IP   Resolved domain name

Figure 8-18: Examining an attack log entry

The following shows the entry in the logs. The attackers were trying to see whether they could run the code located at the URL shown here on the site. This common trick has a decent success rate for attackers.

```
"GET /%20%20//forum/userLogin.php?config[forum_installed]=
```

```
http://www.footballtrainingscrets.info/jim/includes/js/tabs/int1.txt????
```

In this case, you could use Notepad++ to gather up all the entries showing this attack and report it the ISP of record that owns the IP address where the attack originated. You could block the IP address if the attackers were a nuisance, or you could ignore it.

As you can see, Notepad++ is a great tool to use to analyze log files because it opens very large files and has great search options.

Using Log Rotation

As you have seen throughout this chapter, the collection and use of logs is an important task for your CMS website. Logs can be the prognosticator of things to come, or the historical record of things that have passed.

Logs are useful for a short while. Unless you are required (by business or legal requirements) to maintain years of logs, you should maintain about three to four months of your logs. However, this is just a number based on personal experience. Your business needs will dictate the proper time.

Log rotation entails rolling logs over. In layman's terms, log rotation is essentially closing the log files by compressing them and starting new ones. The Linux operating system provides a terrific means to handle this job for you.

Log rotation is driven by a *cron* job (timer) that will wake up and read a configuration file. That file contains a set of instructions to tell the `logrotate` utility what to do with each of the logs.

Additionally, you may be on a web host that supports cPanel, or an equivalent. These applications also provide the capability to set up log rotation.

Setting Up Log Rotation with logrotate

You can perform log rotation manually, and in some cases, set it up in your server control panel.

The WHM Virtual Private Server (VPS) control panel from `cPanel.com` offers an easy means to set up your rotations. In your WHM control panel, you can access the option for log rotation by choosing Main ➤ Service Configuration ➤ Apache Configuration ➤ Log Rotation. The screen shown in Figure 8-19 appears.

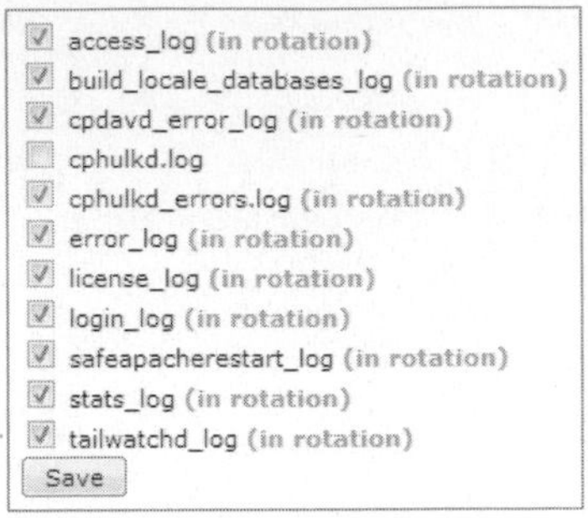

Figure 8-19: WHM logrotate Settings

This particular screen instructs `logrotate` to rotate out all logs, including `access_log`, `error_log`, `login_log`, and many others. However, the `cphulkd.log` is not included in the log rotation. `Logrotate` is by far the easiest method to implement log rotation, but, of course, you must be using the WHM control panel. If you do not have WHM, but have access to your server via a shell, then the method to handle log rotation is through a direct configuration of your `logrotate` application. You can use this application as a process to ease system administration on websites.

Through the use of `logrotate`, you can automatically compress, rotate out, or even e-mail log files. You can treat each log file in your system uniquely. Log files can be handled on a daily, weekly, or monthly basis.

As mentioned earlier, the `logrotate` application is driven by a cron job. It wakes up at a predetermined time and reviews the instructions in the configuration file (`/etc/logrotate.conf`).

Following is an example of the default Fedora release 12 `logrotate` configuration file:

```
# see "man logrotate" for details
# rotate log files weekly
weekly

# keep 4 weeks worth of backlogs
rotate 4

# create new (empty) log files after rotating old ones
create

# use date as a suffix of the rotated file
dateext

# uncomment this if you want your log files compressed
compress
```

```
# RPM packages drop log rotation information into this directory
include /ctc/logrotate.d

# no packages own wtmp and btmp -- we'll rotate them here
/var/log/wtmp {
    monthly
    create 0664 root utmp
        minsize 1M
    rotate 1
}

/var/log/btmp {
    missingok
    monthly
    create 0600 root utmp
    rotate 1
}
# system-specific logs may be also be configured here.
```

This code instructs the system to wake up and rotate access logs weekly, and to only keep a rolling four weeks of logs. Each week, it is to compress the log file using the date as the suffix. Finally, the system is to create a new log.

The rest of the log configuration file instructions handle the system's internal needs. The last line is in place to allow for other configuration options:

```
# system-specific logs may be also be configured here.
```

NOTE The # sign in the configuration indicates a comment. The sign can appear anywhere in the file, as long as it's the first thing in the line.

Following is an alternate version of the configuration file (found using man logrotate while logged in the shell of the server):

```
# sample logrotate configuration file

    compress

    /var/log/messages {
        rotate 5
        weekly
        postrotate
            /sbin/killall -HUP syslogd
        endscript
    }

    "/var/log/httpd/access.log" /var/log/httpd/error.log {
        rotate 5
```

```
        mail admin@domain.com
        size 100k
        sharedscripts
        postrotate
            /sbin/killall -HUP httpd
        endscript
    }
```

In this example, the first command, `compress`, is global, and instructs `logrotate` to compress the files when it rotates them. What follows are the instructions that tell `logrotate` to go through five weekly rotations.

Upon week six, it will delete the oldest one. Additionally, after the log file has been rotated, but not before the compression, it will run the command listed after the `postrotate`: `/sbin/killall -HUP  syslogd` command.

Immediately after `endscript` is where the compression of the file will occur. The next section instructs the `logrotate` for both `/access.log` and `error.log` to be rotated when they reach 100K in size. This particular setup would e-mail the uncompressed (100K) versions of the logs to `admin@domain.com` after five rotations. This way, you can keep a copy locally and "offsite" via e-mail.

The `sharedscripts` command in the last portion of the file means `postrotate` script will run only once for both files — not once for each log. That way, it does its work through one pass.

Manually Setting Up *logrotate* Options

A tremendous number of log options are available to you with `logrotate`. Table 8-4 shows a few valuable ones pulled from the help documents.

NOTE You can see all the commands by logging into your server via a shell and typing **man logrotate**, which shows all the help options available.

Table 8-4: Logrotate Options

OPTION	DESCRIPTION
compress	Old versions of log files are compressed with the `gzip` utility by default.
compresscmd	Specifies which compression utility to use to compress log files. The default is `gzip`.
uncompresscmd	Specifies which command to use to uncompress log files. The default is `gunzip`.
compressext	Specifies which extension to use on compressed log files, if compression is used.

OPTION	DESCRIPTION
copy	Makes a copy of the log file, but won't change the original at all. This option can be used, for example, to make a snapshot of the current log file, or when some other utility must truncate or parse the file.
copytruncate	Truncates the original log file to zero size in place after creating a copy, instead of moving the old log file and optionally creating a new one. See the man pages for more information (for example, man logrotate when logged in a shell).
Create (mode, owner, group)	Immediately after rotation (before the postrotate script is run), the log file is created (with the same name as the log file just rotated). mode specifies the mode for the log file in octal. owner specifies the name of the user who will own the log file. group specifies the group the log file will belong to. Any of the log file attributes may be omitted, in which case, those attributes for the new file will use the same values as the original log file for the omitted attributes. This option can be disabled using the nocreate option.
Daily	Log files are rotated every day.
Dateext	Archives old versions of log files, adding a daily extension like YYYYMMDD, instead of simply adding a number.
dateformat *format_string*	Specifies the extension for dateext using the notation similar to the strftime function. Only %Y, %m, %d, and %s options are allowed. The default value is -%Y%m%d. Also note that the character separating the log name from the extension is part of the dateformat string.
delaycompress	Postpones compression of the previous log file to the next rotation cycle.
extension *ext*	Log files are given the final extension .ext after rotation. If compression is used, the compression extension (normally .gz) appears after extension (.ext).
ifempty	Rotate the log file even if it is empty, overriding the notifempty option (ifempty is the default). This means that an empty log will be treated the same as a log with content in it.
missingok	If the log file is missing, go on to the next one without issuing an error message. See also nomissingok.
monthly	Log files are rotated the first time logrotate is run in a month. (This is normally on the first day of the month.)
nocompress	Old versions of log files are not compressed.
nocopy	Do not copy the original log file and leave it in place. (This overrides the copy option.)

Continued

Table 8-4 *(continued)*

OPTION	DESCRIPTION
nocopytruncate	Do not truncate the original log file in place after creating a copy. (This overrides the `copytruncate` option.)
nocreate	New log files are not created. (This overrides the `create` option.)
nodelaycompress	Do not postpone compression of the previous log file to the next rotation cycle. (This overrides the `delaycompress` option.)
nomissingok	If a log file does not exist, issue an error. This is the default.
notifempty	Do not rotate the log if it is empty. (This overrides the `ifempty` option.)
nosharedscripts	Executes the `prerotate` and `postrotate` scripts for every rotated script.
noshred	Do not use shred when deleting old log files. See also `shred`.
rotate *count*	Log files are rotated *count* times before being removed or e-mailed to the address specified in a mail directive. If *count* is 0, old versions are removed rather than rotated.
sharedscripts	Normally, `prerotate` and `postrotate` scripts are run for each log rotated, meaning that a single script may be run multiple times for log file entries that match multiple files (such as the `/var/log/news/*` example).
	If `sharedscripts` is specified, the scripts are only run once, no matter how many logs match the wildcard pattern. However, if none of the logs in the pattern require rotating, the scripts will not be run at all. If the scripts exit with error, the remaining actions will not be executed for any logs. (This option overrides the `nosharedscripts` option and implies a `create` option.)
shred	Delete log files using `shred -u` instead of `unlink()`. This should ensure that logs are not readable after their scheduled deletion. This is off by default. See also `noshred`.
shredcycles *count*	Asks GNU `shred` to overwrite log files *count* times before deletion. Without this option, the `shred` default will be used.
size size[*G/M/k*]	Log files are rotated when they grow bigger than `size` bytes. If `size` is followed by M, the size is assumed to be in megabytes. If the G suffix is used, the size is in gigabytes. If the k suffix is used, the size is in kilobytes. So, `size 100`, `size 100k`, `size 100M`, and `size 1G` are all valid.

OPTION	DESCRIPTION
weekly	Log files are rotated if the current weekday is less than the weekday of the last rotation, or if more than a week has passed since the last rotation. This is normally the same as rotating logs on the first day of the week, but if logrotate is not being run every night, a log rotation will happen at the first valid opportunity.

logrotate is very much a "fire-and-forget" type of utility after it's up and running.

The next section examines how to use cPanel, which, if you're using a shared hosting account, is likely on your server.

cPanel Settings for Log Rotation

cPanel is a nearly ubiquitous tool in hosting these days. It's one of the most popular applications for web server management. You can use cPanel to set up your log archiving. Although it doesn't offer the same robust features as logrotate, it will easily get the job done.

Log into cPanel and locate the button titled Raw Log Manager. It should look like the icon shown in Figure 8-20. This button takes you to the Raw Log Manager screen shown in Figure 8-21.

Figure 8-20: Access Raw Logs in cPanel

Figure 8-21: Log Rotate settings in cPanel

Note that you should select the option to "Archive Logs in your home directory at the end of each state run." Sometimes the default on hosts is for this option to not be selected. With this box unchecked, only the last 24 hours of log files are saved.

Also note that the Raw Log Manager example shown in Figure 8-21 lists previously archived logs for `SalvusAlerting.com`. Here you can click those and download them, review them, or just delete them.

If you want only one month of logs, then select the option to "Remove the previous month's archived logs from your home directory at the end of each month" (see Figure 8-21). This option deletes the old logs for you.

Using cPanel or another type of hosting control may be far easier for you if you have a small website than using `logrotate`. Additionally, if you do not have SSH access, you must depend on the hosting control system.

Summary

Log files are the historical record of your site. Like other historical documents, they can have great value. This chapter explains the need for keeping logs. It also explores the common log format and combined log format.

By reviewing an FTP log and a standard Apache log, you have the capability of keeping tabs on your traffic.

Tools like SyHunt and AWStats are available to help you make sense of log files, as well as to find trends, keep tabs on potential attacks, and track bandwidth.

Log rotation is a good means to keep your unwieldy logs under control. The three methods explored in this chapter were through WHM, manually crafting a `logrotate` configuration, and using cPanel for shared hosting.

Always keep an eye on our logs and put a plan in place to copy them offline.

In Chapter 9, you will learn about the ins and outs of recovering from a hacker attack. Within your server, you have a web server, e-mail, FTP, and more. Once an intruder breaks through to your site, your cleanup should be your top priority. Chapter 9 takes you on an in-depth tour of that process.

Hack Recovery

When a server or website has been hacked, the impact of the dastardly deed is similar in nature to a criminal breaking and entering into your building. It has a tendency to leave you with an unsettled feeling that your security is bad, and that you are vulnerable to attack.

Although a criminal breaking in to your building is not likely to leave behind a *bug* to listen in on your private conversations, a hacker might. A hacker has many reasons to break into a computer, and leaving behind something like a Trojan horse or key logger to steal passwords is very common.

Dealing with a hacked machine or website is a time-consuming and potentially frustrating venture. In cases such as a theft of credit card information, a hack can also be very costly. The level of frustration, and the cost associated with the hack, can vary, depending on the type of attack. Consider these examples:

- In the event of a kiddie-scripter, who attacks and places some well-known malicious code on the server, dealing with the attack may simply be a matter of cleaning up the malware and patching the code used to get in.

- The placement of a *rootkit* package on your server means you have a lot of work ahead of you getting rid of the virus and fixing the damage.

- As time goes forward, your Joomla!, Drupal, Plone, or WordPress site may targeted to become a zombie, a growing cyber threat.

- As this chapter is being written, a new malware called *Stuxnet* has worked its way into the control systems for electrical generation facilities. This new breed of virus is still being studied for its power. It is unlike almost anything seen before.

▪ Another malware/bot known as Zeus is spreading around the world. For now, it would seem that Zeus is not a prelude to a widespread attack against the U.S., but rather an organized criminal effort. Gaining access to a powerful server such as yours, and, placing it at the disposal of a shadowy group of cyber-mercenaries or state-sponsored hackers, makes for a tempting target.

All of these are *in addition to* the thousands of scripts in use today that are available to attack your site. However, the discussions in this book treat an attack as something that could be much more than a simple defacement. You should treat an attack very seriously, and, obviously, taking a hard stance against security weaknesses will make for better security of your site.

When you are attacked, you should treat it as a hostile act against your server, and you should take all the necessary steps to stop it and prevent it from happening again in the future. Literally, the purpose of this book is to teach you how to integrate good *information security practices* into your daily business operations

This chapter introduces you to a framework to respond to attacks, collect evidence, teach you how to work toward closing holes in your security, and show you how to restore operations.

Activating Your Disaster Recovery Plan

If you are attacked, the key feeling will be some form of panic. Take some advice culled from experience: Do not succumb to that panicked feeling. It will lead to more mistakes, bigger problems, and may cause you to overlook something.

Chapter 6 covers the process of crafting your own disaster recovery plan. In the event of a hack on your website or systems, you will likely *activate* your plan. As you may recall, the implementation of your disaster recovery plan requires that you define the initial actions you will take after you determine there's an issue.

The issue typically is a disruption of some sort in your website or infrastructure operations. This can include an impending disaster. In the activation of your disaster recovery plan, you will notify your team and determine what the outage is. If the outage includes a portion of your site or the entire server, your plan should account for this.

Let's review your general initiation plan.

Why Activate Your Disaster Recovery Plan?

The *why* behind activating your disaster recovery plan means that some emergency situation previously being defined by the plan you created has arisen. This reason could be any number of issues such as power failure, data loss, or, in this example, a cyber attack.

Who Should Activate the Plan?

If you are a one-person operation, then *who* will determine that an emergency exists and declare the emergency will be you. In a larger operation (such as a small or medium-sized company), a documented chain of command is usually in place. When a disaster has been declared, the process should be followed to restore operations.

Another tenet of this activation plan is a defined process to notify the affected personnel in the organization about the disaster. This is the point at which you roll out your communications plan.

How Do You Restore Operations?

The *how* behind implementing the disaster recovery plan depends greatly on what the issue is. In the case of a cyber attack, your procedures should consider doing a full restore from known good backups.

Now that you understand the basics of a disaster recovery plan, take a look at the specifics surrounding the recovery from a hack.

WARNING Depending on when you made your backup, the restored files may still be infected. Trust your backups, but certainly verify that they, too, have not been infected.

Tools for Successful Recovery

As part of your recovery toolkit, you should keep a few things close by. Although you will use most of the tools examined in this section, some (such as a digital camera) may be highly optional.

Virus Scanner

Without a doubt, you should be protecting your desktop machine with a good *virus scanner*. In some cases, the virus scanner may also check for viruses in your files. One preferred virus scanner is Kaspersky available from www.kapersky.com, but you may use whatever you like. However, ensure that you get a reputable commercial virus scanner versus using a free one.

NMAP

Network mapper (*NMAP*) is a free open source utility used for network exploration or security auditing. NMAP is a vital tool for you to know about; it is available from www.insecure.org.

> **WARNING**   Asking for permission from your host before scanning your site with this or other tools is customary (and sometimes required). Your rights to use this may vary in your state, province, or country. Check your local laws before performing any tests with NMAP. Always ask for permission before scanning any site that does not belong to you. Never assume that it's okay.

NMAP produces lots of information about your site, and can help pinpoint problems such as open ports, out-of-date software that is (in some cases) vulnerable, and more.

Nessus Vulnerability Scanner

The *Nessus* vulnerability scanner features high-speed discovery, configuration auditing, and asset profiling, as well as sensitive data discovery and vulnerability analysis of your security posture.

You may choose between a free and commercial version of this scanner at www.nessus.org. The scanner can tell you about a number of things, such as security holes, out-of-date software, and more.

Text Editor

Using Notepad + (mentioned in Chapter 8) is a great method to clean up your CMS source files. Feel free to use any *text editor*, but try to avoid word-processing type applications because they may include special characters that could cause problems.

SSH Client

The SSH client is an optional tool because you may not have Secure Shell (SSH) access. If you do, then you will want to get two utilities:

- *WinSCP* — This is a free open source File Transfer Protocol (FTP) and Secure FTP (SFTP) client for Windows. Available from www.winscp.net, it provides you with a secure method for connecting to your website. It has a great graphical interface, and eases the upload and download of files.

- *Putty* — This tool is used to connect to your server via a shell, and provides a command-line utility to your server. It is available from `www.chiark` `.greenend.org.uk/~sgtatham/putty/download.html`.

Clean Machine from Which to Work

Having a clean machine from which to work is handy for downloading potentially infected files. If you do corrupt the machine, or infect it, you can easily re-image the hard disk and restore the machine to a clean state.

Hand Tools

Having a screwdriver, pliers, nut-driver, and other essential tools for working directly on a server will make your life easier. This only applies if you have physical access to the machine.

Digital Camera

This tool requirement is applicable only if you have access to the server. The purposes for the camera include snapping pictures of damage, recording the cable configuration, and many more uses.

Collecting the Information

You should be aware that what follows is not a detailed method for collecting evidence for submission to a court of law. If you are planning on prosecuting an offender, you should immediately engage a professional forensics company to do proper collection of evidence. *Do not attempt to change anything*; contact a professional. The law requires very specific steps to gather, store, and transport digital evidence.

Additionally, you may easily miss something that a professional would not. If you have any legal questions regarding this process, consult your attorney, because this book is not offering any legal advice.

For the purposes of this discussion, collecting the information is solely for ensuring that the damage is repaired, and changing processes to prevent attacks in the future.

Logs tell you a *lot* about what the hacker did or didn't do. Likewise, the absence of logs could indicate the hacker erased them. To do so would require a higher level of privilege than a typical web application break-in.

> **NOTE** Not all problems in an operation are related to security. Some can be related to *availability*, meaning that the asset (server) was not available, thus impacting the site.

The server (hardware) logs would be of interest to you if you own your own equipment. Today's server equipment can tell you a lot about how the machine is doing. Knowing that a potential memory failure exists on the horizon, or a that disk drive has degraded (starting to fail), will allow you to be proactive and replace the suspect component. For breach purposes, many manufacturers will record in BIOS or firmware whether a case has been opened.

Make a copy of all the log files. Set those aside for now on a flash drive or CD-ROM. The purpose of the logs is to re-create a picture of what happened. You'll learn more about that process shortly.

Copying these logs is very important. Because logs could easily be located in non-standard places, you'll learn more shortly about the generic means to copy them.

Keep in mind a few rules about logs as you go through them:

- If they are not being saved, then clearly you won't be able to get them.

- A compromised server could easily have its logs removed. If you choose not to use log rotation, you could run out of disk space, which could cause other problems.

- Copying logs weekly or monthly, and deleting the old ones, should be fine. However, your company's information security policy will supersede that practice.

System Logs

Each CMS has a different approach to logging needs. Apache/Linux servers will write to the normal error log and access log locations.

Each CMS provides different logging capabilities:

- *Drupal* — Drupal has several functions (depending on the Drupal version and the logs you want to watch) to help you monitor logs. The three of interest are `watchdog`, `dblog`, and `syslog`. Using these (again, these are version-dependent), you can monitor the events recorded in your logs. You can always pull the logs manually from most web hosts. For example, you can view watchdog logs at Administer ➤ Logs ➤ Recent Log Entries (`admin/logs/watchdog`).

- *Joomla Logging* — Most tools for Joomla! are designed for analyzing traffic to your site, and not necessarily for monitoring errors, and so on. To get detailed information for logging, reviewing the `error.log` file or the Apache logs directly is best.

- *Plone* — Plone is based on Python, and the logs for Plone are stored at `var/log/instance.log`.

- *WordPress* — The logging plug-in of choice for WordPress is WPSYSLOG2, available from `ossec.net` (`www.ossec.net/main/wpsyslog2`). This plug-in logs all the system events, including POSTs, failed logins, logins, and logouts. It records new users, profiles, and records to the system log. This very useful tool can help you greatly in monitoring your logs.

Apache Access Logs

One proven means of logging is through Apache. The simplest method to access these logs is to log in to your cPanel control system for your web host. As mentioned in Chapter 8, you should have activated the archiving nightly feature.

Find the *Raw Access Logs* icon. Click it, and one or more log file choices appear, as shown in Figure 9-1. This starts the download process to your local drive, as shown in Figure 9-2.

Raw Access Logs

Please select a raw log to download:
salvusalerting.com

Figure 9-1: Raw Apache access logs from a site

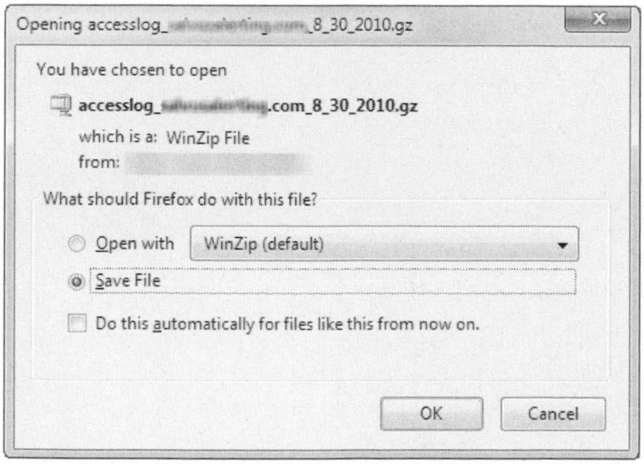

Figure 9-2: Saving or opening log files

In most cases, the download will consist of a compressed file with the extension GZ. Depending on your operating system and tools, you may need to obtain a tool (such as WinZip) to open the file.

You want to review the logs in detail for any correlation to the hack. Such correlations may be repeated requests for files or applications not there. You may see a high number of POSTs in the log file, which indicates an attempt to upload something. The review of logs can be quite daunting at first. However, over time, you'll become accustomed to it.

Take a look at a few examples to help familiarize you with what to look for. Following is an example of a log entry from a Linux server:

```
192.168.1.1 - - [06/Jul/2010:13:49:39 -0400]
    "GET /site/index.php?format=feed&amp;type=rssHTTP/
    1.0" 200 5965 "-" "Mozilla/4.0 (compatible;)"
```

This is a classic example of an Apache log file. As you learned in Chapter 8, this is the common log format. In this case, the visitor is from 192.168.1.1 and is asking for an RSS feed from the site. The 200 indicates all is well.

The following entry shows an attempted attack:

```
xxx.xxx.xxx.xxx - - [23/Jul/2010:01:15:49 -0400]
 "GET /?option=com_xxxxxx&Itemid=12& task=
../../../../../../../../../../../../../../../proc/self/environ%00
HTTP/1.1" 410 296 www.domain.com "-" "libwww-perl/5.834" "-"
```

This example from a log file has been edited to protect the source server. However, you can see from the ../../../../../../../ portion of the file that an attack is attempting to exploit a known vulnerability.

Following is another sanitized example of a server that has been a victim of a *brute-force* dictionary attack:

```
11:22:15 ServerName: Failed password for invalid user dola from
xxx.xxx.xxx.xxx port 57725 ssh2

11:22:15 ServerName: sshd[16667]: Failed password for invalid user
 consuelo from xxx.xxx.xxx.xxx port 39894 ssh2


11:22:16 ServerName: sshd[16670]: reverse mapping checking getaddrinfo
 for xxx.xxx.xxx.xxx.rdns.SourceServer.com [xxx.xxx.xxx.xxx]
failed - POSSIBLE BREAK-IN ATTEMPT!

11:22:16 ServerName: sshd[16670]: Invalid user dolores
from xxx.xxx.xxx.xxx


11:22:16 ServerName: sshd[16670]: pam_unix(sshd:auth): check pass;user
 unknown



11:22:16 ServerName: sshd[16670]: pam_unix(sshd:auth): authentication
 failure; logname= uid=0 euid=0 tty=ssh ruser= rhost=xxx.xxx.xxx.xxx
```

```
11:22:16 ServerName: sshd[16671]: reverse mapping checking getaddrinfo
for xxx.xxx.xxx.xxx.rdns.SourceServer.com [xxx.xxx.xxx.xxx]
failed - POSSIBLE BREAK-IN ATTEMPT!


11:22:15 ServerName: Failed password for invalid user dola from
xxx.xxx.xxx.xxx port 57725 ssh211:22:15 ServerName: sshd[16667]:
    Failed password for invalid user

consuelo from xxx.xxx.xxx.xxx port 39894 ssh211:22:16 ServerName:
    sshd[16670]: reverse mapping checking getaddrinfo
        for xxx.xxx.xxx.xxx.rdns.SourceServer.com [xxx.xxx.xxx.xxx]

failed - POSSIBLE BREAK-IN ATTEMPT!
11:22:16 ServerName: sshd[16670]: Invalid user dolores
    from xxx.xxx.xxx.xxx
11:22:16 ServerName: sshd[16670]: pam_unix(sshd:auth): check pass;

user unknown
11:22:16 ServerName: sshd[16670]: pam_unix(sshd:auth): authentication
failure; logname= uid=0 euid=0 tty=ssh ruser= rhost=xxx.xxx.xxx.xxx
11:22:16 ServerName: sshd[16671]: reverse mapping checking getaddrinfo
for xxx.xxx.xxx.xxx.rdns.SourceServer.com [xxx.xxx.xxx.xxx] failed -
 POSSIBLE BREAK-IN ATTEMPT!

11:22:16 ServerName: sshd[16671]: Invalid user cristian from
xxx.xxx.xxx.xxx
```

Note the POSSIBLE BREAK-IN ATTEMPT entry in the log.

Server (Hardware) Logs

If you're managing your CMS-enabled website on your own hardware, then managing that hardware is as important as the management of the website. The major manufacturers of server hardware all offer some type of software monitoring that talks directly to their servers. The types of things you can monitor and manage vary by manufacturer, but include temperature, power (voltage), status of memory (that is, counting errors leading to failure), hard drive degradation, chassis intrusion, command-line access, and more.

In the event of a break-in to your building, preventing physical access to the machine is important. A dedicated attacker could do a number of things while physically sitting at the machine. For example, the attacker could put a small USB key with a virus onto a machine. The attacker could open the machine and remove parts such as disk drives. The attacker could obtain a password and log on at the machine. Although these actions sound like the stuff of a spy-thriller, they are "real world," and threats like these do exist.

If you suspect or have proof that someone has gained physical access to the server(s), review the hardware logs on the machine for any sign of physical tampering. Ensure that no unwanted USB keys are attached to the server.

NOTE A recent breach of a U.S. military network was traced to a USB key with malware on it. You cannot be careful enough these days.

If you're *sure* your system was not physically tampered with, then proceeding to a check of the hardware logs is okay. However, as a matter of course, regularly performing a physical check of your machines is a good idea.

Network Logs

You can obtain logs from several points in your network. They may be obtained from an *intrusion detection system*, which would tell you about attempts to break in. The *router* or *firewall* logs would keep you in the loop on many items. Generally, you want to copy logs for all devices in your network that may be impacted.

Following is a partial list of events to look for:

- Logins at unexpected times when things should be quiet (such as off hours)
- Sudden jumps in bandwidth that are very out of the ordinary or unexpected (which could indicate someone is copying files down or up)
- A sudden loss of services (which is an easy one, because your phone will quickly ring)
- An increase (before, during, or after) of attempted logins from an unauthorized source
- A list of login names at some point in time just before the hack (perhaps 1 to 24 hours) to ensure that a login was not compromised

Review the logs thoroughly to look for attacks or attempted attacks.

FTP Logs

FTP logs show you who has logged in and out of the server, and with what username. If you find *your* username has been used, yet you know you didn't give it out, then chances are that your desktop has been infected.

NOTE See Chapter 8 for an example FTP log.

IM Logs

Instant messaging (IM) is great tool for companies. Some IM clients can accept downloads or uploads. You want to be sure that a virus or malware was not downloaded into a machine. Scanning *all* local machines (even if there is only one) is important to eliminate them as the source of an attack.

If your information security policy covers the use of IM, you may consider logging software. This is meant less as an intrusion on personal privacy and more about protecting your infrastructure. You should also consider limiting downloads.

IM can let bad things into your environment quickly. As part of your recovery, if you collect IM logging, be sure to obtain all the logs surrounding the attack event.

Reviewing Log Files

Reviewing the Apache log files is made a bit easier with either a text editor, or with a nice tool called *SandCat log analyzer tool* (available from syhunt.com). The latter tool reads through a log file and notes for you possible suspicious log entries. You can then look those up directly by opening the log file in the text editor. The purpose is to attempt to identify a file that was compromised, or a series of comprises. This can lead you to the attack vector.

Procedures for Containment

The following general areas should be considered as prime targets for an attack:

- Operating system breach
- Web applications or website breach
- FTP or Telnet breach
- E-mail services breach

Each of these areas is intertwined, and the sources of attack could be very difficult to track down.

NOTE As you work through a cleanup and restoration, document your steps. For example, if you update a plug-in on your WordPress site, then document it. If you remove a virus, then document what the virus was, where it was found, and the method used to remove it. This is vital, because you may forget or you may not have removed all portions of the attack. The author has worked on sites where the site owner "helped" by cleaning up the damage, and yet they were immediately attacked again — which was worse the second time. By not noting exactly what was changed, the author was unable to discern the original attack point. That particular hacked site took more than a week to clean up. Had the site owner documented what had been done, it would have been a much shorter time.

Before getting into the procedures for containment in these areas of vulnerability, first take a look at two types of hosting: *shared hosting* and *dedicated hosting*. The discussion of dedicated hosting also covers using a virtual private server (VPS) as a dedicated machine.

Shared Hosting Containment

In shared hosting, the server could be breached, or your site could simply be breached. Many times, in shared hosting, you'll likely see a code injection where the bad guys put in some malicious code to spread to other machines simply by a person browsing the website. Or, they may put in a command-and-control application such as a C99 or R57 program (known as a *remote access trojan (RAT) or Root Kit Shell*). The purpose of these evil gems is to use your machine for any number of purposes, including listening in on what you do.

If you are unfortunate enough to be on a shared server that is penetrated, then your immediate options are to restore from a clean backup, or to manually remove the evil files. Your hosting provider can be of assistance by providing you with a list of files that are suspect or that contain viruses.

To be prepared for this event, you should have in advance a clean and up-to-date backup. Your software should be up to date (patched) and you should be changing your passwords every 30 days. As you move into the containment phase, the following steps are commonly followed to address the aforementioned areas:

1. Make an offline copy of your access logs.
2. Isolate and remove the affected code as soon as possible.
3. Change all passwords.
4. Scan files on the server for viruses.

If your site is attacked successfully again, then you may be dealing with a situation that requires you to think about moving web hosts. Sometimes the easiest method is to simply move to a new hosting company.

Dedicated Hosting Containment

Containment and cleanup in a dedicated hosting environment is more time-consuming, but, you typically have a lot more access to the machine, which makes the task of cleaning and protecting the machine easier for you.

NOTE The procedures outlined in this chapter are to be used when logged in as the *root* or *super user* level of your operating system. Take extreme caution and have a full backup before you start. Even if that means your backup is infected, you should still have a copy.

If you have physical access to the machine in a dedicated hosting environment, removing its connection to the network will stop the flow of data to and from the attacker. In the situation where an attacker is using the environment to spam, then disconnecting the machine would certainly stop it.

WARNING If you are intending to bring in law enforcement, then you should not make any changes to the environment, and take every step you can to freeze the data as is. In short, if you are going to take legal action, you must have a security professional gather all the evidence needed before continuing to restore operations. This way, it can be used in a legal case. From here forward, the rest of this chapter will be oriented to a non-pursuit of legal action. This book is not meant to replace or to be legal advice for you.

Because most readers will not have access to the physical server, the procedures discussed throughout this chapter will deal solely with a server at a hosting facility. All the same rules apply for machines you can access.

Operating System Breach Containment

For the CMS types addressed in this book, the operating system of the server will most likely be some distribution of Linux, UNIX, Sun Solaris, or Microsoft Windows. The operating system is the most prized of targets. By controlling the operating system, the bad guy can control the machine.

In fact, in sophisticated attacks, whole portions of a server's operating system may be altered, thus hiding the attack from the administrator. This is done through the replacement of specific functions in the operating system that might help you detect an attack.

The very generic terms for an attack on the operating system is *rooted* or *owned*. Both terms mean that a hacker has gained control of the super user–level processes.

The process a hacker follows is to basically look for or discover weaknesses in your system, and exploit them. Following are several areas that an attacker could use to reach a server:

- Improper or out-of-date firewall configuration
- An unpatched or out-of-date operating system
- Unpatched software components
- Rogue employees
- Desktops or notebook computers connected to a server

- An infected machine on the network
- Physical access to a machine by a malicious person
- Network-attached printers that may be used to assault servers either locally or remotely
- Web, database, or network services that are misconfigured or out of date

A breached server will exhibit odd behavior, such as unusually high loads on the machine, excessive bandwidth, many files open, or super users logged in that should not be. Other signs include software that should not be installed, or unexpected reboots. Many more symptoms could exhibit a server breach. In essence, if the machine is acting strangely, when it normally behaves, then you have a problem.

One area to do a quick review on is the date and time stamp of files. Look to see whether any of the files or folders have recently changed. Although not a guarantee of whether a true hack has occurred, the chances are good that if you have been hacked, this area will note it for you.

Data on a server or site that has been compromised is very often modified by the attacker. Check the FTP archives, directories for users, web pages, and so on for change.

When you are trying to contain an operating system breach, consider the following:

- Using Linux commands on the server
- Updating the server
- Using RKHunter
- Checking for open ports

Using Linux Commands

The intention of this book is not to teach you how to be a Linux operating system administrator. However, a couple of Linux commands are handy to know when dealing with an operating system breach. These are commonly available on most Linux distributions.

The who command can tell you *who* is logged on to the machine. In its simplest form, typing the command who will reveal all the users who are logged in.

When dealing with an operating system breach, the first thing you want to find out is who is on the machine. Log in into your server using PuTTY or another SSH client (discussed earlier in this chapter), and then elevate your login to super user. At the # prompt, enter the **who** command, and you should see something similar to Figure 9-3.

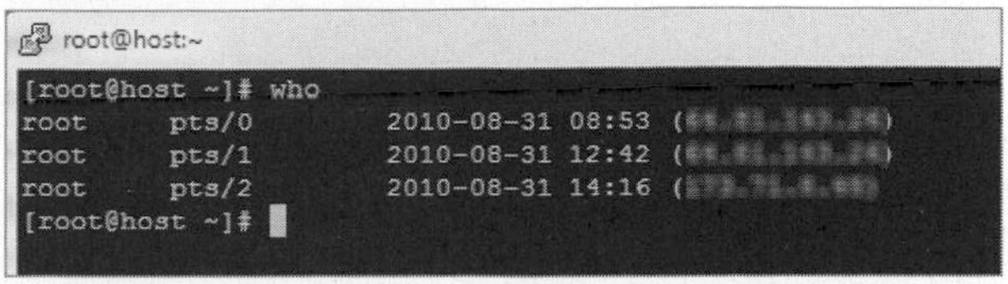

Figure 9-3: Example of using the `who` command

If you find an unauthorized user logged in, then you can take the necessary steps to log him out. Figure 9-3 shows an example of three different Internet providers (IP) addresses logged in as root. If any of those were bad guys, you would be able to take immediate action by terminating their connections and blocking the IP addresses.

What you see here is the *Pseudo Terminal number* (or *PTY number*), who they are logged in as, and what username was used. Most importantly, you see the IP address from where the person is logged in. To locate your PTY, look at your IP address that you are using, and then you'll know which one to terminate.

To terminate or *kill* a PTY, find the number of the PTY with the command `# ps -ef | grep "ssh"`, which will show you all the PID's logged in using SSH. You'll see something like the following:

```
[root@host ~]# ps -ef | grep "ssh"
root      26188      1  0 01:08 ? 0:00:00 /usr/sbin/sshd
root      29740 26188  0 14:29 ? 00:00:00 sshd: root@pts/0
```

The number following root is the PID. Issue the command `kill - 9` *pid*, where *pid* is the number.

If your distribution of Linux does not support the `who` command, consult the `man` pages.

WARNING Be sure you do not log *authorized* users out, such as your host.

If you find that someone has illegally logged in, you'll want to record that IP address.

You'll also want to review the load on your machine from time to time to keep a basic idea of the average load. If your server is hacked and is serving up IRC chats to the underground community, then you'll see an increase in loads. The `top` command provides the capability to take a dynamic look at processor activity in real time. This command enables you to see processes, resources, memory consumption, and the user who initiated the activity.

To find out your load, type **top** at the command prompt, as shown in Figure 9-4.

```
top - 13:59:03 up 55 days,  5:17,  1 user,  load average: 0.19, 0.31, 0.14
Tasks:  62 total,   1 running,  57 sleeping,   4 stopped,   0 zombie
Cpu(s):  0.3%us,  0.3%sy,  0.0%ni, 99.4%id,  0.0%wa,  0.0%hi,  0.0%si,  0.0%st
Mem:    786432k total,   376712k used,   409720k free,        0k buffers
Swap:        0k total,        0k used,        0k free,        0k cached

  PID USER      PR  NI  VIRT  RES  SHR S %CPU %MEM    TIME+  COMMAND
    1 root      18   0  2148  668  580 S  0.0  0.1  0:32.75 init
 1866 root      15   0  4796 3040 1692 S  0.0  0.4  0:02.16 authProg
 3314 root      15   0  2280 1048  820 R  0.0  0.1  0:00.00 top
 3746 root      18   0  8224 5460 1832 S  0.0  0.7  2:23.05 tailwatchd
 3781 root      15   0  4220 2320 1120 S  0.0  0.3  0:08.60 cphulkd
 3797 root      15   0  5616 3744 1284 S  0.0  0.5  0:58.79 queueprocd
 3816 root      33  18  4012 1516  588 S  0.0  0.2  0:01.15 cpanellogd
 5137 root      18   0  7548 4696 1816 S  0.0  0.6  0:00.04 leechprotect
 5138 nobody    15   0 12412 5044 2576 S  0.0  0.6  0:00.25 httpd
 5142 nobody    15   0 12400 4868 2416 S  0.0  0.6  0:00.30 httpd
 5148 nobody    15   0 12448 4880 2392 S  0.0  0.6  0:00.18 httpd
 5254 root      18   0 11964 5148 3108 S  0.0  0.7  0:42.25 httpd
 5712 root      15   0 15936 8072 1288 S  0.0  1.0  1:56.39 cpsrvd-ssl
```

Figure 9-4: top command showing the processes that are running

In this case, you can see that the total load on the CPU is 0.3 percent, the free memory is 409,720 KB, and the machine has 62 total tasks running. Lastly, you can see that one user is logged in.

If your site is extremely busy, you'll see much higher loads. Again, this is not necessarily an indicator that your site is or isn't being hacked, but it's a data point to look at. Monitor your site's performance regularly to gain an understanding of *your* particular traffic pattern.

Updating Your Server

Updating your server may very well be a task your host has taken care of for you. Hosts such as Rochen.com handle the operating systems upgrades for you. Other hosts may handle it differently. If you are tasked with updating your operating system, then the update process is simple in most cases.

At the command prompt type **yum update** (for RedHat/Fedora/CentOs distributions of Linux). This will grab most of the patches necessary to keep your server running optimally and securely.

Using RKHunter

The next step is to check for the presence of a *rootkit*. RKHunter is a great tool for checking whether the system is compromised.

Installing RKHunter is easy; simply type the following at the # command prompt:

```
yum install rkhunter
```

If it's already installed, then you'll get a message similar to the one shown in Figure 9-5.

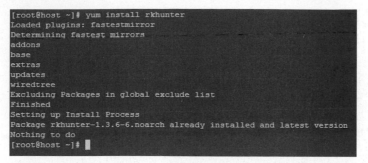

```
[root@host ~]# yum install rkhunter
Loaded plugins: fastestmirror
Determining fastest mirrors
addons
base
extras
updates
wiredtree
Excluding Packages in global exclude list
Finished
Setting up Install Process
Package rkhunter-1.3.6-6.noarch already installed and latest version
Nothing to do
[root@host ~]#
```

Figure 9-5: RKHunter already installed

With RKhunter installed, start it by entering the following command at the command prompt:

```
rkhunter - c
```

RKHunter performs a series of diagnostic checks, looking for known rootkit files, directories, malware, back doors, and suspicious processes. It scans your user accounts and looks for accounts that have the equivalent privileges of root or super user.

> **NOTE** If you're running Windows rather than Linux, you can get equivalent tools to handle those tasks from `http://technet.microsoft.com/en-us/sysinternals/bb842062.aspx`. Download the SysInternals suite.

If directories and processes are running that are atypical, RKHunter flags those and immediately lets you know. If RKHunter finds anything wrong, it displays the various checks in red (very noticeable). If you do find something, you may need to enlist the aid of your hosting company to help remove it.

If all these tests are clean, then you'll be greeted with a message similar to the one shown in Figure 9-6.

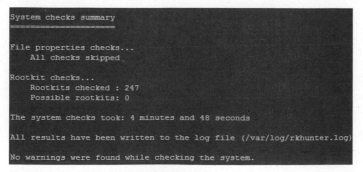

```
System checks summary
=====================

File properties checks...
    All checks skipped

Rootkit checks...
    Rootkits checked : 247
    Possible rootkits: 0

The system checks took: 4 minutes and 48 seconds

All results have been written to the log file (/var/log/rkhunter.log)

No warnings were found while checking the system.
```

Figure 9-6: RKHunter shows "all clear"

Checking for Open Ports

Another basic test you should perform is to see what *ports* are open. RKHunter does check for open ports such as 6666 and 6667, which, unless you are running your own IRC (chat) service, should be closed. However, you should look beyond what RKHunter checks and review all the open ports.

Type in the following at the command prompt:

```
#netstat -az | more
```

This command instructs the server to show you all the open ports. The more command enables you to look at the long list of data more easily by providing a portion at a time, as shown in Figure 9-7.

```
Active Internet connections (servers and established)
Proto Recv-Q Send-Q Local Address          Foreign Address
tcp      0     52 ::ffff:██.██.██.92:22     ::ffff:███.██.█.48:64120
```

Figure 9-7: Active connection to a remote machine

This is a basic connection to your machine. The *Local Address* that has been blurred out here is the server's IP address. The *Foreign Address* is the browsing IP address. This, of course, is simply a basic look. What you don't want to see is machines connecting to port 6667 or 6666, which would show up next to the IP address, such as 192.168.1.182:*6667*. In that case, the action you would want to take is to close ports 6666 and 6667 (assuming they are open).

An easier method to discovering open ports is to use NMAP to scan your system (*with permission from the host or owner of the machine only*) and determine what ports are open. Figure 9-8 shows a view of a server's ports from NMAP. In this example, a variety of ports are open, but, in this case, all is well. If you were to see a system with hundreds of ports open, then you have a bigger problem.

| Nmap Output | Ports / Hosts | Topology | Host Details | Scans |

Port	Protocol	State	Service	Version
21	tcp	open	ftp	PureFTPd
22	tcp	open	ssh	OpenSSH 4.3 (protocol 2.0)
25	tcp	filtered	smtp	
53	tcp	open	domain	
80	tcp	open	http	Apache httpd
110	tcp	open	pop3	Courier pop3d
143	tcp	open	imap	Courier Imapd (released 2008)
443	tcp	open	http	Apache httpd
465	tcp	open	smtp	Exim smtpd 4.69
993	tcp	open	imap	Courier Imapd (released 2008)
995	tcp	open	pop3	Courier pop3d
3306	tcp	open	mysql	MySQL 5.0.91-community-log
8009	tcp	open	ajp13	

Figure 9-8: Output of an NMAP scan

Web Applications or Website Breach Containment

After figuring out who caused the breach, the second step of attack containment is to get rid of the bad and malicious code. This can be a tedious process, depending on the level of attack. Fortunately, in the CMS space, most attacks are related to web applications, which means that the attack is on the CMS itself, or the extensions, modules, or plug-ins. This is a time-consuming, but easy, fix. Let's use the popular Joomla! CMS as an example.

Download the latest version of Joomla!. For example, if you're running Joomla! version 1.5.xx, then download the latest version of 1.5.xx. If you are running production 1.6.xx, then download the latest version of version 1.6.xx. This ensures that any altered files have been fixed by overwriting them with clean copies.

If you have a clean backup, then to contain the attack, you simply conduct the restoration, because this is the safest bet. *This assumes, of course, that you have a recent and clean backup.*

If you do not have a backup, you should create one, even if this means backing up infected files. In some ways, having a dirty backup is much better than having no backup at all.

Assuming you have not changed the core Joomla! files (or Drupal, Plone, or WordPress, if one of those is your CMS of choice), then unzip the downloaded file and upload *over* the current files. This has the effect of potentially wiping out a lot of bad code quickly.

WARNING If you have made any code changes to the stock files, then overwriting the files *will* wipe out those changes.

Next, using a desktop that is protected by a *very* good virus scanning application (such as Kaspersky Internet Security, available at `kaspersky .com`), create a folder on your drive, or preferably on a flash drive that can be easily cleaned.

NOTE Copying files to your local machine has the potential of infecting your machine. Downloading to a machine that you don't care about — one you could easily reformat and re-image — is best.

Download your entire `public_html` or other `www` folder that contains your website. As these files are downloading, the virus scanner will scan each one for malicious code. The file will either be denied the download request, or will be quarantined. This is not meant to clean your server, but rather to locate the files that you will manually clean.

Bear in mind, that as you download the files from your server, you likely will pull a virus down with it. However, a good virus scanner will stop the infected file as it is downloading. Thus, in most cases, you won't really pull the virus onto your machine. Instead, you will get a list of the file locations, making it easy to find them by hand.

After the download completes, locate the report tool in your scanner and note the location of the suspect files. One word of caution is that many attacks paste garbage code or malware into .html, .js, and .txt files. These files may be critical to you, and, thus, deleting them is out of the question. You'll need to manually remove the malicious code.

Using your FTP client, log in and remove the virus files you can get rid of such as rootkit files, banking phishing scam files, and other malware. Next you may need to work on the virus-infected files at the command line.

Let's say you are using a CentOS machine. You open the file by entering the following command:

```
nano filename
```

This opens the editor, as shown in Figure 9-9.

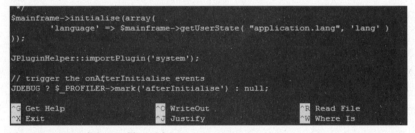

Figure 9-9: Editing a file with nano

This partial screenshot shows some code from Joomla!, and shows a partial list of controls. You would need to edit out the malicious code. If possible, use WinSCP to edit and reload the files. Then press Ctrl+O to save and Ctrl+X to exit.

After cleanup, performing a second scan is a good idea, just in case.

FTP or Telnet Breach Containment

Figure 9-10 shows an example of a remote computer connected to a server via FTP. Here you can see that the Local Address xxx.xxx.xxx.94:21 is connected to a foreign (remote computer) address on port 21. Port 21 is the default for FTP. (Note that the actual FTP addresses have been sanitized in this example.)

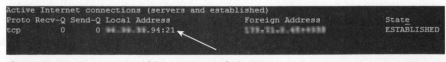

Figure 9-10: Remote machine connected via FTP

You can use this quick test to see whether the intruder has compromised your FTP username and password. If someone is logged in using FTP and no one is supposed to be, then a good chance exists that the bad guy has your FTP. Should you determine that a connection has been obtained, terminate the connection and change the FTP password. Scan the system and all your desktop/notebooks for viruses.

E-Mail Services Breach Containment

Most everyone is familiar with *spam* or unwanted mail that delivers promises of riches, love, fame, and fortune. In fact, according to the MX Logic Threat Center (www.mxlogic.com/threat_center), more than 80 to 85 percent of e-mail sent is spam.

In Chapter 2, you learned about an attacker using open relays as a means to send mail through your server. Or, the attacker can actually add an account to the server.

You can pay attention to a number of symptoms when it comes to your machine's behavior regarding spam:

- *Odd return e-mail coming to you with your name on it* — Knowing you did not send the e-mail is a big indicator that someone or some process has been sending e-mail out from your web server.

- *Remove from mailing list* — You might start receiving reports from unknown recipients asking you to "remove them" from your mailing list. This is an important clue, because you probably know who you send e-mail to on a regular basis. Some mail applications or sending services (such as MailChimp) will handle the "unsubscribes" for you. Receiving a slew of requests to remove people from your mailing list could indicate that mail has been sent from your system to unwanted recipients in some cases.

- *Blocking IP addresses* — Many companies exist that help lower the spam threat by actively monitoring and blocking IP addresses that engage in spam as a business. If you're notified by spam monitoring firms that your IP address has been blocked because of excessive spam, check your SENT mail logs first for evidence, then move up the food chain and locate the spam malware.

- *Bounced and non-deliverable mail* — Lots of bounced messages and non-deliverable reports can mean a few things. One is that if you purchased a list of names, it's likely that the list is not any good for use, and will get you blacklisted as a email sender. Buying a list is never a good idea; you should always build your own. If you did not purchase a mailing list and bounced e-mail is a new symptom, then start looking.

If any of these symptoms occur, you may receive notification from your host that you have exceeded the amount of mail you can send per day. A sure sign that this is happening is when your disk is filling up with spam mail quite quickly in the SENT or TEMP folders.

These are signs that your mail server has likely been compromised, and you should take care of the problem immediately. In most Linux-based e-mail systems, the folders are accessible by the administrator. You can review your folders to see what is in them.

Containing an e-mail breach involves following a number of steps, and lots of cleanup.

Step One: Check for Open Relay Servers

The first step is to ensure that you are not running an open relay e-mail server. Quite a few sites can help you test for open relays on your server.

If you have an open relay, contact your host or e-mail administrator for assistance. You may consider looking at commercial tools available on such sites as DNSSTUFF.COM to assist with your e-mail tests.

Step Two: Scan Your Ports

Next, scan your ports using NMAP (from insecure.org). You should ensure that all the ports are closed that should be closed. Each server is different, so telling you what ports you should open or close beyond the normal 80, 443, 21, and 25 is impossible. Contact your host or network administrator to assist with that. If you find a high number of ports open, then you may have been severely hacked with lots of embedded malware on the server.

Step Three: See Who Is Logging In

To see who is logging in, you must first get to the shell using SSH. After you log on as the root user, type **W** at the # prompt to see who is logged in. If more than one root user is logged in, as shown in Figure 9-11, your server might have been compromised.

Figure 9-11: Unauthorized logon

In the example shown in Figure 9-11, the server was compromised and was sending out thousands of pharmacy spam e-mails a day. As shown in the figure, a quick check revealed that two root users were on.

Should you find yourself in this position, you must first terminate the unauthorized user's session.

To terminate the unauthorized session, you'll need the *Process ID* (*PID*) of the user. To obtain the PID, enter the following command:

```
ps -ef | grep <theusersname>  or  ps -ef | grep sshd
```

This gives you the PIDs of the real root user and the unknown user. Write down both PIDs so you don't accidentally terminate the real root user.

You then terminate a session as follows:

```
kill -9 xxxxxx
```

In this example, xxxxxx equals the user's pid.

Finally, change your password and block the unauthorized user's IP address.

Step Four: Verify That Spam Is Gone

Next, you must verify the spam e-mails have been removed. Because each e-mail system differs in the way it stores and processes a queue, you should consult the manual for your e-mail system. In general you'll see something like what is shown in Figure 9-12.

Figure 9-12: Typical e-mail subdirectory tree

After you click into the mail queue shown in Figure 9-12, you may discover hundreds of e-mails, as shown in Figure 9-13.

Figure 9-14 shows an example of spam that was retrieved from that the example hacked e-mail server's directory. The BCC: field in this particular e-mail contained about 250 e-mail addresses. (Of course, much of the personal information has been wiped out of this screenshot for security and privacy reasons.)

For starters, if you received an e-mail such as this, surely you would realize the United Nations is *not* inviting you to come to a summit. And, unless you are a spammer, and these are in your server's SENT mail box, then finding the offending code or vulnerability is time-sensitive. The longer you take, the more mail that goes out, and the greater the chance that you'll be blacklisted as a sender in many places.

Name	Date modified	Type	Size
1278173471.M39168P10700V00000000000...	7/3/2010 12:11 PM	COM,S=6143%3A...	6 KB
1278175098.M843537P23265V0000000000...	7/3/2010 12:38 PM	COM,S=6267%3A...	7 KB
1278175293.M300072P24485V0000000000...	7/3/2010 12:41 PM	COM,S=6125%3A...	6 KB
1278175408.M514118P24916V0000000000...	7/3/2010 12:43 PM	COM,S=3736%3A...	4 KB
1278175518.M395828P25705V0000000000...	7/3/2010 12:45 PM	COM,S=4696%3A...	5 KB
1278175623.M960490P26264V0000000000...	7/3/2010 12:47 PM	COM,S=4402%3A...	5 KB
1278175829.M56256P27443V00000000000...	7/3/2010 12:50 PM	COM,S=6153%3A...	7 KB
1278175957.M793640P28024V0000000000...	7/3/2010 12:52 PM	COM,S=6275%3A...	7 KB
1278176064.M723632P28504V0000000000...	7/3/2010 12:54 PM	COM,S=6194%3A...	7 KB
1278250029.M799212P22121V0000000000...	7/4/2010 9:27 AM	COM,S=477%3A2,...	1 KB
1278250073.M790156P22283V0000000000...	7/4/2010 9:27 AM	COM,S=475%3A2,...	1 KB
1278320744.M732202P7822V00000000000...	7/5/2010 5:05 AM	COM,S=1989%3A...	2 KB
1278321243.M776505P10130V0000000000...	7/5/2010 5:14 AM	COM,S=12731%3...	13 KB

Figure 9-13: Spam being sent from compromised server

```
Here is a Received: from                          )
         (SquirrelMail authenticated user py       )
      by         .org with HTTP;
      Fri, 2 Jul 2010 17:21:17 -0400
Message-ID: <3f2ca6f106f1996e833a3c951ef4dc3e.squirrel@j          org>
Date: Fri, 2 Jul 2010 17:21:17 -0400
Subject: INVITATION TO UNITED NATIONS SUMMIT
From: "United Nations" <un@un.org>  ◄──
Reply-To: mdgs@un-
Bcc:                        .sg,        ◄──
```

Figure 9-14: Example spam being sent

When you start getting a lot of returned mail like the one shown in Figure 9-14, you've been hacked. In this example, the `Reply-To` field is different than the `un.org` address. The actual purpose for sending these e-mails is actually unknown.

Step Five: Control the Damage

The next step is to review the SENT directory to confirm whether mail has gone out. If so, then the damage is done. Clean out the current and pending-to-send queues, and scan for viruses.

If your situation was that the spam was going out for a very long time, then you might be blacklisted as a sender by several organizations. One major place to check is `SpamHaus.org`. You can enter your IP address in the *blocklist removal page*. They provide a worldwide feed to several spam filtering appliances and companies. If you make it onto their list, you might start getting a lot of legiti-mate mail blocked.

Consider signing up for *e-mail feedback* loops if you send more than a few e-mails. For example, if you have a healthy-sized mailing list of customers, you want to ensure that you get through to them. You can Google *feedback loops e-mail* and find a list of feedback loop forms for major ISPs. Filling these out is pretty simple and easy. Here's a list of a few large ISPs to get you started:

- *AOL* — `http://postmaster.info.aol.com/Postmaster.FeedbackLoop.html`
- *MSN/Hotmail* — `https://support.msn.com` (select Junk Email Partner Program)
- *Yahoo!* — `http://feedbackloop.yahoo.net` (requires a Yahoo! ID to create or sign in to an account)
- *BlueTie* — `http://feedback.bluetie.com`
- *Comcast* — `http://postmaster.comcast.net/feedback-loop.aspx`
- *Cox* — `http://fbl.cox.net/index.php`
- *Hotmail* — `http://mail.live.com/mail/postmaster.aspx`
- *USA.net* — `http://fbl.usa.net/`
- *Earthlink* — E-mail your request to `fblrequest@abuse.earthlink.net` (e-mail request)
- RoadRunner — `http://feedback.postmaster.rr.com` (or send an e-mail to `email-support@security.rr.com`)

For Earthlink and RoadRunner, include the following in your request:

- Your IP address(es) and mailing domain(s) you want to set up on the feedback loop
- Your company's contact information you want to use for the service, including name, e-mail, address, and phone number
- The e-mail address you want feedback transactions sent to so that you may get the reports from recipients marking you as spam

Other control measures include shutting off any type of mail services from your server (not always possible) if you are using an outside provider. This way, your mail server will not be compromised by the bad guys. For clarity, other means for sending mail exist, and this method is not exactly foolproof.

One final point you should be aware of is to check your e-mail folder directory and user list from your control panel. If you see users who have been added that you do not know about, you may want to suspend the user in question.

Crisis Communication to the User Community

During a crisis, a person's comprehension level drops by several degrees. The need to communicate about a disaster in simple terms is important when conveying important information.

Although you probably won't be faced with a large population of people during a hacking event, you might face a lot of support calls or tickets. Learning to speak to these people on a lower comprehension level is vital. This is not to be confused with a drop in intelligence points, but rather means that you must understand that a sufficient distraction occurs in people's minds during a disaster. Preparing your disaster plan ahead of time to include a communications or messaging protocol can help with smooth communications to all stakeholders throughout the life of an outage.

Planning Your Communications

One way to help facilitate the restoration could be to put up a simple "maintenance" message, which will prevent unnecessary interruptions. Other items used to communicate may be scripts to be followed at a telephone call center. If you run a call center, putting up an *Inbound Voice Recording* (*IVR*) will help your clients understand that there's a problem and they should be patient. You may have a forum or blog that you can use to provide updates to your community.

With that said, the following three categories of communication are very important:

- Announcement of the incident
- Communications during the incident
- Post-incident communications

Prepare ahead of time what you will say. This does not mean you should prepare a script for each of the infinite possibilities that could occur. Rather, lay these scripts out in large blocks, such as outage of a server or defacement of a page. One way to generally categorize your scripts might be equipment failure and hacker attack. Of course, a power outage would result in the same client perception as a failing server. Think about the events in this manner.

Understand what you *will plan* to say during a crisis. Although you won't stick to the script verbatim, having a framework for discussion is vital.

Plan communications for your external and internal clients after the crisis has passed.

Here are a few areas to consider for communications:

- Consider how you will reach your team, especially if team members are scattered all over the Internet

- Gather telephone numbers
- Plan a message for your employees, your clients, and for the media
- Craft a message update plan that includes the frequency of communication (for example, hourly versus daily) and set the expectation in the initial message
- Have a single point of contact
- Plan for the post-event messages

The point is keeping your employees calm, your clients feeling safe, and, should the media become involved, having your message crisp and ready. Remember, if you say something to a reporter, it can show up in the paper. Also remember that the people experiencing the effects of the crisis will likely not absorb your message as quickly as you might like.

Review and Prevention

After all is said and done, simply returning to normal operations and carrying on as if nothing happened is an invitation for further trouble. The *After Action Report* (*AAR*) is a report generated to collect all the issues and problems related to the event. The report includes the identification of problems, a proposal for solutions, and recommendations for execution of the proposed fixes. This can be in a template form such as the example presented shortly, or any other form. The key is to develop a means to collect information about what you've learned, and apply that information to update your processes.

As an example, suppose a backup was not completed for several weeks, even though it was set to run automatically on a nightly basis. After a successful attack by a hacker has been properly defended, the AAR shown in Table 9-1 might be generated.

Table 9-1: After Action Report

ISSUE/TASK	RECOMMENDATIONS	ACTIONS TO TAKE	OWNER	DUE DATE
Backup did not run successfully for three weeks, and notifications did not go out.	Update admin's backup procedures to ensure that they are checked daily after the nightly run.	1. Restore cron job.	John Schmitz	4/8/2011

Continued

Table 9-1 *(continued)*

ISSUE/TASK	RECOMMENDATIONS	ACTIONS TO TAKE	OWNER	DUE DATE
Root cause was that the cron job was removed and no procedure existed to notify admins.		2. Update all handbooks.		
		3. Develop a hand-off process for admins so that they know who is checking the backups.		
		4. Document when the backups are occurring.		
Found several extensions and modules out of date on site.	Review and update extensions and check carefully to see whether a hacker was able to shut off cron in advance through one of these extensions.	1. Review whether these items are still needed. If so, update. If not, remove.	Doug Hunt	4/11/2011
		2. Test the site as a user, ensuring that all software works after an upgrade.		
		3. Review cron logs compared to access logs.		

This example AAR looks at the situation that prevented the hacker's victim from doing a restore. In turn, the victim was forced to do a manual rebuild of the site, costing the company time and money.

Your AAR should be integrated into any declared disaster that occurs. This will ensure that lessons learned, problems found, and new systems or software are added to your disaster recovery plan.

> **NOTE** One modicum of advice regarding an event like this in real life is that if you have more than one person, you're a team. A larger team of three or more people will present a challenge in terms of egos. The key is simply this: If you or your team made a mistake (not being grossly negligent), then admit, accept it, and fix it. Many businesses make the mistake of running down the blame path. This does not fix anything.

You can use a spreadsheet, notepaper, or large white boards to capture the AAR items by recording what has been learned, and how to apply that knowledge. An AAR is a powerful tool that you should add to your business processes toolkit as soon as possible.

Preventing further problems is a matter of being proactive. As an example, if your patching processes are lax or non-existent, then you are clearly at risk. Consider prevention as a proactive matter.

Although these points are made in one form or another throughout this book, here are some key points regarding prevention:

- *Patch your systems* — This means all of them, not just your website. If you have any network equipment (such as wireless routers, routers, switches, servers, desktops, phones, and so on), then patch them. They can all become sources of infection or an attacker's entry point.

- *Review your website for unused plug-ins, modules, or extensions* — You might be surprised that you have installed many things you aren't using. Although these unused items may not be a direct security issue today, if you forget about them, they become vulnerable, thus exposing you to unnecessary harm, and possibly leading to your business's security being compromised.

- *Review your log files on a regular basis* — Chapter 8 tells you all about logs. These logs can tell you quite a bit about what is going on, what should not be going on, and who's doing it.

- *Establish an information security policy and follow it* — Consider an information security policy (if you have employees) to prevent accidental infections. Chapter 11 covers this topic in detail.

- *Consider purchasing a PCI (Payment Card Industry) security scan, even if you do not have a PCI requirement* — this scan can tell you a *lot* about your server and your software. It's typically low cost, and companies such as ControlScan.com can offer it to you at a reasonable rate.

- *Get an offsite location that has either a fireproof safe or some other secure, dry storage that you can reach at all times* — This location is good for storing documents such as software licenses and backup media. It should be a place you can reach 24/7.

- *Stay on top of vulnerability information* — Consider purchasing a subscription to SalvusAlerting.com (a company co-founded by the author). This company can handle the "keeping you informed" part of your job.

Prevention is no different than the bi-annual battery change in smoke detectors. You want to ensure that they are always working in the event that you need them.

Reporting Attack(s) to the ISP of Origin

If you have a good set of log files, then reporting the attack is not only easy, it's a very good idea. For example, imagine that your site is being attacked fairly frequently by a specific IP address. So far, the attacker has been unsuccessful, yet these attacks are eating up a lot of your resources because of checking, verifying, and reviewing the logs.

Now, assume that you see the following from the log files:

```
64.XXX.XXX.XXX - - [23/Jan/2011:01:15:49 -0400]
"GET /?option=com_someExtension&Itemid=12&
task=../../../../../../../../../../../../../../../proc/self/environ%00
HTTP/1.1" 410 296 www.yourdomain.com "-" "libwww-perl/5.834" "-"
```

This is an attempt to break into a Joomla! site by attacking a vulnerable and popular extension. In this case, the site had already upgraded this third-party extension because of a published vulnerability. Yet, the bad guy doesn't know that, and continues to shake the virtual doorknob, hoping to get in. The action here is to block the IP address and report it.

You have all the information you need to report the attempted attack. The steps are simple:

1. Locate the ISP who provides the IP address (which, for this example, is shown as 64.xxx.xxx.xxx).

2. Package up enough of the logs to make a case that you are being attacked.

3. Write a polite e-mail to report the incident(s) to the ISP.

Locating the ISP of the Offending IP Address

Visit your favorite WhoIs website to help you track down this information. One favorite is a professional toolset site called DNSSTUFF (www.dnsstuff.com). Another free site is http://tools.whois.net.

Either of these alternatives can provide you with the desired information. For the purposes of this discussion, both were used to verify that they provide the same results. For the offending ISP in the example presented earlier, both tools provide a full page of information on the origin of this IP address, based on the ISP. You are interested in two pieces of the information: the basics about the company (such as contact information) and the ISP's *netrange*.

The netrange confirms that this IP address (64.xxx.xxx.xxx) is in the range of this particular ISP, and, thus, you are reporting it to the correct provider.

```
NetRange:      64.xxx.xxx.xxx - 64.xxx.xxx.xxx
NameServer:    NS2.DOMAIN.COM
NameServer:    NS1.DOMAIN.COM
RegDate:       2008-04-10
Updated:       2008-12-04
RAbuseHandle: technical contact
RAbuseName:    Tech Admin
RAbusePhone:   +1-800-555-1212
RAbuseEmail:   abuse@Domain.com
```

Packaging Up the Logs

One mistake you can make is to send your entire log file out to an ISP or host, who doesn't have the time to read through it. Respect the ISP's time and pull the specifics out of the logs. Following is an example of what to include:

```
64.XXX.XXX.XXX - - [23/Jan/2011:01:15:49 -0400]
"GET /?option=com_someExtension&Itemid=12&
task=../../../../../../../../../../../../../../../../proc/self/environ%00
HTTP/1.1" 410 296 www.yourdomain.com "-" "libwww-perl/5.834" "-"

64.XXX.XXX.XXX - - [23/Jan/2011:01:27:49 -0400]
"GET /?option=com_someExtension&Itemid=12&
task=../../../../../../../../../../../../../../../../proc/self/environ%00

HTTP/1.1" 410 296 www.yourdomain.com "-" "libwww-perl/5.834" "-"

64.XXX.XXX.XXX - - [23/Jan/2011:05:18:49 -0400]
"GET /?option=com_someExtension&Itemid=12&
task=../../../../../../../../../../../../../../../../proc/self/environ%00
HTTP/1.1" 410 296 www.yourdomain.com "-" "libwww-perl/5.834" "-"
```

Notice three nearly identical entries in the previous log entries. The times varied, as if the attacker were trying to get lost in the logs.

Be diligent and locate *all* the possible attacks in the log when reporting. It will strengthen your case with the ISP.

Reporting to the ISP

The following is a good sample e-mail to send to the ISP or host:

```
To: abuse@domain.com
Sub: Abuse report originating from your netblock.
```

```
Dear Sir (or Madam)

We have been receiving a series of attacks on our web site from an IP
address originating in your netblock. The log files are as follows:

<Log files would go here>

Please review and mitigate accordingly as we continue to receive
attacks from this IP.

I can be reached at [email address] or by telephone at [xxx-xxx-xxxx]
between the hours of 8 am and 5 pm, CST.

Sincerely,
Admin Name
```

A polite and brief letter will get you the response you need, and will enable the ISP to track down an infected machine. Many times, ISPs are unaware that a comprised machine is in the network and is attacking people.

Another tip is that *most* hosting companies offer an abuse@domain.com (where domain.com is replaced with the actual hosting company). You can try that first, because it's the quickest. If you get a bounced-back e-mail, a quick call or chat with the host's Technical Support staff can often lead you to the proper e-mail address.

This method usually has a very high degree of success in stopping the bad guy attacks. Occasionally, you'll run into an ISP or host that simply doesn't care, or feels that the attacks are not its issue. In that event, you may need to just block the IP address at the firewall.

Summary

This chapter discusses several key items that you will need when you are hacked. The one key point you should remember is to not panic. Panic only leads to mistakes and errors.

Be prepared in advance for an attack to happen. Make frequent backups of not only your site, database, and other files, but also of the log files.

You learned about a few tools such as NMAP and NESSUS to assist you in discovering problems with your server.

Lastly, having a current communications plan prepared in advance is well worth the time spent crafting it.

You can be prepared and you can be successful in defending against an attack if you follow the steps in this chapter.

Regarding attacks, one key area to ensure you're defensible is your wireless communications. In Chapter 10, you will learn about defending, strengthening, and supporting wireless communications in your network securely.

Wireless Networks

Imagine a scene where you see a car parked near your office on a regular basis. The occupant appears to be still and not really doing much. However, you see this same car and person in or around the same spot daily. You note he has a can of potato chips sitting on his dash. "Odd," you think, and go on about your day.

Soon, you are suddenly hacked out of nowhere. Your security is good, and you're up to date on patching and virus scanning. You even have a strong key on your wireless device.

You may have been a victim of a wireless hack via that can of potato chips. By using his laptop, some easily obtained software, and the potato chip can stuffed with an antenna in it, the bad guy maliciously gathered up your wireless router signals and was able to crack your Wi-Fi key.

The potato chip can (or some variation on the design) houses a powerful antenna. This device is known as a "cantenna," popular with *wardrivers* (those who drive around in vehicles in search of wireless networks). The chip can itself provides what is known as a *waveguide*. It allows the attacker to have a highly directional device. He can literally point it at your general location and gather the signals. This do-it-yourself antenna increases the range of Wi-Fi by miles in some cases. Countless websites are devoted to designing a cantenna, and a commercially available product known as the Cantenna is even available.

The antenna inside is known as a *Yagi* antenna. The original design of this antenna (less the chip can) was theorized in 1926 by Shintaro Uda and Hidetsugu Yagi of Tohoku Imperial University in Sendai, Japan. Their original intent was to transfer wireless energy using this antenna design. The use of a Yagi antenna today is widespread in everything from television reception all the way to military aircraft, and, of course, for sniffing distant Wi-Fi signals.

Since Wi-Fi is a radio, nothing prevents it from broadcasting your corporate secrets outside of your home or office. Radio waves are stronger and can be transmitted farther than you might think. The wireless devices simply don't have the antenna design to pick up the signal from great distances. The Wireless Access Point (WAP) does have the capability to transmit a long distance. This ubiquitous technology is finding its way into many applications and venues, primarily because of the ease of installation and low cost of implementation. Wireless technology has found its way into our telephones, printers, almost all notebook computers, and many desktops.

With regard to wireless applications, the Yagi antenna has proven to be effective in capturing Wi-Fi transmissions from distances that you may not expect, thus providing an eavesdropper with the capability to pick up on your Wi-Fi radio signals from outside your physical premises.

Other viable threats to your infrastructure include the use of Bluetooth devices that are susceptible to a whole array of bad things. You can remedy these potential threats to your security with a little common sense action.

As you can see, wireless signals are a popular target for hackers who are attempting to break into your infrastructure. This chapter discusses how you can safeguard wireless communications in your environment.

In this chapter, you'll take a brief tour of a topic that fills volumes of books today. In this chapter, you'll discover such things as *how to determine the need for wireless*. Many times, companies (and people) will deploy wireless for convenience. Taking into consideration a real need for it will reduce the chances of being hacked by possibly leading you to a decision not to deploy. If you have deployed or will deploy wireless, then understanding the threats and countermeasures to threats will ensure that you have removed (as much as possible) the "open door policy" for hackers.

Using some common tools such as SSL in your CMS will help keep your inflight transmission secure and safe. This chapter introduces you to a few resources you may use to help diminish the target on your CMS.

And, finally, this chapter offers some thoughts on Bluetooth in terms of its threats and countermeasures to threats.

NOTE In the context of this discussion, *Wi-Fi* generically refers to the networking technology that utilizes radio waves to provide wireless network and Internet connections.

Determining the Business Need for Wireless Networks

If you are running a small- or medium-sized business, you are likely to have some type of local area network (LAN). This LAN connects any internal servers you're using, such as Windows servers. Employees probably have desktops that connect to the network, and of course, any wireless networks.

However, you should carefully consider whether you actually *need* a wireless (Wi-Fi) network. After all, today's smartphones, ebook readers, and other devices are all built to take advantage of the presence of Wi-Fi. But do you actually need a wireless network in your workplace?

You should carefully weigh the answers to the following questions to help you get started on the path of thinking about your need for wireless:

- *Do you have any devices such as notebooks that need to connect?* — The first answer that may come to mind is, "Yes, I have a smartphone that *needs wi-fi*." Leaving off the table that your telephone service provider can give you more secure access than Wi-Fi, consider the wireless devices your sales force carries with it. For example, smart marketers today have crafted Wi-Fi– enabled printers. What do you want to bet that many of those will be unsecured after installation? If possible, try to eliminate as much of a "wireless" network in favor of wired network as possible.

- *Do you have outside contractors, vendors, or sales persons who need wireless connectivity?* — This scenario is not at all uncommon. The sales people you may be dealing with face the same problem — how to access their data and the Internet. In this case, providing a separate wireless connection is simple. Be sure you don't put this group on the *same* wireless connection as your network. If you do, you may expose yourself to extraordinary risk.

- *Does your physical setup prevent you from running network cabling?* — Quite often, running and installing cabling in your office or facility may present a challenge. Numerous considerations, such as historical buildings, local permits, costs of installation and support, and so on, come in to play. Suffice it to say that if you are unable to run any hard-line cabling to a desktop or notebook, then a wireless connection is a good alternative.

If your operation has devices that need wireless connectivity, consider starting down this path with an information security policy. Developing a plan and a policy that supports wireless is going to lead to an inherently more secure environment than just operating a wireless router.

NOTE Chapter 11 provides more information about developing an information security policy.

If you must install Wi-Fi, consider going with the latest standard (802.11n as of this writing) and using the strongest encryption possible, (WPA2 as of this writing). If you are running a medium-sized business, you may want to look at Radius to secure your systems. You can learn more about Radius at `http://en.wikipedia.org/wiki/RADIUS`. Additionally, the OpenRadius project (`http://openradius.org`) offers an open source version of the Radius software.

Ensure that you can determine which devices *must* be connected (such as wireless printers) and which devices *would be nice* to connect using wireless (such as a smartphone). For example, consider a notebook computer. They are usually equipped with a 10-base-T Ethernet (cabled) port that allows the user to physically connect to the internal network, which is preferable to a wireless connection.

After you decide that you *need* a wireless network, then moving on to a threat matrix is your next task.

Understanding Threats to Your Wireless Security

As you read in Chapter 1, wireless infrastructures are very susceptible to attack and being breached. In this section, you'll learn about the various components that, when tabulated, represent a *threat matrix* to your wireless network.

The threat matrix is simply a list of threats that may jeopardize your business. By listing the threats and ranking their viability, you can determine where to shore up your systems.

In the fictional setup shown in Table 10-1, the "X" represents the level of threat, and the dash means no threat is present.

Table 10-1: Sample Threat Matrix for Wi-Fi

POSSIBLE THREAT	LOW	MEDIUM	HIGH
Physical access to wireless	X	—	—
Wireless is open	—	—	—
Wireless is locked, but key is short or easy	—	—	X
Employees could install their own Wi-Fi	—	X	X
Signals from Wi-Fi are easily picked up in parking lot	—	—	X
Wi-Fi found on Wigle.net	—	—	X
Wi-Fi router located by window	—	—	X
Overall score	**1**	**1**	**5**

As you can see, this matrix results in a score of "5" in the "High" category, and, thus, this fictional setup is at a high risk of being breached.

Depending on your business, you will obviously design a different threat matrix. For example, if you are in a medical business in the United States, the requirements of the Health Insurance Portability and Accountability Act (HIPAA) and the more stringent requirements of the Health Information Technology for Economic and Clinical Health (HITECH) Act appear in your threat matrix. Another area of concern might be financial data, such as credit or debit card transactions. In the last few years, one high-profile retailer was breached through a wireless system, and millions of card numbers (and dollars) were stolen.

Design your threat matrix in the context of your situation, and follow up on the issues found as soon as possible. Just identifying the threats is only part of the battle, however. You should also understand some of the sources of those threats. The following sections take a look at some common sources.

Misconfiguration

Misconfiguration is a simple, and oft-repeated, mistake. Invariably, it results from opening the box, turning on the device, plugging it in, and walking away.

Leaving default settings on any new device (especially a wireless device) is the equivalent of a misconfiguration. Wi-Fi routers running wide open with default settings are a simple target that deserves to be hacked. Always take the time to change the default settings.

To drive this point home, Table 10-2 shows the default usernames and passwords for *some* Wi-Fi routers and devices. Lists such as these are maintained publically on the Internet, and are easy to find. Being armed with this allows attackers to attempt to log in to your Wi-Fi router. If they are successful, then that hole would allow them into your network. They could add their machine's MAC address, authorizing them to be on the network. They could also change the settings and deny service, or perform any number of other malicious acts.

Information such as this can also be used as a defense. You can use this information to see whether your wireless device is configured to use the defaults, which you can then change to protect your wireless infrastructure.

As discussed in Chapter 1, a weak password is literally the weakest link in your security chain — specifically weak passwords that are easily guessed. Weak passwords are a misconfiguration because they are easy to break. Because many wireless systems do not block multiple attempts, a weak password will be quickly compromised.

You must have a strong password for your systems. If you don't, the common (and often fruitful) technique of brute-force cracking will result in a hacker easily obtaining access to your systems.

Table 10-2: Default Usernames and Passwords for Wireless Devices

MANUFACTURER	PRODUCT NAME	USER ID	DEFAULT PASSWORD	USE
D-Link	DCS-1000	none	none	Internet camera
D-Link	DI-524	admin	none	Wireless broadband router
D-Link	DI-614+	user	(none)	2.4GHZ (802.11B) wireless router
Linksys	WAP54G	(none)	admin	Wireless G access point
Linksys	wrt110	admin	admin	Wireless router
Linksys	WRT54GS	admin	admin	Wireless G access point with speed booster
SMC		None Needed	MiniAP	Wireless router
Netgear	WG302	admin	password	802.11G Wi-Fi access point

This attack looks for common words found in wordlists. Following are some common default passwords found in a wordlist, which an attacker can easily use to compromise your wireless network:

- babygirl
- single
- 1234567890
- qazwsx
- pretty
- pokemon
- hottie
- iloveyou1
- teamo
- iloveyou2
- 987654321
- hahaha
- naruto
- poop

- spongebob
- blessing
- daniela
- blahblah
- princesa
- forum
- christ
- blink182
- Blessed
- 123qwe

This example represents a very small sample of one of the many hundreds of thousands of wordlists out there. Obviously, weak passwords such as these are easy to crack. It's simply matter of checking to see if your passwords (or close variations of them) are available by performing an Internet search.

Dealing with Rogue Wireless Devices

In Chapter 1, you learned about WiFiFoFum, which is a handy software tool that allows you to see and log all the wireless devices in its range. One way to use this tool is to perform an initial sweep of your environment to determine what is there and what should not be there. Deal with those WAPs that should not be there (sometimes known as *rogue devices*) by disabling them, removing them, or securing them.

Disabling rogue WAPs is strictly a policy decision. If your policy states that only your technical staff can deploy Wi-Fi, then any wireless devices attached to your network should be considered rogue devices.

Another device is the pocket Wi-Fi detector. Several different brands are available.

Using one of these tools provides the capability to quickly sweep an area for wireless devices. If they exist, they will show up. WiFiFoFum gives you a good directional finder to locate the occasional under-the-desk wireless device.

Typically, a wireless device that has been sneaked into your network will not conform to your security standards, thus becoming an easy target for hackers.

The frequency you should check for rogue devices is based entirely on your environment. If you have only a few employees, then you should be fine with checking only once in a while. If you have a very large environment, you'll need to consider a more frequent scan.

People

People are clearly the means by which a threat happens. However, if you were to categorize those evildoers, they would fall into two groups:

- *Internal* — This category includes employees or contractors. These people have easy and authorized access to your premises and your wireless network. An employee may foolishly share a Wi-Fi key, or may install FireSheep or another session hijacking tool to exploit the network.

- *External* — This category includes those who want to break in and, of course, the person randomly looking for wireless networks to exploit. These people may be in possession of a stolen device that has a wireless access key on it. Although this key may be encrypted, utilizing the device to gain access to the wireless network is possible.

Your best bet is to define a strong policy to deal with the "people" threat.

Mapping Systems

Part of a dedicated hacker's standard fare is to map your environment. This job requires different tools for different parts of the network.

Mapping the wireless portion of your infrastructure requires a number of tools that are freely available, including the following:

- *Wireless Geographic Logging Engine (WiGLE)* — The www.wigle.net website provides a wealth of regularly updated information, such as the 26,969,388 WAPs that had been reported as of this writing. This, by the way, came from 1,154,921,792 unique observations — that's right, more than 1 billion. Today, this sport or hobby (or whatever you want to classify it as) continues to look out for WAPs, both open and closed.

- *Seattle Wireless* — Another link that provides a well-documented guide and source of parts to build an antenna is Seattle Wireless, located at www .seattlewireless.net/index.cgi/AntennaHowTo.

- *LeWi-Fi* — This tool (located at http://code.google.com/p/lewifi) is a floor plan mapper that enables an attacker to map where the Wi-Fi signals are, their names, and so on.

- *General Defense* — The www.wardrive.net/general/antenna/ website provides the hobbyist and the hacker with a well-documented guide to Wi-Fi defense — and attack.

As you can see, the safe use of Wi-Fi is not simply a matter of turning on a Wi-Fi access point and going on about your day. It does require some preplanning to ensure that it's secured.

Securing the Data in the Air

Originally, Wi-Fi technology was not designed with rigorous security, and, thus, had to progress quite a bit to be fairly secure. Wi-Fi standards are hampered by that "last mile" — that is, from the antenna to your machine.

Securing that last mile is the key your security. It does not take a great deal of effort nor technical skill to handle proper security. This section outlines a couple of points that can form the basis of your security framework.

There are a number of factors involved with securing the data *in-flight* — that is, while its being transmitted in the air from your router to your device.

The first security measure you can take is the use of Secure Sockets Layer (SSL), which will encrypt your data. Deploying a wireless router that supports the WPA2 standard will strengthen you against attacks on your wireless key. Ensuring that you physically secure the access point (that is, putting it up in a high place, or locking it in a room) will prevent tampering. Additionally, changing the System ID (SID) from the defaults, or disabling the broadcast of it, will help reduce exposure of your wireless network.

Having a basic set of wireless security tools will give you a view of how an outsider may look at your wireless network. As you read about some of the tools described here, think about your own infrastructure and how you may be exposed.

Inexpensive Secure Sockets Layer (SSL)

One of the hangovers from yesteryear is the idea that SSL is an expensive tool to implement — not so much in terms of *dollars*, but in terms of the load it puts on your server. Fortunately, that is no longer true. Most modern servers waste more power out of the exhaust fans than they consume by running.

You should consider providing an SSL option for your Drupal, Joomla!, Plone, or WordPress sites for those who need to access it wirelessly. This helps guard against many would-be attacks on your content management system (CMS) via wireless connects.

Each CMS has its own method to activate SSL. To be fair, activating SSL in `.htaccess` and in Apache is possible. Following are some links that provide instructions on how to activate SSL:

- *Drupal* — `http://drupal.org/project/securepages` or `http://drupal.org/node/65890`

- *WordPress* — `http://codex.wordpress.org/Administration_Over_SSL`

- *Joomla!* — `http://forum.joomla.org/viewtopic.php?p=1202073`

- *Plone* — `http://plone.org/documentation/kb/apache-ssl`

WPA2 Standard

WEP is no longer a viable means to prevent wireless hacking. It is susceptible to eavesdropping and other nightmarish attacks. It was introduced in 1997, but, over time, it was quickly determined to be weak.

If you are running a WAP using WEP, check whether your WAP supports other encryption standards. If it does not, consider replacing it right away with a modern WAP.

The current Wi-Fi Protected Access 2 (WPA2) standard emphasizes a lot of security mechanisms (such as unique "keys" and other built-in functions) that make it the most secure wireless technology to date. It implements the mandatory portions of the 802.11i protocol. It has a number of features built into it for backward and forward compatibility, greater strength against attacks, and the support of the Wi-Fi industry.

> **NOTE** For a detailed explanation of WPA2, see `http://en.wikipedia`
> `.org/wiki/Wi-Fi_Protected_Access`. Another good tutorial on the subject
> can be found at `http://www.maxi-pedia.com/wireless+wifi+network+`
> `security+tutorial+101`.

Employing Adequate Countermeasures

Countermeasures are actions you can take to counter the tactics of an enemy. Because, in all likelihood, you'll need a wireless network in your business operation, being able to determine how to protect your wireless network from the bad guys is important. If you learn how to protect the physical and the electronic portions of your wireless infrastructure, you can keep your network safe.

Physical Countermeasures

Take a look around your office. Where is your WAP located? Is it conveniently placed on a desk surface? Or is it mounted up near the ceiling, hence requiring a ladder to reach it?

Protecting the physical device should be the first step in your security plan. For example, if it's sitting on desk surface, it could easily be tampered with, stolen, or unplugged. A better location would be a nearby locked closet. The prime objective of protecting this device is to prevent any type of tampering or changes to settings.

Secure the WAP

Think of your WAP as a doorway leading to your network. This means that if the door is open and unguarded, all types of people will make use of your resources, which is obviously not a good situation.

Securing the WAP is simple and easy. Following are few things you want to consider:

- *Stop telling everyone you have a wireless network* — Even though you probably aren't verbally telling people this fact, the device still broadcasts itself to intended devices. In essence, changing your setting for SSID BROADCAST to NO prevents the device from letting people know it's there. With that said, a very experienced attacker will still be able to find it. However, this countermeasure stops most of the slackers who want to slurp up free Internet.

- *Purchase a modern WAP* — If you've had your WAP for a few years, buy a new one that supports the backward-compatible standards. Look for WAPs that use the 802.11g or 802.11n protocols. These offer the latest (depending on the manufacturer) security tools. Older systems use security protocols that are now broken.

- *Use a high level of encryption (WPA2/802.11i strongly preferred)* — As described earlier in this chapter, use strong password keys, and change them every 30 days or so. If you connect to the network server over a wireless connection, use the Secure Shell (SSH) and Transported Layer Security/Hypertext Protocol Secure (TLS/HTTPS) protocols. In other words, put SSL on your site, as described earlier in this chapter. Using an encrypted virtual private network (VPN) will likely mitigate the effects of tools such as FireSheep.

- *Use MAC filtering* — Every machine that has a network connection has a unique address in it called a Media Access Control (MAC) address. Although faking this address (a process known as *spoofing*) is possible, for the most part, it's a sure thing. If you have a limited number of machines, set MAC Filtering to allow your machines in and everyone else out.

- *Activate any firewall in your wireless router* — The term "firewall" is often confused with Network Address Translation (NAT). The firewall is there to keep *out* bad things. The NAT separates your internal IP addresses from the Internet IP address you have been assigned. If a firewall in your router is available, use it.

- *Create a dedicated segment for your wireless network, and take additional steps to restrict access to this segment* — In other words, make sure this particular network segment is firewalled off from the rest of your network.

- *Check whether the firmware for your WAP and drivers for your wireless adapter(s) are up to date* — Update the drivers if necessary.

- *Test your wireless network for holes on a regular basis* — Learn to use the tools that hackers use. Be sure you stay in compliance with your local laws in terms of testing. You should consult an attorney to learn about your city, state, or country laws regarding this.

- *Enable strict logging on all devices* — Review your wireless log files regularly to be sure you're still safe.

Let's review a few other items that do not appear in this list.

Protecting Your Network Name

If you use a wireless router, look for the Service Set Identifier (SSID), which is effectively the name of your network. If it is set to the default, you are susceptible to an attack. Table 10-3 shows an extract of the top 1,000 SSIDs in use today.

Table 10-3: Top SSIDs

SSID	TOTAL	PERCENT
<no ssid>	2,049,263	7.297
Linksys	1,968,509	7.010
NETGEAR	618,672	2.203
default	578,202	2.059
Belkin54g	262,651	0.935
Wireless	217,717	0.775
no_ssid	213,983	0.762
hpsetup	202,735	0.721
DLINK	162,035	0.577
WLAN	114,317	0.407
home	98,011	0.349
ACTIONTEC	88,473	0.315
<hidden ssid>	74,268	0.264
Free Public WiFi	73,014	0.260
BTOpenzone	61,306	0.218
smc	55,177	0.196
MSHOME	43,881	0.156
BTFON	41,093	0.146
freephonie	39,878	0.142
Motorola	38,052	0.135
SITECOM	37,976	0.135

SSID	TOTAL	PERCENT
ZyXEL	34,749	0.123
FreeWiFi	34,536	0.122
(null)	32,797	0.116
Philips WiFi	31,534	0.112
hhonors	29,894	0.106
Neuf WiFi	29,254	0.104
tsunami	28,927	0.103
tmobile	28,766	0.102
FRITZ!Box Fon WLAN 7170	28,328	0.100
Guest	26,960	0.096
101	26,886	0.095
orange	26,155	0.093
3Com	25,253	0.089
orange12	24,595	0.087
attwifi	22,066	0.078
USR8054	22,009	0.078
Linksys-g	21,923	0.078
SFR WiFi Public	20,318	0.072
Wayport_Access	20,180	0.071
orange14	18,236	0.064
eduroam	17,602	0.062
HomeNet	16,299	0.058
WLAN-AP	15,098	0.053
FRITZ!Box Fon WLAN 7113	14,532	0.051
Customer ID	14,457	0.051

Source: WIGLE.net (www.wigle.net/gps/gps/main/ssidstats)

As you can see from Table 10-3, the second most popular SSID was `Linksys`, which shows an astounding 1,968,509 units found, and Linksys-G had 21,923 units found to date by wardrivers, or 7 percent of all the devices found.

What you can take away from this is that changing or hiding the SSID of your unit is vital for proper wireless security.

Reducing Power Output of a WAP

Many gadgets that people use every day are essentially radios (such as the car radio, satellite radio, cell phones, smartphones, Bluetooth system devices, and more). As you have learned in this chapter, your Wi-Fi router or WAP is a radio.

Radio transmitters are measured in broadcast strength (that is, the amount of power they can output). It's measured in milliwatts, watts, or megawatts (as is the case with your terrestrial car radio). The higher the power (or wattage), the farther the signal will travel. If your Wi-Fi signal can leave your premises through a window or other exit point, a directional antenna like the Yagi can gather up enough of the signal to use it.

One feature that many modern routers support is reducing the power output. Sometimes this is marketed as a "green" approach, but, in reality, it really has nothing to do with the environment. The lower output reduces the strength of the wireless signal and, therefore, lowers the range it will travel with any effectiveness. Although this may fall into the "security by obscurity" category, this feature can be beneficial to safeguarding your wireless network.

To determine whether your wireless router provides this capability, look for one of the following at your router's `Admin` setting:

- RF POWER
- TX POWER
- Lower broadcast power

These generic terms are often used by manufacturers to indicate the product provides the capability for you to reduce power output.

NOTE Be careful about manufacturers' claims for some equipment. Some routers and WAPs may be marketed with the claim that they allow lowering of the power output, but you may discover that they do not. Check with the manufacturers' websites to verify. Additionally, if the manufacturers offer any live sales assistance, you can pose the question via that method.

If you have a high-output router, consider locating it as far into the center of your building as possible. Also, ensure that your transmission range is kept to a minimum. In other words, if you can walk across the street with your laptop computer in hand and connect to your wireless network, then the signal emanating from your wireless network is too strong.

Wireless Security Tools

To better understand how to solve issues identified by your threat matrix, you should understand some of the tools available to the bad guys who want to penetrate your wireless network. This section examines the following example tools:

- FireSheep
- Aircrack-ng

FireSheep

FireSheep is a one-click Firefox add-on tool that can be used to exploit wireless systems. Although this tool is commonly used to target the public Wi-Fi systems (such as your favorite coffee shop), it may work on any wireless network the would-be attacker has access to.

Released in October 2010, this tool is very simple to install, and even easier to use. It works by sniffing the Wi-Fi for network packets, and comparing those to known destinations, such as Facebook.

If used in a setting such as a coffee shop, it provides access to *any* logged-in sessions of many web destinations. In other words, the guy you may see in the coffee shop, posting to his Facebook regularly, is vulnerable to this tool. But you are just as vulnerable.

Suppose you wander in to the coffee shop to check email, drink an overpriced coffee, and then get back to work. In that short time, an attacker using FireSheep could read your mail, change your password, and do any number of things, simply by assuming control of your session.

This same style of attack could apply to your company wireless network.

Aircrack-ng

Aircrack-ng works by capturing several network packets and decoding the Wired Equivalent Privacy (WEP) keys. After enough data packets have been captured, the attacker can use this tool to recover password keys. It implements attacks such as the Fluhrer, Mantin, and Shamir (FMS) attack; the KoreK attack; and the relatively new Pychkine, Tews, and Weinmann (PTW) attack.

In fact, as shown in Table 10-4, the makers of Aircrack-ng offer a whole host of tools that can be used for attacking wireless systems.

Table 10-4: Aircrack-ng Software Tools

TOOL	DESCRIPTION
airbase-ng	A multi-purpose tool aimed at attacking clients as opposed to the access point itself
aircrack-ng	A 802.11 WEP and WPA/WPA2-PSK key cracking program
airdecap-ng	Decrypts WEP/WPA/WPA2 captured files

Continued

Table 10-4 *(continued)*

TOOL	DESCRIPTION
airdecloak-ng	Removes WEP cloaking from a packet capture file
airdriver-ng	A script that provides information and allows installation of wireless drivers
airdrop-ng	A rule-based wireless de-authentication tool
aireplay-ng	Injects and replays wireless frames
airgraph-ng	Graphs wireless networks
airmon-ng	Enables and disables the monitor mode on wireless interfaces
airodump-ng	Captures raw 802.11 frames
airolib-ng	Precomputes WPA/WPA2 passphrases in a database to be used with aircrack-ng
airserv-ng	A wireless card TCP/IP server that allows multiple applications to use a wireless card
airtun-ng	Creates a virtual tunnel interface
easside-ng	An auto-magic tool that enables communication to a WEP-encrypted access point without knowing the key
packetforge-ng	Creates various types of encrypted packets that can be used for injection
tkiptun-ng	Injects a few frames into a WPA TKIP network with QoS
wesside-ng	An auto-magic tool that incorporates a number of techniques to seamlessly obtain a WEP key in minutes

As you can see someone wanting to penetrate your wireless network has many tools at his or her disposal.

Technical Countermeasures

For the highly paranoid, you can do some things to restrict your signals leaving your premises, such as turning off the wireless device or nailing up wire mesh to the walls and grounding it. However, if you need Wi-Fi, but want to be as secure as possible, choose a very modern device that supports the 802.11n protocol or newer. Choose a very strong and random password, and change it every 30 days or more often.

Devices are available to stop transmission of wireless signals, but these work in the same frequency range as cell phones and other devices. To use this type of device, you may want to mount it outside of your premises to kill any outgoing signals. There could easily be legal concerns in this case, as well. You should check with your attorney before using any device that alters transmissions, because this discussion is not offering a legal opinion.

These suggestions are included for educational purposes only, and, of course, if you have this much of a concern, then not using wireless is the best alternative.

Bluetooth Security Considerations

Bluetooth is the technology that allows users to make hands-free calls, use a wireless mouse and keyboard, and annoy people by talking into thin air using earpieces. Bluetooth is a compact "data" radio. It operates on an unlicensed frequency, and transmits at a maximum distance of 100 meters (109 yards). Figure 10-1 shows a typical Bluetooth setup.

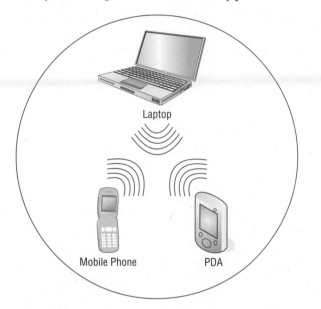

Laptop

Mobile Phone   PDA

Figure 10-1: Example Bluetooth topology (Source: NIST Special Publication 800-121)

In Figure 10-1, you can see the mobile phone, personal digital assistant (PDA), and laptop computer all being "paired." Many laptops today support both Wi-Fi and Bluetooth, primarily because they can be packaged in a single chip. This enables the manufacturers to offer the most options at the lowest cost to you.

Bluetooth security has improved since its inception, and, for the most part, gone are the days of sitting on an airplane and using your laptop to connect to other laptops. This, of course, is rude, possibly illegal, and was a quite frequent practice in the early days of this standard.

Like most technologies, however, flaws have been discovered that have driven the development of new standards. Given its special role in your network, Bluetooth poses a very large potential threat to your website security. If a dedicated attacker can use Bluetooth to gain access to your systems, desktops, or your network, then planting a virus to gain your passwords is a simple matter.

Yet, despite the downsides, Bluetooth can be a useful technology, and can be an effective tool, if you implement proper safeguards.

Bluetooth Pervasiveness

Today, hundreds of devices depend on the Bluetooth standard. A brief search on the Internet reveals devices that are built for the following applications:

- Audio/visual
- Personal computers
- Mobile telephony
- Automotive
- Office equipment
- Audio (as in stereo equipment)
- Medical
- Home

Because this technology is so pervasive in our culture, the chances are good that you have it in your office. Again, the idea of this book is to prepare you for holistically protecting your CMS and infrastructure. You want to protect Bluetooth from any outside (non-authorized) activity at all costs. So, the following sections provide a look at a few security basics.

Bluetooth Threats

If you include a dose of common sense when you use Bluetooth for your applications, you should have minimal problems. In fact, using Bluetooth offers major advantages. Yet, you must recognize and mitigate the risks. The technology and devices are susceptible to many of the same wireless threats that exist for WAPs.

Wireless devices (including those with Wi-Fi and Bluetooth technologies) can be susceptible to a classic "man-in-the-middle" attack or message modification. Unauthorized use of these devices can introduce even more threats.

Following are specific types of attacks identified by the National Institute of Standards and Technology (U.S. Commerce Department) in its guide to Bluetooth security:

- *Bluesnarfing* — Bluesnarfing enables attackers to gain access to a Bluetooth-enabled device by exploiting a firmware flaw in older devices. This attack forces a connection to a Bluetooth device, allowing access to data stored on the device, and even the device's international mobile equipment identity (IMEI). The IMEI is a unique identifier for each device that an attacker could potentially use to route all incoming calls from the user's device to the attacker's device. Rerouting phone calls could be a prank, or a nasty event. Consider upgrading to the most modern Bluetooth devices for telephony applications.

- *Bluejacking* — Bluejacking is an attack conducted on Bluetooth-enabled mobile devices, such as cellular telephones, smartphones, and PDAs. Bluejacking is initiated by an attacker sending unsolicited messages to a user of a Bluetooth-enabled device. The actual messages do not cause harm to the user's device, but they are used to entice the user to respond in some fashion, or add the new contact to the device's address book. This message-sending attack resembles spam and phishing attacks conducted against e-mail users. Bluejacking can cause harm when a user initiates a response to a bluejacking message that is sent with a harmful intent.

- *Bluebugging* — Bluebugging exploits a security flaw in the firmware of some older Bluetooth devices to gain access to the device and its commands. This attack uses the commands of the device without informing the user, allowing the attacker to access data, place telephone calls, eavesdrop on telephone calls, send messages, and exploit other services or features offered by the device.

- *Car Whisperer* — Car Whisperer is a software tool developed by European security researchers that exploits a key implementation issue in hands-free Bluetooth car kits installed in automobiles. The Car Whisperer software allows an attacker to send to or receive audio from the car kit. An attacker could transmit audio to the car's speakers, or receive audio (eavesdrop) from the microphone in the car.

- *Denial of Service (DoS)* — Bluetooth is susceptible to DoS attacks. Impacts include making a device's Bluetooth interface unusable and draining the mobile device's battery. These types of attacks are not significant, because the proximity required for Bluetooth use can usually be easily averted by simply walking away. This is a low threat to you, and could be just considered an annoyance.

- *Fuzzing attacks* — Bluetooth fuzzing attacks consist of sending malformed or otherwise non-standard data to a device's Bluetooth radio, and observing how the device reacts. A device's response being slowed or stopped by these attacks indicates that a serious vulnerability potentially exists in the protocol stack.

Security Recommendations

You do not need to drop your entire Bluetooth device inventory to safeguard your infrastructure. Rather, here are a few common-sense items to help you stay on track:

- A well-formed information security policy (which you will learn more about in Chapter 11) is your friend. In that policy, define what devices and what type of information can be sent over Bluetooth. Remember, just because someone makes a Bluetooth-enabled coffee pot doesn't mean you need to use it.

- Consider discontinuing the use of any older Bluetooth devices. The reasons for this is the later (2008 and beyond) models are more secure and have better encryptions. For example, the original (Class One) Bluetooth radios have a 100 milliwatt (mW) output. This means that anyone within 100 meters (109 yards) can pick up and attempt to attack the signal. Bear in mind that this is an estimate, because there are many other influential factors, such as the device itself, sun-spot activity, materials of the building, terrain, and much more. Don't count on this number being one you can rely on in all situations.

- Ensure that any Bluetooth device used is changed from its *default* settings.

- If possible, turn down the power on the devices to reduce the transmission range.

- Use a very strong PIN or password (device-dependent).

- Set passwords on devices that have a Bluetooth connection in the event of loss or theft. In the event of loss or theft, users should decouple the device from the Bluetooth device.

- Set up Bluetooth devices to be *non-discoverable*. This practice prevents attackers from mapping out your network through them, or knowing the names of the devices.

- Your Bluetooth device likely supports some form of *link encryption*. Activate it, if it exists.

- If you have no need for Bluetooth on a notebook computer, turn it off. This helps save battery life and may prevent a machine from being compromised.

- If a Bluetooth device is not in use, it should be turned off. There is no reason to give someone a window of opportunity.

Although you can use many other tactics, these should suffice for most organizations.

Summary

In this brief tour of wircless security, you were introduced to many concepts and possibly new ideas. You gained an understanding of threats to your wireless security, and how to build a threat matrix. You were introduced to various tools that can be used to secure or attack your Wi-Fi connection, and, of course, the danger of not changing default passwords.

You learned that you should use SSL with any wireless network. You also learned how to find information regarding activation of SSL for each CMS covered in this book.

This chapter exposed several key points to building out your secure infrastructure, and you learned about Bluetooth security countermeasures.

Chapter 11 shows you how to develop an information security policy.

Information Security Policy and Awareness

Your information security policy is a document that describes how you will deal with specific information security situations. This could define what the acceptable use of your e-mail system is, or it might dictate whether you can read employee e-mail. Today, a good information security policy will cover the gamut of information, such as e-mail, Instant Messaging (IM), backup storage, and acceptable use of company resources (meaning desktops, notebooks, servers, Internet connection, and so on).

An information policy is built to guide the employee, as well as to protect you and your company from inadvert problems. Often, the employee excuse of *"we didn't know"* tends to work, and, sadly, it forces you to document all of your policies. Although people tend to gloss over employee policies, the information policy document will serve to push the burden of responsibility back onto the employee or user community.

Your information security policy should cover the responsibility of each person. The information policy also should cover license information (such as if you find pirated software, what to do), as well as what can or cannot be plugged into your network, such as an outside notebook or any other unauthorized device.

Awareness also falls into the information security category. People are often unaware of what is going on around them. This is a "perfect storm" situation for a social engineer (that is, someone who uses specific social techniques to get past another person's defenses). A classic social engineering technique is to call someone in the company and fool him or her into helping the caller by providing a password. Unfortunately, this method works very well. Training your staff in proper phone screening can help to avoid this issue.

This chapter covers two aspects of the information security spectrum. The first half of this chapter provides an in-depth view of the information security policy itself. Although you won't find here a full written plan, the discussion can help guide you to developing your own. The second part of the chapter helps you to develop a strong defense against social-engineering techniques and takes a look at the situational awareness paradigm.

Establishing an Information Security Policy

The information security policy can be a single document stating what is and is not acceptable concerning what information can be divulged to whom. It may also be a collection of policy documents. The purpose of the information security policy is to protect you and your business from harm caused by the actions of employees, contractors, customers, and others who violate the rules.

Following are the particular policy areas examined in this section:

- Overall information security policy
- Internet use
- Remote access
- Acceptable e-mail use
- Instant messaging
- Social media network use

Although this list of examined topics is not exhaustive, it's meant to get you started on the proper path. This section covers a basic framework for your information security policy. Take the time to discuss the information presented in this chapter with your staff as it relates to your business and technical needs.

To begin, let's start with the overall information security policy.

General Information Security Policy

The primary document you will create is the information security policy. This document is typically delivered to employees for acknowledgment and signature. Its scope covers the use of the company's information resources.

The policy should be updated from time to time as your technology needs change. It's important that the employees read the policy document and acknowledge an understanding of its contents by signature.

This type of document typically covers the following areas:

- Violations
- Management's responsibilities
- Employee responsibilities
- IT (or your technical staff) responsibilities
- Acceptable use of resources
- Unacceptable use of resources
- Password policy
- Software installation policy
- External equipment/installation policy
- Social networking policy

Sections within the overall information security policy document tend to cover these areas, which represent many of the normal delicate areas in IT. However, keep in mind that, as your IT evolves with new technologies, your policy should also cover new technologies, cover new issues, and address various yet-to-be-determined threats.

Violations

Make a clear definition statement for what will happen in the event of violations. This should cover whether disciplinary action will occur, and may even contain to what degree.

An example statement may be written as follows:

"Violations of this information security policy may result in disciplinary action in accordance with company policy. The failure to observe and maintain the guidelines of this policy could result in the employee's being subjected to disciplinary action up to and including immediate termination. The severity of the employee violation will dictate the level of disciplinary action. These violations include (but are not limited to) actions that result in liability or harm/loss to the company, or repeat violations of the policy."

Of course, you should draft your own statement of what will happen in the event of violations.

Management Responsibilities

The roles of management should be spelled out to describe the expectation that you have for them in regard to this policy. For example, supervisors and managers should be responsible for reviewing the contents of this document with their direct reports. Further, managers must put into place the standards and controls to ensure employee compliance with this policy.

Employee Responsibilities

The employee responsibilities section of your security policy will be specific to your environment, but should include coverage of several common areas that span across companies.

Many systems in IT are simply *communications* tools of one form or another. Therefore, at all times, the employee must observe a sense of decorum and professional behavior in his or her use of the IT systems.

This policy should state that the employee has full responsibility for any file (text, music/audio, video, and so on) that he or she sends or uses with the company's computer and network systems.

In today's electronically oriented society, stressing to employees what copyrighted materials are is important. Ensure that copyrighted material is not unlawfully sent out or distributed using company resources. The idea that sharing a digital resource is wrong often tends to escape some employees. Your company could be on the hook financially for such behavior.

Be sure that the employee is fully aware of company policies regarding the security of information such as price lists, customer lists, road map information, or anything else deemed confidential by the company.

IT/Technical Staff Responsibilities

Be sure to cover the basic scope of your IT or technical staff's mission. This includes the setting of technical security standards, such as virus scanning, spam filtering, and so on. You should also spell out how IT is also responsible for providing assistance as needed to the employees with regard to technology.

Acceptable Use of Resources

Define for your staff what you will deem acceptable use of company resources. For example, web browsing for company purposes should be fine, whereas you may not want employees spending time on an auction site for personal use. Alternatively, you may not care. It's all a matter of what you deem as acceptable.

You may also want to clarify for your staff the appropriate use of e-mail and other communications tools. Do you care if they send personal e-mails over the company e-mail systems? If not, then state it. If you do care, ensure that you state that the e-mail system is to be used for company business purposes only. As you will discover later in this chapter, many companies deem e-mail that is sent and received as company property. Be sure to consider that when drafting your acceptable use policy.

Unacceptable Use of Resources

Unacceptable use of resources could be practically anything, because different companies have different views of what is and is not acceptable. However, it is the opposite of acceptable use. This section of your information security policy details what is clearly not up for negotiation.

Define in this section of the policy the overview of what you will not accept (for example, racism, viewing or sending pornographic material, using company resources to run the employee's own business, and so on).

This section should tie back into the violations section of your policy.

Password Policy

Define the password standards, the length of time between password changes, who the employee may give his or her passwords to, and why. You might consider adding to this a process or policy to guide the employee on procedures to follow in the event of a compromised password.

Software Installation

Depending on the nature and size of your business, you may want to restrict any installation rights to your IT administrative staff. Write out the policy for installing software, such as "software may be requested through the change management process and will be installed by IT."

Spell out the policy on software licensing. That is, if software is licensed commercially, the company should have proof of that license before installation occurs.

The goal of this part of the security policy is to prevent employees from attempting to install software they were given, downloaded, or brought in from another source. The installation of this software could open you up to legal or technical liabilities.

External Equipment/Installation

You should have a general policy to prevent the installation of external devices such as wireless routers or switches or any other unauthorized devices. The policy should prohibit any unauthorized installation of equipment to your network. The reasons are simple. It could cause a disruption to service, it could be a security risk, or it might very well be an intentional security vulnerability (such as a sniffer).

Internet Use Policy

Without a clearly defined policy, employees will not consider the Internet connection to be company property. You must define how firmly you want to control employee behavior in terms of Internet use.

Unless a legitimate business reason exists, you should include in your policy that browsing or surfing any sites that display or promote pornography is considered a violation of company policies that will result in immediate termination. This is one area you cannot waver on at all. That type of activity can lead to lawsuits and other legal trouble.

Additionally, your Internet use policy should extend to prohibit any site promoting hate, racism, and so on.

Remote Access Policy

Remote access is commonplace today with both open source and commercial applications. The remote access policy primarily defines acceptable use for remote access, the security standards expected for the remote machine, and the type of software to be used. In addition to these items, you'll want to cover any legal violations and provide a disclaimer for damages to the user's machine or loss of data. For example, is the employee responsible if a hacker breaks into your network through the user's remotely connected machine? Clearly, this is a tough question, but one that should addressed.

Lastly, in the remote access policy, consider including what the rule will be for access costs. Today, the typical means of remote access is through the employee's ISP. Define whether you will reimburse the employee for costs incurred for the IPS. Write this into your policy upfront so that there will be no questions later.

Acceptable E-Mail Use

E-mail can easily let in all kinds of attacks. The use of your company's e-mail system by and large should be rigidly defined. At a minimum, your policy should address the points shown in Table 11-1, and clearly spell out the company's position.

Table 11-1: E-Mail Policy Description

POLICY	DESCRIPTION
Defining employee responsibilities	E-mail can reduce productivity. The employee policy should be to ensure that e-mail doesn't replace traditional communications and, thus, impact employee productivity. The employee is clearly responsible for anything sent from his or her e-mail address. The employee should never transmit any copyrighted material without permission. This can include music, videos, or e-books. The employee should not disable any virus protection systems for any reason. Lastly, you should define in your policy what non-public information is, when it should be allowed to be sent, and to whom.
Defining "spam"	The policy should state what is considered "spam." The policy should contain a statement to never create or send spam.
Defining a response to the receipt of spam	You're likely running a spam filter that helps capture and slow the flood of spam. However, a possibility always exists of spam getting through. Spam is sent for mostly nefarious reasons, and the payload is often viruses, phishing scams, and other things that could hurt your IT systems. Your policy should define a procedure for dealing with spam that slips through your e-mail defenses.
Opening of spam	Define the process the employee should follow if he or she inadvertently opens an e-mail that contains harmful contents. Occasionally, people will open a spam and, without proper safeguards, the contents could quickly spread evil through your network.
Chain e-mail	The policy should instruct the employee to not forward or send chain e-mail letters (or equivalents). Without a doubt, this is not only annoying, but can be a drag on your resources. This should include jokes, humor, or any type of photos that may be deemed inappropriate.
Sending of malware	Any intentional transmission of malware or viruses should be strictly forbidden in all circumstances.
Denial of service	The policy should state that the employee should never engage in any activity that could cause a denial of service.
Phishing	Your policy should contain rules against alteration of the e-mail headers for the purpose of deceiving the receiver. This is typically known as *phishing*.
Contents of mail	The policy needs a clear statement prohibiting the sending of any hate, racist, sexually oriented, or pornographic images.
Illegal mail	The policy must contain statements that define not sending e-mail that contains any illegal information (for example, copyright violations or disclosure of trade secrets), harassing messages, or threatening messages.
Encryption	Some e-mail systems encrypt e-mail before sending. Some countries do not allow encryption. Be aware of this issue and address it in your policy if needed.

Define for your employees your company's position on the sending of political e-mails during an election season. By and large, a company resource such as e-mail should only be used for company purposes, and the transmission of political messaging is a recipe for trouble and wasting time.

The final point is to define the nature of ownership of your e-mail system and the e-mail passing through it. As part of this ownership policy, you should establish the right to review any and all e-mail that is sent through your e-mail system. (This part of the policy may require a review with your legal counsel.)

With respect to external clients, you want to cover the responsibilities for any e-mail sent to them through your website. This responsibility would be covered separately in your privacy policies.

Instant Messaging Policy

Instant messaging (IM) has become such a critical part of our society that countless applications are in use. IM is a wonderful resource to communicate with clients, co-workers, vendors, or others. The challenge with IM is that it represents a two-way street. It can allow in malware, or it can be used to transmit out company information.

You should standardize on a company-wide IM platform. Choose one that fits your needs and is fairly secure. Beyond that design, your policies should account for the following:

- *Scope of IM usage* — Typically, for business reasons, you should define the acceptable purpose of IM, such as customer care, vendor communications, and so on.

- *Prohibited use* — Define what the prohibited usages of IM are.

- *IM etiquette* — People tend to get brave and dumb behind a keyboard. Be sure you cover rules such as not discussing confidential or sensitive company business or information. Further, be sure that employees are careful about not opening or accepting any attachments. Additionally, IM conversations should never be considered private. The possibilities of eavesdropping are too great. Be sure that employees never ask for anything such as credit card numbers or passwords over IM.

- *Compromised accounts* — Define in your policy what actions should be taken if an employee believes (or you have reason to believe) an IM account has been compromised.

- *Fees* — Determine how (or whether) you reimburse your staff for any commercial IM services.

- *Care and feeding of IM* — Define who takes care of issues for IM users.

- *Monitoring of IM* — If you need to monitor IM and capture the traffic, you may need to inform your users and employees.

Social Media Networks

The use of social networks today is as common as using the telephone. Most everyone has used or heard of Facebook, Twitter, and other social media networks.

The social media network is also a means for a hacker to gain vital information about you or your company. Define your policy regarding the use, posting, and distribution of company information on social networks.

The social media network should be considered as completely public (that is, 100 percent of the time). There are simply too many ways into a social media network, and, thus, too great of a chance that information can be released that should not be.

The next section provides a primer on increasing your awareness as it relates to information security. Most people are so inundated with information (such as advertising, news, interruptions, and life in general) that they tend to ignore their surroundings. The problem is compounded by a plethora of techniques employed by what are commonly known as *social engineers*.

Social Engineering

The idea behind social engineering is to manipulate how the human mind works, to the advantage of the attacker. A hacker may deploy many tools, but they tend to fall into some very observable categories. Table 11-2 shows a few tools in the social engineer's toolkit.

Table 11-2: Social Engineering Tools

TOOL	DESCRIPTION
Framing	The framing technique is used to *frame up* a particular thought, such as "75 percent real fruit juice." Okay, what's the other 25 percent? The idea of framing is to get your mind headed in a specific direction. That direction is likely not one you want to go in if it's a social engineer doing the talking.
Incentives	Using incentives is a timeless technique. In fact, it's used quite legitimately on a regular basis. Think about "35 percent off" of that item you *have to have*. The incentive, of course, is less money for them and more money for you! At least, that's how it's presented. This incentive can also be social; for example the homeless guy who holds up the "will work for food" sign. The incentive is that you can absolve the feeling of guilt he may be creating in your mind by giving him some money. A social engineer can use incentives in relation to his or her desired attack. The attacker needs to know what incentive will work on you. It could be any number of things, such as money, social influence/pressure, or something that plays on your personal value set or ideals.

Continued

Table 11-2 *(continued)*

TOOL	DESCRIPTION
Reciprocity	Although it can be tricky to use, reciprocity can work very well when a social engineer plays it right. The reciprocity ploy does take some time to set up because the target (that's you) must feel that you owe the perpetrator. An example might be where someone calls in and pretends to provide "help" to the target, such as, "This is Matt from the phone company. I proactively have reset your phone passwords. Can I get your current password to test?" The grateful target will want to pay back the perpetrator, and so comply with the request.
Scarcity or time-limited	Much like the "35 percent off" example, the *scarcity* play is used by sales people as a social engineering technique all the time. A simple example is when sales person can get you that deal, but you must provide a signed purchase order *today*, because the sales person's boss is going to pull the offer. Although this is complete nonsense, the technique works so well that it's a standard one used in vendor/customer relationships. For the social engineer, the time-limited or scarcity problem comes into play in an "urgent" situation. The perpetrator places a call to the target to obtain the information. The perpetrator explains that she must have this report in *tonight*, or else she may lose her job (or other bad things will happen). She might say that she is unable to get into the server, into the site, or wherever. If you could *help* her, she would be most grateful.
Authoritarian play	Clearly, authoritarian play refers to the normal behavior of submitting to authority. If your boss calls and is irate, and tells you to get something done *now*, chances are you'll jump on it. This is a very common ploy used by social engineers. They will pretend to be sent by the boss or, in some cases, they pull off the sham of making you think they are the boss. Your inner desire to stay out of trouble with the manager could motivate you to comply.
Getting to "yes" by commitment	The "getting to 'yes' by commitment" tactic is a very sneaky one that you often see used in an infomercial. The concept is that if the perpetrator can get the target to say "yes" to something that is in line with that person's ideals, then the target is likely to say "yes" to another question that is in line with the initial commitment. The typical "Do you like to save money every time you shop?" is a ploy to get you to say "yes."
	For example, a social engineer will start with something small, building in the question-and-commitment scenario with the target. Typically, this is a public proposition that continues to escalate until the attacker has the target committing to what he or she wanted. The target's desire to save face will usually prevent him or her from backing off of the commitment. It's a powerful technique.

TOOL	DESCRIPTION
Liking or being liked	Deep within all humans is a desire to be liked or wanted. In return, people tend to like other people. This means of information gathering is used in one or two ways. The first is when the social engineer is *charming*, which can be a powerful tactic to get the desired information. It could be used as a negative, in the sense of *taking away approval*. More often, though, the former and not the latter is the method used, especially in a seductive manner such as compliments paid. This will cause the target to linger, desiring more compliments. People like positive reinforcement — the proverbial "carrot-on-a-stick" method. The social engineer will flatter a target by playing to the person's emotions and feelings, lowering their defenses enough to get them to divulge information. This dirty trick works on people from many cultures and age groups.
Social proof or groupthink	Another common tactic of marketers is *social proof*. The general thought is that if the *crowd* likes it, it can't be wrong! An example of this is a statement such as, *"Nine out of ten dentists recommend brushing your teeth as a means to prevent cavities."* You might think, "Well, yes." But you likely never stopped to think why that *tenth* dentist feels the opposite way. In the social engineering space, the attacker uses groupthink to get you thinking that the decision he wants you to make is wise and is supported by many people. Therefore, *it must be right*! Right? If the attacker can get you to buy into it because it goes along with popular wisdom, then you own the decision and will go along with it.

Social engineering is a well-known and well-used means to extract information. Train yourself and your employees to question unusual situations, and to remain vigilant in the workplace environment.

Having Situational Awareness

If you were in a combat situation, you would experience *situational awareness*, which means that you would be extremely aware of what's going on around you in any direction — what your fellow soldiers are doing, and possibly what the enemy is doing. The nature of combat demands that you keep a strong vigilance of your surroundings, but in everyday civilian life, people tend to lose focus and not be vigilant at all.

You and your employees should develop a sense of awareness regarding your office, your network, and the company perimeter in order to protect the company from hackers.

Situational awareness is important because people tend to *leak information*. A skilled social engineer can pick up your employees' lack of vigilance and get more information. For example, a good Samaritan may open a door for a stranger without question, or an overly helpful person may not challenge a person during a phone conversation who says he or she works for the president of the company. These are examples of where situational awareness would be handy to have.

Usually, if you pay attention to your surroundings, you are not surprised when things happen. You may see things build up to something. it, The buildup doesn't catch you off guard, and gives you an opportunity to prevent damage.

If a hacker desires to gather information or penetrate a building for the purpose of hacking a company's systems, then he or she can deploy a number of different *social engineering techniques*. These are actions taken for the specific purpose of fooling someone to gain something from him or her. In social engineering techniques such as a *Ponzi scheme* or a *confidence-man ploy*, which is a scheme where the con artist gains your confidence to deceive you, the idea is to get past your natural defenses to get something from you.

Additionally, a hacker wanting to enter a company's building needs to know as much as possible about the people, the way they dress, the cars they drive, the guards, security systems, trashcan locations, and more.

Using the information gathered online, over the phone, and from your employees combined with knowledge of your company's physical perimeters, the attacker can construct a false persona to use with social engineering techniques to gain the information he is seeking from your company.

Vulnerable Security Points

The following sections cover points of vulnerability that are general in nature, but could represent a threat to you.

Front Door

"Hold the door, please," a well-dressed gentleman says with a briefcase in one hand and cardboard carrier with four large cups of steaming-hot coffee in the other. You smile and hold the door because he looks like he's late for an important meeting. You move on your way to your desk because you are late yourself and are glad you made it without too much fanfare. You don't give the guy a second thought.

Who was he? Did he have a badge? Do you know him? This situation has been played out many times through both penetration testing and real-life hacker exploits. It is a technique to play on your sympathy. If your company has a policy for badges and clear identification of who's coming in, then you should have challenged him and asked for identification.

Develop and cultivate an awareness of everyone who is entering and leaving your company premises. Who is following you into the building? Why are they there? Where are they going? What is their business? Do they have an appointment?

Asking these questions does not make you paranoid; it makes you aware and smart. People are often afraid to challenge someone because they fear that the person may be someone important who could take it the wrong way and make life difficult. However, if that person is an executive and you challenge him or her for identification, then you should be thanked. A vigilant employee can save the day.

Asking for an ID from someone is perfectly fine. If the person cannot produce it, then a polite escort to the guard for further assistance is usually all it takes. If the person is legit, the guard can track down the right party for him or her. If not, then the guard can follow whatever procedure is in place to take care of the intruder.

Following are some basic rules for awareness regarding door entrances:

- Be aware of who follows you into a building, and encourage employees to do the same. Figure out whether you know the person or whether he or she looks familiar.

- Notice whether someone following you into your building has a badge or not (if your company has badges), and ask the person to produce the badge or show an ID.

- Know the procedure for escorting an unbadged or unfamiliar person to the guard. If the person is a visitor, you could politely ask him or her to go check in at the front desk.

- If you are the boss, make sure you have a physical security policy in place, and ensure your employees know what the policy is.

Trash Receptacles

Another interesting area to be aware of in regard to security is when carrying out trash to a dumpster. Do you see someone *always there* about the same time emptying a can? Is someone parked nearby? Digging through the trash is a very *powerful* means of information gathering. Trash can yield passwords, customer lists, internal memos, e-mails, source code, sales figures, and more.

This type of information can make someone very knowledgeable about your company, sometimes so much so that he or she can easily pass for an employee. Consider establishing a policy to either shred all paper (cross-cut like confetti) or utilize an outside service to handle destruction of paper. In the area of electronic waste, there are a number of third-party services that will provide certified destruction. Hardware devices are prime targets for data loss.

Before sending out drives for destruction, use the free software product called *Darik's Boot and Nuke* ("*DBAN*") from www.dban.org. This tool is designed to wipe out data on hard drives very thoroughly. Using this in combination with the physical destruction of the drive is a sure-fire guarantee that the data is not retrievable.

Cars

Remember the fictional wireless hacker from Chapter 10? He used his parking spot near the building to monitor the wireless transmissions from outside your building. The information he gathered enabled him to break into the wireless network.

The guy in the Chapter 10 was simply picking up "free" signals from his location. From a hacker's point of view, he's safe — he's not trying to physically gain access to the building.

If the hacker wanted to gain access to the building, he would want to get closer to observe the target. Strange cars that are continuously parked in your parking lot or that are constantly driving around and scoping out the building are cause for vigilance.

The hacker wants to gain information about the building, the people, security, cameras, telephones, deliveries, and more. If he is to successfully penetrate your building, he'll need a full scope of what he's facing.

Following are some types of information a stranger in a "parked car" might be after:

- Where are the main and back entrances?

- Where are the designated smoking areas?

- Do the doors require badges for entrance?

- When do guards patrol?

- Does the area have frequent law enforcement patrols?

- How many times a day or week does the company receive deliveries?

- Are cameras mounted on the building, and are they stationary or do they move?

- Are the cameras wireless? If so, they may be able to be hacked into, and would give the hacker the same view as the guards.

- Is the loading dock door open? Is it guarded?

- Are other businesses nearby? If so, can the perpetrator pretend to be looking for the business if he's caught?

This list merely scratches the surface of possible points of interest to an attacker, but you can probably imagine how the information he could gather can compromise your company's security, either physically or wirelessly.

Fire Exit or Smoke Break Area

Most buildings today in the United States are non-smoking. That means that smokers must go outside or to a designated smoking area. In many buildings, the fire exit is often a place for employees to smoke because it's easily accessible. Similar to the "hold the door please" scenario mentioned earlier, the smoking areas are a prime target for building penetration.

Imagine the scene where a person comes walking toward a smoking area, holding a pack of cigarettes. He's *patting* his pockets in a manner familiar to all smokers, looking for a lighter. A fellow smoker might quickly offer him a light. The bad guy may strike up some small talk with the new acquaintance and, being friendly, the other person would respond. After all, he's just taking a smoke break! If the bad guy has done his homework, he'll know quite a bit about the inner workings of the company — enough so that he could *pass off himself* as an employee of the company.

His purpose, of course, is to either follow you or someone else in. He may stay for one more quick smoke while you return to work. He might casually smoke another as he waits for someone else to come out who didn't know the bad guy had simply walked up. At this point, the bad guy merely taps out the smoke as the other person walks out, and then he walks in. Mission accomplished.

Employees

People are clearly the biggest threat to your network. In this case, "people" are defined as *employees*. A break-in often occurs via an employee either by accident or intentionally. One very well-known case of an employee doing something wrong is the alleged behavior of the soldier who delivered documents in the WikiLeaks scandal. According to the charges filed, he allegedly accessed the government networks and removed documents for delivery to an unauthorized person.

This scenario has been repeated at all levels millions of times. People inside your company are very likely your largest threat.

The author once had job in the defense industry that used a proprietary network in a building that routed communications to terminals (before PCs were everywhere) from the mainframe. This network was very sensitive to physical changes (that is, putting something on the network that was not supposed to be on it could cause it to fail).

The author received a trouble ticket stating that part of the robotic manufacturing network had failed. He traced it down to a terminal that had been attached that shouldn't have been. He found out a *manager* had taken it upon himself to add it and avoid the process of applying for installation.

Following the process to remove the terminal and letting the person know how to properly request access, the author continued about his business. A mere few hours later, the robots in manufacturing had lost their connection again. Returning again to the manager's location, the author found that the manager had decided to ignore the previous admonition and put the terminal back on. Removing it restored proper operations. After that, the recurring problem was handled directly with the manager at a more senior level in the organization.

In this example, when the manager attached the terminal, it broke the connection to the robots that delivered parts to the manufacturing line. This caused a stop in production, thus causing delays in delivery of the product to the customer. Hence, the network was fine, but the cause of the failure was the *person* who was deliberately installing equipment he should not have.

Your policy should clearly cover situations where employees decide to take things into their own hands. In the event of someone's adding equipment to the network, adding a wireless router, or plugging a home laptop into your network, you'll have to decide on the actions to take. Consider each scenario and lay out the proper procedures, accompanied by the consequences for not following procedure.

Blatant violations like information theft should be treated as a criminal act, and be dealt with by your policy. Other items such as innocently plugging in a notebook computer may just require a discussion about safety of the network, virus scanning standards, and so forth.

Rogue Devices

Numerous online sites sell *hardware keyloggers* that plug into a USB port. The purpose of these innocuous-looking devices is to capture, record, and send out electronically what was typed. These devices are basically a hardware equivalent of a Trojan horse. This type of technology has been used in various forms for many years across many types of computing platforms.

Take the time to periodically check desktops and keyboards for any devices plugged in that you don't recognize. Obviously, if you don't know what it is, you should investigate and remove it if it is unneeded.

Along those same lines, train employees to never insert a "found" USB key or other device into a workplace computer. Dropping a USB key containing malicious code in a place an employee can find it is a form of social engineering, as is simply asking an employee to insert it — a technique that works more often than you might think.

Phones

One of the more popular social engineering attacks (but by far not the only one) is the caller who phones in and pretends to be someone in need of assistance, such as for a forgotten password. This type of hacker attempt can run from a nice "please help me" kind of conversation all the way to a hostile or possibly threatening call.

Summary

This chapter covered two key operational areas for your business — the development of a solid information security policy, and increasing your situational awareness.

Policies are designed to guide your employees on the proper use of your information systems (such as server, websites, e-mail, browsers, instant messaging, and so forth). Policies should also cover the use and misuse of confidential information. You should establish a policy on the type of equipment that employees can install into your network, and how they can use remote access.

The second half of this chapter covered the *dark* side of information gathering through social engineering techniques. The idea you must adopt is to pay attention to what is going on around you. The techniques deployed are very simple to detect and defeat. However, without any awareness that they are occurring, you and your employees can often be tripped up by them.

Security Tools, Port Vulnerabilities, and Apache Tips

This appendix examines a collection of tools, backdoor Trojan horse port listings, and tips for the Apache user.

Security Tools

This section provides an overview of common security tools.

Nmap

The GNU/GPL tool Network Mapper (Nmap) from `http://insecure.org` is one of the best security tools available today. It can operate on a single machine or on a very large network. It discovers what services are running and what operating system is being used. It also reveals a lot about a firewall or packet filters in place. In essence, it's very effective in mapping your network.

You should become familiar with this tool and learn to use it.

WARNING Never scan networks you do not own or have permission to scan. It can be considered a hostile act. In other words, use this tool for your administrative purposes only, and do not use it to hack or attack any other networks or servers.

After you install Nmap on Windows machines, it runs via the graphical user interface (GUI). To begin using Nmap, enter your host name or IP address in the Target box. Next, select the type of scan from the Profile drop-down.

Using the drop-down box in the GUI, you may select from among popular combinations of scanning. These preconfigured options are only a handful of the many combinations. They represent many of the normal commands you'll use. When you make a selection, a command is entered in the *Command box*. For example, if you select the Intense Scan option, the following command is entered:

```
nmap -sS -sU -T4 -A -v -PE -PS22,25,80 -PA21,23,80,3389 domainname.com
```

This command breaks down as follows:

- `-sS/sT/sA/sW/sM` — TCP SYN/Connect()/ACK/Window/Maimon scans
- `-sU` — UDP scan
- `-T4-T<0-5>` — Set timing template (higher number is faster)
- `-A` — Enable OS detection, version detection, script scanning, and traceroute
- `-v` — Increase verbosity level (use `-vv` or more for greater effect)
- `-PE/PP/PM` — ICMP echo, timestamp, and netmask request discovery probes
- `-PS/PA/PU/PY[portlist]` — TCP SYN/ACK, UDP, or SCTP discovery to given ports (scans the ports)

Following is a description of the other Profile options:

- *Intense Scan plus UDP* — This produces the following command:
  ```
  -sS -sU -T4 -A -v -PE -PS22,25,80 -PA21,23,80,3389
  ```
- *Intense Scan, all TCP ports* — This produces the following command:
  ```
  -p 1-65535 -T4 -A -v -PE -PS22,25,80 -PA21,23,80,3389
  ```
- *Intense Scan, no ping* — This produces the following command:
  ```
  -T4 -A -v -PN
  ```
- *Ping scan* — This produces the following command:
  ```
  -sP -PE -PA21,23,80,3389
  ```
- *Quick scan* — This produces the following command:
  ```
  -T4 -F
  ```
- *Quick scan plus* — This produces the following command:
  ```
  -sV -T4 -O -F --version-light
  ```
- *Quick traceroute* — This produces the following command:
  ```
  -sP -PE -PS22,25,80 -PA21,23,80,3389 -PU -PO
  ```

- *Regular Scan* — This conducts a default Nmap scan
- *Slow comprehensive scan* — This produces the following command:

```
-sS -sU -T4 -A -v -PE -PP -PS21,22,23,25,80,113,31339
   -PA80,113,443,10042 -PO --script all
```

NOTE For more information on these options, see `http://nmap.org/svn/docs/nmap.usage.txt`.

Telnet

Although Telnet should be removed from your server, it's great as a testing tool and still the norm for connecting to specific types of network gear. Telnet is a very old protocol that allows you to connect to a machine and issue commands. By default, Telnet runs on port 23.

To start using Telnet on a Windows 7 machine, click Start ➢ Accessories ➢ Command Prompt. At the command prompt, type **telnet**. The TELNET> prompt appears.

To Telnet to another machine, enter the following:

```
O machine name port
```

Replace the `machine name` with the IP or hostname and the port number.

Telnet can be used to connect and send e-mail on misconfigured servers. For example, the following command will attempt to connect you to the Mail Services:

```
telnet machine name 25
```

If you are successful in connecting, you can often send unauthorized e-mail through the server. This is also a means to check for open relays in your mail system.

Following is a list of common parameters used with the Windows version of Telnet:

- c — Close the connection.
- d — Display operating parameters.
- o — Connect to hostname (defaults to port 23).
- q — Exit (quit) Telnet.
- set — Set options (see set ? for more information).
- sen — Send strings (commands) to server.
- st — Print status information.

- u — Unset options.
- ?/h — Help.

Netstat

Netstat is a very valuable tool for troubleshooting and observing what is going on with your network. You can use this tool any time to view network connections, routing tables, the statistics of an interface, and more.

Following are common options for Netstat:

- -a — Displays all active Transmission Control Protocol (TCP) connections, as well as the TCP and User Datagram Protocol (UDP) ports on which the computer is listening.

- -e — Displays Ethernet statistics, such as the number of bytes and packets sent and received. This parameter can be combined with -s.

- -i — Displays network interfaces and their statistics.

- -n — Displays active TCP connections. However, addresses and port numbers are expressed numerically, and no attempt is made to determine names.

- -p — Shows which processes are using which sockets.

- -r — Displays the contents of the IP routing table.

- -s — Displays statistics by protocol. By default, statistics are shown for the TCP, UDP, Internet Control Message Protocol (ICMP), and IP protocols. If the IPv6 protocol for Windows XP is installed, statistics are shown for the TCP over IPv6, UDP over IPv6, ICMPv6, and IPv6 protocols. The -p parameter can be used to specify a set of protocols.

- -v — Sets verbose mode.

- -V (uppercase) — Displays the version information.

- -h — Displays help.

WireShark

WireShark is known as a *sniffer*. It listens in on the network connection and captures each packet. According to the website www.wireshark.org/about .html, "Wireshark is the world's foremost network protocol analyzer. It lets you capture and interactively browse the traffic running on a computer network. It is the de facto (and often de jure) standard across many industries and educational institutions."

You should become familiar with this powerful tool. It is an excellent tool for network and server administrators to use to troubleshoot issues.

WARNING Only use WireShark on a corporate network if you have permission. *Never* use this tool for any illegal or unethical tasks (such as capturing passwords). Only use it for the proper administrative needs.

Currently, WireShark is available for the following platforms:

- Windows Installer (32-bit)
- Windows Installer (64-bit)
- Windows U3 (32-bit)
- Windows PortableApps (32-bit)
- OS X 10.5 (Leopard) Intel 32-bit .dmg
- OS X 10.6 (Snow Leopard) Intel 64-bit .dmg
- OS X 10.5 (Leopard) PPC 32-bit .dmg

After you download it, follow the installation instructions for your platform. For Windows, you must install WinPcap (included with the installer) or the captures will not work.

The Windows installation is a fairly simple point-and-click process. Unless you have other reasons to do so, you should choose the defaults.

On a Windows machine, you start WireShark by clicking its corresponding icon.

Open the Capture ➤ Interface selection from the toolbar. This will provide a list of installed network interface cards (NICs) on the machine. Your machine may have a wired NIC and a WIRELESS NIC, and each will be listed. Choose the NIC from which you want to collect packets and click Start.

As the collection process starts, you will see the collection window filling up with packets. These listings show the IP source, IP destination, protocol, and other information about the packet. Using this information can enable you to locate all kinds of problems on your network, such as bad NICs and illegal traffic (hackers).

WireShark can capture many protocols that are used for various devices. For example, the most common packet you would be TCP/IP for your normal Internet traffic. Voice over IP (VoIP) would have a different protocol. Select or deselect the protocols for which you want to capture information.

After you collect enough packets, you can review errors, warnings, and other information WireShark has found. Errors can indicate software or configuration issues. For example, if you're troubleshooting a network storm, the noted errors can be used to track down the offending device. WireShark can also detect problems such as bad patch cables that could be causing network issues such as slow performance.

One very powerful feature is the capability to search for specific information. For example, you could search for all the traffic from a network that was bound to or from `mail.google.com`.

Backdoor Intruders

Table A-1 shows a list of known (as of this writing) ports and the backdoor viruses and Trojans that try to use these ports. Many of these may be old, but given that virus writers tend to reuse each other's code, tracking the historical viruses is important. This compiled list from `www.sans.org/security-resources/idfaq/oddports.php` and other sources is one you can cross reference if you believe you have been hacked.

Table A-1: Common Ports and Backdoor Intruder

PORT NUMBER	TROJAN NAME
2	Death
20	Senna Spy FTP server
21	Back Construction, Blade Runner, Doly Trojan, fore, Invisible FTP, Juggernaut 42, Larva, Motlv FTP, Net Administrator, Senna Spy FTP server, Traitor 21, WebEx, WinCrash
22	Shaft
23	Fire, HacKer, Tiny, Telnet, Server, TTS, Truva, Atl
25	Ajan, Antigen, Email, Password, Sender, EPS, EPS II, Gip, Gris, Happy99, Hpteam, mail, I love you, Kuang2, Magic, Horse, MBT
31	Agent 31, Hackers, Paradise, MastersParadise
41	Deep Throat, Foreplay or Reduced Foreplay
48	DRAT
50	DRAT
59	DMSetup
79	CDK, Firehotcker
80	AckCmd, BackEnd, CGI, Backdoor, Executor, Hooker, RingZero
81	RemoConChubo
99	Hidden Port
110	ProMail trojan
113	Identd, Invisible, Deamon, Kazimas
119	Happy99

PORT NUMBER	TROJAN NAME
121	JammerKillah
123	Net, Controller
133	Farnaz
142	NetTaxi
146	Infector
146	(UDP) Infector
170	A-trojan
180	(TCP/UDP) amanda
334	Backage
420	Breach
421	TCP Wrappers, trojan
456	Hackers Paradise
513	Grlogin
514	RPC Backdoor
531	Rasmin
559	(TCP/UDP) teedtap
605	Secret Service
666	Attack FTP, Back Construction, Cain & Abel, NokNok, Satans Back Door, SBD, ServU, Shadow Phyre
667	SniperNet
669	DP trojan
692	GayOL
777	AimSpy, Undetected
808	WinHole
911	Dark Shadow
999	Deep Throat, Foreplay, Reduced Foreplay, WinSatan
1000	Der Späher / Der Spaeher
1001	Der Späher, Der Spaeher, Le
1010	Doly Trojan
1011	Doly Trojan
1012	Doly Trojan

Continued

Table A-1 *(continued)*

PORT NUMBER	TROJAN NAME
1015	Doly Trojan
1016	Doly Trojan
1020	Vampire
1024	NetSpy
1026	nterm
1042	BLA, trojan
1045	Rasmin
1049	/sbin/initd
1050	MiniCommand
1054	AckCmd
1080	WinHole
1081	WinHole
1082	WinHole
1083	WinHole
1090	Xtreme
1095	Remote Administration Tool - RAT
1097	Remote Administration Tool - RAT
1098	Remote Administration Tool - RAT
1099	Blood Fest Evolution, Remote Administration Tool, RAT
1170	Psyber, Stream Server, PSS
1200	(UDP) NoBackO
1201	(UDP) NoBackO
1207	SoftWAR
1212	Kaos
1234	Ultors Trojan
1243	BackDoor-G, SubSeven, Apocalypse, Tiles
1245	VooDoo Doll
1255	Scarab
1256	Project, nEXT
1269	Matrix
1313	NETrojan

PORT NUMBER	TROJAN NAME
1338	Millenium Worm
1349	Bo dll
1434	(UDP) MS-SQL
1492	FTP99CMP
1524	Trinoo
1600	Shivka-Burka
1777	Scarab
1807	SpySender
1966	Fake FTP
1969	OpC BO
1981	Bowl, Shockrave
1999	Back Door, TransScout
2000	Der Späher, Der Spaeher, Insane Network
2001	Der Späher, Der Spaeher, Trojan Cow
2023	Ripper Pro
2080	WinHole
2115	Bugs
2140	The Invasor
2140	(UDP) Deep Throat, Foreplay-Reduced Foreplay
2155	Illusion Mailer
2234	(TCP/UDP) directplay
2255	Nirvana
2283	Hvl RAT
2300	Xplorer
2339	Voice Spy, OBS!!! namnen, har, bytt, plats
2339	(UDP) Voice Spy, OBS!!!, namnen, har, bytt, plats
2345	Doly Trojan
2565	Striker trojan
2583	WinCrash
2600	Digital RootBeer
2716	The Prayer

Continued

Table A-1 *(continued)*

PORT NUMBER	TROJAN NAME
2773	SubSeven, SubSeven 2.1, Gold
2801	Phineas, Phucker
2989	(UDP) Remote Administration Tool, RAT
3000	Remote Shut
3024	WinCrash
3127	mydoom
3128	Squid Proxy
3129	Masters Paradise
3150	The Invasor
3150	(UDP) Deep Throat, Foreplay, Reduced Foreplay
3456	Terror trojan
3459	Eclipse 2000, Sanctuary
3700	Portal of Doom, POD
3791	Total Solar Eclypse
3801	Total Solar Eclypse
4000	Skydance
4092	WinCrash
4242	Virtual Hacking Machine, VHM
4321	BoBo
4444	Prosiak, Swift Remote
4567	File Nail
4590	ICQ Trojan
4950	ICQTrogen (Lm)
5000	Back Door Setup, Blazer5, Bubbel, ICKiller, Sockets des Troie
5001	Back Door Setup, Sockets des Troie
5002	cd00r, Shaft
5010	Solo
5025	WM Remote KeyLogger
5031	Net Metropolitan
5032	Net Metropolitan
5321	Firehotcker

PORT NUMBER	TROJAN NAME
5343	wCrat Remote Administration Tool
5400	Back Construction, Blade Runner
5401	Back Construction, Blade Runner
5402	Back Construction, Blade Runner
5512	Illusion Mailer
5550	Xtcp
5555	ServeMe
5556	BO Facil
5557	BO Facil
5569	Robo-Hack
5637	PC Crasher
5638	PC Crasher
5742	WinCrash
5760	Portmap Remote Root Linux Exploit
5882	(UDP) Y3K RAT
5888	Y3K RAT
6000	The Thing
6006	Bad Blood
6272	Secret Service
6346	(TCP/UDP) BearShare
6400	The Thing
6666	Dark Connection Inside, NetBus worm
6667	ScheduleAgent, Trinity, WinSatan
6669	HostControl, Vampire
6670	BackWebServer, Deep Throat, Foreplay
6711	BackDoor-G, SubSeven, VP Killer
6712	Funny trojan, SubSeven
6713	SubSeven
6723	Mstream
6771	Deep Throat, Foreplay, Reduced Foreplay
6776	2000Cracks, BackDoor-G, SubSeven, VP Killer

Continued

Table A-1 *(continued)*

PORT NUMBER	TROJAN NAME
6838	(UDP) Mstream
6883	Delta Source DarkStar
6912	Shit Heep
6939	Indoctrination
6969	GateCrasher, IRC 3, Net Controller, Priority
6970	GateCrasher
7000	Exploit Translation Server, Kazimas, Remote Grab, SubSeven 2.1 Gold
7001	Freak88
7215	SubSeven, SubSeven 2.1 Gold
7300	NetMonitor
7301	NetMonitor
7306	NetMonitor
7307	NetMonitor
7308	NetMonitor
7424	Host Control
7424	(UDP) Host Control
7597	Qaz
7777	Tini
7789	BackDoor Setup, ICKiller
7983	Mstream
8080	Brown Orifice, RemoConChubo, RingZero
8787	BackOrifice 2000
8988	BacHack
8989	Rcon, Recon, Xcon
9000	Netministrator
9325	(UDP) Mstream
9400	InCommand
9872	Portal of Doom, POD
9873	Portal of Doom, POD
9874	Portal of Doom, POD

PORT NUMBER	TROJAN NAME
9875	Portal of Doom, POD
9876	Cyber Attacker, Rux
9878	TransScout
9989	Ini-Killer
9999	The Prayer
10067	(UDP) Portal of Doom, POD
10085	Syphillis
10086	Syphillis
10101	BrainSpy
10167	(UDP) Portal of Doom, POD
10520	Acid Shivers
10528	Host Control
10607	Coma
10666	(UDP) Ambush
11000	Senna Spy Trojan Generator
11050	Host Control
11051	Host Control
11223	Progenic trojan, Secret Agent
12076	Gjamer
12223	Hack'99 KeyLogger
12345	cron/crontab, trojan, GabanBus, icmp_pipe.c, Mypic, NetBus, NetBus Toy, NetBus worm, Pie Bill Gates, Whack Job, X-bill
12346	GabanBus, NetBus, X-bill
12349	BioNet
12361	Whack-a-mole
12362	Whack-a-mole
12623	(UDP) DUN Control
12624	ButtMan
12631	Whack Job
12754	Mstream
13000	Senna Spy Trojan Generator

Continued

Table A-1 (continued)

PORT NUMBER	TROJAN NAME
13010	Hacker Brasil HBR
14500	PC Invader
15092	Host Control
15104	Mstream
15858	CDK
16484	Mosucker
16660	Stacheldraht
16772	ICQ Revenge
16969	Priority
17166	Mosaic
17300	Kuang2 the virus
17449	Kid Terror
17499	CrazzyNet
17777	Nephron
18753	(UDP) Shaft
19864	ICQ Revenge
20000	Millenium
20001	Millenium Millenium (Lm)
20002	AcidkoR
20023	VP Killer
20034	NetBus 2.0, Pro NetRex, Whack Job
20203	Chupacabra
20331	BLA trojan
20432	Shaft
20433	(UDP) Shaft
21544	GirlFriend, Kid Terror
21554	Exploiter, Kid Terror, Schwindler, Winsp00fer
22222	Donald Dick, Prosiak
23005	NetTrash
23023	Logged

PORT NUMBER	TROJAN NAME
23032	Amanda
23432	Asylum
23456	Evil FTP, Ugly FTP, Whack Job
23476	Donald Dick
23476	(UDP) Donald Dick
23477	Donald Dick
26274	(UDP) Delta Source
26681	Voice SpyOBS!!!, namnen, har, bytt, plats
27374	Bad Blood, SubSeven, SubSeven 2.1 Gold, Subseven 2.1.4, DefCon 8
27444	(UDP) Trinoo
27573	SubSeven
27665	Trinoo
29104	NetTrojan
29891	The Unexplained
30001	ErrOr32
30003	Lamers Death
30029	AOL trojan
30100	NetSphere
30101	NetSphere
30102	NetSphere
30103	NetSphere
30103	(UDP) NetSphere
30133	NetSphere
30303	Sockets des Troie
30947	Intruse
30999	Kuang2
31335	Trinoo
31336	BoWhack, Butt Funnel
31337	Back Fire, Back Orifice (Lm), Back Orifice, Russian Baron, Night, Beeone, BO client, BO Facil, BO spy, BO2 cron/crontab, Freak88, icmp_pipe.c

Continued

Table A-1 *(continued)*

PORT NUMBER	TROJAN NAME
31337	(UDP) Back Orifice, Deep, BO
31338	Back Orifice, Butt Funnel, NetSpy, (DK)
31338	(UDP) Deep, BO
31339	NetSpy, (DK)
31666	BOWhack
31785	Hack 'a' Tack
31788	Hack 'a' Tack
31789	(UDP) Hack 'a' Tack
31790	Hack 'a' Tack
31791	(UDP) Hack 'a' Tack
31792	Hack 'a' Tack
32001	Donald Dick
32100	Peanut, Brittle, Project, nEXT
32418	Acid Battery
33270	Trinity
33333	Blakharaz, Prosiak
33577	PsychWard
33777	PsychWard
33911	Spirit 2000, Spirit 2001
34324	Big Gluck, TN
34444	Donald Dick
34555	(UDP) Trinoo (for Windows)
35555	(UDP) Trinoo (for Windows)
37651	Yet Another, TrojanYAT
40412	The Spy
40421	Agent 40421, Masters Paradise
40422	Masters Paradise
40423	Masters Paradise
40426	Masters Paradise
41666	Remote Boot, ToolRBT, Remote Boot, ToolRBT

PORT NUMBER	TROJAN NAME
44444	Prosiak
47262	(UDP) Delta Source
50505	Sockets, des Troie
50766	Fore, Schwindler
51966	Cafeini
52317	Acid Battery 2000
53001	Remote Windows, ShutdownRWS
54283	SubSeven, SubSeven 2.1 Gold
54320	Back Orifice 2000
54321	Back Orifice 2000, School Bus
57341	NetRaider
58339	Butt Funnel
60000	Deep Throat, Foreplay or Reduced Foreplay, Sockets des Troie
60068	Xzip 6000068
60411	Connection
61348	Bunker-Hill
61466	TeleCommando
61603	Bunker-Hill
63485	Bunker-Hill
64101	Taskman, TaskManager
65000	Devil, Sockets, des Troie, Stacheldraht
65432	The Traitor, (=th3tr41t0r)
65432	(UDP) The Traitor, (=th3tr41t0r)
65534	/sbin/initd
65535	RC1 trojan

Apache Status Codes

This section provides information about status codes used with Apache. The descriptions are grouped according to the numbers of the codes.

1xx Series

This class of status code indicates a provisional response, consisting only of the Status Line and optional headers, and is terminated by an empty line.

Following are specific codes in this series:

- 100 Continue — HTTP_CONTINUE
- 101 Switching Protocols — HTTP_SWITCHING_PROTOCOLS
- 102 Processing — HTTP_PROCESSING

2xx Series

This class of status code indicates the action was successfully received, understood, and accepted.

Following are specific codes in this series:

- 200 OK — HTTP_OK
- 201 Created — HTTP_CREATED
- 202 Accepted — HTTP_ACCEPTED
- 203 Non-Authoritative Information — HTTP_NON_AUTHORITATIVE
- 204 No Content — HTTP_NO_CONTENT
- 205 Reset Content — HTTP_RESET_CONTENT
- 206 Partial Content — HTTP_PARTIAL_CONTENT
- 207 Multi-Status — HTTP_MULTI_STATUS

3xx Series

Codes in this series indicate that further action needs to be taken by the user-agent in order to fulfill the request. The action required may be carried out by the user-agent without interaction with the user if (and only if) the method used in the second request is GET or HEAD. A user-agent should not automatically redirect a request more than five times, because such redirections usually indicate an infinite loop.

Following are specific codes in this series:

- 300 Multiple Choices — HTTP_MULTIPLE_CHOICES
- 301 Moved Permanently — HTTP_MOVED_PERMANENTLY
- 302 Found — HTTP_MOVED_TEMPORARILY
- 303 See Other — HTTP_SEE_OTHER
- 304 Not Modified — HTTP_NOT_MODIFIED

- 305 Use Proxy — HTTP_USE_PROXY
- 306 unused — UNUSED
- 307 Temporary Redirect — HTTP_TEMPORARY_REDIRECT

4xx Series

Codes in this series indicate that the request contains bad syntax or cannot be fulfilled. The codes indicate a case where the client seems to have erred. Except when responding to a HEAD request, the server should include an entity containing an explanation of the error situation, and whether it is a temporary or permanent condition.

Following are specific codes in this series:

- 400 Bad Request — HTTP_BAD_REQUEST
- 401 Authorization Required — HTTP_UNAUTHORIZED
- 402 Payment Required — HTTP_PAYMENT_REQUIRED
- 403 Forbidden — HTTP_FORBIDDEN
- 404 Not Found — HTTP_NOT_FOUND
- 405 Method Not Allowed — HTTP_METHOD_NOT_ALLOWED
- 406 Not Acceptable — HTTP_NOT_ACCEPTABLE
- 407 Proxy Authentication Required — HTTP_PROXY_AUTHENTICATION_ REQUIRED
- 408 Request Time-out — HTTP_REQUEST_TIME_OUT
- 409 Conflict — HTTP_CONFLICT
- 410 Gone — HTTP_GONE
- 411 Length Required — HTTP_LENGTH_REQUIRED
- 412 Precondition Failed — HTTP_PRECONDITION_FAILED
- 413 Request Entity Too Large — HTTP_REQUEST_ENTITY_TOO_LARGE
- 414 Request-URI Too Large — HTTP_REQUEST_URI_TOO_LARGE
- 415 Unsupported Media Type — HTTP_UNSUPPORTED_MEDIA_TYPE
- 416 Requested Range Not Satisfied — HTTP_RANGE_NOT_SATISFIABLE
- 417 Expectation Failed — HTTP_EXPECTATION_FAILED
- 418 I'm a teapot — UNUSED
- 419 unused — UNUSED
- 420 unused — UNUSED
- 421 unused — UNUSED

- 422 Unprocessable Entities — HTTP_UNPROCESSABLE_ENTITY
- 423 Locked — HTTP_LOCKED
- 424 Failed Dependency — HTTP_FAILED_DEPENDENCY
- 425 No code — HTTP_NO_CODE
- 426 Upgrade Required — HTTP_UPGRADE_REQUIRED

5XX Series

Codes in this series indicate that the server failed to fulfill an apparently valid request. The codes indicate cases in which the server is aware that it has erred, or is incapable of performing the request. Except when responding to a HEAD request, the server should include an entity containing an explanation of the error situation, and whether it is a temporary or permanent condition. These response codes are applicable to any request method.

Following are specific codes in this series:

- 500 Internal Server Error — HTTP_INTERNAL_SERVER_ERROR
- 501 Method Not Implemented — HTTP_NOT_IMPLEMENTED
- 502 Bad Gateway — HTTP_BAD_GATEWAY
- 503 Service Temporarily Unavailable — HTTP_SERVICE_UNAVAILABLE
- 504 Gateway Time-out — HTTP_GATEWAY_TIME_OUT
- 505 HTTP Version Not Supported — HTTP_VERSION_NOT_SUPPORTED
- 506 Variant Also Negotiates — HTTP_VARIANT_ALSO_VARIES
- 507 Insufficient Storage — HTTP_INSUFFICIENT_STORAGE
- 508 unused — UNUSED
- 509 unused — UNUSED
- 510 Not Extended — HTTP_NOT_EXTENDED

.htaccess settings

The .htaccess file is a configuration file that can be placed on a per-directory level when you're running Apache Web Server software. Within this file, you can tweak and set very specific Apache directives.

This section describes a few of the more popular .htaccess settings. Many of these examples are courtesy of Perishablepress.com. For more information, see the following resources:

- http://www.htaccess-guide.com
- http://httpd.apache.org/docs/2.2/mod/quickreference.html

WordPress users should visit `http://perishablepress.com/press/tag/security/` to see various `.htaccess` samples. Joomla! users should visit `http://snipt.net/nikosdion/the-master-htaccess/` to learn about specifics for using `.htaccess` to better secure Joomla! sites.

Blocking IP Addresses

Following is an example of blocking IP addresses from visiting your site:

```
<Limit GET POST PUT>
 Order Allow,Deny
 Allow from all
 Deny from xxx.xxx.xxx.xxx
 Deny from xxx.xxx.xxx.xxx
 Deny from xxx.xxx.xxx.xxx
 Deny from xxx.xxx.xxx.xxx
</Limit>
```

Blocking Bad Bots

A class of malware that attacks websites is *bad bots*. These malicious creatures either break in or gather information used to break in. Blocking them is a regular and frequent task. Fortunately, `.htaccess` provides a simple method to do it.

For a good example to use to block bad bots in `.htaccess`, see `http://perishablepress.com/press/2010/08/09/2010-user-agent-blacklist` and copy down the directives from 2010 User-Agent Blacklist.

Protecting a Specific File

The following example protects a specific file from all visitors except your IP:

```
Block all visitors except your IP or IPs
<Limit GET POST PUT>
 Order Deny,Allow
 Deny from all
 Allow from first ip address
 Allow from second ip address
 </Limit>
ErrorDocument 403 path/custom-message.html
<Files path/custom-message.html>
 Order Allow,Deny
 Allow from all
</Files>
```

Requiring SSL on Your Site

The following example shows how to require SSL on your site:

```
SSLOptions +StrictRequire
```

```
SSLRequireSSL
SSLRequire %{HTTP_HOST} eq "domain.tld"
ErrorDocument 403 https://domain.tld

# require SSL without mod_ssl
RewriteCond %{HTTPS} !=on [NC]
RewriteRule ^.*$ https://%{SERVER_NAME}%{REQUEST_URI} [R,L]
```

Deploying Custom Error Pages on Your Site

Replicate the following patterns to serve your own set of custom error pages. Simply replace the /errors/###.html with the correct path and filename. Also change the ### preceding the path to summon pages for other errors.

NOTE Your custom error pages must be larger than 512 bytes in size, or they will be completely ignored by Internet Explorer.

Use the following to serve custom error pages:

```
ErrorDocument 400 /errors/400.html
ErrorDocument 401 /errors/401.html
ErrorDocument 403 /errors/403.html
ErrorDocument 404 /errors/404.html
ErrorDocument 500 /errors/500.html
Provide a Universal Error Document
```

Use the following to provide a universal error document:

```
RewriteCond %{REQUEST_FILENAME} !-f
RewriteCond %{REQUEST_FILENAME} !-d
RewriteRule ^.*$ /dir/error.php [L]
```

Disable the Server Signature

Use the following to disable the server signature:

```
ServerSignature Off
```

Limit Server Request Methods to Get and Put

Use the following to limit server request methods to GET and PUT:

```
Options -ExecCGI -Indexes -All
RewriteEngine on
RewriteCond %{REQUEST_METHOD} ^(TRACE|TRACK|OPTIONS|HEAD)
RewriteRule .* - [F]
```

Prevent Access to the .htaccess File

Add the following code block to your `.htaccess` file to add an extra layer of security. Any attempts to access the `.htaccess` file will result in a 403 error message. Of course, your first layer of defense to protect `.htaccess` files involves setting `.htaccess` file permissions via CHMOD to 644:

```
<Files .htaccess>
 order allow,deny
 deny from all
</Files>
```

Prevent Access to Multiple File Types

To restrict access to a variety of file types, add the following code block and edit the file types within parentheses to match the extensions of any files that you want to protect:

```
<FilesMatch "\.(htaccess|htpasswd|ini|phps|fla|psd|log|sh)$">
 Order Allow,Deny
 Deny from all
</FilesMatch>
```

Prevent Unauthorized Directory Browsing

Prevent unauthorized directory browsing by instructing the server to serve an `xxx forbidden - Authorization Required` message for any request to view a directory. For example, if your site is missing its default index page, everything within the root of your site will be accessible to all visitors. To prevent this, include the following `.htaccess` rule:

```
# Disables Directory Browsing
Options All -Indexes
```

Conversely, to enable directory browsing, use the following directive:

```
# Enables Directory Browsing
Options All +Indexes
```

Likewise, this rule will prevent the server from listing directory contents:

```
# Prevent Folder Listing
IndexIgnore *
```

Finally, you can use the `IndexIgnore` directive to prevent the display of select file types:

```
# Prevent display of select file types
IndexIgnore *.wmv *.mp4 *.avi *.etc
```

Acronyms and Terminology

Table B-1 provides a list of common security acronyms.

Table B-1: Acronyms

ACRONYM	MEANING
APF	Advanced Policy Firewall
AES	Advanced Encryption Standard
ACL	Access Control List
ASP	Active Server Pages
BIOS	Basic Input/Output System
BSIG	Bluetooth Special Interest Group
CGI	Common Gateway Interface
CISSP	Certified Information Systems Security Professional
CISO	Chief Information Security Officer
CISP	Cardholder Information Security Program
CLI	Command Line Interpreter
CMS	Content Management System

Continued

Table B-1 *(continued)*

ACRONYM	MEANING
CoLo	Co-location Facility
CSU/DSU	Channel Service Unit/Data Service Unit
DCE	Data Communications Equipment
DDoS	Distributed Denial of Service (attack)
DES	Data Encryption Standard
DHCP	Dynamic Host Configuration Protocol
FDDI	Fiber Distributed Data Interface
FTP	File Transfer Protocol (application layer)
GBIC	Gigabit Interface Converter
Gbps	Gigabit per second
HTML	Hypertext Markup Language
IANA	Internet Assigned Number Authority Organization
ICMP	Internet Control Message Protocol
IMAP	Internet Message Access Protocol
IOS	Internetwork Operating System
IP	Internet Protocol (Internet layer)
IP Address	Internet Protocol Address
IPS	Intrusion Prevention System
IRC	Internet Relay Chat
ISDN	Integrated Services Digital Network
ISP	Internet service provider
JAXP	Java API for XML Parsing
JDBC	Java Database Connectivity
JDK	Java Development Kit
Kbps	Kilobits per second
LAN	Local area network
LDAP	Lightweight Directory Access Protocol
LLC	Logical Link Control
MAC	Media Access Control
MAN	Metropolitan Area

ACRONYM	MEANING
Mbps	Megabits per second
MIB	Management Information Base (SNMP)
MTA	Mail Transfer Agent
NIST	National Institute for Standards and Technology
NIC	Network Interface Card
NOC	Network Operations Center
OSF	Open Software Foundation
OSF	Open Systems Foundation
OSI	Open Systems Interconnection
OSI	Open Source Initiative
POP3	Post Office Protocol version 3
POTS	Plain Old Telephone Service
QoS	Quality of Service
RAID	Redundant Array of Inexpensive Disks
RAM	Random Access Memory
RBOC	Regional Bell Operating Company
RIP	Routing Information Protocol
RIP	Routing Interface Protocol
SEO	Search Engine Optimization
SMTP	Simple Mail Transfer Protocol
S/MIME	Secure MIME (e-mail)
SMNP	Simple Network Management Protocol
SMTP	Simple Mail Transfer Protocol
SOA	Start of Authority
SSI	Server Side Includes
SSL	Secure Sockets Layer
TCP	Transmission Control Protocol
TCP/IP	Transmission Control Protocol/Internet Protocol
TLS	Transport Layer Security
UDP	User Datagram Protocol

Continued

Table B-1 (continued)

ACRONYM	MEANING
URL	Uniform Resource Locator
W3C	World Wide Web Consortium
WAE	Wireless Application Environment
WAIS	Wide Area Information Server
WAN	Wide-area network
WAP	Wireless Access Protocol
WebDAV	Web Distributed Authoring and Versioning
WEP	Wireless Equivalent Privacy
Wi-Fi	IEEE 802.11 (Wi-Fi Alliance)
WTLS	Wireless Transport Layer Security
WPA	Wi-Fi Protected Access Security
WWW	World Wide Web

Table B-2 provides a list of common security terminology.

Table B-2: Security Terminology

TERM	EXPLANATION
Access Control Lists (ACLs)	An ACL is a database that tracks the resources a user (or a machine) has access to use. If a user does not appear in the ACL, then the user won't be granted access to the systems in question.
Agent	A program used in distributed denial of service (DDoS) attacks that send malicious traffic to hosts based on the instructions of a handler. You might also see this called a *zombie* or *bot*.
Audit trail	A record showing who has accessed your server during a given period of time.
Availability	This means that you ensure timely and reliable access to your information systems. You might say a site has high availability if it is never down.
Backup	A copy of files and programs made to facilitate recovery, if necessary.
Baseline security	The minimum of security controls required for safeguarding your IT resources.
Baselining	The monitoring of resources to determine typical utilization patterns so that significant deviations can be detected.

TERM	EXPLANATION
Blended attack	Malicious code that uses multiple methods to spread.
Boundary router	A router located at the organization's boundary to an external network, such as the Internet.
Brute-force password attack	A method of accessing an obstructed device by attempting multiple combinations of numeric and/or alphanumeric passwords.
Buffer overflow	A programming error that could allow more input being placed in a buffer area in memory that could cause a crash. Additionally, it could allow someone to exploit this to insert code to control a system (that is, malicious code being placed into the memory location of the crashed or flawed program for execution).
Buffer overflow attack	See "Buffer overflow."
Business Continuity Plan (BCP)	Documentation of a predetermined set of instructions or procedures that describe how an organization's business functions will be sustained during and after a significant disruption.
Brute-force password attack	A method of accessing a locked system or website through attempting multiple combinations of numeric and/or alphanumeric passwords. This is particularly effective in sites and systems using weak passwords.
Certification Authority (CA)	A trusted third party that issues and revokes public key certificates.
Common Vulnerabilities and Exposures (CVE)	The list of publicly known IT system vulnerabilities.
Compromise	Disclosure of information to unauthorized persons. It could be a violation of the security policy of a system in which unauthorized intentional or unintentional disclosure, modification, destruction, or loss of an object may have occurred.
Computer security incident	A violation or imminent threat of violation of your computer systems, or a violation of your information security policies.
Computer virus	Code that usually performs some unwanted function as a side effect, typically with an additional "payload" that triggers when specific conditions are met (such as information theft or data destruction).
Confidentiality	The property that sensitive information is not disclosed to unauthorized individuals, entities, or processes.

Continued

Table B-2 *(continued)*

TERM	EXPLANATION
Contingency plan	Management policy and procedures written to maintain or restore business operations, including computer operations, possibly at an alternate location.
Cookie	A piece of information supplied by a web server to a browser (along with a requested resource) for the browser to store temporarily and return to the server on any subsequent visits or requests.
Countermeasures	Actions, devices, procedures, techniques, or other measures that reduce the vulnerability of an information system.
Cross-Site Scripting (XSS)	An attack technique that involves attacker-supplied code sent into a user's browser. Once there, the rogue code will execute as if the user were the one operating it. Overall, this event is devastating for desktops.
Data integrity	Data that has not been modified using unauthorized or unintended ways.
Denial of Service (DoS)	The prevention of authorized access to resources or the delaying of time-critical operations. The time factor depends strictly on your tolerance for downtime.
Dynamic Host Configuration Protocol (DHCP)	The protocol used to assign Internet Protocol (IP) addresses to all nodes on the network.
Disaster Recovery Plan (DRP)	A written plan for returning your systems, software, and operations back to working or near working states following a disaster or loss.
Exploit code	A program that allows attackers to automatically break into a system.
False positive	A false report about malicious activity.
Firewall	A gateway that limits access between networks in accordance with local security policy.
Incident handling	The documented process to mitigate damage from an attack or loss.
Least privilege	The security objective of granting users only the access they need to perform their official duties.
Malicious code	Software or firmware intended to perform an unauthorized process that will have adverse impact on your systems or data. This could be a virus, worm, a Trojan horse, or any other code introduced for malicious reasons.

TERM	EXPLANATION
Non-repudiation	Assurance that the sender of information is provided with proof of delivery, and the recipient is provided with proof of the sender's identity, so neither can later deny having processed the information. This is akin to a certified letter through the postal service.
Nonce	A value used in security protocols that is never repeated with the same key. For example, challenges used in challenge-response authentication protocols generally must not be repeated until authentication keys are changed, or there is a possibility of a replay attack. Using a nonce as a challenge is a different requirement than a random challenge, because a nonce is not necessarily unpredictable. The use of a nonce is part of the Secure Sockets Layer or (SSL) transaction.
Phishing	Tricking individuals into disclosing sensitive personal information through deceptive computer-based means.
Port scanning	Using a program to remotely determine which ports on a system are open (for example, whether systems allow connections through those ports). See also "Scanning."
Public key	The public part of an asymmetric key pair that is typically used to verify signatures or encrypt data. It is a cryptographic key that is used with a public key cryptographic algorithm. The public key is uniquely associated with an entity and may be made public. In an asymmetric (public) cryptosystem, the public key is associated with a private key. The public key may be known by anyone and, depending on the algorithm, may be used to verify a digital signature that is signed by the corresponding private key, encrypt data that can be decrypted by the corresponding private key, or compute a piece of shared data.
Public key certificate	A digital document issued and digitally signed by the private key of a Certification Authority (CA) that binds the name of a subscriber to a public key. The certificate indicates that the subscriber identified in the certificate has sole control and access to the private key.
Remediation plan	A plan to remediate vulnerabilities in your infrastructure. This is done in lieu of a forthcoming fix (in most cases).
Rootkit	A set of tools used by an attacker after gaining root-level access to a host to conceal the attacker's activities on the host, and permit the attacker to maintain root-level access to the host through covert means.

Continued

Table B-2 *(continued)*

TERM	EXPLANATION
Salt	A non-secret value that is used in a cryptographic process, usually to ensure that the results of computations for one instance cannot be reused by an attacker. Random data of some form is gathered and added to the computational process.
Scanning	The sending of packets or requests to another system to gain information to be used in a subsequent attack.
Secure Sockets Layer (SSL) and Transport Layer Security (TLS)	Secure Sockets Layer (SSL) is a protocol developed by Netscape for transmitting private documents via the Internet. SSL works by using a public key to encrypt data that's transferred over the SSL connection. Most web browsers support SSL, and many websites use the protocol to obtain confidential user information, such as credit card numbers. By convention, URLs that require an SSL connection start with `https` instead of `http`. TLS is an Internet standard based on SSL version 3.0. Only very minor differences exist between SSL and TLS.
Spoofing	Sending a network packet that appears to come from a source other than its actual source. This involves the capability to receive a message by masquerading as the legitimate receiving destination, or masquerading as the sending machine and sending a message to a destination.
SQL injection	An attack technique that exploits applications that have not checked for proper input. The attacker can supply SQL statements to the application and, if successful, the attacker can cause the instructions to be executed against the database. Note that this is a popular attack.
Virtual Private Network (VPN)	A logical network that is established at the application layer of the Open Systems Interconnection (OSI) model, over an existing physical network, and typically does not include every node present on the physical network.
Vulnerability	Weakness in an information system, system security procedures, internal controls, or implementation that could be exploited or triggered by a threat source.
Vulnerability assessment	Formal description and evaluation of the vulnerabilities in an information system.
Warez	A term widely used by hackers to denote illegally copied and distributed commercial software from which all copy protection has been removed. Warez software often contains viruses, Trojans, and other malicious code and, thus, is very risky to download and use (legal issues notwithstanding).
Zombie	A program that is installed on a system to cause it to attack other systems.

Index